Critique of Freedom

critique of freedom

OTFRIED HÖFFE

TRANSLATED BY NILS F. SCHOTT

THE CENTRAL PROBLEM OF MODERNITY

The University of Chicago Press
Chicago and London

The University of Chicago Press, Chicago 60637
The University of Chicago Press, Ltd., London

Published 2020
Printed in the United States of America

29 28 27 26 25 24 23 22 21 20 1 2 3 4 5

ISBN-13: 978-0-226-46590-6 (cloth)
ISBN-13: 978-0-226-46606-4 (e-book)
DOI: https://doi.org/10.7208/chicago/9780226466064.001.0001

Originally published in German as *Kritik der Freiheit. Das Grundproblem der Moderne* © Verlag C.H.Beck oHG, München 2015.

The translation of this work was funded by Geisteswissenschaften International—Translation Funding for Work in the Humanities and Social Sciences from Germany, a joint initiative of the Fritz Thyssen Foundation, the German Federal Foreign Office, the collecting society VG WORT, and the Börsenverein des Deutschen Buchhandels (German Publishers & Booksellers Association).

Library of Congress Cataloging-in-Publication Data

Names: Höffe, Otfried, author. | Schott, Nils F., translator.
Title: Critique of freedom : the central problem of modernity / Otfried Höffe ; translated by Nils F. Schott.
Other titles: Kritik der Freiheit. English
Description: Chicago : The University of Chicago Press, 2020. | Includes bibliographical references and index.
Identifiers: LCCN 2020026483 | ISBN 9780226465906 (cloth) | ISBN 9780226466064 (ebook)
Subjects: LCSH: Liberty—Philosophy. | Civilization, Modern—Philosophy. | Philosophy, Modern. | Ethics, Modern.
Classification: LCC B824.4 .H6413 2020 | DDC 123/.5—dc23
LC record available at https://lccn.loc.gov/2020026483

⊗This paper meets the requirements of ANSI/NISO Z39.48-1992 (Permanence of Paper).

Freedom in free association

For Evelyn

Contents

Preface

Freedom is humanity's highest good. It constitutes human dignity. Not surprisingly, freedom in various ways shapes all human history. It therefore assumes a preeminent position in two respects, anthropologically and with regard to a specific age. To understand this double status, we must overcome a widespread but narrow conception of freedom. Freedom is not just a political topic and, merely as a supplement, one of personal responsibility.

To take on the much vaster theme of freedom is to engage with a tricky and convoluted phenomenon. For example, freedom is constitutive of the human being, and nonetheless, it remains a task still to be accomplished. And for accomplishing this task, in turn, modernity has elaborated a highly sophisticated, multifaceted project.

There is, however, skepticism toward this project, and thus toward freedom. In evidence, skeptics cite the negative consequences of modernity and the flip-sides of the project of freedom. This book takes such skepticism seriously. It subjects freedom and, with it, modernity to a judicative critique. For, without possessing an exclusive right to it, modernity is of overwhelming importance for freedom, while, inversely, freedom in its numerous versions plays an outstanding role in modernity. My study thus conceives of itself as a contribution both to a philosophical anthropology and to a critical theory of freedom and modernity. And because furthermore, it understands itself to be a reflection on the situation of our time, it joins the tradition of a truly practical and political philosophy.

I have developed reflections toward a critical theory of freedom and modernity in earlier works, namely, in *Categorical Principle of Law: A Counterpoint of Modernity* (1990), *Morality as the Price of Modernity* (1993), and *Kant's Critique of Pure Reason: The Foundation of Modern Philosophy* (2003). In this book, I continue my discussions from *The Art of Life and Morality* (2007) and the interpretation of *Kant's Critique of Practical Reason: A Philosophy of Freedom* (2012) with the aim of outlining a more comprehensive theory.[1]

Though obliged to the towering thinker of freedom Immanuel Kant, this study does not seek to develop a Kantian theory. On the one hand, it finds inspiration, where that makes sense, in other philosophers. On the other hand, the term "Kantian" evokes options this book undermines. Unlike many of the alternatives popular today, this study sees itself as opposing neither a Hegelian nor an Aristotelian theory. Overall, it is ultimately not concerned with an interpretation of classic and contemporary thinkers but with the issue of freedom and the issue of modernity, with their content, their constructive potential, but also with their ambiguities.

Starting with the wide range of topics it addresses, such an undertaking is undoubtedly ambitious. It seeks to contribute to critical social theory as well as to critical legal and democratic theory and to a theory of personal freedom; moreover to furnish some elements, at least, of a critical theory of technology and environmental protection, of medicine, and of education; and, not least of all, albeit only briefly, to sketch a freedom theory of science and art. I can only hope that in not all too simple a manner it lives up to Nietzsche's demand from the early notebooks: "set goals for yourself, *lofty* and *noble goals*, and come to grief in their pursuit!"[2]

Once again, I must thank the following: the Fritz Thyssen Foundation, whose grants allow this professor emeritus to maintain a staff; the University Carlos III in Madrid, where a *Catedra de Excellencia* allowed me to present first drafts of several chapters to a knowledgeable audience of colleagues and doctoral students in the spring of 2013; Dr. Wolfgang Hellmich and Moritz Hildt, MA, whose many comments have helped make this study clearer; Annika Friedrich, BA, who helped in the editing; and not least of all, Heike Schulz, MA, who has a detective's talent for deciphering handwritten texts.

Tübingen, late summer 2014

Otfried Höffe

1

Putting Freedom and Modernity to the Test

Freedom is of constitutive significance for human beings in general and for modernity in particular. The thesis that guides this book is that for both, freedom is the highest good. To be sure, there are many reasons to doubt this thesis. Neither the principle of freedom nor the project of modernity — nor, therefore, their conjunction — may hope for spontaneous approval. Instead, people love to talk, in the second case, about postmodernity, which includes a notion of postdemocracy and a skepticism about progress (even if such talk is heard less and less), and, in the first, about freedom as an illusion. The situation we find ourselves in thus suggests that we put freedom to the test and reassess modernity in a way that aims for a critique, in the word's original, juridical sense.

I do not, accordingly, mean critique as a charge or an accusation, nor do I mean its flat-out opposite, a defense. I intend to subject freedom, modernity, and their conjunction neither to a rejection nor to an apology but rather to a judge's critique. Rather than fall into radical pessimism or an equally radical optimism, I seek out and weigh arguments for and against them: what potential legitimization, what potential limitations do the principle of freedom and the project of modernity comprise? More precisely: what do they promise, from increased opportunities, to expectations, to hopes? To what extent do they keep their promises? Where might they be abused, and what are their downsides and their dark sides? What unreasonable demands do they make?

These questions come together in a guiding question, the question of whether what has become a fashionable skepticism ought not to make us skeptical in turn, whether we may not, based on more precise diagnoses and, of course, in a conceptual and argumentative effort, advocate a renewal of both the principle of freedom and the project of modernity.

To do so, we must first be clear about the many facets of what this includes: What kind of freedom counts? And what kind of modernity are we talking about? Then we must look for what kind of legitimacy they have maintained or may have lost, discover what threats and dangers they entail, in order finally to explore possibilities of regenerating them without heroic pathos.

A way of thinking committed to the principle of freedom is commonly called liberalism. When for the purpose of regeneration, such a way of thinking adopts elements of the Enlightenment, it may be called "liberalism in the spirit of Enlightenment" or, succinctly, "enlightened liberalism." That is the kind of liberalism this study advocates.

1.1
CONSTITUTIVE AND PERIOD-SPECIFIC MEANINGS

As an essential aspect of modernity, the principle of freedom serves modernity to show that it does not pursue a new goal per se but rather seeks to bring about the flourishing, preferably even perfection, of a basic anthropological intention: freedom, precisely.

Renouncing the principle of freedom thus amounts to putting more at stake than just the project of modernity or the insights of modernity's great thinkers. It also poses a threat to the essence of the human as we know it. That is why we should not lightheartedly give up a principle essential both anthropologically and for modernity. Marx in any case was probably right, at least socially and politically, when he claimed that "no man combats freedom; at most he combats the freedom of others."[1] According to the *first* and *fundamental* thesis of this book, freedom counts as an integral part of the unique nature of the human being in three respects: as a reality, as a task, and as a desire.

Because renouncing it has grave consequences, we should familiarize ourselves with the principle of freedom before we dismiss it. In doing so, and this is the *second* thesis, we encounter threats and dangers that do not necessarily insist on a dismissal but indeed on immanent improvements.

Be they individuals, groups, or institutions — all who have found freedom risk losing it again. Freedom, along with modernity, appears as a multilayered goal exposed to internal tensions. In some respects, it even appears to be self-contradictory. But why shouldn't we accept these three characteristics and conceive of freedom as a (1) multifaceted phenomenon, (2) charged with internal tensions, and (3) shot through with contradictions?

For this is true as well: many enterprises and visions of, once again, humanity in general and modernity in particular are inspired by an idea of freedom. This inspiration stands out all the more clearly when we add three closely related concepts: emancipation, self-determination, and autonomy. It then becomes obvious that at the basis of the second concept to guide this book, modernity, we find visions such as reason and Enlightenment, progress as well, that have been shaped essentially by the idea of freedom. Whether we look at the Enlightenment as a liberation from superstition or from the tutelage of church and state, at the emancipation from natural constraints and arduous labor through new knowledge and skills, at the curtailment of privileges, control of political power, democracy as a self-determination of those concerned — despite some skepticism about modernity, these and other processes typical of modernity continue to be appreciated. Above all, these processes can be brought together in the common *expression* "freedom"; and that speaks in favor of, precisely, this expression. They hardly come together, however, in a common *concept*.

The conception of freedom as a constitutive aspect of the human, a conception that has found in modernity its highest visionary shape yet, at least does not presuppose a homogeneous conception of freedom. That is the *third* thesis. Reassessing modernity via the principle of freedom on the contrary demands that we begin by elucidating the ambiguity of the principle. And because its different meanings are debated in different discourses, we must bring together discourses that have so far remained isolated but are equally important to our topic, such as those about technology and environmental protection, medicine, education, and religious tolerance, as well as the threats from religious fanatics; about markets and capitalism, privacy, data protection, and media democracy; and about the ambitious claims of the neurosciences.

There is another phenomenon that speaks in favor of the double task of reassessing modernity by means of the principle of freedom and of operating, in this reassessment, a regeneration. Even if we conceive of the history of the last few centuries as a history of freedom, and of modernity as a project of freedom, we often find one conception involved in them to be hopelessly naive. Whether explicitly or implicitly, some visionaries of freedom (and similarly of modernity) believe in a linear *progress* thanks to which the extent of freedom will steadily increase and finally lead to a comprehensive and perfect "realm of freedom." In reality, we find phenomena that contradict the optimism that reigned for so long and even turn it into pessimism.

Phenomena that foster pessimism include, for example: (1) dilemmas, that is, situations of constraint in which to make a decision is to speak out in favor of one freedom and simultaneously against another freedom; furthermore, (2) a dialectic of self-endangerment, that is, an increase of freedom turns into a loss of freedom or encourages an abuse of freedom; and not least of all, (3) aporias in the attempt to gain freedom and liberties and to preserve such gains.

Such negative phenomena must not, however, lead us to minimize or even forget such gains. In any case, there are still pathbreaking innovations being made, for example in information technology, molecular biology, and the neurosciences, or, in different ways, in international law. Yet these domains are not exempt from the cited trio of dilemmas, dialectic, and aporias. That is why, without losing any of their luster, freedom and modernity must reinforce their readiness for self-critique and reform. An attitude that allows for such a learning process is what I call, as mentioned, an "enlightened liberalism" (see also chapter 5). And those who want to hold on to the expression "modernity" may speak of a "regenerated modernity."

This study discusses three aspects of freedom. According to its first, normative aspect, freedom is the quintessence of heroic visions, that is, the interlocking principles of reason, enlightenment, and emancipation, whose interplay I call the "freedom project of modernity." According to the second, largely empirical aspect of lived processes of freedom, these processes consist in the attempt to make as much as possible of one's vision a reality, an attempt that comes up against difficulties, dilemmas, and aporias. The third aspect, finally, the project of freedom regenerated through self-critique, tries to preserve as much as possible of the visionary project of freedom in the multifaceted program of an enlightened liberalism.

It will readily be objected to the view of freedom's superior value that, at least in our time, the difficulties inherent to it have led to freedom losing some of its value and that approval of freedom has become less significant. And indeed, social ethics and social philosophy have long moved justice to the foreground. It seems that theories of freedom must cede first place, philosophically and politically, to theories of justice.

There are other contenders such as the already-mentioned concept of progress, as well as a process of rationalization and, in a different way, a process of secularization. There is also a functional differentiation of society said to amount to a de-moralization. There is globalization. And, not least of all, there is a widely diagnosed progressive disempowerment of the human being: the geographical disempowerment of the Copernican turn, the evolutionary disempowerment of Darwin's theory, and the psychological disempowerment brought on by Freud, which the neurosciences push all the way to an allegedly irrevocable dismissal of freedom and responsibility.

Why does freedom nonetheless deserve the significance it has as a guiding concept? Why can it still be declared to be the supreme value? As a mere topic of study, "theory of justice" does not call the principle of freedom into question; neither does even the dominant definition of justice in terms of equality.

It would be possible, after all, to claim that there is a tension between freedom and equality, to consider this tension to be necessary, and to call for a constant conciliation of freedom and equality claims. Yet in the work of the great legal theoretician Kant and of the most important theoretician of justice in the last few decades, John Rawls, who was inspired by Kant, justice and freedom belong essentially together (as we will see in chapter 7, for example). This does not, of course, exclude that tensions arise between the two aspects.

Various doubts may be raised against the other contenders. The justification of the progress thesis can no more be assessed wholesale than that of the rationalization process thesis, and if they are justified with respect to particular aspects, there are various different facets of freedom to respond to them. Insofar as there is a process of secularization, it largely owes its existence to the acknowledgment of liberties [*Freiheitsrechte*]. At best, then, the alleged disempowerments describe half the truth, as we will see. And the functional differentiation of society does not entail a de-moralization.

There are thus three arguments in favor of freedom as a guiding concept. According to a first, still superficial argument, the range of topics of today's dominant debates must be extended. According to a second, more important argument, economic and social theory neither should subject the concept of freedom to a neoliberal reduction, nor should they, to oppose such a reduction, renounce the concept of freedom. And neither in matters of law nor in matters of morality should we let some brain researchers and psychologists argue freedom away.

A third argument is even more essential, and it designates the *fourth* thesis of this book: in examining freedom, we also examine the guiding concepts and presuppositions of other debates. The debate concerning justice that Rawls rekindled, for example, assumes responsible persons who, free from external restraint (negative concept of freedom), seek as great a measure of freedom as possible to realize their personal plans for their lives (positive concept of freedom). In employing concepts such as liability, responsibility, and guilt, criminal law presupposes freedom, a point that in different ways also applies to civil law, politics, science, the economy, research and medicine, and, not least of all, art, literature, and music. They all suppose freedom even if it is not an unbounded freedom, and along with freedom they assume that humans are responsible for themselves, before themselves and before others.

The notion that freedom is a concept essential but not specific to modernity, that it is constitutive of humanity in all ages, points to the *fifth* and *last* thesis. The concept contains a revolutionary explosive force, namely, the potential of a universalization that it begins to develop only in the course of modernity: when the privileges of certain groups are suspended, freedom becomes *the* characteristic of human beings merely because they are human.

1.2
FREEDOM — A PERPLEXING CONCEPT

The fact that freedom can endanger itself really emerges only in the course of the modern history of freedom. Yet inner tensions have accompanied freedom from the beginning. One of these tensions is named in this paradoxical quotation from a modern theoretician of freedom: "Man is born free, and everywhere he is in chains."[2]

This opening sentence of the first chapter of *The Social Contract* (1762) leads Jean-Jacques Rousseau to the core of the concept of freedom with its many and often perplexing facets. It asserts five claims about freedom to which the next sentence and the context add three more claims. They all turn out to be plausible.

1. According to the thesis that the human being "is" born free, freedom is not a mere idea or even an illusion but a reality.
2. The one who is born free is "man," or the human being. As Rousseau writes elsewhere, "To renounce one's freedom is to renounce one's quality as man, the rights of humanity, and even its duties."[3] Freedom, then, is not a concept tied to a specific age. Even if we may consider it to be the key principle of modernity, it is of greater, anthropological significance. It is a constitutive aspect of the human being.

   A look at the history of ideas will confirm this point. The concept neither falls from the sky, nor is it discovered or even invented by the modern age. It lifts the human being out of the continuum of nature. A sign of the special position of the human, it characterizes not just modern Europeans but the human as human, that is, every human being in every culture and every age. Our age of globalization benefits from this fact. Because freedom is not the privilege of a specific culture, because it is thus not tied to the West, its significance cuts across different cultures. Freedom is of intercultural, even general, universal, we may also say cosmopolitan significance.
3. According to Rousseau, this freedom has a perplexing characteristic, namely, that everywhere, we perceive its exact opposite. Although humans are born free, everywhere we find them to be enchained. Albeit free by "nature," from a social-political perspective, they live in relationships that are often experienced as coercive.

As experience teaches us, partly going beyond Rousseau (who is thinking of superficialities like fashion and luxury), such chains can be not just of an external, social, and political nature but also of an internal, mental, even neuronal nature. Strict determinists even claim that these chains, which bind us so tightly, cannot be unlocked or forced open, that we are not free at all. Should the determinists be right, should freedom indeed be an illusion, our life and coexistence would be changed to the core. It would radically put into question the dominant self-evident conceptions of freedom, responsibility, and, as the case may be, guilt as well. Should strict determinism not be justified, however, should Rousseau's thesis about our lying in chains be correct, then we must infer two things.

4. Even though it is an aspect of the human from birth, freedom does not seem to have full reality but to be real only as a mere disposition, as the kind of potentiality that in many places, allegedly even in all places, lacks actualization. Undoubtedly many of the dispositions human beings are born with, such as the disposition to walk or to talk, must nonetheless be developed. In that sense freedom, too, might be something inborn that must nonetheless be developed, something that loses the mode of a mere disposition and becomes a reality only in being developed either definitively or at least to a previously unknown extent.
5. According to Rousseau, however, it is not just still-developing human beings, that is, children, who are in chains but adults as well. To that extent, it seems, actualization never seems to be fully reached. Instead, certain chains always remain.
6. "One believes himself the others' master," Rousseau declares in the next sentence, "and yet is more a slave than they." In the Templar's assertion in *Nathan the Wise* that "not all who scorn their chains are free," Lessing offers a variation of this statement. And in *Elective Affinities*, Goethe has Ottilie note in her diary: "No one is more a slave than he who thinks he is free without being so."[4]

"Master" and "slave" are social, more precisely, legal and political concepts. Many of the debates about freedom today, of course, are not concerned with these concepts but with freedom of action and freedom of the will, that is, with the freedom of responsible persons, with personal freedom. Yet an author of such significance for the thinking of freedom as Rousseau studies other and quite numerous fields, as many other philosophers before and after him have done—let me cite only Aristotle and Kant by way of example. If we do not want to unduly narrow down the debate, we thus have to discuss not just personal but also economic, social, and political, as well as scientific and artistic freedom.

7. According to Rousseau, Lessing, and Goethe, it is possible to be "more" of a slave. Freedom thus appears as a comparative term. And in fact there are,

depending on personal and cultural development, different degrees or stages. Some people live more freely than others, and some communities and some cultures allow their members more freedom than others.

8. In its most common form, the determinism that declares freedom to be an illusion concerns only personal freedom. According to Rousseau, however, self-deception and illusion exist in the case of social and political freedom as well.

1.3

THE DUAL CORE

Despite a wealth of phenomena of freedom it is possible to note a modest commonality, namely, the distinction between a negative and a positive meaning. There the expression "independence" designates the negation of coercion and being determined by others, of intrusion and tutelage, here the positive ability to set goals of one's own and to choose the means to attain them, that is, the self-determination that allows for a life according to our own conceptions.

In some phenomena, however, the two perspectives are hard to separate, for example, the moment a person suffering from asthma is able to fill his lungs unhindered. And the very moment the East Coast colonies rid themselves of British rule, they are free to politically determine themselves. Nonetheless, one of the two meanings, namely, negative freedom as independence from coercion, as freedom *from*, enjoys a certain primacy, for reasons that are partly conceptual, partly normative, but also partly due to the evolution of the idea of freedom.

In Rousseau, a conceptual primacy begins to emerge whose gist is later affirmed by Isaiah Berlin in his famous lecture "Two Concepts of Liberty": that the freedom of human beings does not lie in being able to do what they want but in not having to do what they do not want to do.[5] This primacy must not, however, be amplified into an exclusive conception that unnecessarily accepts merely the negative concept of freedom and dismisses the positive one. Since someone who can do what he wants is free as well, the modest claim of a simple primacy is more persuasive: to be free in the positive sense, one must be independent of coercions that might exist, not entirely independent but nonetheless free from an overwhelming power.

The conceptual primacy and the normative one it already contains are joined by a further normative primacy: those who have the right to be free from overwhelming coercions are not for that reason obligated positively to make use of their freedom.

According to philosophers such as Kant, there is, third, an evolutionary priority for the negative concept of freedom. Kant advocates it both when it comes to the history of the species and when it comes to the history of the individual. The most violent passion of the natural human being—both of the so-called savage, that is, an early phase in the history of the species, and of the newborn child—lies in an inclination toward freedom that understands freedom as independence from all coercion.[6]

The pattern of negative freedom can already be found in the subhuman domain: a bird freely flying in the air remains free even when it is hungry or cold. A dog let off its leash, too, is free. An opposite example is the wild animal that, locked up in a cage in a zoo, is unable either to move in its accustomed environment or to develop according to the laws of its species and of self-preservation.

Analogously, people who leave a confinement behind are free (be it prison, internment, a home, an orphanage, or oppressive debt); others are free when they escape iron rules and intransigent protocols, flee a yoke or other forms of dependence. And sometimes we say at a funeral, without cynicism, "He's truly free now." Negative freedom (with its conceptual and normative priority) here can be something someone is given, by forgiving a debt for example, or by setting him free from oppressive responsibilities. Above all, it often has a dynamic character: it is obtained in a process, in a becoming free of ties, and this proves to be emancipatory.

According to positive freedom, the freedom *to*, the subject in question—a natural individual, a group, or a political community—can finally do or not do what it likes. This includes the possibility of "overdoing it" in one form or another. Free in the positive sense, in any case, are those who motivate and orient what they do and do not do and go down that road on their own. And internally free are those who live in accordance with their convictions without fear, who maintain their dignity, namely, that dignity whose core is a self-respect that is not reducible to the human dignity protected by constitutions. For this dignity can be lost without losing one's (human right of) human dignity.

In the negative sense, we are all the more free the fewer requirements, ties, and constraints there are, which is why negative freedom has that comparative character mentioned earlier: because we can be independent to a greater or a lesser degree, we have to speak of different degrees, perhaps also stages of freedom.

Those who concentrate on the negative side of freedom like to bring it down to volition, to doing or not doing as we please. What they mean is more than an option we have in mind or a wish that overcomes us. What they also mean is the opportunity, preferably also the right and the power, to actualize an option. Freedom then becomes a realizable potential. Of course, a resistant reality may assert itself in opposition, financial limits, for instance, or limited talent, not least the resistance and deficits of external nature. Realizing the potential for freedom may moreover be hindered by other people or by custom. And not infrequently, we get in our own way because we get involved in something that makes other things, which often are more important in the long run, more difficult or that even prevents them. An unlimited freedom, pure arbitrary freedom, is refracted at both internal and external limits, now natural, now social, now personal limits. Generally, then, only those are free in a livable and experienceable sense who understand freedom to be more than a mere arbitrary freedom.

Both core meanings, negative as well as positive freedom, have a vast spectrum of applications. A popular song says that our thoughts are free, suggesting that nothing and no one can censure them, that they may wander as they please. This negative freedom of thinking as we please thanks to the human imagination transforms into a positive freedom when it creates free worlds of thought in which we emancipate from the outside world. Already in the simple form of daydreams we liberate ourselves from the often oppressive world of the everyday. And gifted writers—and, in different ways, painters, sculptors, and composers—bring forth new worlds of their own making released from the narrowness and the constraints of reality. The positive freedom thus practiced is once more a comparative concept. Those who have more imagination and greater creative power can act more creatively and originally, more free of thought and free to create than those who only take up, copy, or reproduce what others have produced.

Another example is that of the glider pilot who realizes his dream and as if weightlessly flies in the plane he has built himself—for him the feeling of absolute freedom.

Research, in turn, is referred to as free already when it is not subject to political restraints. It is free to a greater degree where it frees itself from economic requirements. These two levels of negative freedom, however, only transform into positive freedom where research follows its own laws alone, where it refuses to be tied to any kind of utility and thereby becomes an end in itself (see section 9.1).

Free in the personal sense and to a particularly great degree are those who not only emancipate themselves from previously dominant rules but also reject the external "vanities of the world" such as power, wealth, and celebrity, and to an even greater degree those who overcome the power of internal desires as well. Yet those who, for example, renounce property but do not live this renunciation ascetically and instead celebrate it as an artistic performance may not lay claim to such freedom. They push themselves into the foreground and at the same time subject themselves to a different constraint, namely, that of having to achieve something spectacular. Moreover, and this too makes them unfree, their own vanity comes into play.

Are only those free — and are they free at all — who live according to a principle of permanent preliminariness, that is, who pursue an activity they soon give up in favor of a second, this one to be given up later for a third, who choose anew time and again but make these choices on the condition that they will soon be revoked again? Or is it, rather, those who unreservedly decide on something and those who thanks to careful life planning have no need, for the most part, for spectacular emancipation? It is in this sense that the Danish author Peter Høeg can declare in his novel *The Quiet Girl*: "True freedom is freedom from having to choose, because everything is perfect just as it is."[7] People who come close to this great freedom are often recognizable by their gaze and their attitude: internally free people convey lightheartedness and deep peace.

Another novel, Jonathan Franzen's 2010 *Freedom*, however, conveys a very different message. Freedom may indeed be something that cannot be taken away and something worth living for. But there is also something we might consider a curse of freedom: we must decide, on a wife, on a car, on a profession. And cruelly, we often end up more unhappy after the decisions we have made than we were before. Mere freedom does not make us happy. For that, we need things that lie beyond freedom or that belong to a demanding conception of positive freedom, for example an activity that entirely fulfills us, or friendship and love.

Finally, there is an attitude toward life of a moral order that belongs to positive freedom, the capacity and readiness for generosity. For the Greeks already, it is a sign of the (morally) free man that he manages his material resources neither avariciously nor profligately but sovereignly and thus generously.[8]

1.4
A LOOK AT THE HISTORY OF IDEAS

Ever since Antigone's appeal to "the immutable unwritten laws of Heaven . . . not born today nor yesterday,"[9] European culture has contained an impulse skeptical of authority. This impulse helps freedom become one of the concepts guiding the Western mind that form in ancient Greece, are enriched by Roman, Christian, and also Germanic notions, and achieve in modernity the overwhelming, ultimately singular position that makes them first the signature of the age and finally the core of a universal juridical morality.

From the perspective of conceptual history, the legal and political meanings play a special role.[10] For, etymologically, the expression "free" and "freeman" go back to an Old Germanic word, "frija," in Old Icelandic "frjâls," which means "free-necked." That person is free whose neck is not placed in a yoke, who in other words does not serve someone else as a serf or a slave but serves only himself.

The expression "free" is related, moreover, to "dear" and "friend." It goes back to the Indo-Germanic root "prai," which means "protect, take care of, hold dear, love" and points to "friend." From this root, Germanic develops "frei" as a legal concept: those are "free" who belong to the "dear" and are therefore protected, the members of the clan and tribe, the "friends." According to the Grimm brothers' *German Dictionary*, "free" first corresponds to the Latin *privus*, which expresses *singulus*, *sui juris*, and to the Greek *idios*. Accordingly, the freeman "owns himself"; he is "sui juris, does not belong to anyone else."[11]

Similarly, in Greek thought those are called free who live for their own sake, not for another's. According to this definition, which Aristotle surprisingly cites not in the *Politics* but in the *Metaphysics*, the human is an end in itself.[12] This counters two popular but false assessments, for the notion, so essential to the modern self-conception, that the human being is an end in itself is articulated much earlier, and the premodern beginnings are to be found not just in Judeo-Christian thought but in pagan antiquity as well.

As a legal and political concept, freedom initially, in the Greek as in the Roman as well as in the Germanic world, has merely a particular meaning: only the "free" have the privilege of being full members of the community. Unlike nonprivileged, even disfavored persons, those in bondage and the hereditary subjects, the serfs and slaves, they live for their own sake, independent of an external power.

Because this legal privilege characterizes the members of a community of blood and tribe, the freeman is also distinct from the foreigner. Unlike the latter, he is protected from harm and oppression by others. It is for this reason that in this old European legal concept, the two basic meanings form a unity: in a negative respect, the freeman is released from foreign power; in a positive respect he is protected against foreign power by means of a shared power. Added to this is the further positive meaning that the freeman participates, with equal rights, in the political life responsible for exercising the shared power.

Since the protection that the community of law offers its "full members" rests on reciprocity, the free are "all in the same boat." Consequently, there is an intrinsic link between the concept of freedom and that of solidarity, which explains the already-mentioned etymological kinship with "friend": since the free know each other, work with each other, and mutually support and protect each other, they tend to be bound in friendship among each other.

Not just individuals, but social units too can be ends in themselves. In that sense — according to a second, once more clearly premodern meaning — the classical Greek *polis*, a kind of city-republic, claims for itself autonomy: self-determination as self-legislation. The freedom meant here — incidentally a double freedom, internal freedom as opposed to tyranny and external freedom as independence from foreign rule — the Greek city-state distinguishes itself with great self-confidence from polities such as the Persian Empire. Since Herodotus,[13] that is to say for two and a half thousand years, our continent has defined itself via its political culture, as a liberal democracy it has defended militarily, if needed, since the battles of Marathon, Salamis, and Plataea. At the same time, the concept of freedom acquires a new opposite: in domestic policy, the freeman is distinct from the slave; in foreign policy, the Greek man (of course only the free Greek man) from the non-Greek, denigrated as barbarian.

In late antiquity, when the Greek city-state has long lost its political freedom, the then-leading philosophical school, the Stoa, develops a radically new meaning of freedom that is certainly neither social nor political. This conception, which quickly begins to exert immense influence, expands the concept of freedom and at the same time foreshortens it. It consists in the deeply apolitical notion of a purely internal freedom, and this freedom is understood to be the epitome of a personal way of life independent of law and politics.

Freedom is given a different meaning — albeit not a fundamentally new one, since it too is apolitical — by Christianity. According to the letter to the Romans, Christ liberates humanity both from sin and from being subject to death. The same apostle, Paul, writes to the Galatians: "For freedom Christ has set us free"; and to the Corinthians, "where the spirit of the Lord is, there is freedom."[14] These passages theologically superelevate the Stoic concept of inner freedom. With this superelevation, freedom enters the philosophically and theologically difficult field of allegedly freedom-promoting but, at least at first sight, only freedom-endangering factors, namely, predestination and divine grace. The new, religious or theological concept, however, leaves one thing untouched: the exceedingly high, even unsurpassable, superlative rank assigned to freedom.

Although its significance is primarily personal, Christian freedom also has a social and political but by no means revolutionary content. Because true freedom —Christian freedom, precisely — relativizes the weight of social orders, Paul does not advise the runaway slave Onesimus to emancipate himself from his (Christian) master, Philemon. Rather, as he tells the Corinthians, "let each of you remain in the condition in which you were called . . . for whoever was called in the Lord as a slave is a freed person belonging to the Lord."[15]

On the one hand, then, the religious superelevation counteracts the weakening of politics implied in a merely personal concept of freedom — from the religious perspective, the difference between master and slave does not apply; on the other hand, however, it affirms and even amplifies it. Because from the religious point of view, everyone is already a freeman, legal liberation seems to be of no consequence and may thus be dispensed with. Surrendering to the given and not resisting a legal discrimination, however, is possible only on the implicit condition *in dubio pro positivo*, when in doubt, in favor of the factually given. According to another apostle, Peter, renunciation, accepting one's fate, is even what is called for. Christian freedom does not prove itself in protest against state power but in obedience to it.[16]

1.5
MODERNIZATION

In a long process that perhaps still has not concluded, modernity gradually abolishes all privileges. Seen through the lens of the concept of freedom, this is not a mere coincidence. For natural persons, the elementary meaning of freedom is action that takes place of one's own accord, of one's own free will (Greek *hekōn*, Latin *sua sponte*). Obviously, this capacity is not tied to the legal status of the freeman, and for that very reason, it has revolutionary potential. According to our fifth thesis, the concept of freedom in the theory of action has the potential to be universalized and thereby to abolish all privileges and to make freedom, in the course of a longer history, the characteristic of all human beings.

In premodernity there is another important notion besides the ancient Stoic conception of inner freedom, namely, the notion of the human as made in the image of God to be found in Judaism (but not foreign to other cultures). Christianity abolishes the ethnic limitation of Judaism. And yet, for centuries, all three — Stoa, Judaism, Christianity — barely draw legal consequences from their conceptions of freedom. It is in modernity, essentially, that freedom transforms from a particular privilege into a universal claim with broad social and political consequences. Each individual human being and every political community — albeit only now — demand freedom, as the earlier quote from Marx suggests.

Neither individual nor legal nor social reasons can permanently legitimate special rights. That is why they cannot be maintained in the long run and are lost. This is the decisive modernization: each human being and each political community are entitled to freedom; now that freedom is a prerogative of every human being simply because she is human, the expression loses its prior, in a neutral sense discriminating force. The corresponding development, namely that, according to Hegel, first one, later a few, later again many, and finally all are free, could take place linearly. Yet factual history features breaks, setbacks as well, but then again, fortunately, progress too, now steady, now in leaps.

The major emancipatory steps are familiar: through abolishing the privileges of the nobility, the clergy, and all other estates, supplemented by the abolishment of slavery and related institutions like serfdom, first the middle classes, later the workers, and finally — in many places the most important bearer of modernization — women obtain equal rights. At the end of this process, every human being has become a free legal subject simply for being human. Thanks to the end of colonialism and satellite states, polities too achieve freedom, even if often only in matters of foreign policy. For often, civil wars rage within, and dictators rule, and where corruption thrives, formerly wealthy polities descend into bitter poverty.

The double meaning of "freeman" discussed earlier persists in these processes of emancipation to this day: both legal and political freedom consist in being rid of the action and power of others and at the same time in securing this being rid by means of a shared power, usually through the legal order and the public authorities responsible for it. In that regard, as the earlier quote from Rousseau suggests, rules and authorities entitled to impose constraints — certain chains, precisely — belong to freedom. The legitimacy of these chains is what Rousseau inquires into.

While many debates about freedom consider only a few aspects, Kant and the German Idealists (Fichte and Hegel more so than Schelling, who is not interested in the law and the state) manage to bring its various facets together and at the same time expand on them. Here at the latest freedom becomes a key concept of (Western) modernity in which ethics (personal freedom), social philosophy (economic, social, and science freedom), and political philosophy (freedom in domestic and foreign policy) as well as the philosophy of religion (inner freedom), theoretical philosophy (starting with its criticism of determinism), and not least of all the philosophy of art (aesthetic autonomy) find a common, albeit very complex denominator: freedom has become the comprehensive fundamental concept of modernity.[17]

In the course of the development thus sketched, freedom comes to have enormous weight. As the focus of the modern self-conception, freedom highlights the individuality and autonomy of the human being; it changes social and political relationships and their institutions; it boosts the rise of the sciences and promotes the liberalization of the economy; from the notion of freedom develop the human rights that expand from, initially, a primarily negative conception—human rights as defensive rights—to, later, a positive and participatory conception, namely, positive liberties and rights to political participation. And, not least of all, modern art, including literature and music, conceives of itself as free in seeking to be answerable only to itself.

For all these superior concepts, of Freedom with a capital F, we must not forget the less spectacular yet existentially indispensable ones. Thus, some want to be delivered from worries or liberated from loneliness. Others want to secure the freedom of everyday life, that is, move in the streets without danger and live in their home without fear of violence; run a business without paying so-called protection money; sell their products without the threat of large-scale counterfeiting. On the principle "my home is my castle," we demand for ourselves a private sphere that no one, neither other people nor businesses nor the state, is allowed to intrude on. This includes the right—now threatened both by private and by state actors—not to be tracked and spied on (see below, section 12.1).

1.6
AMBIGUITIES AND SELF-ENDANGERMENT

Great achievements are borne by visions, albeit less by the necessary placelessness of enthusiastic utopias than by visions oriented toward reality. Is the principle of freedom to be counted among such visions? A diagnosis of modernization certainly falls short if it turns a blind eye to the already-mentioned phenomena of ambiguity and self-endangerment. The first ambiguities, of course, are independent of modernity.

The flipside of the fool's liberty to speak without "mincing words" is that the speaker is precisely taken for a fool and thus not taken seriously. A similar ambiguity is experienced by people relieved of tasks and responsibilities. Politicians and others in so-called positions of responsibility who do not leave office of their own accord but for external reasons, who involuntarily relinquish the habit of being in demand and having demands made of them, are simultaneously free and unfree. The smart ones among them are glad about the relief; the less smart ones suffer from withdrawal; and those who have practical wisdom, although they experience both, in the end reach, often quite painfully, a positive assessment.

Free, in any case, are those who shed responsibilities and the constraints that come with them; unfree are those who do not shed them voluntarily, personally, but find this to be imposed on them from the outside. And, at the latest, when one becomes free of all responsibilities and moreover of all ties and resources, emancipatory freedom loses all positive value: because they have nothing left to lose, those who have lost everything undoubtedly do not have an enviable freedom. Understandably, people who suffer this kind of radical loss tend to despair. The feeling of no longer being able to lose anything, however, can also heighten freedom.

Because certain ambiguities and self-endangerments are specific to historical ages, a theory that seeks to account for them must not be static but, as a dynamic and flexible theory, understand human history as an open process. To this end, it is helpful to organize the more recent centuries into three phases such that a new survey of modernity, insofar as regards its historical development, can be presented as a dialectical three-step process. In the first phase, the *thesis*, freedom dominates, in the course of a universalization, as a powerful vision of a richer, better, more beautiful future. Here, images full of pathos predominate, such as the painting *Liberty Leading the People*, which Delacroix paints about the French July Revolution of 1830, the overthrow of the reactionary king Charles X. There is no less pathos in the line from the revolutionary workers' song "Brothers, to the sun, to freedom!"

In the next phase, the *antithesis*, the ambiguities and self-endangerments at issue here emerge and by and large cause the pathos of the first phase to disappear. The vision of freedom and modernity becomes modest; more trenchant criticism even sees only the negative aspects. In the first third of the twentieth century, authors like Georg Trakl are downright obsessed with decay, albeit not with regard specifically to freedom. Something similar can be said of Oswald Spengler's two-volume *The Decline of the West* (1918/1922), a general philosophy of the history of civilizations that becomes a veritable long and best seller.

The scenarios of decline sketched by economic historians such as Niall Ferguson are less trenchant. For they limit the decline, geographically to the greater European–North American region and thematically to its (alleged) loss of economic and, subsequently, political power. Surprisingly, they sideline the considerable scientific-technological-medical and the cultural (literary, musical, artistic, architectural, design) potential. Moreover, they underestimate the long-term attractiveness of democracy, rule of law, and human rights.

The self-endangerments inherent to freedom and modernity play a more significant role only later in other authors, for example in Hans Jonas's late response to Ernst Bloch's three-volume *The Principle of Hope*. Jonas's search for "an ethics for the technological age," his once-much-praised study *The Imper-*

ative of Responsibility, is willing even to accept an ecological dictatorship.[18] This readiness—which constitutes, after all, a betrayal of the principles of freedom and democracy on which modernity is based—has, however, carelessly been overlooked by enthusiastic followers of Jonas.

The negative antithesis, which fortunately is rarely inclined toward despair, ought today to be succeeded by a third theoretical phase, by the kind of *synthesis* that undertakes to deal with the self-endangerments. If it succeeds, the negative pathos, a skepticism in the guise of prophecy, can be pushed back in favor of a renewed but this time more modest pathos, a "liberalism in the spirit of the Enlightenment" and a "regenerative liberalism."

As our first example of ambiguity and self-endangerment, let's take a technical innovation that has borne modernity, Gutenberg's invention of metal movable type. Within a short time, it leads to a reduction in price and consequently to a faster circulation of books and other printed matter. Insofar as this breaks the hegemony of the small number of monastic and aristocratic libraries, a merely technological freedom, the free manipulation of type, turns into an initially cultural and subsequently political freedom. A large part of the population gains free access to printed materials that, because of widespread analphabetism, are furnished with expository illustrations and picture stories.

This free access in turn helps the Reformation, a liberating event, acquire immensely greater notoriety. For its part, however, this event contributes to the outbreak of the religious wars of the sixteenth and seventeenth centuries, which are unquestionably inimical to freedom. Yet fortunately, these conflicts bring forth a capacity for overcoming dangers as they inspire international law and motivate the peace treaty concluded in Münster and Osnabrück in 1648. In overcoming a long period of war, the Treaty of Westphalia undoubtedly makes a contribution to freedom. In this case, the effect is enhanced by the agreement's creation of a legal framework for Europe that, despite the many subsequent violations, serves as a model for a liberal coexistence of different nation-states.

Gutenberg's invention is an example of a complex history of freedom insofar as the process just sketched out can be organized into five phases. (This of course does not preclude taking it as exemplary of other histories, of course, especially the history of education.) (1) Gutenberg's technological freedom promotes (2) cultural and political freedom that in turn (3) sets a process of freedom, the Reformation, in motion, which, however, (4) grows into an evident loss of freedom, wars, which fortunately (5) are ended with a peace, that is, a gain in freedom. In this introductory sketch, we may disregard the need to assess each of these phases in more detail, especially the fact that the Reformation cannot be regarded as a pure event of freedom.

A second example: freedom over against external nature, the freedom to subdue the earth, has by now led to a risk society that severely curtails freedom. Whether mastery of nature must necessarily result in a risk society remains to be seen, as does how it is possible in a risk society to maintain or regain a maximum of freedom (see section 2.5).

A third example is concerned with legal freedom. At the beginning, it is largely limited to negative liberties, especially freedom from violence exercised by other people. The insight, however, that actual freedom requires positive liberties as well, combined with the aim of diminishing social inequalities, has led to the creation of a welfare state that, for all its legitimacy, endangers freedom in three respects. First, the ever-denser social legislation and more intricate bureaucracy that come with the expansion of the welfare state create barriers, constraints even. Second, the welfare state—initially intended as a subsidiary—and the notion of helping people help themselves threaten to lead to a state whose help weakens the capacity for self-help because it makes the recipients of aid dependent.[19]

In this way, a life in security and prosperity undermines the very meaning of security and prosperity, freedom. At the end, freedom, which in the French Revolution comes first, loses this primacy and is relativized, in some cases even displaced, by the two other, initially subordinate, principles of equality and fraternity (or solidarity, in gender-neutral terms).

There is a further danger the relevant theory, the theory of the citizen, does not even notice. Many citizens no longer even perceive their polity as a community, as something in common to which they are to contribute. Instead, they merely make claims, demands, replacing solidary reciprocity with ego-centered one-sidedness. Finally, the ever-increasing costs of the welfare state lead to enormous debts that put a burden on the next generation and severely restrict its possibilities to invest in freedom.

A fourth example: the second danger posed by the welfare state may in part be due to the undoubtedly legitimate overcoming of all class privileges, but it cannot be reduced to it. The state citizen—who is by no means necessary and has therefore emerged only slowly—threatens to whither into a "downsized citizen," someone who might participate in elections and pays taxes, given sufficient income, but who otherwise does not contribute to the common good. And both habitual nonvoters and citizens who do not pay taxes for extended periods of time do not even contribute the minimum. They thus degenerate into something they are allowed to become as state citizens but which may nonetheless be branded by the term "downsized citizen." They become the kind of minimal citizen that the modern struggle for freedom unquestionably does not aim for (see chapter 13).

The digitalization of the world provides a fifth example. For undoubtedly it expands our room for agency, which is a gain in freedom. Yet media addiction and private, business, and political abuse in turn restrict freedom.

A sixth and last example is concerned with personal freedom, which begins with freedom of action and reaches a philosophical summit — perhaps even an apex that can be improved on only in detail but in principle cannot be exceeded — in Kant's ethics of the will. Personal freedom is already endangered by a preponderance of social morality that sidelines duties toward oneself. Moreover, personal morality is opposed by processes of naturalization, partly philosophical, partly in the individual sciences, that now implicitly, now explicitly and emphatically declare freedom to be an illusion and make the related concepts of responsibility and guilt disappear.

From this broad spectrum of topics, this book selects the five domains that are the most important for the human being and at the same time represent the main aspects of the project of modernity. In each of these domains, humanity's and modernity's interest in and potential for freedom are especially great, but so, at the same time, are the endangerments of freedom, along with modernity. Even if the five domains do not cover the entire field of human freedom and threats to it, they nonetheless offer more than just a few examples of the problem. I begin with the human being as a creature of nature who wants to become free, not of nature in its entirety, but of its constraints, the constraints of both outer and inner nature (part I). Then I look at the human being as an economic and social being who seeks to overcome economic unfreedom with its extensive scarcity of goods but also to gain social freedom (part II). As a kind of interlude, the following part examines the human being as seeking knowledge, pursuing science, and creating art (part III). This is followed by an investigation of the continuation of the human's social nature in its political nature, which demands legal freedom as well as freedom in domestic and international policy; this also includes a look at the digitalization of the social world and its surveillance (part IV). Finally, I examine the freedom that distinguishes the human being as responsible person insofar as all the other aspects of freedom are based on it — this is personal freedom (part V).

These five domains, which can be further differentiated, are not simply juxtaposed or merely complementary. Nor do they form an ascending or descending hierarchy, the fundamental importance of personal freedom notwithstanding. Nonetheless, there is an arc extending from the first part, in which freedom finds its highest form in the education aiming at morality, to the last part, personal autonomy, which also culminates in morality, now defined as freedom of the will. The domains developed in between interlock, and only in working together and with each other do they justify and explain the freedom that distinguishes the human being in its dignity and that modernity has elevated to the level of a principle. In parallel, they indicate the complicated nature of this freedom, including its endangerments.

1.7
ON METHOD

The attempt made here to subject modernity to a reassessment or critique guided by the principle of freedom is not an empirical but a philosophical endeavor. As I announced in the preface, it belongs to an, in the emphatic sense, practical and political philosophy. For that reason, it seeks to avoid two kinds of one-sidedness: getting lost in details, however pertinent, and proudly withdrawing to discussions of principle alone. As a contribution relevant to its time, it combines fundamental philosophical reflections with case studies and commentary on the contemporary situation. Where the essay, for the sake of the argument's completeness, recurs to earlier studies, these are named in the notes.

The basic methodological principle of all practical philosophy is *sōzein ta phainomena*, saving the phenomena. To this end, philosophy learns about relevant experiences, and here empirical study plays an essential role. And against a lack of historical awareness rampant in many places, systematic philosophizing does not refuse instruction from the history of philosophy, either. For the cues from the history of ideas—and this is the second methodological point—endow systematic reflection with a dimension of historical depth and contribute to its clarity. According to a further philosophical method, the task sometimes is also to make classic passages speak, such as the quotation from Rousseau.

As I hinted at in the preceding section, freedom contains a potential—a technological, economic, social, and scientific, a legal, political, and not least of all artistic potential—whose deployment in the course of modernity is not wholly positive. Its modern actualization thus not only has beneficial consequences but also causes difficulties and has downsides that disavow the principle of freedom and of modernity itself or at least their splendor. This study, in any event, takes *di-aporesai* as its third methodological principle, acknowledging and working through difficulties.

Aporias, however, do not have to be understood literally as dead ends. The reassessment undertaken here in the form of a judicative critique instead takes them as embarrassments and paths not yet opened. It does not see difficulties as reasons for despair but as occasions for reflection. It seeks the roots of the difficulties and to this end gives a precise diagnosis. And it develops this diagnosis, on the pattern of determinate negation, into a solution, that is, a therapy.

In discussing possible aporias the question of their consequences for freedom arises: for its assessment, for its appreciation, for its future viability. Undoubtedly, beside its twofold anthropological and epochal significance, the notion of freedom has a third, existential meaning. That is why the topic does not fall under the purview of philosophy alone but that of considered everyday reasoning, of political debate, and of course of numerous individual sciences as well.

Finally we must not forget great authors. I have already mentioned Lessing and Goethe; a third, Friedrich Schiller, becomes an honorary citizen of the young French republic for his freedom plays. Unlike what some provocation-loving authors think, however, neither any single one of the extraphilosophical authorities nor their combination has sole jurisdiction. Beginning with clarifying the concept via provocative attempts at obstruction all the way to the constructive labor of thinking, no thorough reflection, no veritable critique of freedom and modernity can do without philosophy.

PART I

Freedom from Natural Constraints

There are two things René Descartes, one of the pioneers of modern philosophy, expects of the investigation of nature he helped to found, and both are relevant to freedom: an "effortless" enjoyment of the fruits of the earth and a liberation from "an infinite number of diseases, both of the body and of the mind."[1]

Descartes's superlatives, "effortless" and "an infinite number," clearly go too far. Still today, almost four hundred years later, and even in the wealthy West, neither an effortless enjoyment nor the liberation from infinitely many diseases seems within reach. The countersuperlative that both goals remain forever unattainable is more convincing. Nonetheless, the brilliant success of an ever-expanding research into nature can hardly be contested, neither in the domain of facilitating labor through engineering, including the new information technologies, nor in the domains of health and prolonged life expectancy through medicine, medical technology, and pharmaceutics. These are joined by a third domain Descartes hints at in his later acknowledgment of a Stoic life maxim. The principle of not fearing death points to the domain of education and self-education.

All three domains are constitutive for the human being, the principle of freedom, and the project of modernity. Yet they are often overlooked, which is why this book places them at the beginning and discusses their relevance to freedom, first the emancipation from the constraints of external nature operated by means of (science-based) technology in a broad sense (chapter 2), then the achievements for freedom of (also science-based) medicine (chapter 3), and finally the emancipation not from but with regard to an inner nature that takes place by means of education and self-education (chapter 4).

In engaging nature, modern freedom reveals its double essence. As liberation from natural constraints, as emancipation, it stands up to a recalcitrant outer and inner nature. In that respect, it serves negative freedom, which, of course, turns into positive freedom, that is, culture. Now, what is true of freedom and many other basic concepts relevant to the human being is true of culture as well. It is not for a lack of clarity but because of the many facets of the matter in question that the concept is polysemous. To take our first methodological principle seriously, to save the phenomena, is to accept its variety of meanings.

The Latin word *cultura*, from which the word "culture" derives in many European languages, already has three basic meanings. "Culture" means (1) working on, maintaining, planting; (2) agriculture, working the land; finally (3) education and training. Later, the word also designates what comes out of these and other activities. "Culture" then means both (4) the entirety of the manifestations of the collective life of a group, people, or society and (5) the collective defined by these manifestations itself.

This first part of the book focuses on two of these meanings. Both designate dynamic activities such that culture takes place as a process, a cultivation. The first cultivation happens as an ultimately collective activity that by means of technology arranges the natural environment according to the interests of the human being. I call this process *oikopoiesis*. The second cultivation consists in an activity relating to the individual, that of developing each person's talents and skills. We may, for the moment, call the first task an external cultivation (chapter 2), the second task an internal cultivation (chapter 4), with the achievements of medicine, along with pharmaceutics and medical technology, forming a field in between (chapter 3). For all three tasks, I lay out—not always formally but always in terms of content—the series of reflections I presented in section 1.6, that is, I sketch first the potential for freedom (thesis), then the endangerments of freedom (antithesis), and finally a renewed freedom (synthesis).

2

External Cultivation: Technology

2.1

THE CONCEPTS OF TECHNOLOGY AND NATURE

To avoid misunderstandings, we have to explain what phenomena the terms "technology" and "nature" describe before we reflect on technology's potential for freedom over or against nature.

The expression *tekhnē*, or technology, originally designates an intelligent ability, an art in the sense of artistry or craftship. According to Aristotle's decisive definition, it is a capacity for making something according to rules that can be taught and learned, to produce tools and goods, for example, as well as to create works of art or restore a patient's health. The corresponding activity is called *poiēsis*, producing or making, as distinct from *praxis*, acting in the narrower sense.

While in antiquity, technology was a craft, "modern" technology is conducted on the basis of research that ever further penetrates the "secrets of nature." Technology transforms from a craft into a science of engineering that, in the terms of Descartes's *Discourse*, seeks to make the human being the *maître de la nature*, the lord and master of nature.

Undoubtedly, the capacity for reason and language belongs to the essence of the human being. Without technology, the human is a deficient being; it is with the help of technology that humans liberate themselves from numerous natural constraints and subject (external) nature to their will. Technology both bears on emancipation — it liberates from constraints — and has positive, constructive significance. Not just the Suez Canal, the moon landing, and ever smaller yet more powerful computers, but ancient aqueducts and Gothic cathedrals, too, are technical masterpieces.

Looking at reality with open eyes, however, also means acknowledging that there is technology designed from the start for aggressive and destructive goals and purposes, that is, ever more refined weapons including poisons and procedures aimed at destruction. And it does not ignore that technology designed for constructive ends can be repurposed or abused: almost every technology can be developed into a weapon or employed as one directly. And the interests of terrorists, organized crime, or a given country's enemies are too great to prevent possibilities from quickly becoming realities.

Fortunately, there is an opposite direction as well. Nuclear energy can be used not only militarily but peacefully as well (although nuclear energy peacefully intended, too, is anything but without dangers). Unmanned aerial vehicles, so-called drones, were initially developed to carry and launch weapons and are being deployed that way. But they can also be used, for instance, to detect the source of a major fire.

Both destructive technology and the abuse of constructive technology, however, are all too obvious phenomena. We will therefore leave them aside here, but not those phenomena where even a freedom potential with positive intentions turns into unfreedom.

The concept of technology thus clarified, let's turn to the concept of nature. The expression has two fundamentally different meanings. Formally, "nature" means the essence of a thing, including the human being, which can be captured in concepts and, in some domains, in laws. Materially, in contrast, nature concerns the entirety of all perceivable givens not produced by the human being but, precisely, given. They include inorganic and organic matter as well as plants and animals, and, when considered as an organism, the human being, too. For the perspective of technology, the second, material meaning of "nature" is of special importance.[1]

2.2
AGAINST THE ROMANTIC VIEW OF NATURE

Humanity has had an ambivalent relationship with material nature since its beginnings. The "romantic view" only looks at the creative and vital aspects, the ones that are positive for freedom. It sees that in the course of natural history—this is the creative aspect—life in the first place, then ever more powerful forms of life, finally a being of freedom, the human being, emerges. And nature—this is its second, vital achievement—provides all these organisms with the means of life. The romantic view (in the colloquial sense of "romantic"), third, also sees the cosmos, the well-ordered organization of nature (the original meaning of "cosmos") as well as what is beautiful and awe-inspiring about it, as a phenomenon that transcends everything ordinary, purposive, and calculable.

When, prompted by the theme of technology, we focus on the human being and its environment, nature is characterized not merely by the aid it gives or its beauty. At first, humans can make immediate use of only a small part of nature, caves they crawl into, for example, or berries they eat. A larger part must first be arranged to suit their purposes. The work this necessitates shows nature to be resistant and recalcitrant, which, first, makes working on nature necessary and, second, makes this work arduous.

Importantly, nature abounds in destructive power.[2] Even those groups that in German are called *Naturvölker*, "natural peoples," cannot escape the terror of nature. More than that, since they lack developed technology and are thus much more exposed to destructive nature, they in many places offer sacrifice, even human sacrifice, to placate the gods, the rulers of nature, because they lack a knowledge of causes.

A technically highly developed civilization can never tame the destructive forces once and for all. It remains subject to—not infrequently devastating—natural forces, which prompts skepticism concerning the romanticizing talk, which goes back to Rousseau,[3] of nature's wisdom and the demand to revere it: although nature at times bestows food and shelter in abundance, the happy symbiosis, eternal peace between nature and humanity, does not occur in reality. Nature itself, to be sure, is neither cruel nor benevolent. Rather, it is the embodiment of givens whose interplay of laws and external conditions creates ever-new constellations. To the human being, however, nature shows itself as constructive, destructive, or deficient. It is for this very reason that the first conception of cultivation, the technically supported work on nature to further human interests, is indispensable.

A freedom perspective on nature presupposes the ambiguity evoked earlier. That which is indispensable to life, nature, often simultaneously proves to be a threat, first to bare survival, then to a secure and pleasant life, finally only to the luxurious life. Moreover, humanity is distinguished by wanting ever more. Probably since its beginnings, undoubtedly as it progressed (as witnessed by Plato's description of the affluent *polis* in the *Republic*)[4] and immensely amplified in modernity, both the individual human and the collective turn out to be insatiable gluttons rarely content with the resources nature provides, which suffice for being able to live.

Of course even people who are not as greedy have a demand for technology. They bring it about by the interplay of three factors: (1) thanks to their intelligence humans react, (2) now for the purpose of bare, then of the pleasant and secure, then of the good life, (3) to the challenges of nature in a constructive way. It is because of these factors that nature poses three fundamental challenges to the human and that, from a functional perspective, there are three basic kinds of technology: In the name of the human being's self-assertion, a defensive technology — in elementary fashion the construction of levies and the planting of avalanche forests — seeks to tame the destructive forces of nature. An economic technology — in the form of domesticating animals and plants for the purpose of higher and more secure yields — opposes the situations of scarcity and lack resulting from the deficits of nature. From clothing, habitation, and household tools, to ships and land craft, to airplanes and the means of information and telecommunications, finally, a compensatory technology makes up for shortcomings that are partly specific to the species, partly specific to individuals.

All three kinds reduce the dependence on natural constraints and, simultaneously, expand our own creative leeway. Technology thus enhances both negative and positive freedom. Moreover, it is indispensable to the human, not in every but in many regards, as the following thought experiment shows. Imagine someone who, in search of a great adventure, undergoes extreme survival training. Even that person lives on more than just unboiled water and natural berries and mushrooms. For example, he is equipped with clothing to defy the elements; he brings along devices for boiling water and, generally, for calling help in extreme emergencies; rarely will he go without an emergency food ration; and not least of all, he'll carry basic first aid equipment. For modern man, even the most adventurous, the return to the state of nature is permanently cut off. The same is true of the American television show *Born in the Wild*. For this alleged birth in the wilderness, there are midwives and EMTs standing by in the case of an emergency, and the closest hospital is not far away — the wilderness degenerates into a mere backdrop.

Finally, we must not forget that changing nature for one's own purposes is not a human invention. It can already be found among subhuman organisms, in all species, even, and is, for all of them, literally vital. For a use of nature that changes nature begins with breathing and continues with the metabolism, including the process of digestion. The early civilized peoples already, even more so the advanced civilizations, and, in another advance, modern civilizations, go far beyond this, far beyond also the — if we're honest — highly rudimentary use nonhuman primates make of tools. Only human beings practice more than a primitive form of technology.

2.3
OIKOPOIESIS

Where nature offers resources, it is used in a variety of ways by even the most modest societies, which turns the initially untouched given into an increasingly cultivated nature. We have been living in the geological era in which the human (*anthropos*) has become the major driving force of ecological and even geological processes, the Anthropocene, much longer than atmospheric chemist Paul Crutzen supposed in 2002.

The cultivation taking place here is evidently a process of freedom in both of the core meanings. As an (albeit never final) overcoming of dangers, it enhances negative freedom. Insofar as yields are increased and work processes made easier, as, moreover, jobs, conveniences, and wealth are created, the use of nature has emancipatory character. Insofar as it creates a new kind of lifeworld, however, the other, positive freedom grows.

These observations oppose an overestimation of European modernity. From a fundamental point of view, European modernity accomplishes the same thing as stone age cultures and their predecessors. The boarders of nature are always already its rational, both technical and economic "exploiter." What comes to characterize modern civilization is the agenda Francis Bacon, the prophet of modern natural research, announces: in the technical engagement with nature, an enormous expansion, enhancement, and concentration of fighting dangers, facilitating work, and increasing yields is taking place.

The use of nature typical of modernity can be illustrated exemplarily by the forest. As the history of language shows, it originally was anything but a place of refuge for romantics fleeing the city. Related to the expression *Wild*, the German word for forest, *Wald*, at the beginning means the land that is uncultivated, moreover not subject to any lord, the ungoverned wilderness. Now, the wild forest has long been tamed, in many places also threatened by destruction. Above all, it is no longer ungoverned but is instead technologically cultivated by public or private owners. While indeed attempts are made, partially in avalanche and protective forests, comprehensively in so called primeval forests and national parks, to renature forests, this itself is a cultural process.

The despoliation of nature, incidentally, begins much earlier, in ancient Babylon, for example. And the extinction of many large animals owing to the inhabitants of North America was so massive that the corresponding geological epoch is being referred to as a Pleistocene overkill.[5] It seems the point must be generalized: whenever a culture does not, as the ancient Egyptians did, live quite obviously from the "flourishing" of nature (in their case, the periodic flooding of the Nile), it behaves quite ruthlessly.

In the self-conception of some modern thinkers, their respective present is superior to everything in the past—"the world has never been better than it is today." Where they no longer consider this superiority to be positively possible, authors like to switch to a negative appreciation. As prophets of penitence, their diagnosis of the threat is often apocalyptic, and they declare that "the world has never been worse than it is today." A more placid ethics puts this self-assessment into question. Even if it recognizes today's dangers to be greater than earlier ones, it sees in contemporary crisis phenomena an element of the *conditio humana*, albeit one interwoven with dangers specific to the age.

In a process we may call *oikopoiesis*, natural nature is arranged (*poiesis*) to suit the purposes of the human being, to become, ultimately, the *oikos*, the home and homestead of the human. A wise humanity of course leaves enough of noncultivated nature for it to be enjoyed as counterimage to technical and social constraints. For even where so-called natural landscapes have long been converted into cultivated, artificial landscapes, it is still possible to experience something also called "nature," the other of the everyday: instead of the noise or even just background noise of engines and machines, there is the burbling of water, the whispering of trees, the twittering, warbling, chirruping, and warning of birds, furthermore the sunrise in the mountains and by the sea, clear air, the taste of salt, the movement of the waves, the play of the clouds—what confronts the human in all these phenomena is what is literally nonhuman, not inhumane but never created by the human, an admirable if not always benevolent force of its own. When the process of *oikopoiesis* that is euphemistically called "culture" does not live up to its implicit promise progressively to improve the conditions of human life, in any case, forceful countermaneuvers are called for.

In many respects, a new technology is indifferent to freedom. The state of technology at a given moment does shape the structure of society, obviously the economy and professional life, less obviously but no less profoundly social and communal life with its forms of communication. Yet the changes thereby taking place become relevant to freedom only once they make work easier, for example, or create convenience or wealth. A new technology, however, can also result in great suffering. A prime example is the invention of the power loom, which—as we know from Gerhart Hauptmann's *Weavers*—deprived countless people of their jobs and families of their livelihood.

Other examples of the threat to freedom inherent in the loss of jobs include the introduction of robots in automotive and mechanical engineering and the digitalization of the world of communication. At the same time, the labor market in these domains splits into well-paid jobs requiring higher qualifications and badly paid ones demanding only lower qualifications.[6]

But to return to *oikopoiesis*. Of course work on nature that aims at establishing a home must not take place arbitrarily. Such an ethics of nature and technology, however, is not our topic here; technology's potential for freedom is. This potential manifests in a progressive mastery of nature that not only serves freedom but also threatens it. For on the one hand, the vitality of nature is endangered even from an exclusively anthropocentric perspective; on the other hand, great new risks emerge. Both phenomena reveal the dream occasionally dreamed of a self-liberation through technology to be purely an illusion. In reality, the service to freedom often enough turns into a threat to freedom (see below, sections 11.1 and 11.3).

There are many and varied reasons for this transformation, both external and internal to technology. The reasons external to technology begin with an overly optimistic diagnosis that sidelines (negative) side effects. The much-needed research on risks, too, is being neglected (see section 2.5). The causes internal to technology include a potential for excess on the part of technology: thanks to the life energies released by means of technology, what began as self-assertion turns, as if by itself, into a simplification of life and later into luxury.[7] With the same necessity, the struggle against hardship at some point turns into convenience; overcoming scarcity turns into excess and wastefulness.

Finally, there is an intermediate phenomenon that is based on the difference between maximization and optimization. Maximal improvements are sought in ever more specialized domains, and this almost naturally leaves aside the question of optimization, the decisive question for the value a development has for the human being: does this improve the *oikos* as a whole?

Nonetheless, on balance the great technical developments offer humanity more opportunities than risks. To cite the most salient example: the fires we are able to light likely have warmed more than they have scorched, and devices like knives and hoes likely have made work easier much more than they have endangered other people. Here a variant of Occam's razor—"entities should not be multiplied unnecessarily"—may apply: the simpler diagnosis, as opposed to unnecessarily convoluted ones, may be the better one. But it remains to be verified whether the on the whole positive assessment also applies to the newest developments in medicine, say, or digital networking.

2.4
PROTECTION OF NATURE VERSUS PROTECTION OF THE ENVIRONMENT

To oppose the devitalization of nature, we can still go back to a basic idea articulated by a philosopher who, although he does not develop an explicit theory of how to deal morally with nature, introduces a persuasive basic principle. In the *Critique of Judgment*, Kant, without naming the author, takes up Descartes's notion of humans as the "lords and masters of nature." He calls the human the "titular," that is, legitimate "lord of nature." This right, however, is his only as a moral being and therefore includes the duty to cultivate nature—which for Kant means both inner, thinking nature and outer, material nature—according to the standards of morality.[8]

In reality, of course, the human in the progress of external culture has developed more and more into a predator, even into the most dangerous predator on the planet. Here we cannot but agree with a contemporary of Kant's, the philosopher and theologian Johann Georg Hamann, who in his *Brocken* [literally, *Chunks*] declares: "Man consumes infinitely more than he needs—— and devastates infinitely more than he consumes."[9] Our own age is no exception. In despoiling nature, including overhunting and overfishing as well as poisoning and not least through climate change, it severely disturbs the previous equilibrium. Hence the best way for humans to bring order to nature is to call themselves to order, which is to say at the very least to restrict their predatory freedom enormously.

Restricting the predatory aspect does not, as overzealous critics of technology think, mean giving up technology as a whole. For the broad spectrum of modern technology comprehends not just the destructive forces that severely aggravate ecological crisis phenomena. It also contains counterforces that, moreover, have become so essential that without their deployment humanity today is no longer able to survive. Two indications must suffice: on the one hand, the detrimental consequences, such as an excess of pollutants and waste and the exhaustion of resources can no longer be managed without relevant technologies, recycling and waste treatment. In addition, the world's population continues to grow; the per capita need for habitation, for material infrastructure (streets and roadways; train, electricity, phone, and gas lines; etc.), not least of all for water and energy increases. Just for energy, the lifeblood of modern civilization, worldwide demand is expected to double by midcentury, even triple if modeled on the per capita demand in the United States and Canada. On the other hand, unless per capita demand were drastically reduced, the world's population could not even be fed without technical help. Given an increase in population and a decrease in agricultural land, the struggle against hunger in the world cannot be conducted without the development of nutrient-rich high-calorie foodstuffs, that is, a technological achievement in the wider sense.

And many, if not vital then life-simplifying technologies, from traffic lights, elevators, kitchen appliances, and vehicles for public and private transportation, to computers and ever more powerful mobile and smart phones, to glasses, dentures, medication, and surgical tools, are so profoundly interwoven with the fabric of everyday life that, although in "modern" societies, it might be possible to do without one or another of these technologies, practically no one today can live without all of them. In that regard, the announced third restriction of freedom already exists today: a de facto dependence on the technosphere.

The conclusion to be drawn from these findings is evident. It contradicts a thesis that now superelevates, now underestimates technology, and that conservative thinkers skeptical of technology such as Werner Sombart, Ernst Jünger, Martin Heidegger, and Hans Freyer come close to:[10] while in earlier times, humans prayed to God, they now idolize technology. In reality, technology is considered powerful because there is practically nothing that might not be improved, which is why the researchers' republic in Francis Bacon's scientific-technical utopia *New Atlantis* is called "College of the Six Days' Work." For six here is the number of the incompleteness and imperfection that characterizes all human technology, creation without the perfection of the seventh day on which "God saw that it was good." Yet everyone is aware that the omnipotence responsible for this perfection is never found in human works, technology included. And nobody, anyway, expects from technology any of the other properties usually attributed to God, such as justice, wisdom, and mercy.

A sober assessment grants technology an enormous gain in freedom without being silent about the costs.[11] The indispensable task, the taming of the predator in the human, does not by any means demand renouncing technology of whatever kind it may be.

What is necessary, in turn, is a restriction that here, to simplify and by way of example, I call "environmental protection" in a positive sense. It has two aspects that are particularly important, climate protection and environmental protection in the narrower sense. In both respects, a sustainably environmentally friendly technology is necessary. Profound conflicts arise here that modernity's freedom project must not marginalize: Germany is paying for the energy transition, the quick phase-out of nuclear energy, with higher energy prices, with greater dependence on other countries, with new power lines and windmills that interfere with nature and the aesthetics of the landscape, and not least of all with a setback in climate protection efforts. And from a political perspective, an energy and environmental policy conceived as a model for the world is, for the moment, hardly accepted to be an example worth emulating anywhere in the world.

In addition, a climate protection policy fixated on the reduction of carbon dioxide (CO_2) competes with a protection of nature that in order to protect certain biological species and ecosystems leaves nature untouched by human interventions. The competition is apparent already in a historical fact: by using coal to furnish the vast amounts of energy required by eighteenth- and nineteenth-century industrialization, the previously immense pressure was taken off the forests. In this example, although that was not the motivation back then, it is the protection of nature that wins over the protection of the environment. As Jens Soentgen writes in a summary, without "the carbonization of the economy," which came with enormous CO_2 emissions, the reforestation of large swaths of central Europe would not have taken place.[12]

A second, current example for the competition between climate protection and the protection of nature is the question what certain natural spaces are to be used for: to build solar energy plants, to grow biomass, or to protect nature in the area. While the protection of nature advocates for leaving forests as natural as possible—no trees are to be felled, pests like bark beetles are not to be fought, and woody debris is always to be left on the ground—climate protection sees forests as resources for regenerative energy production and considers forests left in a natural state to be a socially and politically inadmissible luxury. The consequence is unavoidable: because renewable energies need enormous amounts of space, the competition between climate protection and the protection of nature is, first, unavoidable and will, second, at least in densely populated high-consumption regions such as central and western Europe, likely be lost by the protection of nature, bar some rather symbolic exceptions.

For optimistic ecologists the sad consequence of this situation is that either CO_2 is declared "the universal indicator of the good condition of the environment" or the universal indicator is renounced to maintain the existing plurality of values and resolve competition between values by negotiation and compromise, not by priority rules enshrined in law.[13]

A third example of competition is the unconventional method of producing oil and gas by fracking. Arguments in favor of fracking include a (relative) energy independence and a lowering of energy prices combined with a decrease in unemployment; arguments against it include renewed consumption of land and dangers for the ground water.[14]

2.5

MAJOR RISKS

There is a further threat that a technology oriented by freedom poses to freedom, the notorious "major risks." Having discussed them in detail elsewhere,[15] I would like to limit myself here to presenting an addendum to those earlier reflections that becomes necessary within the framework of a study on freedom. We must not restrict use of the term "major risk" to the technical domain. There are major global political risks such as stocks of weapons of mass destruction kept at the ready; there are political-economic risks that have led to numerous crises, not just the Great Depression, and political-financial risks that finally prompted the Great Recession across the globe and, in Europe, the Euro crisis, which started in 2009. Nor must we ignore the major risks in domestic policy, and thus social risks, that have led to a slowdown in investment in a situation of high national debt and, in many countries, to high levels of long-term unemployment.

There are some voices demanding that we not even expose ourselves to major risks. On that reasoning, however, there should be no cities like San Francisco and metropolises like Istanbul constructed in regions with seismic activity. And the atomic bomb had better not been developed at all, especially since it was clear at the time already that both Germany and Japan had practically lost the war.

The question of whether we ought to get involved with the technology related to major risks is not at issue here. But one thing is evident where freedom is concerned: a society has the right to take such risks only if it publicly debates risks and opportunities, if it prepares such debate with rigorous risk assessment and follows up with efficient measures.

At a minimum, the indispensable risk assessment must explore what kind of dangers are threatening and then decide whether these previously unclear and thus in part uncanny dangers can be transformed into clear, manageable, and controllable risks. Not least of all, it has to assess the cost — personal and social, ecological and cultural, and even aesthetic — at which such control might come. In all cases, a society whose policies build on both kinds of research, regular science and risk assessment, is immune to the danger of a pessimism that considers the combination of science and technology with democracy and rule of law — in short, modern civilization — to be a terrible mistake.

What threatens, of course, is the opposite danger once more, namely, that the comprehensive and unbiased perception of reality is sacrificed to prior political considerations. On March 11, 2011, an earthquake of a magnitude of 9.0 shook Japan. It was immediately followed by a series of tsunamis that had two consequences: damage to the nuclear plant in Fukushima that led to a nuclear meltdown in three reactors, and a devastation that killed twenty thousand people and destroyed the homes of hundreds of thousands.

A fair perception of this catastrophe would have acknowledged from the outset that 9.0-magnitude earthquakes are improbable in Germany. Moreover, it would have looked at both catastrophes. In Germany, however, the second, the devastation, had no emotional impact worth mentioning. Reactions were restricted to Fukushima, and an energy transition was declared—rashly, already from the perspective of political craftship—which, moreover, no longer focused on the previously prevalent topic of climate protection. And because the selective perception was shaped by prior political decisions, there was no serious engagement with the final report on Fukushima published by the United Nations Scientific Committee on the Effects of Atomic Radiation.[16] For the conclusions of the report did not correspond to expectations; they were that the radiation released in Fukushima had no immediate effect on the health of the population; cancer risk has not recognizably increased; and no statistically demonstrable health damage is expected for the future.[17]

An unbiased assessment may very well remain skeptical toward this result, highly disturbing for opponents of nuclear power. It may, moreover, bring up the risks of nuclear waste disposal that, in Japan and across the world, have been ignored since the beginnings of the use of power plants fueled by atomic energy. We should, however, rely on valid arguments as well as, in addition, advocate an open-ended public debate and concede that the energy transition—and this is why it may be qualified as rash—has economic, foreign policy, and aesthetic costs that had not been seriously thought through and calculated. One important point, meanwhile, namely, that atomic energy be used as a transitory bridge technology, that is, one to be employed only temporarily, had long become a consensus view.

2.6
A PRELIMINARY SUMMARY

The fact that this chapter ends with the topic of major risks must not be mistaken for tacitly proffering the view that on balance, the freedom potential of technology is negative. Neither de facto nor necessarily does technology ultimately threaten humans more than it benefits them. On the contrary, people living in the societies that are most developed in this respect enjoy their technological achievements in a way and to an extent that makes them the envy of other countries: the simplification of work by machines, the reasonably secure provision with food thanks to an enormous increase in yields based on agricultural technology and science, and, barring pollution and congestion, ever faster, safer, and more comfortable means of transportation (which for many bring extra enjoyment), as well as information and communication technologies that were quite simply unimaginable just a few years ago.

Even so-called natural peoples are not content with the nature imposed on them, a fact that relativizes their widely held self-conception as a mere part of nature: in using equipment for fishing and hunting, in acquiring clothing and shelter through the use of tools, in searching for means against illness and obtaining fire, not least in working on nature, these peoples already maintain an, in many respects, technological civilization.

Finally, this, too, is true: humans do not have to relate to technology like a sorcerer's apprentice, losing control of the tools, means, and procedures they develop because these devices would develop a power of their own. Phenomena with such an autonomous power potential do indeed exist. Skeptics can point to the major risks just evoked; additional examples will be given later in this book. Nonetheless, technology not merely remains, as indicated, indispensable for humans. In the course of history, it has also significantly increased freedom. It has facilitated numerous goals and purposes for humans, moreover gifted them with relief and gains of time that could be converted into freedom. No longer at the mercy of an overwhelming nature, humans with the help of the three dimensions, defensive, economic, and compensatory technology, have been able immensely to increase their freedom potential and, in many respects, turn the earth into an, on the whole, familiar home. That is why general pessimism or despair are not called for in confronting modern technology.

Those, however, who believe it possible to develop a technology divested of all ambiguity and safe from abuse fail to recognize that tendencies toward ambiguity and abuse, or at least the danger of dependency, are inherent to technology. Moreover, they fall prey to an illusion of omnipotence. The alternative, a realistic vision, understands the meaning or purpose of technology, *oikopoiesis*, as an open process, never perfect and always in need of improvement.

3

Medicine

Understanding medicine (along with pharmaceutics and medical technology) as a contribution to freedom from nature is not an obvious notion. Yet once entertained, it easily meets with agreement, because both the general meaning of freedom and its paramount importance in the project of modernity are quickly evident, even if the issue here is no longer external nature in the usual sense but nature in the human being. And unlike classic technology and engineering, the focus is no longer primarily on physics and, later, chemistry but on biology and, more generally, the entirety of the life sciences, in addition to, of course, physics and increasingly medical and information technology as well.

This shift in the guiding science(s) aside, there is a commonality with the "usual" technology: since early modernity, both of them have been based on intensive natural research. According to one mathematician, physicist, and metaphysician, that is to say, someone engaged in basic research—the already mentioned René Descartes—medicine even belongs to the most important drivers of natural research. Even more important is another argument: medicine aids in situations that threaten the human not as a cultural being but already as a natural being. That is why, in cases of illness and accidents, that is, of dangers for the human constitution, already the cultures whose practices, by the standards of modern medicine, count as primitive appreciate the relevant experts, the proverbial medicine men. In addition, medicine, though not exclusively, of course, is responsible for the significant rise in life expectancy that has taken place over a number of generations now.

Now, medicine contributes to freedom from nature insofar as the three possibilities of falling ill, suffering an accident, and dying rather young evidently restrict freedom for precultural as for cultured people: all other conditions being equal, a healthy person is more free than a sick one, and an ill person whose breathing difficulties and pain are being relieved is more free than one who does not receive treatment. The person who recovers from an accident is more free than the one who continues to suffer from an accident's consequences. Finally, someone who expects a longer life is more free than someone who must die at a young age.

In all three cases, there is a higher degree of both basic kinds of freedom, negative and positive. Those concerned are subject to fewer constraints such that there are more possibilities for their actions and life projects, which is why medicine's contribution to freedom appears exclusively to be positive.

Since medical discoveries and inventions are helpful so often and in so many ways, we may even speak of a progress relevant to freedom. This progress is spurred by a change that, viewed across the centuries, has revolutionary character: while the salvation of the soul used to have the highest priority, it has now been replaced by health, and it is only a slight exaggeration to say that medicine has replaced metaphysics and theology.

Nonetheless, a closer look via the theory of freedom finds uncertainties and ambiguities that public debates have brought to wider attention. There are, moreover, phenomena in which different freedoms enter into competition.

I concentrate here on the two phases of life that are existentially the most significant and in which medicine has had the most spectacular success. Salient from the perspective of freedom in the one phase, the beginning of life, are assisted reproductive technology (ART) and preimplantation genetic diagnosis (PGD) and in the other, the end of life, the medical prolonging of life and euthanasia, which relates to a problem — suicide — that is not primarily medical but highly relevant to freedom, which is why I will discuss it in greater detail. In both domains, medicine contributes to a liberation from natural constraints but also conjures up conflicts between freedoms. Both topics are broad, and I will focus on a small number of aspects. I begin, though, with a general reflection.

3.1
ETHOS PLUS ETHICS

Because of uncertainties and ambiguities, moreover because of competing freedoms, there has for a while now been a need for medical ethics. This need even continues to grow, as is evident in numerous ethics councils and ethics commissions as well as the professional and public debates that partly precede, partly accompany, partly comment on the recommendations these institutions make.

The fact that the members of these commissions, above all physicians, legal scholars, theologians, and philosophers, as well as psychologists, seek to meet this demand suggests two things: their willingness to take on social responsibility and their readiness to work interdisciplinarily. This achievement must not make us overlook that the call for medical ethics is extraordinary—almost as extraordinary, as I've had occasion to remark, as a hitherto healthy person's visit to the doctor[1]—because the medical profession, one of the oldest in human history, has since antiquity protected itself against the abuses that threaten the art of the physician, as they do all skilled activity, by means of solemn commitments. The most famous of these, (1) patient welfare (*salus aegroti*), which in its caritative aspect is also called "duty of care," (2) nonmaleficence (*nil nocere*), and (3) respecting the will of the patient ("informed consent"), are obligations that are both specific to individual tasks and morally uncontested. As moral truisms, however, they do not require interdisciplinary ethics commissions, never mind philosophical justification. Rather, it is better to rely on exemplary physicians, nurses, and researchers—their model is enough.

That there is nonetheless a need for said commissions and that a discourse about fundamentals requires a professional medical ethics follows from the fact that the principles just named might be self-explanatory but no longer suffice for new sets of problems. In that sense, the call for ethics is the symptom of a crisis, albeit not in the dramatic sense that society is following bad practices but in the sense that medicine is confronted with having to make fundamentally new kinds of decisions. This is where the freedom ambiguity sets in: there are ever more options that expand freedom yet at the same time, and this restricts freedom once again, there is a constraint to make ever more complicated decisions. In these decisions, from a third freedom perspective, freedoms may compete and might have to be weighed against each other.

Understandably, the new possibilities, for example that human life might be prolonged or begun thanks to medical support, conjure up not only great hopes but deep-seated fears as well. Not just because of this emotional reaction but also because of the difficult state of affairs, the three sides, physicians along with scientists, patients along with their families, and society via its laws, would be making it too easy for themselves if they claimed license freely to dispose of the new possibilities.

Undoubtedly one may appeal to the usual arguments for freedom of decision even when it comes to previously unknown options: on the medical side even to a duty, the task of curing, on the research side to the basic right of the freedom of research, on the patients' side to the right of self-determination, and on the legislator's side to political humanity and liberality. But the humanitarian mission and the three freedom aspects do not give rise to an unlimited power of disposition over human life. An unrestricted license to dispose is opposed by another aspect of freedom that indisputably ranks as a principle of ethics and law. It consists in the inviolability of human life and incontestably comes before science's freedom of research and personal freedom of decision.

Speaking in favor of a therefore not unlimited but far-reaching right of disposition is the fact that neither the beginning nor the end of human life is simply a natural event. There are conflicts as well; in the case of abortions, for example, the conflict between the rights of the mother and the life of the fetus. The question also arises whether research that uses embryos is allowed; it destroys human life but in the long run can serve therapeutic purposes. Moreover, we have to think about whether we should be allowed to examine the human germline with the goal of manipulating it; such examinations entail risks that are difficult to assess but also give rise to diagnostic and therapeutic hopes.

Finally, there is at least an ethical question mark to be applied to medicine concerned with healthy people, from Botox injections to breast enlargements and facelifts to so-called performance enhancement, that is, medications such as "stimulants" for pilots, surgeons, and CEOs but also for actors, musicians, lecturers, examinees, and many others.

While we must not overestimate this more recent field, medicine for the healthy, we must not forget that medicine primarily serves other purposes, namely, curative, preventive, and palliative. When it acts on behalf of the healthy in other ways than with check-ups and obstetrics, its image changes, and so does medicine's contribution to freedom. The one side, patients, no longer goes to see physicians primarily as helpers in distress but as service providers for special requests that to people in real distress appear as superfluous luxuries. The other side, the physicians, are threatened by a commercialization that increasingly focuses on profit.

Only because on these and other issues, it is not possible without further ado to say what the three guiding goals of medicine demand, what patient welfare, nonmaleficence, and respect for the patient's will, in combination with self-evident principles of law, require as the result of an immense increase in knowledge and ability—on the pattern of "morality as the price of modernity"[2]—there is a need for what was previously dispensable, namely, both a veritable medical ethics and ethics commissions. Since these are expected to issue precepts and above all prohibitions, in any case suggestions to determine actions, the leeway and hence the freedom the medical profession as a whole and, not infrequently, patients, too, have in making decisions is being restricted.

Add to this social restrictions on freedom. When there is the possibility to diagnose a child in the womb with trisomy 21 (Down syndrome), for example, how free is a woman to continue a pregnancy despite this diagnosis? Does not social pressure arise, which it takes a lot of courage to oppose and nonetheless carry the baby to term, when such examinations are common and most women have an abortion? And does she not only subject herself to social criticism but must expect the child later to be rejected as well?

A fair and above all appropriate assessment of modern medicine begins with those of its achievements that are practically free of ambiguity. These include strict hygiene, which, starting with the significant lowering of maternal and infant mortality rates, is beneficial to freedom in a variety of ways. They continue with the invention of antibiotics and sophisticated diagnostic procedures and equipment and are far from exhausted even when we reach numerous surgical innovations.

3.2
END OF LIFE I: TERMINAL CARE

Skepticism toward modern civilization must not lead us to deny a success story for which medicine is not solely but certainly coresponsible, a veritable mortality revolution: life expectancy has risen significantly. To be sure, it has not gone very far beyond the age already reached by ancient writers and philosophers. Like Solon, Sophocles lived to be ninety years old, Pythagoras probably longer, and Plato died in his eighty-first year. What is new is that the higher life expectancy benefits large parts of the population.

Happily, people do not merely grow older. They also—and this continues the gain in freedom that lies in the mortality revolution—people stay fresh longer: physically, mentally, and not least of all socially and emotionally. The popular complaint that our societies are growing too old or even senile is a distortion of reality because true aging now sets in much later than it used to. Seen that way, people are growing younger—sixty-year-olds today are far from old. The onset of grave illness and need for care has shifted more and more. And, again in distinction from antiquity, even the restrictions of freedom that come with a grave illness or dependence on care can often be alleviated: not only socially, via proper care, but also medically, pharmaceutically, and technically, via optical, hearing, or walking aids, for instance.

The freedom gains of modern medicine including pharmaceutics and technology are thus enormous. Yet to know that they are not able to avoid all blemishes, it is not necessary to take Jules Romains's comedy *Knock* seriously, in which an ambitious physician and crafty judge of character succeeds in turning a healthy rural population into an army of permanent patients.

The not just fictional but factual flipside of many treatments begins with their in part significant side effects. Not only is the body weakened; new risks arise as well, and, not least of all, emotional as well as mental changes take place that in turn have emotional consequences for spouses, parents, and children, and colleagues, too. All this diminishes freedom, which is why sometimes, on balance, abstaining from treatment seems the more appropriate option.

Furthermore, people prefer dying at home, in familiar surroundings. Since there, however, the simplest preconditions for appropriate medical treatment often are not met, most people spend their last weeks and months in a nursing home, hospital, or hospice.

Sybille Lewitscharoff, Büchner Prize winner and prominent author, cites both positive and negative examples of the different ways of dying. In the first part of her notorious Dresden speech, in any case, she presents models that could hardly be more different: the tenderly beloved grandmother, who maintained "dignity, confidence, and friendliness" and thereby deprived the death brought by a cancer of "its terror"; the father, an "extremely generous social person" and a gynecologist who, during one of his depressive phases, hanged himself in his office and "even permitted in this horrible kind of death that my mother had to find him like that"; and an eighty-eight-year-old friend of the mother, who severely injured herself in a fall at home, was taken, "after several hours of agony," to the hospital, "where she immediately fell into a coma and would surely have died had one allowed her to do so." When, after an "elaborate reanimation show" and an "absolutely horrifying year in an atrocious home," she finally died, she died as "a rebellious angry person."[3]

Indeed the impression arises in some places that the human being is no longer allowed to die, for severely injured and dying persons are saved with all available means or treated until the very last moment with experimental cures even when the only appropriate aid would be palliative care. Such care, however, is called for in the name of freedom as well: a dying person suffering from thirst, nausea, or constipation may receive support for what remains of his or her physical freedom, the vital functions, and breathing difficulties and pain may be relieved as well.

Similar things can be said for the emotional and social aspect of freedom. To respond to the anxiety and restlessness of dying persons, their isolation, resignation, and depression, that is, to restrictions of the freedom the dying can still have, an accompaniment is desirable that supplements the relieving of pain with emotional and social support. Only in this way are the dying respected as human beings who until their last breath have the right not to have their dignity violated and instead their freedom strengthened as much as possible.

Dying persons need and deserve not help to die but help in dying, that is, care, support, and love. In addition, not only the dying but their families, too, deserve help. A medical culture of dying also includes the task of not raising false hopes. Some still follow the maxim of Goethe's and Schiller's personal physician. Christoph Wilhelm Hufeland demands that physicians spread life at all times and in all situations and that they maintain the illusion of hope for the patient even where no hope exists anymore. It is better, both more honest and more dignified, to put hopes straight that cannot be fulfilled. Rather than put on an act of omnipotence and rush into treatment for the sake of treatment, humane physicians admit, where that is necessary, the overwhelming power of death and at the same time their own powerlessness. This includes tactful explanations; for even if it is easier, "naked honesty" is also unmerciful.

In today's age of high-performance, even omnipotent medicine, it is necessary to recall that everyone involved must learn once more something they would prefer to repress: both doctors and nursing staff as well as patients and their families must existentially accept the finitude of the human being.

3.3
END OF LIFE 2: SUICIDE

The topic of suicide raises the issue of freedom from natural constraints, but not only. It also reaches into the fifth part of this study, personal freedom. But of course it has its place here, in the domain of medicine. Whether here or there — because of its great relevance for freedom, it demands a thorough and thus comprehensive discussion.

The Concept

When it comes to suicide and assisted suicide, the very terminology is a matter of contestation, particularly in German. Traditionally, one speaks of *Selbstmord*, self-murder, which evokes a serious crime when no such thing is at issue. To avoid the misleading association, some prefer the expression *Selbsttötung*, self-killing, yet killing is still a crime, which is why others again prefer speaking of *Freitod*, "voluntary (literally: free) death," or *mors voluntaria*, to emphasize a double self-determination: ending one's life in freedom and ending it with a right to this freedom.

This purely positive assessment, however, is contested. German, a language as tolerant as it is, in some respects, lacking in self-confidence, therefore hides behind the borrowed term *Suizid*. Yet that word recalls *homo-cidium*, homicide, and *sui-cidium* thus means nothing but self-killing — the association to be avoided is maintained. To remain neutral in this normatively charged conflict, one may speak of "laying hands on oneself," "dying by one's own hand," or, to emphasize the relevance to freedom, "voluntary death [*Frei-Tod*]."

Whatever the expression employed—what is meant is that someone does not wait for a "natural death" but rather puts a nonnatural end to his or her own life. Among all the organisms we know, this possibility is available to human beings alone. It proves that humans do not simply exist but relate to themselves and that, in this relationship, they have a power of disposition that is literally radical, that reaches to the very roots of life.

In the case of dying by one's own hand, freedom is at stake not only in a radical but simultaneously in an ultimate way. Someone who lays hands on himself without constraint and after careful consideration, that is, in fact, freely, acts destructively, in the literal sense, and irreversibly. He proves his freedom to himself but at the same time loses it; he freely puts an end to his freedom. It is not, in any case, false pathos to say: veritable existence is at issue here; death by one's own hands is, to a high degree, an existential problem.

Although suicide is a deeply personal act, it also has, like everything that is human, a social side. People willing to commit suicide do not shrink into Robinsons living on desert islands without companions. Generally, they have family, perhaps also a partner, moreover acquaintances and neighbors, perhaps even friends who—anything but indifferent to a death brought about voluntarily—are being deeply affected. People who learn from someone close to them that they seriously no longer want to live feel coresponsible. When that person takes his or her life without talking to me, moreover, especially in the case of parents, children, and partners, there is damage done to the relationship of trust. And persons that are being involved against their will, railroad engineers, for example, are traumatized for life.

A Look at Reality

For both reasons—because suicide is a specifically human and because it is an ultimate, quite simply irrevocable act—its normative assessment is of particular significance. Before we embark on such an assessment, however, we are well advised to take a twofold, social and personal, look at reality.

Let's begin with the social. Ever since the landmark study by French sociologist Émile Durkheim,[4] we have known that suicide involves cultural particularities. It is because of them that in the West, especially in central Europe and there particularly in Switzerland, the suicide rate is much higher than in Buddhist, Hindu, or Islamic countries while in one particular other country, South Korea, with its culture shaped by neo-Confucian thought as well as by thinking in terms of success and competition, it is particularly high. And we must not overlook that there is, in Islam in particular, a tradition of suicide attacks in which one's own voluntary death is combined with a grave homicide, the killing of innocent people.

There are probably a number of factors responsible for the higher suicide rates in Europe. One factor, a strengthening of freedom and of the right to live one's life autonomously, modern society may be proud of. Other factors, though, may hardly be said to be exclusively positive, neither the dissolution of personal relationships nor the diminishing of religious ties, and not the low capacity for working through suffering either.

A second, personal look starts from the experience that humans have a natural interest in being alive. The wish to put an end to one's life thus generally comes about in fundamental life crises. Empirical suicide research does not doubt there might be a death freely chosen after a sober assessment, a so-called *Bilanzsuizid*, but it rarely encounters it in real life. In the vast majority of cases, suicide is committed by people who despair of the meaning of life. Either they do not see anyone who understands them and is reliably on their side, or they suffer from a progressive terminal illness and particularly from unbearable pain. There is in any event good reason, in cases of suicide, generally to suppose a severe restriction of freedom and above all a last appeal to other people or to society.

A socially responsible society therefore not only inquires into the causes of suicide. It also takes preventive measures and tries to help those in (psychological) distress even more. That young people who are lovesick or have trouble at work are not to be left to themselves should be a matter of course. From an ethical point of view, in any case, suicide prevention, caring counseling for people at risk of suicide, and palliative care as well hospice work deserve a clear priority.

A Look at the History of Philosophy

The moral assessment of suicide (which is rarely wholly free) is contested. According to Plato, humans do not dispose of their own lives. There is only one exception, namely, that the polis condemns someone like Socrates to death and, to avoid sullying itself, to killing himself. In his late work the *Laws*, however, Plato distinguishes between two kinds: suicide in the case of incurable shame that makes life unbearable and suicide committed out of laxness and cowardly despair.[5] In the second case, he calls for a lonely, inglorious funeral at a place without a name. Aristotle thinks similarly. According to him, "to die to escape from poverty or love or anything painful is not the mark of a brave man, but rather of a coward."[6]

While for Plato and Aristotle, suicide is not a prominent topic, it takes centerstage in postclassical philosophy, in Epicurus and the Stoics. Because these thinkers are much more interested in the concrete living of life, they push back against the polis's power claims just evoked, which consider suicide a self-murder and condemn it like all murder. Instead, they emphasize personal freedom. Epicurus, who encourages a steadfast enjoyment of life, explains: "Necessity is an evil, but there is no necessity to live under the control of necessity."[7] The Stoic Seneca follows Epicurus and grants reason the right to counsel giving up one's life or to terminate the community with the body when one thinks it right to do so.[8]

The countermovement begins not with Christianity but already in Neoplatonism, that is, already with philosophical and not religious reasons. It condemns self-killing as a precipitous intervention in the perishing of the flesh.[9]

According to the great Christian thinker Thomas Aquinas, three arguments speak against suicide. The first is a natural law argument concerning personhood: the argument of self-preservation extended by that of the love with which everyone is to meet him- or herself. The second is of a social-ethical nature: suicide is an injustice toward the community of which every human being is a part. Only in third position is the theological argument that suicide opposes God's decision about life and death.[10]

In his essay *Of Suicide*, David Hume seeks systematically to refute these arguments: first, self-destruction no more violates the divine will than self-preservation does since in both cases, the action takes place with forces given by God. Second, any possible social duty lapses at the latest when one's own life becomes unbearable. Finally, once life becomes a burden, self-destruction falls within legitimate self-interest. Hume's contemporary Jean-Jacques Rousseau has a more differentiated and dialectical view of the matter. In his epistolary novel *Julie or the New Heloise*, a resolute defense of the freedom to death is followed by a no less resolute contradiction: the apology of a dutiful active life in the service of others is to prompt an about-turn.

According to the most important figure of reference for today's debate about the foundations of moral philosophy, it is a duty "to preserve one's life"; moreover, "everyone has an immediate inclination to do so." Kant does not deny that "adversity and hopeless grief" may rob us of "the taste for life" entirely. In the opposition between duty and inclination, however, only those act truly morally who even then "preserve [their] life without loving it." Nonetheless, Kant does not consider suicide a criminal offense.[11]

A few more views may be mentioned. Kant's admirer and critic Arthur Schopenhauer says about suicide: "Far from being a negation of the will, this is a phenomenon of a strong affirmation of will."[12] According to Hegel's great antagonist Kierkegaard, despair—an advantage of the human over the animal—is the "sickness unto death" that precludes any coming to an end: as "the eternal," the self is incapable of "self"-destruction.

Schopenhauer's "student" and critic Friedrich Nietzsche demands with the pathos that characterizes his "book for all and none" that we strive to die neither too early nor too soon, but rather "at the right time!" and moreover in the right way, as a "consummating one . . . victorious, surrounded by those who hope and promise."[13]

Let's skip a few generations and pick up again in the middle of the twentieth century. In his 1942 essay *The Myth of Sisyphus*, Albert Camus rejects suicide for an existential reason: in a world devoid of meaning, life is the only human value, such that its negation would signify the victory of the absurd over the human. The human in revolt must live to protest against the absurdity of existence: for him, "a premature death is irreparable."[14] The contrary position, of course, also has its proponents. Thus, the philosophers Karl Löwith, Karl Jaspers, and Wilhelm Kamlah, and the theologian Karl Barth, as well as the author Jean Améry advocate the freedom to one's own death. For Améry, suicide is a "resounding no to the crushing, shattering *échec* of existence."[15]

Any conclusive assessment of suicide from the perspective of freedom depends on the concept of freedom at stake. Mere freedom of action does not exclude the possibility of suicide. If freedom is also held to include the openness and uncertainty of the future, however, then voluntary death contains a moment of negating freedom. The same is true when the social is seen to be constitutive of freedom. And from the perspective of unalienable human dignity, human life maintains its irrevocable right also in situations of suffering, illness, and humiliation. The mere right, however, is an authorization, not a duty. Without additional arguments, human dignity does not oppose voluntary death.

An Assessment from a Juridical-Ethical Point of View

The debate merely sketched here about the moral-philosophical assessment of suicide may be perplexing. But perhaps an enlightened liberalism may nonetheless give a twofold piece of advice. On the one hand: follow the maxim *in dubio pro libertate*, when in doubt, in favor of freedom. Since there are respectable reasons to oppose a prohibition on suicide, the personal assessment of freedom should be a matter at individuals' discretion. Leaving it to them must not, however, result from indifference toward the fate of our fellow human beings. It must be joined by a commitment to give a maximum of aid and renewed sense of life to persons inclined toward suicide. On the other hand, personal morality and the legal morality that the state can assert by force, if necessary, must be strictly distinguished. The history of ideas furnishes material for reflection on this point.

After Christian synods in late antiquity had declared voluntary death a crime, codified sanctions post mortem were introduced in many places, ranging from physical mistreatment of the corpse via denying a ceremonial burial to confiscating possessions. Yet almost half a millennium ago already, the *Constitutio Criminalis Carolina* of 1532, a precursor of modern codes of criminal law, no longer provides sanctions for killing oneself. Two and a half centuries later, toward the end of the eighteenth century, Prussia renounces sanctioning suicide attempts; only suicide assistance remains punishable.

Even when, later, suicide is struck from the list of legal crimes elsewhere, a sense of strangeness lingers in societies' consciousness. It extends to the one willing to commit suicide, further to the location where the act was done, and to all persons connected with him and the act. Society, Durkheim observes in 1897, grants absolution for something that, fundamentally, it rejects.

By now, the following point is no longer contested in legal ethics: the human being's natural interest in life does not contain a duty toward society or the state; the human being does not owe it to them to stay alive. Abolishing punishments for attempted suicide, rather, is one of the achievements of the criminal law reforms inspired by the European Enlightenment. Even if one has a responsibility to go on living, toward partners, parents, or children, perhaps also toward very good friends or because of an office one has assumed, there is no legal, and certainly no civil or criminal, legally enforceable, duty.

On the other hand, politics rightly consider a high suicide rate to be alarming. For they have a duty enshrined in human rights to protect human beings' natural interest in life.[16] Because suicide, insofar as it is an expression of a fundamental life crisis, is clearly to be distinguished conceptually from the *Bilanzsuizid*, an expansion of suicide prevention does not contradict permitting suicide.

Generally, judging voluntary death is a difficult weighing of rights because two moral principles that, taken by themselves, are uncontested oppose each other. Self-determination advocates in favor of the "liberal" solution, namely, that a person capable of making judgments be allowed to decide for him- or herself whether to go on living in a difficult situation. As already mentioned, however, empirical research on suicide shows that in the vast majority of cases suicide is attempted or committed by people who despair of the meaning of their lives. Theirs is not a veritable self-determination but a strong restriction of freedom and in particular a final appeal to their fellow beings or to society. What is called for, therefore, is less the principle of self-determination than an obligation to give aid in an emergency. One may not, in any case, rashly suppose a suicide to be a *Bilanzsuizid*.

To summarize our findings so far: from an ethical point of view there are three conceivable positions toward voluntary death. The first, a fundamental prohibition, has been advocated by many moral philosophers since Plato. Yet it essentially concerns — it only concerns — the responsibility of the human being before his conscience or before God, not the domain of the responsibility of the state. It is not a prohibition of legal ethics but merely one of virtue ethics that, moreover, is not accepted by all moral philosophers.

Within the frame of a different sets of laws, general personal rights, one is allowed to live one's life autonomously. This includes — this is the third and convincing ethical option — permission to put an end to one's life oneself. At issue is a highly personal, a private action in the strict sense of the term. If someone wants to end her life in full freedom and as her explicit wish, no one, and certainly not the state with its coercive power, has the right violently to prevent her.

Yet even this third option does not apply without restrictions. Suicide prevention is practiced, and for good reason, for people in state custody, prisoners, as well as patients in hospitals (not just psychiatric wards). The reason lies in the duty of care toward people whose freedom, one supposes, is restricted, restricted because of a limited ability for insight and judgment due to a situation-bound instability. In the case of prisoners, a public interest, namely, that sentences are executed, also plays a role.

Suicide Assistance

In legal terms, especially in terms of criminal law, the intervention of a third party fundamentally differs from an action taken by oneself. There is a basic, insurmountable difference between "taking one's life oneself" and "helping someone, at his request, to take his life." It consists in going beyond the domain of personal rights and entering — at least in addition — the domain of criminal law. Assistance by a third party in suicide thus requires very good justifying reasons.

The Swiss National Advisory Commission on Biomedical Ethics convincingly declares that "respect for the autonomy of a person determined to commit suicide does not in itself provide a reason to help him or her carry it out." The "additional motive" may consist in an extreme case of care, "the desire not to abandon the person concerned, and to provide support."[17] Since assistance in suicide is not part of medical activity, when physicians decide to assist in suicides they do so not as physicians but as a familiar human being. Before they offer this kind of assistance, of course, they reflect on possible alternatives. Above all they must ensure that they are dealing with persons fully capable of judgment whose desire for suicide fulfills three conditions: it is well considered, came about without external pressure, and is enduring.

Recently, assisted suicide organizations have become active even for people who do not suffer from a disease immediately leading to death, and numbers are rising. Mentally ill people, in Belgium even children, are granted suicide assistance. One organization, moreover, seeks to be active in state-subsidized retirement homes and fights for the availability over the counter of the barbiturate usually employed, pentobarbital sodium. In addition, it advertises its "service offer."

Another cause for concern is that organized acts of assisted suicide are usually preceded by only very few meetings between those seeking to commit suicide and those willing to assist. And not least of all, we must acknowledge that regulations that put the threshold for access to suicide assistance rather low and which are euphemistically called "liberal" build up enormous pressure on particularly vulnerable people, such as chronically ill or severely disabled persons, or children: the self-determination that does indeed exist can be counteracted by economic, societal, and not least of all interpersonal constraints. Therefore, this final remark: even if a legislature does permit organized suicide assistance, it must not neglect and in fact must ameliorate the implementation of other tasks, that is, suicide prevention, counseling of people at risk of suicide, and palliative care, as well as the work of hospices.

3.4

BEGINNING OF LIFE I: REPRODUCTIVE AUTONOMY

Suicide is only partially a medical topic, namely, in the case of possible assistance from a physician. Matters are different, as the very term suggests, in the case of medically assisted procreation. Let's begin with some general thoughts.

While the complaint about societies growing too old is, as mentioned, misleading, there is a dramatic decrease in the numbers of groups who enrich every society: children and adolescents. The threat is not society growing too old; it is its lack of rejuvenation. This development, to be sure, is not so dramatic as to threaten the continued existence of humanity. But where, as in Europe, there are more people over sixty than there are people under fifteen, spontaneous liveliness diminishes. In this situation, the topic of medically assisted procreation has additional currency.

A second thought: there is no duty to bring children into this world. However, giving life to a new human being—and "give" is the appropriate word here—should be welcomed for a number of reasons, namely, because one considers human life to be worth living and because inherent to all life, including human life, is a temporal finitude that cannot be overcome by omnipotence fantasies about an infinitely long life. Humanity continues to exist only if it brings ever-new generations into the world.

There have been people before who did not want to procreate. Yet it is probably for the first time in human history that this lack has increased so much that the question arises whether a generalization of this lack would not make the life of all people difficult to bear when they grow old, retire, and need help and care.

Let's take a look first at the history, which Barbara Orland aptly describes as the "normalization of reproductive medicine since the 1970s." What used to be fate is now treated with acknowledged sterility therapies. Thanks to them, what used to be a holistic practice "has transformed into a modular procreation" that by technological means "separates 'physical love' and begetting in those directly involved." This produces what Blumenberg called "the seemingly unproducible," namely, "self-evidence."[18]

Unwanted childlessness is an "age-old" social phenomenon. It has usually been felt to be particularly painful and has brought social and economic disadvantages especially for women, who generally have been the ones to be blamed. As male offspring was preferred, the concern with having a "son and heir" is well familiar from the private sphere via agricultural, artisanal, and industrial enterprise to politics (from Henry VIII to the Iranian shah Mohammad Reza Pahlawi).

People who still today want to have children but cannot have them—a sixth of Europeans, according to estimates, remain childless without wanting to be such—are now being offered so enormous a gamut of possible aid that one increasingly wonders: are we allowed to make use of all these possibilities?

The answer that everything that can be done will sooner or later be done anyway is not just rash; it is cynical. Fortunately, it does not apply to reality. Euthanasia directed against life allegedly "unworthy of living"; the "breeding of humans" feared after the birth of the first "test tube baby," Louise Brown, in 1978; a eugenics that thanks to targeted intervention in the genome claims to bring about a new kind of human being allegedly better adapted to modern civilization—they are and remain prohibited. Such prohibitions, of course, do not support a wholesale veto against new medical possibilities. For why should a rational living being renounce its capacity for rationality as a matter of principle in so existentially crucial a wish as bringing a new life into the world? Does not here, in a profoundly personal domain, a freedom of procreation suggest itself, that is, a reproductive autonomy, according to which the decision to have children at all and, in the case of infertility, to seek medical help is one's own decision?

Undoubtedly, in many countries today it is possible to remain childless without having to fear pity or low esteem, as used to be the case. But one may also have children. And if that is not possible the natural way, one may, if one so wishes, get medical help.

Whether naturally or with medical assistance — in the end, it is the same thing that should be decisive: during the pregnancy, we are to do everything within our means for children to be healthy. And even if they are not born healthy, we are to give them all the care and security they need and help them acquire that which helps them master even a difficult life: self-confidence and trust in the world.

Medically assisted procreation does not in the least endanger any of this. There might be pathos in saying this, but once born, a child has every claim to human dignity and human rights. Moreover, all experience disavows the claim that fulfilling the wish for a child with medical help puts the child in a worse position. The very decision is rarely taken easily, the procedure itself is not without hardship, and even all these troubles do not guarantee success. Why, then, given this emphatic desire for a child, should there be any danger from the parents, during pregnancy or after birth, for the decisive criterion, the welfare of the child? And why should the child later, when it comes to learn of the medical help, feel diminished in its well-being? Thanks to heightened care, the chances for security and confidence in the self and the world are certainly not diminished, and the child will experience itself as fully accepted.

The speech by Lewitscharoff already cited, in its second part on the beginning of life, may be taken as a willful rejoinder, as an objection to medically assisted fantasies of omnipotence and a warning against modern humanity pushing itself too far. Humans will never fully be masters of their fate anyway. Of course, an organism capable of reason and language does not have humbly to accept all destinies, and Lewitscharoff does *not* say it must. Where the line is to be drawn, when, as the author approvingly says, "excellent health care" is to be made use of, is thus a question of an increasingly difficult weighing of goods.

In questions of medically assisted procreation, everyone is free to draw very narrow limits for themselves personally. An open, liberal society, however, allows for drawing the limits differently as well. In any case one should not, even in a case rightly considered to be highly problematic, surrogacy, articulate one's "disgust" as unvarnished as Lewitscharoff does, especially if one admits one's own disgust "in those cases" to be "stronger than reason," because one is hurting the legitimate feelings of others who think differently. Moreover, one is lacking something one demands from others: "any form of differentiated intellectuality."[19]

The legislative must in any event acknowledge that procreation — both the wish to procreate as well as the wish not to — is a highly personal matter. In confronting this intimate domain, every legal order with coercive power must exercise rigorous restraint. If the state seeks to intervene nonetheless, the burden of proof rests with it. There are several good reasons it might seek to intervene: where the basic rights of others are threatened, that is, where reproductive autonomy violates another's freedom, where there is injury to the common good, or where society is being overtaxed with regard to social security systems, the legislative not only may but must intervene. Violence and fraud obviously violate human rights. But given a certain age and free, reciprocal consent, neither violence nor fraud applies.

There is, however, another condition that must be met. The welfare of the child must not be endangered; it must not even be restricted. Even if medically assisted procreation takes the beginning of human life out of the natural nexus, away from the sexual experience of the parents and the development of the embryo in the womb alone, and moves part of it to the medical laboratory, the welfare of the future child must be the primary concern. And this welfare is to be understood not only in medical but in mental and social terms as well. Indisputably, the child has a right to an intact genome, to be influenced only in case of severe damage. Further, it has the right to a regular maternity and the right, within the given possibilities, to develop within an intact relationship with the mother/the parents.

Whether in the case of infertility medical assistance takes place by means of extracorporeal insemination, via a sperm donation or an egg donation — medical assistance as such does not endanger the welfare of the child. The insight that it is not possible despite many attempts to have children naturally can be painful. Those concerned react in different ways. Some accept their infertility as fate and renounce having children of their own. Others adopt children. Others again seek their calling as teachers. An open, enlightened liberal society leaves these options entirely to those concerned. Their freedom of decision also includes the possibility to seek medical help to fulfill their wish for a child. If the process of artificial insemination, which is never easy, is successful, the child finally being born is an intended child in the emphatic sense, and it may count on its parents' aid and care and on a higher, rather than lower, chance to find security, self-confidence, and trust in the world.

Skeptics nonetheless raise questions, for example: is a fifty-year-old single woman to be allowed to have children thanks to modern medicine? Is so late a pregnancy not even against nature? An attentive look at the world teaches us two things. First, women who became pregnant naturally in their late forties could give birth to healthy children already two generations ago, long, that is, before today's medicine. Second, single fifty-year-old women know that it is often more difficult for them to raise their child. Their decision will thus usually be well considered. Since the 1990s especially, both the number of pregnant women over thirty-five years of age and the age of these pregnant women have gone up. Yet with age, these women's risk of chromosomal abnormalities increases. That is why it is advisable to inform women that the wish for children is fulfilled more easily and with less danger in younger years.

Another question raised: are same-sex couples to be allowed to have children? And a third (the last one here): is surrogacy to be permitted? A "surrogate mother" is a woman who conceives a child by an artificial procedure and brings it to term for another woman. The ovum may come from the surrogate mother, from the woman in the couple of parents seeking to have a child, or from a third woman.

Even someone who has no fundamental objections to surrogacy and can imagine, for example, a sister or cousin to be a legitimate surrogate will not deny the enormous difficulties it poses, which are not as much medical as they are personal and social. First, in reality it will hardly be very close relatives who will be willing to serve as surrogate mothers but women from poorer backgrounds, whose economic situation will thus be exploited. Moreover, second, so personal a task as maternity should be shielded from any danger posed by commercialization.

Two further problems are even more serious. In our legal orders, third, termination of a pregnancy under the conditions stipulated by law is not punished. If, now, a disability were to develop in the fetus during the pregnancy, an abortion would be allowed, which would raise the undoubtedly conflict-laden question: who may decide the legitimate termination or nontermination of the pregnancy, the surrogate mother or the intended mother? And the additional question: if the intended mother decides in favor of an abortion but the surrogate mother refuses it, is the intended mother allowed to refuse acceptance of the child?

Not least of all, fourth, a close emotional relationship is likely to develop between the surrogate mother and the developing child that may lead her to no longer wish to give the child away once it is born.

Because of these profoundly existential difficulties and conflicts, even those who have no fundamental objections should opt against surrogacy. For the moment, it cannot be claimed — to be cautious — that it constitutes a reasonable kind of reproductive autonomy.

3.5
BEGINNING OF LIFE 2: PREIMPLANTATION GENETIC DIAGNOSIS

How are we to assess this topic? In some quarters, there is a pronounced tendency toward pathos and drama when it comes to preimplantation genetic diagnosis (PGD). One side considers this medical innovation a blessing, the other a curse. Strictly speaking, it is only a diagnostic procedure that is used primarily in parents for whom there is a high risk that their children will suffer from a grave hereditary illness. The procedure then helps them have a child who is not genetically burdened with the disease in question. Such a procedure reduces the fear of a severely disabled child being born; it expands the parents' possible choices and contributes to freedom in these two respects especially.

Yet the question of the freedom of the unborn child also poses itself: are parents allowed to restrict or even disregard the rights of the unborn? This question obviously leads to the highly contested topic of abortion, but this is not the issue here.[20]

Before we begin to address these questions, we must make a distinction that clearly separates preimplantation genetic diagnosis from the possible selection of embryos based on the diagnosis. The physician merely conducts the diagnosis, which is usually followed by informing the woman or the parents about relevant matters of reproductive medicine and human genetics. The diagnosis is made only a few days after the artificial insemination of the ovum and before (*pre-*) its implantation or nonimplantation in the uterus. These initial activities must be strictly distinguished from the selection between several embryos that might follow. In the former case, the responsibility lies with the physician; in the latter it lies with the persons consulting the physician alone, especially the woman who will carry the child to term, possibly the father as well.

Preimplantation genetic diagnosis, which has been employed since the late 1990s in many European and non-European countries, has been prohibited in Germany under the provisions of the 1990 Embryo Protection Act. New research and changed examination procedures, however, allow for meeting an important condition of this law, namely, not to act on totipotent embryo cells. For, beginning on day four, embryos are only pluripotent. It has also become possible to take cell samples without the danger of injury to the embryo or of diminishing the likelihood of implantation in the uterus.

Nonetheless, in the eyes of its opponents, PGD violates three of the highest constitutionally protected values: the human dignity of every child, including those with genetic defects; the right to life of embryos of which, most often, several are destroyed when a PGD is performed; and the prohibition on discrimination, since PGD is said to discriminate against those people who live with the hereditary illnesses that can be avoided through preimplantation diagnosis. Not least of all, opponents fear the slippery slope of expanding the number of cases in which PGD is indicated.

Even if this last fear were unfounded and PGD were to remain strictly limited, the threefold violation, if it applies, amounts to an egregious breach of preeminent constitutional principles. The consequence would have to be what is analogously the case for suspected tax evasion: persons who travel from Germany abroad would have to be prevented from doing so at the border or be prosecuted upon their return. A country that prohibits PGD, moreover, would have to strongly protest against the states that allow PGD, for example against Belgium, France, and the United Kingdom, against the Netherlands, Sweden, and Spain, further against the United States and Israel, and, in the case of European states, file suits in the European courts.

Because the critics do not do any of this, the question imposes itself whether they really consider a violation, an egregious breach of the fundamental values of Western constitutions to be taking place. Or might there not be an ethical and above all a constitutional justification for allowing preimplantation genetic diagnosis within narrow limits? Proponents of a restricted authorization cite above all the interests and rights, ultimately the freedom of the parents. This normative justification is also at the basis of the legislation in most countries that allow preimplantation genetic diagnosis.

How are we to evaluate the arguments in favor? For couples who bear a high risk that their child will suffer from a grave genetic illness — this undoubtedly does not include Down syndrome — in addition to going through the experience of miscarriages and stillbirths, lifelong care for a gravely ill child can pose a problem they are subjectively, and often objectively as well, unable to deal with. The problem is aggravated when there already is another gravely ill child to take care of. Moreover, the problem is one that goes beyond the parents' expected life span. Furthermore, caring for seriously ill children can have lifelong negative consequences for other children a couple might have.

Not least of all, the alternative that is legal in many countries, a "pregnancy on probation" with a later, pre*natal* genetic diagnosis, is more problematic for parents physically, psychologically, and above all also ethically than a preimplantation diagnosis.

On the one hand, legislators should not deprive a couple who would otherwise, because of the possibility of a gravely ill child, have renounced the wish for a child of the freedom nonetheless to have a presumably healthy child by means of preimplantation diagnosis. On the other, a couple should also have the right to give life to a child presumably born with serious genetic defects. Parents must remain completely free to make that decision, which presupposes that they not be socially discriminated against.

Concerning a fundamental question of relevance here, the moral status of the embryo, it is biologically indisputable that the fertilized egg cell represents human life, for it is an exemplar of the species *Homo sapiens* that is being born and not one of another species. Yet the question from what point onward and with what intensity human life in its earliest stages of development is worthy of protection cannot be answered with insight from biology and medicine. Questions of ethical evaluation come into play here, questions that in recent years have been discussed in detail around the world and have led, for example, to the so-called *Fristenlösung*, the German law permitting an abortion within the first three months of pregnancy. These debates notwithstanding, two positions continue irreconcilably to oppose each other.

The one side demands for the embryo the same protection of life and dignity from the very beginning as that of a born human being. The other side advocates for legal protection that gradually grows in the process of the embryo becoming human, all the way to birth. Moral philosophers and legal ethicists should of course enter into this fundamental dispute. Yet since the debate has repeatedly and in a great variety of ways been had in many parts of the world without the conflict being resolved, legislators come up against the question of how to situate themselves over against these opposite positions that refuse a resolution.

A first answer practically goes without saying: the legislative has no originary ethical competency, which is why ethical restraint imposes itself. Hence it is hardly justifiable to declare the ethically disputed position that the earliest embryo is entitled the same protection of life and liberty as a greatly developed fetus or a born human being to be legally binding and even to pertain to criminal law.

Legislatures, moreover, must avoid contradictory evaluations. Yet there is an evaluative contradiction when the legislature permits implantation inhibitors and prenatal diagnosis, more than that: when it even permits, on certain conditions, the termination of a rather advanced pregnancy but prohibits preimplantation diagnosis as a matter of principle. In addition, in matters that remain ethically contentious, a state governed by a constitution and the rule of law considers its citizens' freedom of conscience, in the case of PGD that of the woman, to be a very high good particularly worthy of protection.

Not least of all, in so highly personal a domain as reproduction, a great measure of freedom in the form of self-determination in "reproductive autonomy" imposes itself. This civil liberty belongs to the core of how we personally conceive of and live our lives. It does not prohibit the legislator, however, from imposing strict limitations on the domain in which preimplantation diagnosis is indicated. For that reason alone, occasional talk about PGD as a means for breeding humans, that is, in effect, a modern form of eugenics, is a gross exaggeration. Desiring a child that is not foreseeably being born with a serious hereditary illness is something fundamentally different from operating a positive selection.

Like one woman's individual decision in favor of PGD, another woman's decision to make use neither of preimplantation nor of prenatal diagnosis must be respected. Moreover, based on the experience we have, there are no more negative effects on the integration of and support for people born with hereditary illnesses to be expected from authorizing preimplantation diagnosis than the authorization of prenatal diagnosis has had. On the contrary, the readiness to help people with mental, physical, or intellectual restrictions has significantly increased.

Today, many contemporaries wonder if there isn't more than one progress in medically assisted procreation that we would do better to do without. Behind this thought is the question: What kind of medicine makes human sense and is thus worthy of support, and what kind might not? In the case of preimplantation diagnosis, this question is undoubtedly not easy to answer, but one thing can be said: severe hereditary diseases that lead to stillbirths or to the likely death of the infant within days of being born have been known for centuries. Before there was the possibility of preimplantation diagnosis, the parents concerned had to decide whether it would not be better to have no children at all. The chance opened up by preimplantation diagnosis that they might have a child of their own that does not run the danger of developing a severe hereditary disease brings them a significant progress in human freedom.[21]

After these reflections, even a preliminary summary of the value modern medicine has for freedom is not an easy task. Two things, however, should be beyond dispute: medicine offers humans an ever-richer potential for liberating themselves from natural constraints. And the larger share of aids, for example those to combat infant and maternal mortality, to cure innumerable diseases, and to rescue many victims of accidents, are not merely welcome but also beyond ethical doubts. Especially in the two liminal areas, the beginning of life and its end, though, the gain in freedom displays a paradoxical ambivalence. That which expands freedom also increases responsibilities and demands decisions, which already contains a certain constraint. Moreover, one's own freedom can enter into competition with the freedom of others. How far medicine may in that case continue to liberate from natural constraints is a question for which there is no all-comprehending answer. Instead we must discuss the various types of cases one by one, such as these reflections attempt to do.

4

Inner Cultivation: Education to Freedom

Many debates about modernity ignore the topic. In fact, however, education and its study, pedagogy, play an essential role both historically, for the age of Enlightenment, and in the project of modernity overall. The freedom aspect is indispensable here. A critique of modernity according to the principle of freedom thus enters into the topic, and in articulating one goal of education, the responsible citizen in a democracy, it anticipates later parts of this book.

4.1 FROM DISPOSITION TO REALITY

Humans live not only with an outer but also with an inner nature. The term designates that part of the *conditio humana* that is not yet formed socially and culturally and that is, in that respect, "natural." Of course all real human beings are formed socially and culturally, and speaking of the natural human being is thus an abstraction. Yet this abstraction aids in defining the factors that, on the individual level, newborns and, on the collective level, humanity need in order to become, in the former case, autonomous persons and, in the latter, responsible societies. The necessary process of education, which includes self-education—on the individual level in the progress of one's biography and on the collective level in the history of humanity—supplements external cultivation with an internal one.

Since external cultivation takes place within the framework of freedom of action, it presupposes a significant degree of internal cultivation, and we might well have begun our discussion with the latter. For without a preceding education, all there is, is the small, subhuman, instinct-like aspect of mastery over nature. Internal cultivation not merely supplements external cultivation; it is its precondition.

Undoubtedly, the human in the course of internal cultivation overcomes a number of barriers to freedom. Even more importantly, because more fundamentally, internal cultivation opens up for humans a previously inaccessible world, the basic level of personal freedom, namely, freedom of action (see in more detail part V below). Without internal cultivation, humans do not even have a potential for freedom, and they certainly are not actually free beings: they merely have dispositions. Education, including formation, does not simply expand or amplify in this or that respect a freedom already given in principle. Rather, we then enter for the first time a world, the real world of free action, that we subsequently, in the course of education, discover more and more. Education, however, also places limits on freedom.

Like so many things in human life, freedom once developed can be abused, which is why education is needed here too. This education, then, is not an education to freedom but an education to make the right, especially the upright use of freedom.

Internal cultivation, too, is not free of ambiguities; for example, constraints are imposed for the sake of freedom. This ambiguity will even turn out to be immanently necessary; it is of a fundamental nature and in that regard not specific to any particular historical age. Education can abolish constraints that are unnecessary for humans becoming selves, that perhaps even counteract their freedom. Beyond that, it should follow the principle that, in Kant's terms, "from earliest childhood the child must be allowed to be free in all matters." A pedagogy committed to freedom accepts two, but only two, limits to freedom: the child must neither harm itself nor, according to the principle that freedom must be compatible with the freedom of all, impede the legitimate freedom of others.[1]

This is what distinguishes a pedagogy in the spirit of freedom from an (exclusively) antiauthoritarian education that seeks to avoid all kinds of constraint. A maximation of the freedom from constraints that neglects the guiding purpose of a rational education, namely, a responsible exercise of freedom, harms children and adolescents. We must not, however, equate the *anti*authoritarian education propagated in connection with the so-called student revolution of 1968 with the *non*authoritarian agenda of progressive education developed especially in the first third of the twentieth century by educators such as John Dewey, Célestin Freinet, and Maria Montessori, and later A. S. Neill, as well as the psychologist Jean Piaget.[2]

Humans from birth have only numerous dispositions, nothing more, toward the meaning and purpose of internal cultivation, the development of an autonomous person capable of leading a responsible and at the same time free life. These, as noted, are mere possibilities that are to be realized and that, once mere dispositions have become a potential, must be made actual.

The human being has since antiquity rightly been considered a being endowed with a capacity for reason and language, furthermore a social, more precisely, juridical and political being. And among the other defining traits, the most salient feature with regard to freedom and responsibility is that the human being is a moral being. All these definitions, however, apply to the human, both the individual and the species, only as a kind of germ, as dispositions, precisely, that are to be developed for them to become real and ultimately to thrive. In this regard, the human initially is not an *animal rationale* but only an *animal rationabile*, nor is the human an *animal politicum* and *animal morale* but only an *animal politicabile* and an *animal morabile*.

In all these cases, the *-abile* is given in three respects: whether we look at reason, at the political, or at the moral: humans are, first, capable of them—they have these dispositions; they are, second, called on to develop these dispositions and have an inner drive to do so; and, third, they must develop in that direction, which includes making an effort for the sake of which there is a task to be fulfilled, an ought or an imperative.

When we take a closer look at these dispositions—for example: the human endowment with organs and instinct does not tie us to any specific environment—the human being appears as a generalist open to the world, capable of and called to freedom. Humans are capable of performing an almost unlimited number of things; not subject to the constraints of a narrowly circumscribed environment, they have an infinity of options. This presupposes, however, that in addition to, and in many respects also prior to, external cultivation they subject themselves to an inner cultivation.

Immanuel Kant, a philosopher of paramount importance for both freedom and modernity, provides a refined theory of this cultivation. In so doing, as we will see, he proves to be a thinker experienced in and smart, even wise about the matters of life.

Kant is usually seen only as a theorist of knowledge and objects, in addition as a philosopher of morality, religion, history, and politics, including law and the state, perhaps also as a theorist of biology and art. But even those familiar with Kant often underestimate him as a philosopher of education whose lecture course on pedagogy and other texts are still of relevance today. Education in Kant is the object of the highest appreciation; he considers it the source of "all the good in the world."[3] The theory of education, pedagogy, forms an essential part of Kant's philosophy of freedom, a part that he presents in a persuasive manner and whose rich variety of perspectives has rarely been attained since.[4] The Königsberg philosopher is thus the right author to draw on for a judicative critique of modernity that includes the principle of freedom when it comes to discussing the question of the internal cultivation for the purpose of freedom, the question of education.

Those who take Kant's reflections seriously are safe from following pedagogical fads. They will not only reject the idea of an (exclusively) antiauthoritarian education; they will also refuse the countermodel that, following the shock provoked in 2001 by the results of the PISA study—in which school performance in countries like Germany at best attained the international average—placed cognitive and thereby economically utilizable skills at the center of primary and secondary school pedagogy. A pedagogy inspired by Kant is equally safe from other dangers, such as overprotecting children and seeing in every child an intellectually gifted one, as well as the danger of neglect.

According to the basic idea of Kant's pedagogy, "our species" is to be led "from the lowest step of animality gradually up to the highest step of humanity, and indeed through the human being's own art, albeit one extorted from him."[5] The corresponding process has two dimensions, the collective development of humanity in the course of its history and the individual development in the course of each individual's biography. Since the discussion of the first dimension will be tied into parts II and III, I concentrate here on the second, individual dimension. According to Kant, this latter is both specific to the human being: "The human being is the only creature that must be educated," and indispensable: "The human being can only become human through education."[6]

One might object to this specific meaning of education that other highly developed animals such as other primates teach certain rules of conduct to their young. Kant did not know of such observations, but even if he had known, he would likely have discounted the objection with the argument that teaching certain rules of conduct is hardly more than a preliminary and deficient step in the (four-step) process of teaching and learning that the internal cultivation of the human being, its education, consists in.

We will return to this point in discussing Kant's four steps of education. In any event, Kant's second thesis is significantly more important: even if a certain education takes place already among subhuman species, the decisive point for a freedom-oriented theory of education is that humans become veritable beings, namely, beings capable of freedom and morality, only on the basis of a (four-step) education.

Finally, another aspect is likely absent in subhuman beings: the true education of the human is content neither with individual private welfare nor with a collective welfare, the welfare of the state, for example. That is why Kant calls it cosmopolitan: it serves the human being as a citizen of the world. Without being declared irrelevant, the other two goals of education, private and collective welfare, are being relativized; although they are important, the ultimate decision is made according to a different criterion. The purpose of the true education is "the best for the world and the perfection to which humanity is destined," where the best for the world is considered to be an idea that also benefits "our best private condition."[7]

4.2
FOUR STEPS

An ultimately cosmopolitan education, according to Kant, takes place in four steps. It begins (1) with a preliminary step, disciplining; continues with two main steps, (2) cultivating and (3) civilizing; and ends (4) with the decisive, the cosmopolitan education that aims at moralizing. When Kant speaks of moralizing, of course, he does not mean the partly excessive, partly misplaced chastising commonly associated with the term today.

It is to be expected that Kant, the great moral philosopher, would ultimately orient education toward morality. The other three steps are therefore more remarkable because they do not tie education to a single task, morality: the human is to become not just a moral being.

To avoid misunderstandings concerning the second step, we must remember that his concept of cultivation is a narrow one. In his pedagogy, external cultivation plays no role, and internal cultivation names not the entire process of developing human dispositions but only a well-defined part.

The already-mentioned task education has concerning freedom must be reflected in its method and its didactics: people must not be "merely trained, conditioned, mechanically taught" but must rather be "actually enlightened."[8] According to Kant's Enlightenment conception, they must not be subjected to certain authorities but rather be brought to think for themselves, to seek "the final touchstone of truth in oneself."[9] In that sense, the principles that determine our will, which Kant calls "maxims," "must originate in the human being himself" and thus freely.[10]

Here, now, are the four steps.

(a) Disciplining

The preliminary step of education proper is to overcome "the animality in humanity."[11] It consists in a paradox that an exclusively antiauthoritarian education naively overlooks: a certain constraint is required because when we lack all discipline we are incapable of "choosing for ourselves." It is understood that it is needed not as an end in itself but merely for the sake of freedom. Those humans who most approximate natural humanity, both very young children and so-called primitive peoples, are characterized, according to Kant, by a "savagery," not acknowledging precepts of reason and following every whim.[12] As the Greek playwright Menander puts it succinctly: "he who gets no flogging gets no training."[13]

We may leave aside here the question whether the description of primitive peoples as "savages" really applies and the preliminary question whether we may indeed meaningfully speak of primitive peoples as opposed to civilized peoples at all. For education, it is the reference to children that counts. And children *prior* to all education do indeed prefer subjecting themselves to the notions and "nonsense" of the moment and, in their impetuousness, endanger themselves and others. This double danger may be present for the children of other primates as well, which is why their adults "discipline" them. This discipline, in their case, however, is not an element of thinking for themselves; rational reflections of a technical, pragmatic, or moral nature likely remain inaccessible to nonhuman primates and other more developed animals.

We also have to agree with Kant that those who, like later proponents of an exclusively antiauthoritarian education, neglect the first step, disciplining, harm children more than those who neglect the second step, cultivating. The argument that convincingly makes the point is that cultivation can be caught up on later—discipline cannot.

In a rarely noticed process of liberation, namely, an emancipation that is not one from external powers such as social constraints or tradition, children are to tame their instinct-like savagery and thereby become free from inner constraints. According to an observation of Kant's that is confirmed by everyday experience as well as by scientific research (and that, moreover, recalls Aristotle's concept of the *bios apolaustikos*, a life of pleasure defined as "slavish," *andrapodōdēs*), children initially live under a "despotism of desires."[14] The pedagogically decisive alternative, therefore, is not either freedom or constraint but either "despotism of desires" or its overcoming, that is to say either a constraint that negates freedom or a constraint that makes freedom possible.

Kant voices his objection against the "despotism of desires" or "savagery" without any moralizing undertone. Education does not aim at becoming free from sensuous nature. On the contrary, Kant even grants the drives a positive significance since "nature has given" them to us "in order not to neglect or even injure the determination of the animality in us."[15] Animality does not mean inhuman perversions or bestialities but driving forces the human shares with the animal. These forces, for example the need to eat and drink, the need for protection from the elements, or the need to procreate, are not to be neglected or even violated; humans are simply to become free of any unacceptable overwhelming power. That is why in disciplining, "the will of children must not be broken but merely directed."[16]

Negative freedom, emancipation operated in the form of disciplining, does not of course suffice for an education to freedom, in this case the capacity to choose by oneself. After overcoming a barrier, we need something positive, a constructive potential. The three main steps of education serve the development of this potential, that is to say, positive freedom. Incidentally, they correspond exactly to the three kinds of imperatives familiar from Kant's *Groundwork of "The Metaphysics of Morals."*[17]

In Kant, "imperative" names not just any kind of rules of conduct but principles determined by (one's own) reason, binding principles that nonhuman primates lack because they lack shared reason.[18] Kant distinguishes technical imperatives, the "rules of skill" that serve various kinds of purposes, both from pragmatic imperatives, "counsels of prudence," that aim at one's own happiness and from categorical or moral imperatives, the "commands (laws) of morality."[19]

The first main step of education, cultivating, enables us to accept the technical imperative; the second, civilizing, to accept the pragmatic imperatives; and moralizing, finally, to accept the categorical imperatives. The imperatives thus designate three levels of freedom such that disciplining prepares humans for the three steps of increasing freedom: for the technical freedom made possible in cultivating; for the pragmatic freedom made possible in civilizing; and not least of all for the moral freedom that moralizing aims at, the freedom of the will (more on this in chapter 17).

(b) Cultivating

We must not think of this first main step of an education committed to freedom, cultivating, in terms of what we usually mean by "cultivated" today, in terms of good manners, of paying attention to what is going on in the world outside one's profession, and, rather than being fixated on making a living, of being open to matters without immediate use that are "beautiful," such as music, art, and literature. Kantian cultivation serves to develop skills that enable us to do what we might want to achieve later.

If the rules of conduct other primates teach their offspring also aim at skills, there might be cultivation there, too. Yet compared to what human children are educated to do, this is so narrow and simple a form that the expression "cultivation" is clearly going too far. Nonhuman primates and other highly developed animals might, as Kant insists, achieve a potential for positive freedom. And yet it is hardly possible to claim that "because of the multitude of purposes, skillfulness becomes, as it were, infinite."[20] A good education, in any case, conveys a versatile skillfulness that alone frees humans from being tied too closely to the needs of the present and prepares them for a changing world.

It is not without interest to draw up a list of abilities, knowledge, or goods that education aims for. Yet with the exception of reading and writing, as well as calculating and an elementary understanding of law, such a list is of secondary significance and both beholden to its time and guided by particular interests. In that respect, every "canon" runs the danger of a narrowing down predicated on the historical situation, a danger that Kant, wisely restraining himself, does not fall prey to.

The *Groundwork* affirms the objection to narrowness and the plea for openness with an undoubtedly wise principle: because we do not know when we are young what we ought later to be able to do, "parents seek above all to have their children learn *a great many things* and to provide for *skill* in the use of means to all sorts of *discretionary* ends."[21]

(c) Civilizing

In the case of the second main step, civilizing, we again have to prevent a misunderstanding. We must not think of civilizing in terms of a civilization opposed to a superior culture. The opposition between a merely economic-technical civilization and an intellectual culture is foreign to Kant. In having the step of civilizing follow that of cultivating, he even inverts the ranking and silently considers cultivating to be of a lower rank than civilizing.

To do justice to the expression "civilizing," we best start with its core, the *civis* or citizen, where being the citizen of a state, though not irrelevant, is not the only important thing. What it aims at is the human as a social being. Although disciplining does not take place through the individual itself, although like all education it has a social dimension, Kant does not claim here that the human becomes a free being only in society. He does not narrow his appreciation of the social down to the exclusivity so widespread today. He merely declares that the human being as a free being ought to become a social being as well. This is the task of civilizing, which aims for a comprehensive socialization that includes several important partial aims.

First, humans are to become "prudent." Kant, realistically and without reservations, includes something here that clearly expands the leeway of freedom of action but seems to contradict the more sophisticated concept of freedom, freedom of the will or moral freedom, because it seems to permit what the guiding moral aim prohibits: using the human being as a mere means. For the sake of one's own prudence, he says, we ought to do something that undoubtedly amounts to an instrumentalization of the kind prohibited by the categorical imperative, his formula concerning the human as a purpose: one ought "to use all human beings for one's own final purposes."[22]

Such conduct, of course, is immoral only if "merely," that is, exclusively, an instrumentalization takes place. The passage in question, however, does not make that claim; it declares only that the human being as a social being may indeed be asocial as well.

As we know from Kant's famous anthropological formula, the antagonism of "unsociable sociability,"[23] our philosopher intertwines intersubjectivity and subjectivity. He thereby implicitly rejects two tendencies that dominate today's ethics and social philosophy as much as they shape public debate. He contradicts the inclination toward equating morality with altruism, which makes all egotism seem immoral. Even more strongly, he opposes the widespread tendency to reduce morality to social morality and ethics to social ethics. Yves-Marius Sagou, whose interpretations of Kant are worth reading, thus gives voice to only half of the truth when he says of civilizing that "it bridles an unbounded competition." The point is correct if amended: "a harmony . . . and a rejection of competition would prevent culture from progressing."[24]

Kant considers two kinds of prudence. One of them, "worldly prudence," is not a cosmopolitan kind of prudence. Instead it consists in a capacity that clearly marks itself off from a mere altruism but extends the legitimate freedom to act in "the art of using our skillfulness effectively." In almost Machiavellian terms Kant here includes a poker player's capacity for making himself "impenetrable" while being able to see through others, as well as the capacity—which, however, is to be exercised only "sometimes"—to conceal one's faults.[25] Already in his moral philosophy, in the *Groundwork* for example, he speaks of the skill to influence others to serve one's own purposes.[26]

Something else is hardly less surprising: in the *Groundwork*, Kant assigns a lower rank to worldly prudence than to the other kind of prudence, private prudence. The latter counts as superior for the clearly not altruistic reason that it combines all the purposes for which one seeks to influence others to one's own enduring advantage. Ultimately, then, in becoming civilized, we do not serve our fellow human beings alone but ourselves as well, namely, the aim that guides us naturally, our own welfare. While thanks to worldly prudence we succeed in the social "world," private prudence ensures that social success serves our own ("private") long-term happiness. In both respects, civilizing belongs to enlightened self-interest.

In more amiable terms, society for Kant, though not primary, is nonetheless also a system of being mutually useful to each other or, in less amiable terms, of reciprocally using the other. Freedom to act in any case requires a social compatibility for which Kant names three levels that remain convincing today: (a) elementary compatibility ensuring that the human is "well suited for human society"; (b) going further, being "popular"; and (c) going further again to achieve something that serves both society and oneself, namely, being "influential."[27] The task thus is first to fit in, then to acquire a reputation, finally to obtain influence and power.

Besides prudence, Kant in the second main step, civilizing, insists on two partial aims, on "manners" and "politeness." "Manners" does not refer to table manners and forms of address, "politeness" not to docility. For Kant suggests as the guiding principle for politeness and manners, and simultaneously as criterion for civilizing: "We must not annoy one another; the world is big enough for us all."[28] This likely means two things: on the one hand, people are not to carry the competition they stand in with each other too far such that possible opponents do not become enemies but remain civilized competitors. On the other hand, where we merely bother each other, we ought better to get out of each other's way. This must of course not lead us to remain "alone" by ourselves. Kant on the contrary puts great store by sociability and friendship.[29]

(d) Moralizing

Kant is not Knigge. To be sure, the quickly (and still) famous but rarely read two volumes *On Human Relations* the baron published in 1788, shortly after Kant delivered his lectures on pedagogy, go far beyond the dance school etiquette associated with Knigge's name today.[30] Yet, opposing any reduction of education to civilizing, however sophisticated it may be, Kant clearly demonstrates that as a moral philosopher, he values a third main step: after the freedom of action thematized up to now, what is at issue now is freedom of the will. The issue at this highest level of education, of moralizing, is selection: human beings "should not merely be skilled for all sorts of ends," they must not become jacks of all trades who know how to do all things but also, unconscientiously, get involved in all things. Instead, they are to learn something that, according to everything we have come to know so far, is inaccessible to higher-developed animals. They are to acquire the morally good disposition with whose help one "choose[s] nothing but good ends."[31]

In provocatively opposing the reduction of morality to a social morality, Kant as his lecture course on pedagogy proceeds begins with duties we have toward ourselves. Even in the "Doctrine of Right," in the theory, that is, of what humans owe each other that may be enforced by coercion, the categorization of legal duties begins with a legal duty toward oneself. The duty to enter into a state of law is now preceded by the duty to be a juridical being and to "assert . . . one's worth as a human being in relation to others."[32]

Freedom thus imposes duties. The addressee of the first duty, however, is not the other; on the contrary, duty is first of all a duty toward oneself. The reason for this primacy is both moral and rooted in the subject matter. The duties we have to ourselves in order to be able to assume the usual duties, those toward others, are not merely additions; they are systematic as well as evolutionary requirements. Accepting this duty is an act of free acknowledgment (see section 17.3 below).

According to Kant's *Pedagogy*, the duties toward oneself—now a plural, no longer a singular as in the "Doctrine of Right"—do not consist in trivialities such as "fine clothes." They are about something binding thanks to whose acknowledgment "the human being [has] a certain dignity within himself which ennobles him before all creatures." The "duty not to deny this dignity of humanity in his own person" includes the duty not to succumb to drink, to avoid all kinds of immoderation, but also, and this recalls the duty in the "Doctrine of Right," to affirm and respect oneself, not to "grovel . . . before others."[33]

The *Pedagogy* explicates the "duties to others," which it cites only in second place, as "reverence and respect for the rights of human beings." They must "be instilled into the child at a very early age" because the right of human beings, Kant, usually so sober, writes, is nothing short of the "apple of God's eye on earth." For example, a child meeting a poorer child must not "haughtily push . . . it out of the way or away from itself." Should this happen nonetheless, we are not to admonish the child or appeal to its pity, but, Kant uncompromisingly states, we "must treat it just as haughtily and noticeably."[34]

Finally, Kant finds fault with something of great significance for the guiding theme of civilizing, its core of educating citizens, namely, that schools are lacking "something which would nevertheless greatly promote the formation of uprightness in children, namely, a catechism of right." By way of example, Kant discusses "someone who should pay his creditor today" and "is touched through the sight of someone in need and gives him the sum which he owes and should now pay." Kant's uncompromising answer to the question "Is this right or not?" is "No! It is not right."[35] For this example belongs to the legal duties we owe, which as such unrestrictedly deserve priority over meritorious extras, virtue's commands. As obligatory virtues, Kant names honesty, decency, and pacificity; as meritorious virtues, in turn, magnanimity, beneficence, and self-control.

Within the framework of the task of moralizing, Kant considers it to be "immensely important . . . that children are taught from youth to detest vice" and not to leave this task to the preacher, to the church, or to another religious community.[36] For what counts in this detestation to be taught is also the right reason for the detestation, and this reason lies not in mere fulfillment of duty but in an acting out of duty that goes beyond legality. For that, for morality, it does not suffice to act out of an awareness that God has prohibited vice. The place of an external, theonomous justification that was widely held at the time and is still advocated today — something is a vice because God prohibited it — is taken by an intrinsic justification that already expresses Kant's notion of a freedom of the will that outdoes freedom of action. Moreover, from God's point of view, too, vice is "detestable in itself," for as "the holiest being," God "demands that we should practice virtue because of its own inner worth and not because He demands it."[37]

Moral Refinement

At each of the three main steps of education, human beings according to Kant acquire a specific value; they undergo a process of moral refinement. Education to skillfulness "gives him value in relation to himself as an individual. But by means of formation towards prudence he is formed into a citizen, thus receiving public value."[38] Once more Kant is thinking not only of the state citizen concerned with public affairs, nor merely of the economic citizen. Thus indifferent to the alternative economic citizen or state citizen, the citizen in the expanded concept acquires "a public value" that has the two dimensions of asserting oneself in competition and being a fellow citizen. In opposition to a merely social conception, a rational citizen is both a competitive and a cooperative being. Citizens must fit in with society and the polity but only in such a way as to be able to continue pursuing their own goals.

On the highest level, moral education, the human being "receives value in view of the entire human race."[39] At issue is less the species of the human than its essence, *humanitas*.

One might want to neglect all other goals of education in favor of the one that surpasses them all, moralization. The danger in that case, however, is that, put in the terms of the theory of freedom, one is educated toward a freedom of the will without freedom of action. The result would be an honest and helpful human being, upright in every way but otherwise unfit for life. Kant avoids the danger already by having moralization be preceded by the three steps just outlined: the taming of savagery, the development of a versatile skill set, and civilizing including practical wisdom.

This antecedence has a necessary basis in the subject matter; it results from the difference between capacity and willingness: to be honest, one must have something to say; to be helpful, one must know how to help someone in need. In a *before*—to be understood in a systematic sense—humans must be able to choose purposes in the first place, then acquire capacities and skills to pursue them, and not least insert their pursuing of purposes into living together with their peers. Within this frame, they choose, thanks to a good attitude, only purposes that "are necessarily approved by everyone and which can be the simultaneous ends of everyone."[40]

Here, too, we find a parallel between Kant and his alleged antipode, Aristotle. It is not by accident that the form of life Aristotle develops in the *Nicomachean Ethics*, the form in which the ethical virtues—from, say, collectedness to valor and generosity to justice—and the dianoethic virtue associated with them, *phronēsis*, are practiced, is called *bios politikos*. As in Kant, so in Aristotle everyone can agree to this "political form of life." Everyone who dedicates himself to the theoretical, contemplative life needs it. And where it is universally practiced, a moral communality emerges beyond the difference between community and society.

4.3
PLAYING AND WORKING

Kant diverges from the ethics predominant today in a further respect. While today, an ethics of the economy and of labor plays a role only within the vast field of applied ethics, for Kant it constitutes, via the indispensable obligations of pedagogy, an integral component of a general ethics.

Kant does not fall prey to an economistic reduction here that would merely prepare children for the contests of the economy. Even leaving aside here the fact that only those are professionally successful who know how to cooperate at least as well as they know how to compete, Kant's concept of labor is not purely economic. For him, work includes all "occupations for which forces are required." He also declares, "The child should play," and he continues: "it should have its hours of recreation."[41] A Kantian pedagogy vehemently objects to an education that trains economic citizens too early, more vehemently still to one that makes this its exclusive goal.

Within the frame of cultivating the mind, free culture takes up significant space, and according to Kant, free culture is "only a play" and "should be play." Kant considers spoiling and pampering children a threat. We may leave the question aside whether the threat comes more from mothers, as he supposes, or from fathers. The decisive and at the same time insightful point is that one should let children jump and run around, that is, play freely without always being afraid "that they might be injured."[42]

Put in more general terms: children, if they are to become free personalities, must be allowed both, to move of their own accord and in so doing experience what possibilities they have and where their limits are. On this principle, a child who in learning to walk falls on a step should not be made to wear a helmet. Instead, one should grant children such experiences through which they learn to master their own bodies and thereby to acquire the best protection from risks. Children in any case must be allowed to explore a resistant environment, both a natural and a social environment, autonomously, on their own.

In this, in a pedagogy committed to freedom in a Kantian spirit rejecting widespread one-sided views, lies the prudence, even wisdom about life I claimed it to have at the beginning of this chapter.

The fitness for life that counts in Kantian cultivating includes a fitness to be a citizen. To it belongs the capacity to subject oneself to the constraint of laws, and to this end to "feel early the inevitable resistance of society" and nonetheless "to make good use of his freedom."[43] The capacity to work and to exercise a profession constitutes an integral part of this freedom-despite-___.

According to Kant, it is also part of freedom not to depend on the provision of others. The philosopher considers it a matter of course that the future citizen is an economic citizen insofar as he makes his own living. Children should not think that later, the way they are used to from home, "they will receive food and drink without having to be responsible for it."[44] On the contrary, it is "extremely important that children learn to work from early on. It is of the greatest importance that children learn to work."[45]

For Kant, work has anthropological significance: "The human being is the only animal which must work." And for him, this *must* is not a constraint alien to human essence. He answers the question, "whether heaven would not have cared for us more kindly if it had let us find everything already prepared so that we should not need to work at all," with a clear no, "for the human being requires occupations [*Geschäfte*]." It is wrong to imagine "that if Adam and Eve had only remained in paradise they would have done nothing there but sit together, sing arcadian songs, and observe the beauty of nature" because "boredom would have tortured them."[46]

The task of learning to work must, as noted, not be understood in purely economic terms. Kant is concerned not only with the capacity for making a living but also with the capacity for seeking more in life than play and rest. Above all, even the economic aspect, the capacity for a profession, forms part of the wider goals of education, of autonomy and independence, thus of freedom.

The emphasis on the capacity for work and a profession is likely addressed to two target audiences in particular. Since in his day, no generous welfare state existed yet, Kant does not address the one group, the large majority of the population and its task of sufficiently incentivizing all those growing up to be capable of work and a profession in the future. For lack of a developed welfare state, this task was self-evident in everyday experience. Kant focuses only on the other group, the sometimes-so-called privileged. He, who himself came from a humble background, would not consider today's playboys and glamor girls to be privileged and therefore not envy but probably pity them: they remain what already announces itself in the terms "boys" and "girls" and what, on Kant's view, threatens the children of rich parents and of princes, namely, "children throughout their entire lives," that is, not autonomous, dependent, not actually free.[47]

And those who are highly educated but unable to make a living on their own, too, remain lifelong children in this sense. Without putting too fine a point on it and yet quite clearly, Kant rejects, for students at all levels, an education that aims only at formation [*Bildung*] but not at training [*Ausbildung*]. The corresponding demand that the one must be joined to the other may still serve as a decisive principle for schools and universities: formation and training must go hand in hand.

4.4
EDUCATION TO PERSONALITY

Let's summarize internal cultivation. A pedagogy committed, on the Kantian model, to freedom brings the different goals of education together in a guiding goal that remains modern, even exemplary, beyond the age referred to as modern. In this guiding goal, a general antipaternalism grows into a plea for freedom and endows internal cultivation with its essential purpose, one alien even to the more advanced animals: an education to personality.

A single post-Kantian author may suffice to confirm the enduring relevance of this endeavor. In the eighth chapter of his "introduction to the philosophy of education" entitled *Democracy and Education* (1916), the philosopher, educator, and social reformer John Dewey, whose democracy-oriented theory of education had worldwide influence, names three general aims. All three are not far from Kant's goals: developing human capacities, the social usefulness of the educational process, and cultural, personal growth in the sense of enhancing the capacity for understanding meanings and working with them creatively. Dewey does not pursue Kant's final goal, morality.

By Kant's guiding aim, personality, we are to understand a freely acting being, which evokes the four steps of education: (1) liberated from the despotism of desires, humans are capable of exercising their will to control their natural driving forces; equipped (2) with (almost) infinite skills and capacities, including (3) practical wisdom and the capacity for social life, they are able to pursue independently chosen purposes that are compatible with the purposes of others. And finally, when education fully succeeds, (4) they acquire a "disposition to choose nothing but good ends."[48]

Not least of all, free action comprises the ability to make one's own living, which means that in a Kantian pedagogy we find the three roles of the citizen I distinguished in an earlier work: the economic citizen, the state citizen, and the world citizen, understood morally on the Kantian model.[49] In explaining his general aim of a personality, Kant specifically stresses three tasks: (1) the freely acting being is able to sustain itself; (2) it is a member of society; and (3) it has an inner value for itself. In these tasks, we can recognize the three roles of the citizen, in the first the economic citizen, in the second the state citizen, and in the third the world citizen.

At the same time, like Kant, we should reject any education that pursues only one goal exclusively, an economism, for example, that focuses on the capacity for a profession alone; also a privileging of the communicative and the social that sees humans only as social beings; finally an "idealist moralism" that pays attention only to each person's sense of self-worth. On the contrary: because a level-headed education considers morality to be the dominant, but not an inclusive goal that comprises everything else, it is not content with the task of moralizing. Instead of seeking freedom of the will without freedom to act, it addresses all three dimensions. A well-considered internal cultivation aims at three dimensions of freedom: at a capacity for a profession, at a capacity for sociability, and beyond that, but by no means instead of it, at the highest goal, the capacity for morality.

PART II

Freedom in Economy and Society

The title is famous. Ever since the 1922 publication of Max Weber's "outline of interpretive society" as *Economy and Society* (the title chosen by Marianne Weber), the two expressions are difficult to separate. Conceptually, of course, the separation is possible, even if "society" refuses a conceptual fixation. The connections, however, are so close, the correlations so numerous and intense that the two expressions belong together like (albeit not identical) twins. The second part of this study in any case treats both and in so doing, by way of the topics chosen and the way they are being discussed, overcomes such fixed alternatives as "Kant or Hegel" and "Aristotle or Kant." The introductory sketch of this study's guiding thread, enlightened liberalism (chapter 5), is followed by exemplary reflections on economic freedom under the heading "Market and Capitalism" (chapter 6), on the free society (chapter 8), and, articulated as a question, on justice in the name of freedom (chapter 7).

5

Enlightened Liberalism

Labeled as neoliberalism and discredited, the thinking that takes up the banner of freedom, liberalism, rings false in the ears of many. To keep this study from being caught in the maelstrom of negative assessments and at the same time ensure that critics of liberalism do not have to confront too simple an opponent, it is advisable to develop a secure position. As I announced in the introduction, I call this position enlightened liberalism. A liberalism worthy of esteem subjects itself to a regeneration for which it adopts elements of Enlightenment. This includes an expansion of the range of topics it addresses, which I have begun with the first part, the freedom from natural constraints, and will continue in parts III–V.

5.1
IN THE SPIRIT OF ENLIGHTENMENT

Explaining the term is easy. "Liberalism" is the name of a thinking whose central issue is freedom. Closer observation, however, finds "liberalism" to be just as ambiguous as its key component, *libertas*, freedom. Usually, in the footsteps of John Stuart Mill, liberalism is not concerned with "the so-called Liberty of the Will" but with "Civil, or Social Liberty," that is to say, "the nature and limits of the power which can be legitimately exercised by society over the individual."[1] This purposely multifaceted book, however, does not omit freedom of the will, no more than it does freedom from natural constraints or the freedom of the sciences and of art.

By no means limited to the economy, liberalism conceives of itself as a social and political theory and as a movement that, in a first sketch, we may characterize as three-dimensional: it is a theory of the economy, of society, and of government. In all these domains, liberalism trusts in the development, as free from constraint as possible, of the dispositions and strengths of individuals. From this development, it expects a progress or, more modestly, an improvement in these three domains: in the economy; in society including science and culture; and in government, including law and the state.

The backdrop is what we may call, in the shallow sense the term has today, a "metaphysics" of liberalism, of a liberalism inspired by the spirit of the Enlightenment: with the courage to make use of one's own reason and with the right to live one's life according to one's own convictions — provided one does not violate this same right on the part of others — liberalism counts on a pluralism of forms of life on the basis of a pluralism of values. Skeptical toward ultimate truths, it supposes, even for values, a legitimate competition that we ought to enter into for the "better," but only ever tentatively better, values to impose themselves. There is just *one* restriction most liberal thinkers provide for: they consider the juridical morality of democracy and inviolable civil rights and liberties to be nonnegotiable, indispensable. Beyond that, it might be personally necessary and, in certain communities, especially among families and friends, even desirable in some respects to decide between competing values. But this is not always required either in society or in government.[2] Against the background of the history of ideas sketched in section 1.4, liberalism, preshaped by the Enlightenment of the seventeenth and eighteenth centuries, in the nineteenth century becomes the decisive herald and champion of a liberal economic system (economic liberalism), of an increasingly open society (social liberalism), and of a democratic constitutional state or a constitutional democracy (political liberalism). The spectrum of liberal thinking extends between the two extremes of the night-watchman state content with enforcing peace, order, and security, that is, with a narrow domain of negative freedom, and a robustly social liberalism that is also concerned with citizens' positive freedom and, for their sake, transfers a varied set of tasks to the state. There are many forms in between, for example Judith N. Shklar's "liberalism of fear" that pursues "only one overriding aim: to secure the political conditions that are necessary for the exercise of personal freedom."[3] For the sake of this aim, Shklar, though not explicitly, subscribes to Kant's famous principle of the universal compatibility of freedom.

With the expression "enlightened liberalism," I am referring to a large family of theories and agendas (I will cite historical examples in the next section) characterized by three aspects. All three conform to core elements of the Enlightenment: an empirical, even anthropological challenge; a normative, even moral attitude; and a moral-political response. Two further aspects are connected with these three: a social responsibility that overcomes the extreme of the "night-watchman state," the exemplary form of nonenlightened liberalism (section 5.2), and that develops, thanks to self-criticism, a capacity for regeneration without which no liberalism may count as enlightened (section 5.3). The notion of enlightened liberalism I defend here, however, does not share some Enlighteners' tendency toward boundless optimism, the overrating of science to be found already in Bacon and Descartes, and the belief that the human being can be not just educated but perfected.

An enlightened liberalism, *first*, is allergic to any ideological and authoritarian politics that resists reality; instead, it prefers to trust experience. This begins on an elementary level with two experiences of anthropological significance. In the first part, I discussed one of these, the anthropological experience that humans must obtain and maintain their freedom through an engagement with external and inner nature. We must now discuss the second, the experience that human beings are characterized by their twofold nature as cooperative and competitive beings.

On the one hand, humans depend on their peers, on a multifaceted cooperation that begins with reciprocal aid and extends via the facilitation of work through a division of labor and specialization to mutual acknowledgment and even love and friendship. On the other hand, competition and conflict dominate, and they dominate already because such important things as goods, services, even the affection of friendship and love are scarce. Scarcity is among the fundamental experiences of liberalism. In its enlightened form, it also expects humans to want to distinguish themselves before others and not least of all anticipates the threat of envy and jealousy.

Now, looking at the growth rates of the 1950s and 1960s in particular, one might consider scarcity a temporary fate, that is, a problem that can be overcome and whose solution will lead to the fabulous Cockaigne where milk and honey flow, where grilled pigeons fly right into the mouths of the sluggish, and where laziness is considered the highest virtue and diligence the greatest vice. In truth, scarcity has accompanied humanity since the beginnings. And neither scientific-technological nor economic innovations nor their combination can suspend an element of the human condition, the *anthropological law of scarcity*, because the following are and will remain notoriously scarce: the land on which humans live; the fruits of heaven and the earth they enjoy, in part immediately, in part after processing them; also extraordinary talents, outstanding capacities, and the willingness to take risks and accept hardships; services, jobs, and capital, moreover positions of influence and the esteem of one's peers; not least of all, the attention of the public is scarce, and fame in posterity anyway.

To be sure, enlightened liberalism is willing to learn from concrete experience to answer the question of how best to deal with the double nature, the conflictual-cooperative or cooperative-conflictual nature of the human. But because it knows that experience cannot furnish the ultimate standard, it needs, *second*, a normative criterion to guide an experience that is not free of internal contradictions. Enlightened liberalism here advocates an individualism of a particular kind. It does not, as some critics claim, champion a disconnected individualism that sees only an isolated individual who has severed all economic and social, cultural and political ties, depends on nothing and no one, and rests entirely in itself.

Enlightened liberalism promotes, and this is its normative and even moral aspect, only a *legitimizing individualism*. On this view, everything social is not an end in itself; ultimately, rules and institutions and especially their power of constraint are legitimized only by the individuals concerned. According to the liberal principle *volenti non fit iniuria* (literally, "to a willing person, injury is not done"), what counts is free consent, even, in the case of ultimate principles, the kind of free consent by each and every one that can be expected only where every individual can on balance count on an advantage.

This condition, an advantage for everyone that is not just collective but also distributive, is met by the realm of the social if, *third*, it is able to connect to basic patterns whose visionary force is the foundation for the attractiveness of enlightened liberalism. On the one hand, we are to seek peace and for that reason to subject to enforceable rules, that is, the law, and the law is to be bound to principles of political justice, to negative and positive liberties, to public authorities, their democratic legitimation, and their horizontal and vertical separation. On the one hand, we are to give space to the free play of forces, to the in part economic, in part political, in part also scientific and cultural market from which a great thriving is to be expected, namely, a wealth of goods and services, of science, medicine, and technologies, of political agendas, of music, literature, art. The first vision, the vision of freedom, law, and justice, is joined by a second vision of multidimensional wealth such that an age-old dream of humanity may be realized: "they shall beat their swords into plowshares, and their spears into pruning hooks."[4] Physical violence, in any case, is to be transformed into economic and cultural force and freedom to be enriched by wealth, science, and art.

In connecting the two basic patterns, democratic rule of law and free play of forces, enlightened liberalism implicitly, without using the term, follows a principle from social ethics, the principle of subsidiarity: what individuals are able to do in free cooperation is not to be taken over by the state. This results in a shift of the burden of proof enlightened liberalism tends to apply: the state may take over only those tasks that individuals by themselves or with others can either not accomplish at all or accomplish only in a significantly worse manner.

5.2
FROM ADAM SMITH TO JOHN RAWLS

Although the individualism liberalism advocates initially pertains only to method, not to social theory or social ethics, it is often reproached wholesale, without addressing its various guises, with being socially insensitive. A short look at prominent thinkers of classical liberalism suffices to discount the reproach. Since this is primarily a systematic, not a historical study, only a few proponents can be discussed here. Some important authors, from John Locke to Alexis de Tocqueville to, for example, Isaiah Berlin and Charles Taylor, are missing. (On some of them, however, see section 8.1.)

The first one to be cited as proof of an alleged lack of social sensitivity is usually Adam Smith. In fact, however, Smith not only held a chair in moral philosophy for many years and wrote an influential theory of moral sentiments that centers on sympathy, an emphatically social sentiment. Even later, in the famous economic theory published in 1776, *An Inquiry into the Nature and Causes of the Wealth of Nations*, he does not advocate a free market in order to favor entrepreneurs and "capitalists" and an increase of their profits. On the contrary, as the very title announces, he is concerned with wealth, which means more than material riches. And above all, the group this wealth is being referred to is not a small group or class. It is not those who are well off but all together, a given polity or nation. Smith is concerned with collective wealth, a collective welfare of which he believes that it will emerge by itself thanks to the free market, namely, thanks to the division of labor, competition, and self-interest.

That Smith's interests were social and social-ethical becomes clear when we compare his book to another work that was very influential at the time. Two generations before Smith, Bernard de Mandeville, a physician practicing in London and author of the famous satirical *Fable of the Bees*, in his 1723 *Essay on Charity and Charity Schools* advances the deliberately provocative thesis directed against Shaftesbury that the wealth of a nation is produced where a mass of poor, ignorant, and modest people work for the rich.[5]

Smith holds the exact opposite: "No society can surely be flourishing and happy, of which the far greater part of the members are poor and miserable." Moreover, "it is but equity" that those who through their labor ensure everyone else's living "should have such a share of the produce of their own labour as to be themselves tolerably well fed, clothed, and lodged."[6] According to

Adam Smith, economic rationality—a nation's material wealth—and what is morally desirable—cheap goods in relation to high wages—go hand in hand. For profits, he says, are low, wages in turn high and prices low, which is why contemporary workers are doing better than people in other cultures.[7]

Another prominent proponent of liberalism is Jeremy Bentham, a lawyer's son who became a jurist himself but was primarily committed to social and political reforms. In *An Introduction to the Principles of Morals and Legislation* (1789), he advocates a methodically rational government on the basis of experiential data about the needs and interests of people. His self-assessment that his normative principle, the utilitarian principle of the greatest happiness of the greatest number, made him the "Newton of the moral sciences" is certainly exaggerated. Uncontestably, though, his utilitarianism is directed against the concentration of power and wealth in a small, privileged class—the nobility, high clergy, and jurists. For in the calculation of the greatest happiness, each and every one counts, and they all count the same.

After a meeting with James Mill, John Stuart's father, the "Benthamites" formed as a political group whose demand for fundamental reforms earned them the name "Philosophical Radicals" and whose *Westminster Review* was a major influence on public debate.[8] Bentham rejects the notion of basic and human rights as supposedly "anarchical fallacies" because their appeal to a suprapositive authority allowed for turning against positive law, opening the floodgates to arbitrariness. Nonetheless, the French Revolution made him an honorary citizen to honor his ideas for reform.

Among the reforms Bentham demands are a more humane treatment of prisoners (instead of retribution, prevention and rehabilitation); an equally humane legislation concerning the poor; abolishing the House of Lords; and the vote for every citizen ("everybody to count for one, nobody for more than one")—Bentham imposes one single but, given contemporary practices, hardly insignificant restriction: insofar as the citizen be able to read.

The liberalism Bentham advocates for the economy is clearly less social. In his economic treatise with the telling title *Defense of Usury* (1787), he declares that everyone is the best judge of his own interests. He also does not reject all kinds of colonization, which he considers legitimate when it absorbs the surplus population of the "mother-country" and its economic activity increases the wealth of the world.[9] That the colonized population might be impoverished, also that its political sovereignty disappears, is of no importance for the utilitarian Bentham. For, over against an increasing collective welfare, here the welfare of humanity, veritable considerations of justice have no role to play in his utilitarianism.

The most important document of early German liberalism comes from an important scholar and cultural policy advocate. In *Ideas for an Attempt at Defining the Limits of the Efficacy of the State* (1792), a twenty-five-year-old Wilhelm von Humboldt castigates an authoritarian state concerned with the physical and moral well-being of his subjects as "the most oppressive despotism." The, according to Humboldt, only legitimate task of the state, maintaining order and security, may sound like a mere night-watchman state. Yet Humboldt is calling for promoting the "true end of Man," namely, the "highest and most harmonious development [*Bildung*] of his powers to a complete and consistent whole."[10] His liberalism, too, thereby acquires a social accent and at the same time a new quality. Unlike Bentham, he conceives of individual freedom not as a static goal but as a dynamic task. The educational liberalism advocated by Humboldt, which ties schooling to much more than a (humanist) curriculum, namely, to a truly human education, is not a supplement to the economically liberal *Homo oeconomicus* but an alternative to it.

Just parenthetically: a few years later, Humboldt comes to lead the Prussian educational system; for a while, the paths of power and of the mind run parallel, and it is only a slight exaggeration to say that, for one of those rare moments in world history, a philosopher-king appears. In one person, intellectual elite and political power combine.

Humboldt proves to be an enlightened liberal in his report *On the Draft of a New Constitution for the Jews* (1809). While other reformers support only a step-by-step movement toward equality, Humboldt demands granting Jews (1) all civil liberties (2) immediately and (3) without restrictions. The only school of freedom, he says, is freedom.

The most important theorist of English social liberalism, John Stuart Mill, adopts Humboldtian notions and amplifies the liberal elements in Bentham. Influenced by Harriet Taylor, his future wife, he even develops sympathies for socialism. Thus he advocates the progressive transformation of private property into cooperative and state property; he demands equal rights, freedom of association, and company shares for workers as well as breaking the economic and political hegemony of the landed nobility. Later, however, Mill's sympathies for socialism cool off. As a member of Parliament from 1865 to 1868, he advocates policies we might call "social-liberal."

According to Mill, attaining the overall aim that all citizens be able freely to develop their personalities requires a political framework, which is why the state must be granted a great deal of influence. Inspired by Humboldt among others and also in a Kantian spirit, Mill writes that humans are to develop their talents and capacities, since, as he puts it in *Utilitarianism*, "it is better to be a human being dissatisfied than a pig satisfied."[11] For that reason Mill advocates something that is a matter of course in today's democracies, namely, compulsory and expanded education. Although the state should not found schools, it is to constrain parents to send their children to school and severely punish those parents who refuse that task.

Mill also demands laws restricting child labor. Moreover, to prevent exploitation and damage to workers' health, the state is to monitor citizens' labor time. Furthermore, it is to fight poverty but in such a way as not to create new dependencies. And by promoting emigration, the state is to act against overpopulation, which is said to endanger social peace. Mill of course overlooks that the resulting colonialism does injustice to the colonized population. On the contrary, he—for thirty-five years an official with the powerful East India Company, which held the monopoly for trade with India—considers colonization a civilizational gift.[12]

With particular vehemence, Mill demands that the "almost despotic power of husbands over wives" be broken, namely, by granting women "the same rights, and . . . the protection of law in the same manner, as all other persons."[13] From the ultimate result of this process, equal rights for women in family and society, he even expects a progress of moral attitudes that would entail the "moral regeneration of mankind."[14]

In a way that surprises us today, Mill on the one hand supports equal rights for women and a universal franchise that explicitly includes women. Although he is a staunch democrat, he also, on the other, probably as an enthusiastic reader of Darwin, holds the unquestionably elitist view of granting the educated and the wealthy a greater share of the vote.[15]

With *Principles of Political Economy* (1848) Mill writes the most important work in nineteenth-century anglophone economic theory. Also aimed, as the subtitle has it, at "applications to social philosophy," the author seeks to update Smith's *Wealth of Nations* by taking up new knowledge in the field, namely, from David Ricardo and his own father, James Mill.

Mill here turns against utopian socialists who want to replace free competition with the state. Because individual human beings act selfishly and at the same time are the best judges of their personal interests, the nonintervention of the state (laissez-faire) brings about a twofold optimization: an efficient activity of the state, of importance to the utilitarian Mill, and, important from a liberal perspective, the strongest incentive for the development of the individual. Mill rejects, however, the "economistic" view of the priority of the economy; primacy lies with government alone.

For Mill, a proponent of hedonism, it is a matter of course that amassing riches is not an end itself; all wealth instead is to serve the (correct) enjoyment of the present. And as a utilitarian, Mill demands a just distribution of goods, accepting, unlike communism, a moderate inequality in distribution as just.

The third edition of the *Principles* includes a new chapter, "On the Probable Future of the Labouring Classes," that, influenced by the 1848 revolutions, harbors great sympathies for socialism (which, however, will later cool off considerably in *Chapters on Socialism*).[16]

Unlike Smith, Mill does not want to leave the distribution of a society's riches to an invisible hand—although Smith, as noted, uses the not just pecuniary term *wealth*. It is instead to be subject to the notion of justice. That is why property one has not worked for, an inheritance, for example, which does not fall under the concept of private property, is to be heavily taxed and the income thus generated be used for the public good.[17] Mill also pleads for a stake of the workers in their companies. The minimum of income required for life and health is to remain free of tax; the rest, however, is to be taxed proportionally. Mill suggests a rate of 10 percent. Mill would not consider the progressive tax rate in effect in many places today and a marginal tax rate, including Church Tax and Solidarity Supplement, of over 50 percent, as in Germany, to be too inimical to great wealth. Rather, it is an unwise policy on the part of the state because it hinders industry and diligence, and, moreover, it is unjust because it punishes the people who work harder.

The main work of Mill in social philosophy and the philosophy of law, *On Liberty* (1859), is a manifesto against the puritanism of Victorian society. The author here extends his social economic liberalism with a political liberalism that begins with a radical juridical liberalism. Mill demands freedom of thought and of speech and passionately defends each human being's right freely to elaborate his convictions and freely to fashion his own life in accordance with them. For in opposition to Auguste Comte's notion of a "social system" that amounts to "a despotism of society over the individual," he argues that nobody is accountable to society for actions in which only one's own interests are at stake.[18]

Mill fears that democracy could terrorize individuals' consciences, which he emphatically rejects as a "tyranny of the majority."[19] The only justification for restrictions on freedom on the part of the state and of society is one that, as noted, Shklar takes up: protecting others from harm. Self-government, democracy, does not mean that everyone is governed by himself but that everyone is governed by everyone else, and that can mean governed by a disliked mass.

Mill's second political essay, *Considerations on Representative Government* (1861), rejects two basic conceptions of the essence of government as one-sided: both the voluntarist conception according to which the state is a product of the human will to serve specific purposes and the historicist conception that sees in the polity "a sort of organic growth from the nature and life of that people."[20]

The book, however, does not stop at defining the essence of government. Mill is looking for a criterion for good governance and finds it in the increase, on balance, of citizens' intellectual, moral, and practical capacities. On this standard, which means not as a matter of principle and merely in most cases, democracy is the preferred form the state is to take. Mill moreover ties this preference to a condition, the public casting of the vote. It alone, he says, guarantees that one is voting not in one's own interest but in accordance with the public good. Mill does not see that such a public vote would promote the tyranny of the majority and thus contradict one of his own basic interests.

The *Considerations* remains one of the most important contributions to the theory of democracy and to a deliberative conception of government. Mill advocates a parliament elected on the basis of popular sovereignty. He supports the separation of powers and oversight of the executive yet entrusts the task of legislation not to parliament but to a committee of the best and brightest to manage the affairs of the country. Finally, Mill champions a rule of the educated from which the entire polity could learn and ultimately profit.

Mill seeks to prevent a possible deformation of democracy under the conditions of mass democracy. He supports protecting minorities and discusses the threat increasing bureaucratization poses to political freedom. He pleads for tolerance, and his commitment to equal rights for women makes him an important forerunner of feminism.[21]

The most prominent representative of recent liberalism is probably John Rawls with his *Theory of Justice* (1971). As his theory is widely known, a short reminder will suffice. Chief among his soon-famous principles of justice stands, uncontested, a variant of a Kantian principle: everyone has the same right to the most comprehensive total system of the same basic liberties that is compatible with the same right on the part of everyone else. This principle, which advocates both liberal civil liberties and democratic participatory rights, is expanded via a second principle to include a significant amount of welfare state elements. While it does allow for economic and social inequalities, it nonetheless does so only on the condition of equal opportunity and on the second condition that the social and economic organization benefit those with the lesser opportunity.[22]

Rawls's second main work bears liberalism in its very title.[23] In *Political Liberalism*, Rawls seeks to show that pluralistic societies are indeed capable, in a process he calls "overlapping consensus," to agree on the exact normative conditions they need both despite and for their pluralism. To do so, they require neither religious or ideological views, which are in dispute anyway, nor a philosophical justification.

This last aspect places Rawls, without him pointing it out, in the tradition of American pragmatism. The three great representatives of pragmatism, Charles Sanders Pierce, William James, and John Dewey, explicitly renounce ultimate justifications and absolute certainty. Similar to the way in which they put knowledge at the service of life, so in Rawls, philosophy contributes to the process in which the political life of liberal polities reassures itself.

Also permeated by the spirit of pragmatism but even more skeptical of philosophy than Rawls's genuinely political liberalism is Richard Rorty's notion of "liberal irony."[24] To oppose the always looming threat that philosophy will move only on well-trodden paths, Rorty emphatically seeks a corroding, de-constructive thinking that, on his view, paradoxically has a constructive effect. In the language of traditional philosophy, Rorty represents an extreme epistemological and language-theoretical relativism that accepts no eternally valid truth criteria and disputes philosophy's ability to make any binding truth claims. The remaining possibility, a decision, is made in favor of Western liberal democracy—exemplified by Rorty's home country, the United States—of which the Left, too, where Rorty explicitly situates himself, should be "proud." For if the nations do not act, then there will be no progress beyond "nationhood" toward a "global polity," a cosmopolitan order in a Kantian spirit.[25]

With his liberal irony Rorty rejects both liberal metaphysicians, among whom he also counts Jurgen Habermas because of his faith in a communicative reason not bound by time and coincidence, and illiberal ironists like Michel Foucault who are lacking a sense for the advantages of liberal societies.[26] For Rorty, liberal people consider cruelty the worst thing humans do; and ironic people accept that even central considerations and needs are contingent rather than capable of (ultimate) justification. Finally, solidarity, Rorty's third guiding concept, characterizes those who consider vulnerability to humiliation the only social bond humans need and who lead their lives accordingly.

Because of its extreme relationalism, Rorty's ironic liberalism even does without human rights and instead bets on an increasing sensitivity for the pain and humiliation of others. Perhaps because he considers the stable and tested political institutions of his country to be too self-evident, he does not particularly highlight the division of powers that is nonetheless indispensable to constitutional democracies. And if the sensibilization to the pain of others is not to be left to chance, it is helpful for a liberal society—which Rorty, too, wishes for—if it considers a core of this sensibilization to be a binding duty, and legally and politically grants this core—for example, the protection of life and physical integrity and the prohibition of torture, moreover freedom of religion and of the press and other liberties as well as equal rights for women and men—the status of fundamental rights that can be sued for if need be. The question whether these rights can be given a justification, perhaps even an ultimate justification as human rights—and I do not share Rorty's extreme skepticism on this point (see section 11.2)—may be transferred from law and government to philosophical discourses.

It is probably more persuasive, not just for philosophers but generally, if the hopes of the solidary liberalism Rorty advocates are granted more than contingency. Rorty in turn can expect agreement from the enlightened liberalism propounded here when he encourages the Left to give up its "revolutionary" and eschatological rhetoric in favor of a "reformist and pragmatic" attitude and to "get back to the business of piecemeal reform within the framework of a market economy" and representative government.[27]

This brief look at the history confirms two things: that "liberalism" in the singular does not exist and that there is a proud series of liberal motifs dominated not by the notion of a night-watchman state but by a quartet of driving forces.

Even the first voice, classical *economic* liberalism, is concerned not with the particular interest of entrepreneurs but with the common good in the form of higher wages, lower prices, and the wealth of society as a whole. Here, the core element, the free market, does not deserve wholesale criticism already because the adoption of market-economical elements in non-Western countries like China in the twenty years from 1990 to 2010 has reduced the number of people living in poverty by half. According to the United Nations, the first thirteen years of the twenty-first century even saw the fastest decrease in poverty in human history. Even those skeptical about this "good news"—the Asian Development Bank, for example, considers some of the data to be overly optimistic—will hardly be able to claim that economic liberalism has had no success in combating poverty.

The second voice, *social* liberalism, advocates pluralism and tolerance, among others, and opposes the terrorizing of consciences. A further voice, *political* liberalism, is concerned about civil liberties, and by no means only the negative liberties but—as the necessary precondition of actual freedom—positive liberties as well. It usually also insists on popular sovereignty and oversight over the executive that begins with the separation of powers.

It is difficult to find a name for the fourth voice, for the interest in a personality with highly developed capacities and a character of its own, including a right to idiosyncrasy and even eccentricity. Taking the notion of education not in a narrow institutional but in the emphatic sense, we might speak here of *educational* liberalism.[28]

These different kinds of liberalism are united by a common leitmotif that has the status of a fundamental criterion: because ultimately, what counts is the infinite value of every human being, and, namely, every singular but not singularized and isolated human being, each individual's freedom must be promoted.

5.3
A VIABLE LIBERALISM

Born in the age of the *philosophes*, in the Enlightenment, modern liberalism considers a further element to be indispensable. The (1) reference to experience, (2) legitimizing individualism, and (3) the free play of forces within the framework of the constitution and the law are joined by (4) a self-criticism relevant to action that is visible in a willingness to change when confronted with new challenges. Without this element, without a reflective regeneration, liberalism is not viable; above all, without this element, it does not deserve being called enlightened.

Let's take an example. No liberalism ossified at the stage of the night-watchman state can claim the honorific "enlightened." In any case, this variety can at most be found in American debates. The liberalism dominant in Europe, in contrast, has long expanded to include political participatory rights and social rights that serve a function in maintaining freedom and democracy. In consequence, criticism of orthodox old liberalism and even of its neoliberal restoration has become a thing of the past here. Reflective regeneration is needed in other areas. Four challenges are of particular importance. I will quickly sketch them here and discuss them in detail in the chapters that follow.

The *first* challenge has to do with the argumentative strategy that is of significant import for all further challenges that regard content: liberalism's basic elements must be legitimized in an interculturally understandable language. This task imposes itself already as a matter of policy. As far as we know, liberal thought emerged in the West. To explain the value of this thinking to non-Western cultures, more than that: to convince them of this value, we must not limit ourselves to an argumentation beholden to Western culture alone. Another reason, however, is more important and ultimately the only decisive one: respect for the value proper of other cultures demands that we engage not in culture-specific but in intercultural discourse with them.[29]

The first challenge with regard to content, the *second* challenge overall, has been familiar since the rise of the movement for environmental protection (see section 2.2 above). It can of course begin with the ecological dimension, but it far exceeds this dimension. Undoubtedly, economic liberalism must expand to include an ecological liberalism and where necessary be corrected by it. In addition, there is the "new social question." Without marginalizing the "old social question," that is, without absolving ourselves from the enduring task of regulating how we provide against the hardships that can come with illness, old age, or unemployment and of preventing poverty and pauperization, we must no longer sideline our responsibility for future generations. For them, we must preserve the achievements of civilization and culture and, as has happened in the past, expand them with new achievements.

This demanding task concerns at least six areas: (1) culture, including language, literature and art, music, architecture, science, medicine, and technology; (2) material and educational infrastructure: from roads, waterways, railroads, airports, canalization, and so on, to the health-care system to the education system and the architectural quality of cities; (3) legal and social institutions; (4) the economy, particularly investments and an appropriate accumulation of capital rather than of debt; (5) the environment, including the aesthetic and recreational value of the landscape (only then is it possible to speak of an ecological liberalism); and not least of all (6) demographics.

Whether a polity lives up to this task is evident for example in the relationship between state spending on consumption and spending on investments. The opposition here is not one that pertains to budgetary law; by consumption I mean spending that primarily benefits the current generations whereas investments serve future generations. The distinction concerns for example the relationship of the share of the gross domestic product represented by health-care spending to the share represented by spending on education. Experience shows what social statistics confirm: that the health-care system largely benefits those who are older, which is why it falls on the side of consumption more than it does on the side of investment. Now, the share of GDP spent on health care increases while the share spent on education stagnates at best.

Since beside health care it is primarily spending on employment, social programs, and retirement, in addition interest paid on the national debt, that have an inordinate impact on public finances while public investments have decreased enormously, government in practice prioritizes the older over the younger generations. This is what the injustice between the generations consists in to which humanity, since the Club of Rome's 1972 report *The Limits to Growth* and the emergence of the environmental movement, has tried to become sensitive. We must not gloss over the fact that governments act differently, that they pursue an obviously unjust policy of waste and indifference: the old enrich themselves at the expense of the young. This enrichment goes back to a past that, through increased national debt (debt that is, however, not incurred for the sake of investments), has shamefully restricted the leeway for public investments.

The *third* challenge is a desire for "civic society and civic virtues." Classical liberalism relies on a clear division of labor. For fear of morally overtaxing the citizenry, it provides for just laws and institutions such that citizens can make do without justice and can follow their mere interests. This division of labor—just institutions and justice-indifferent citizens, or rule of law instead of morality—overlooks that citizens must first create the institutions and then fill them with life. For only free people produce and preserve a free society. To that end—according to the third challenge—the classical division of labor must be abolished. In addition to the just institutions, a civic society with civic virtues is needed (see section 8.4).

The *fourth* challenge is so obvious that I can limit myself here to merely citing it: globalization. Just one aspect should be mentioned because it is often marginalized: globalization must not be reduced to its economic aspects. Weapons development, environmental damage, terrorism, and organized crime have long gone global, too. Fortunately, we do not live only in a global violent community but, even more so, in a global cooperative community as well. To the latter belong not just the economic, finance, and labor worlds but also tourism, the world of science, medicine, and technology, of education and training, of literature, music, theater, and the fine arts, also of (world) religions and of sports. Finally, we live in a global community with a common destiny, a worldwide community of misery and suffering.

An enlightened liberalism that seeks, thanks to reflective self-criticism, to remain viable today thus faces at least four challenges: the necessity of intercultural discourses, the new social question, a demand for civic virtues, and the many facets of globalization. A liberalism proves to be capable of regeneration and viable, in any case, only if it opens up to intercultural discourses and confronts the three challenges: the new social question with a shift of the state's responsibilities and spending in favor of (not merely economic) investments;

the demand for civic virtue by strengthening free civic sense and civic society; and, finally, globalization through a cautious development of fair worldwide cooperation, including political institutions, in the direction of large regional intermediary levels such as the European Union and ultimately of a subsidiary and federal global legal order that may in the end be called a world republic (see chapter 15).

6

Free Market: Vision or Illusion?

Humanity knows more than one form of organizing visionary forces committed to the principle of freedom. In addition to three-dimensional cultivation, that is, the visionary forces of technology, medicine, and education (part I), there is constitutional democracy. There, politically necessary rule is exercised by those concerned themselves and tied to civil rights and liberties, to negative and positive freedoms (part III). A third vision, one of the oldest social inventions, the market, allows human beings to conduct the work and business necessary for them as well as all forms of competition freely and autonomously, without restrictions imposed by a third party. As regards labor, the market supplements the freedom potential of technology. While the latter's contribution to freedom consists in devices and procedures that make work easier and increase its yield, the market's free play of forces ensures that the management necessary for the liberation from hunger is efficient and that the talents required can unfold. The market makes it possible for competition to take place peacefully and thereby to stimulate innovative achievements.

The two new visions, democracy and the market (new when compared to cultivation), do not exclude but supplement each other. In a preliminary definition: the rule of law in a democracy fixes the binding framework within which the market may unfold. At the same time, from a formal point of view, democratic government itself, because of the competition inherent to it, has market character, since both people and organizations, namely, political parties, not least of all programs and platforms, perhaps ideologies, compete with each other: for votes, offices, and access to public funds. Although both forms of organization are visions of freedom, they run the danger, in several respects and on certain conditions, of threatening freedom.

For some time now, there has been a further vision that mediates between democracy and the market, the civic society with the civic virtues of civic-mindedness sketched in section 5.3.

In the course of European modernity, the market has entered in so close a connection with a particular economic form, capitalism, that it is scarcely possible to delineate the market as a form of organization, the market economy, from capitalism, since both the market and capitalism bear three identical structural characteristics: institutionally, private property; motivationally, increasing and even maximizing profits; and, in terms of their coordinating mechanism, the free formation of prices. The first characteristic comes with decentralized decision-making; the second, the striving for profit, entails an undreamed of dynamism but also turns practically everything and everyone, not just goods but also services, and thus workers, as well as resources, into objects of trade, into commodities.

Capitalism—for some a polemic concept but here, for the moment, a neutral term—emerges neither only in modernity nor exclusively in Europe. Nonetheless it is less common, both historically and geographically, than the market. To be able to fathom the opportunities but also the limits the complex "market and capitalism" implies for freedom and yet be brief, I discuss the market as a more comprehensive, not exclusively economic phenomenon (section 6.1); talk about the value (section 6.2) and nonvalue (section 6.3) of the market; turn to the social market economy (section 6.4); and point to a number of noneconomic markets (section 6.5). In a final section, I offer a first discussion of capitalism in the currently dominant form, finance capitalism (section 6.6); further reflections follow in chapter 7.

6.1
MARKET AND CAPITALISM

To discuss the market, let us begin with a look back at its history. Originally, the German *Markt* (from Latin *mercatus*) designates the hawking activity of Roman peddlers in the age of Caesar. More generally, "market" refers to the public offering of goods, trade or public selling, and furthermore the large open space in a town reserved for that purpose. From a sociological perspective, according to Max Weber, modern towns arise only with markets; every town is a marketplace.[1] Because of its anthropologically paramount significance, the institution of the market can be found in practically all cultures, for example in the form of bazaars.

When markets specialize, there are, depending on the goods, fish markets, corn markets, beef markets, moreover labor, currency, and capital markets that are not bound to a place. Depending on the frequency with which goods are offered, there are daily, weekly, annual markets. The markets that serve the wholesale trade are called (trade) fairs.

At the beginning, as *agora* among the Greeks and as *forum* among the Romans, the market has no economic meaning yet. It names the site where the people assembles, the place of the political public. Only later does it expand to become the place of merchants without, of course, relinquishing its political significance, and it is only much later that the economic sidelines the political aspect.

In Europe, but probably elsewhere as well, markets are set up especially at the intersections of important trade routes as well as at river crossings (as in Ox*ford* or Frank*furt*) and around castles or monasteries. Often, urban settlements developed around the trading place that are endowed with special privileges, the market rights protected by a special "market peace." These were of such importance that the right to establish markets was claimed as a privilege by the Frankish and German kings, although they could bestow this right on others.

Finally, an organizational conception developed from the geographical and legal as well as the economic meaning: the market as an institution. There, seller/supplier and buyer/consumer meet and, via the balancing out of supply and demand, form the prices of all traded goods, at the beginning especially wares, soon services as well, later also money and financial instruments.

The market is that form of organization that is guided by exchange, rational price formation, and especially by increasing—according to the notion of the *homo oeconomicus* even maximizing—profits. Markets are considered free when they meet three conditions. First, the necessary institutional preconditions must be given, namely, "private" rights of ownership or of disposal must exist, rights that are neither collective nor otherwise "public." Not everything, however, must be privatized. Second, within them, neither monopolies nor oligopolies must exist; instead, unhindered cooperation and complete competition must reign. And third, rules imposed from outside should ensure that the basic forms of economic practice, cooperation and competition, unfold in fairness.

In reality, however, freedom of markets is never completely given. "Freedom of markets" is not an absolute but a comparative concept, and an absolutely free market is neither desirable, nor has it ever existed. Today, in any case, there are almost exclusively lawfully regulated and not absolutely free markets. For this real form of organization, which is at the same time the only one considered legitimate, the name "social market economy" has become common, where the qualification "social" is once more a comparative characteristic.

Markets lose freedom when sellers or buyers make arrangements among themselves, further, when the state awards a monopoly to certain suppliers, as was longtime the case with postal and telecommunications services, or when it grants concessions or licenses, mining rights, say, or establishes education standards. The state also appears as limiting freedom when it decrees certain prices, such as fixed prices, maximum or minimum prices, or imposes rent control or minimum wages. Not least of all, it limits freedom when it grants the privileges of a (tax-funded) public broadcaster to certain radio and television stations.

Where such restrictions of freedom enable, enhance, or secure the freedom of citizens for the long term, they undoubtedly make sense from the perspective of a theory of freedom. Where and how that is the case obviously depends on the concrete conditions, among which we must not overlook operational costs and the danger of abuse and corruption.

The three conditions of free markets — the existence of private rights of ownership and of disposal; the nonexistence of monopolies, oligopolies, and trusts; and the fair conduct of cooperation and competition — are not met by markets spontaneously, purely naturally. Rather, it is the legal order that permits, prohibits, or limits private property; proscribes monopolies, oligopolies, and trusts; and establishes, particularly in commercial law, including corporation law, insurance law, and so on, binding rules for financial transactions. In this sense, the market is to be tied in with a liberal legal order, which does indeed restrict the freedom of markets but not freedom as a whole. On the contrary, it allows for and promotes the freedom of economic subjects. And in achieving greater private profits, it also achieves a greater social profit, for example by subsidizing or supporting people not successful in the markets.

6.2
VALUE . . .

European intellectuals like to associate the free market with capitalism, and both are often held in ill repute. Astonishingly, the criticism that dominates is usually directed at the pure, merely free market. To consider the market, as Axel Honneth does, to be highly dangerous,[2] or even to fear, as many do, a "dictatorship of the market," or more recently, a dictatorship of capital, however, is to misjudge reality. For what predominates in reality is a social market economy that may well deserve criticism, but a criticism that is much more differentiated and probably more difficult to sustain.

Already the most famous theorist of the market, Adam Smith, does not sing the praises of entrepreneurs' unlimited profits, as we saw (section 5.2). Instead, like Plato before him,[3] he begins with the value of the division of labor and specialization, which are said to contain a potential for cooperation and sociability. Marx and Engels will doubt this value because in the ideal society they favor, the communist society, everyone explicitly no longer has "one exclusive sphere of activity." Instead, it is to be possible for everyone "to do one thing today and another tomorrow, to hunt in the morning, fish in the afternoon, rear cattle in the evening, criticise after dinner . . . without ever becoming hunter, fisherman, herdsman or critic."[4]

This is not to dismiss Marx and Engels out of hand. A fair look shows these quotes to contain two aspects. On the one hand, even in communist society, people remain economic citizens who as such are likely to appreciate the economic and social advantages of the division of labor and of specialization. They will therefore welcome a developed economy and within that economy prefer concentrating on one activity, on either hunting or fishing or rearing cattle. On the other hand, prudent people will reject the suggestion that they are only (specialized) economic citizens, since a charitable interpretation of the critic's activity cited by Marx and Engels detects within it a claim to responsible citizenship. Perhaps it also includes the right, as a moral personality, to possess a dignity beyond any price.

Back to Adam Smith. Not unlike Plato, Smith considers that "the greatest improvement in the productive powers of labour, and the greater part of the skill, dexterity, and judgment with which it is anywhere directed, or applied, seem to have been the effects of the division of labour."[5] Smith was probably right about it not only in his own time but generally. Because in the course of modernity especially, the desired result of the free market economy, the lowering of costs, its contribution to an offer of goods and services and to their efficient distribution to meet demand, has benefited a large part of humanity: the market grants a broad swath of the population a previously unknown, even undreamed of measure of prosperity.

Going beyond Smith, let's summarize the not unjustly much-praised advantages. The market stimulates those two basic forms of human coexistence that predominate also among politicians, artists, scientists, and intellectuals, as well as, to no negligible extent, among philosophers: cooperation and competition. Cooperation already, competition all the more so incite creativity, boldness, and effort. Through its demands, the market promotes autonomy, motivation, supply guided by demand, and efficient distribution. Moreover, it encourages a work ethic, including self-discipline and the stimulation of skills and of a willingness to work. It also contains the incentive to renounce certain things in the present for the sake of one's own future.

On the other hand, the market not merely stimulates these extraeconomic drivers of the economy. To a large extent, it already presupposes them, such as the willingness to develop one's talents and to employ one's skills to enhance one's own human capital. This in turn leads to a growth in productivity, and not just economic but also social and cultural, in the long run political productivity, too.

Undoubtedly, the immediate profit lies with those who make the effort: the entrepreneur gains customers willing to pay, the politician gains votes, and the author gains book buyers. In addition, they develop their capacities and gain what ultimately counts for human beings, that is, not money but respect, both respect from others and respect for themselves.

Traditional economic theory has had surprising difficulty in thinking the progress that characterizes economic history. The economic balance models were static. Yet already a hundred years ago, Joseph Schumpeter in *The Theory of Economic Development*, using the example of Henry Ford, shows how great entrepreneurs break the balance by means of an innovation driven by daring and creativity.[6]

A recent example is information technology (see also section 12.1). It is not due to (subsidized) research programs. It even makes do without traditional companies' initial conditions or at least their conditions for success, without, that is, the combination of patented inventions with a significant amount of capital. The factors responsible for its success are ones that rash criticism of the market prefers to marginalize: the creativity and originality spurred by the free market. It must be ungrudgingly acknowledged: these founders are entrepreneurs of genius.

What emerges here is a radically new kind of capitalism whose very newness has gone largely unnoticed. In traditional capitalism, money—called "capital"—is to yield a high return. In the new capitalism, it is quite simply the mind, namely, a brilliant business idea, that yields this return, which, moreover, is unimaginably high: not the 5 to 10 percent major companies are content with nor the 10 to 15 percent small businesses expect to gain. The returns are unimaginably high even by the standards of so-called vulture funds: within two decades, inventors who started out practically without capital have joined the exquisite "order" of billionaires.

It sounds almost obscene, and yet it is hardly an exaggeration: the highest yields have come out of the partnership between the market and the mind. On the side of the market, two factors account for these yields, first the provocation of creativity, which challenges the mind in the sense of original ideas, and second, prices determined by a very large demand, which have also made many athletes and crime writers and certainly the author of the Harry Potter novels superrich.

The first factor of economic progress, destructive innovation, is joined by a second that, again, must neither be passed over in silence nor be underestimated as to its impact: the Great Depression, the economic crises of the 1850s, 1870s, and 1890s, as well as a number of other crises, most recently the financial crisis that began in the United States in 2008, caused, among other things, by waves of world-economic liberalization since the Bretton Woods Conference in July 1944. They all expand the dynamic by a second factor, the shock of crises, in addition to the "Creative Destruction" due to great entrepreneurs.[7]

The succession of ever-new innovations that results from entrepreneurial spirit and shock is by no means limited to material things. Marx charged capitalism with an "unlimited extension of the working-day."[8] This diagnosis is contradicted by the de facto development, by the progressive shortening of the working day, week, and year. At the same time, the market proves its viability, but, as apologists of the pure market overlook, it maintains this viability only under the favorable marginal conditions that must be fixed by the polity. While one indispensable element of these conditions, the welfare state, operates a redistribution, the market ensures what the welfare state is interested in as well: that there is as much as possible to redistribute.

There are other achievements like the promotion of education, at least of job training. This today also includes knowledge of foreign languages and a capacity for lifelong learning as well as social and cross-cultural skills. In turn, workers who cannot keep up with more advanced qualifications and entrepreneurs who cannot keep up with the improvements of products get into trouble. There is another advantage: with higher prices, the market opposes the wasting of natural resources and thus turns out to be ecologically beneficial as well.

Hasty criticism, finally, likes to overlook something indicated by the development of places of trade into urban settlements: while the exclusively economic market might begin with a merely economic reciprocity, it soon overcomes this thematic limitation. Even where economic cooperation is all there is, people who otherwise would never have had anything to do with each other enter into networks. They commit themselves to contracts, and if, as is usually the case, the contracts are kept, so valuable a good as trust emerges: markets develop a peaceful and civilizing effect.

I will discuss the flipside, the promotion of excessive competitiveness and conflict, in a moment. But the flipside is the reverse of another side: even a purely economic market is not an arena of pure egotism. Without presupposing altruism, even with skepticism toward it, markets are an institution of reciprocity; in Adam Smith's much-cited words: "Whoever offers to another a bargain of any kind, proposes to do this. Give me that which I want, and you shall have this which you want, is the meaning of every such offer. . . . It is not from the benevolence of the butcher, the brewer, or the baker that we expect our dinner, but from their regard to their own interest."[9]

6.3
. . . AND NONVALUE

Now for the flipside. Only a naive apology of the free market relies completely on its self-healing powers. In reality, markets left to themselves develop, in addition to inequality, oligopolies, monopolies, and trusts, which weakens competition and achieves the opposite of a free market: the improvement of products slows down, and instead, prices rise for consumers and profits for entrepreneurs.

Such distortions of competition, paradoxically, are a demand of economic rationality: given the necessary power, one either makes more profit by the same means or makes the same profit by staking less. Because of this "law of rational anti-competitive behavior,"[10] competition that promotes the common good does not arise spontaneously but requires guiding counterforces that create a framework to promote the common good.

These counterforces do not all have to be enforceable through coercion. Quite a few things are brought about simply by praise and reprimand, respect and disrespect. For even in purely economic exchanges, trust and reputation prove to be nonmaterial and yet precious "goods" that are easy to lose but difficult to regain. Both smart business people and smart customers thus do not put the immaterial goods in jeopardy; already below the level of authorities that can exercise coercion, they create an atmosphere promoting the common good.

Yet where such incentives do not suffice, an enforceable legal order is required. Such a legal order has the right, first of all, to guarantee personal property and free competition, then to ensure fair rules of competition that maintain the delicate balance between the markets and state oversight. Finally, there are things that money cannot buy—not contingently but as a matter of principle. All cultures are aware of this fundamental limit of the market, the Western ones at the latest since the early philosophers Socrates, Plato, and Aristotle. No need to wait until 2012, for Michael Sandel's pathos-filled plea for the "moral limits of markets." But there is no harm in repeating it.[11]

The counterconcept to the market stressed by Sandel but acknowledged since Rawls at the latest, justice, must of course not be understood in too material terms if we are to avoid committing the error made by the opponents, an economistic reduction. Yet, even if the reminder is welcome, what is new is not that no one, however rich they be, can purchase vitally important things like respect and self-respect, like friendship and love, like a sense of security and feeling at home. And the notion, according to Sandel advocated occasionally by some overzealous economists, of auctioning off votes, is likely to be rejected without much debate both in the theory of democracy and in its practice.[12] European readers of Sandel, moreover, should not forget that while it might be possible in the United States to speak of unfettered markets and triumphant capitalism, that is hardly the case in Europe's democratic welfare states.

The most important limit of the market, in the eyes of constitutional democracies, is drawn by human rights and human dignity. What I mean here is not that they protect from the market—that is the task of the welfare state. Something more fundamental is at issue. Because of their absolute inner value, these human rights and human dignity stand above all prices and therefore have no place, as a matter of principle, in the world of prices, on the market. If nonetheless they are being traded there, they have already lost their essence, their absolute value.

To offer human dignity and human rights on the market is to commit a category mistake; it mistakes the essence of both sides. Not just under today's, under any conditions, the market fails here. Whether barter, money, or capital economy, whether Western or Eastern, premodern or modern preferences apply: markets and human rights are quite simply incompatible with each other. Yet since human rights by their very concept pertain to the human being as such, they are, without compromise, normatively superior to the market and to all political rule. The authority they demand by their very nature differs fundamentally from that of the market and limits the power of the market: constitutional democracy (see chapter 11).

6.4
ECO-SOCIAL MARKET ECONOMY

Human rights comprise such rights as the right to property and to a free development of one's personality. These include a free participation in economic life in the forms of consumers' freedom to choose an occupation or of free enterprise. Not content with negative liberties, however, the notion of human rights also demands additional restrictions of the market for the market's vision of freedom not to revert into unfreedom.[13]

To avoid this reversal and to ensure that the market is free, already internally but externally as well, for the one who ultimately counts, the individual, a sensible polity expands its responsibility in matters of economic policy and commits to the guiding concept of a social market economy,[14] which is far from being a thing of the past, especially considering its dynamic rather than static nature. Thanks to this guiding notion, the economic form that has come to dominate in western and northern Europe is a mixed form of private and social economy: to counterbalance the grave deficiencies of pure market and private economy, it has created public social security, a progressive income tax, and other measures to redistribute wealth. And education policy is concerned with targeted support.

In the case of the goal of bringing about justice within a generation, we may also speak of an intragenerationally just freedom because the welfare state in addition ensures a public system of education and, not least of all, equal opportunity as regards freedom. With respect to future generations, there are also the protection of the environment and other intergenerational tasks. That is why what is needed is not a "merely social market economy" but an "eco-social market economy," moreover, a market economy that, beyond ecological matters, defends a comprehensive intra- and intergenerationally just freedom.

There is thus a particular affinity of enlightened liberal democracy not with the simple market economy already but only with a social and ecological market economy. But the latter's real cost in freedom must not be passed over, neither the financial cost, which in many places has already led traditional welfare states to amass enormous debts that restrict the ability to invest, nor that soft totalitarianism created by a freedom-disrespecting bureaucracy. For a market economy to be legitimate, it does therefore not suffice to be ecological and social; it must, in addition, be subject to the criterion of compatibility with freedom. What is required is thus a weighing of four aspects, the market, the social, the ecological, and freedom.

That this weighing is difficult, that it will hardly lead to a simple, objective solution, is evident. Instead, a relatively wide spectrum of legitimate possibilities is to be expected. This includes, for example, the question how far the right to property extends: is it legitimate only for consumer goods or also for means of production, and if the latter, just for specific ones or for (almost) all of them? The question of the extent of competition, too, remains open: is it to apply even to the educational and the health-care system, and if so, only to the basic organization or to individual institutions such as schools, universities, and hospitals as well? There is legitimate leeway, too, where the establishment of social and environmental standards and their balancing with incentives to autonomy and individual initiative is concerned.

Because the necessary balance between the two poles of eco-social market economy, the eco-social and the market, is not easy to find, imbalances threaten. In a first imbalance, a fixation on redistributing wealth overlooks that the wealth to be redistributed must first be created. This danger is parried by policies establishing marginal conditions, in part legal, in part economic, that allow businesses to grow profitably despite international and even intra-European competition. Policy must also ensure that the profits actually yield the taxes that are to finance collective projects.[15] Not least of all, it must not marginalize the increasing inequality of fortunes, especially the emergence of ever more of the superrich.[16] That is especially the case when huge fortunes promote an "heiristocracy," a rule of heirs, which is not a matter of indifference when it comes to justice, and neither does it benefit entrepreneurship and thus indirectly the common good because many rich heirs tend to avoid the daring of entrepreneurial enterprise.

As regards the necessary balance, especially the area of welfare programs and jobs, the second threatening imbalance is an exclusive focus on either the tasks of the polity or those of individuals. Those who primarily pay attention to the polity emphasize, like Honneth does, that those who do not find their place in the labor market both disappear from the community of state responsibility and lose their participation in democratic corporations. This danger has grave consequences, and it is indeed a danger; Honneth and others who proffer similar arguments, however, exaggerate it. They underestimate or even remain silent about the fact that in Europe's democratic welfare states, there remains a measure of social security, including health insurance and housing subsidies, that may not allow for a bountiful life but does allow for more than mere subsistence. One of the results: not a few people prefer the "welfare" status to work (work that pays little more).

As far as participation in democratic corporations is concerned, one must not forget those corporations that are as good as independent of the workplace: families, for many immigrants extended families; religious communities; clubs for sports and other hobbies; not least of all neighborly relationships. Political participation is not tied to a job; knowledge of the language is much more important and, not least of all, a kind of connection with the (host) country that is made more difficult by the "generous" granting of dual citizenship.

These objections do not contest the importance of the topic. They merely advocate for a judicatively open debate. Such a debate acknowledges that we have for a while been living in societies shaped by labor and by professional life, which places demands on both sides. On the one hand, making job creation possible ought to be the top policy priority. On the other, the young generation ought to learn what Kant already pointed out (see section 4.3), namely, learn to provide for themselves as much as possible. In discursive language, this principle takes the form of "helping others help themselves," in the rhetorically more powerful language of a proverb, "give a man a fish, and you feed him for a day; teach a man to fish, and you feed him for a lifetime"—and, we may add, he enjoys greater self-respect and, moreover, the respect of his peers.

6.5
NONECONOMIC MARKETS

Not just economic theorists, philosophers, too, advocate competition; in modernity, for example, thinkers from Montesquieu to David Hume and Condorcet to Kant. In *The Spirit of the Laws* (1748), Montesquieu speaks of the civilizing force of commerce, which replaces the war of the passions with the compromise between diverging forces.[17] And according to Kant, the human being is destined fully to develop all its natural dispositions aimed at the deployment of reason. This takes place, besides through targeted support, once more via competition, since such competition "awakens all the powers of the human being, brings him to overcome his propensity to indolence, and, driven by ambition, tyranny, and greed, to obtain for himself a rank among his fellows."[18]

Kant rightly is not thinking just of economic competition because the beneficial effects of competition are apparent not only in the economy. The market can be understood in a formal and at the same time expanded sense that, in concentrating on a core independent of the economy, acquires a much wider field of application.

In this new, formal understanding, the market remains a spontaneous and moreover anonymous institution of control, a form of organizing supply and demand. As noted, however, its application is not limited to goods, services, and financial products, and the control takes place not only via money or capital. According to the expanded conception, there is also a market of ideas where methods and (hypo-) theses from the humanities, sciences, medicine, and technology compete with each other for acknowledgment, ultimately even for the common good. Guided by the idea of truth, the common good is here not defined in material terms, as increasing wealth, but as an increase in insight or objective knowledge, and in certain cases in terms of humane applicability (see section 9.3).

Moreover, there is an artistic market in which musicians (composers and performers), writers and actors, painters, sculptors, and architects compete among themselves for attention and acknowledgment. A nice example for artistic competition spurring on the highest achievements is the competition for perfection and fame between two outstanding painters of the Renaissance, the melancholic loner Michelangelo and the elegant, sociable Raphael. Both are at first working (among other places) in Florence and are later, just a few years before the iconoclasm of the Reformation on the other side of the Alps, called by Pope Julius II to Rome, where they create, reciprocally stimulating but also competing with each other, world-famous works of art. Michelangelo paints the pope's private chapel, the Vatican's Sistine Chapel, with the story of creation, the prophets, and the (prophesizing) Sibyls, as well as the Last Judgment on the wall behind the altar. Raphael for his part glorifies the triumphs of the church in the papal apartments in the Vatican, the *stanze*.[19] We must, nonetheless, not overestimate the factor of competition. Michelangelo and Raphael owe their enormous productivity first of all to their artistic genius, then also to the support from princes (including princes of the church).

Another example is the Italian city-republics competing for cultural splendor, like the German principalities later, which has led to a host of outstanding buildings, parks, and museums. In Germany, together with Austria and Switzerland, it created the area with the world's highest density, then and now, of theaters and opera houses.

Even criticism of the market has its market, which is why such criticism, when it asserts itself as criticism in principle, succumbs to a pragmatic contradiction: it rejects what in rejecting it lays claim to.

The market, in both the narrow and the broadened sense, is also found in the media, in publishing, radio, and television (where the criterion of ratings rules everything), not least of all in the new internet media. Even politics, especially in a democracy, bears market characteristics, since people, parties, and platforms vie for attention in the media and for support from citizens.

This has no bearing on the fact that in other respects, market and polity remain antipodes: when it comes to their legitimizing bases, different property rights oppose identical civil rights; there, the goal consists ideally in particular welfare, here in the public's; and the procedure, to simplify, on the market consists in exchange, in the polity in debate, the medium there in money, here in power.

The fact that money controls the common, economic market is not suspended on the market in the expanded sense, not even on the artistic and the market of ideas: books are intended to be bought; authors want royalties, publishers a profit. There is an additional means of control, which indeed often stands in the foreground and which, above all, tends to be more scarce than money: reputation. It undoubtedly conforms to the second structural characteristic, the maximization of profit: the reputation is to be increased, even maximized, and to turn into fame. Also scarce is the medium with which the political market is controlled, the combination of power, influence, and popular support.

The market is thus a much more far-reaching and in consequence a much more significant organizational force than is usually assumed. Nonetheless, we must not forget what we said earlier, that such vital things as loyalty, trust, and friendship can neither be bought with money nor be subjected to the principle of profit maximization.

Often only in a secondary and nonessential sense, the economic component enters into the markets of the new kind as well. Academic and artistic achievements, for example, are often acknowledged not just by honors but also by awards; publications not only receive favorable reviews but also generate large sales; music and theater performances bring in royalties; success at the voting booth leads to more money and indeed to lucrative offices.

Noneconomic markets, too, require marginal conditions that ensure the freedom of the market and prevent distortions of competition. Since political rule contains a high potential for preventing the proper functioning of the market, the systematic starting point here consists in negative liberties as defensive rights against the state: the minimal condition for academic and artistic freedom of the market—in short: for freedom—consists in freedom of speech (combined with the rejection of censorship) and the freedom of art and science, research and teaching. The responsibility of another defensive action, the prevention of plagiarism or even fraud in academia, lies with the academy itself. The freedom of the political (market) in turn comes together in the notion of participative or republican democracy (see below, section 11.5).

Undoubtedly, it takes more for music, art, and the sciences not just to be freed from obstacles but to receive the means to actually develop: on the one hand institutions for music, art, and the sciences, including public debates, and, on the other, financial means. These can come from public coffers, for example as public funding for orchestras, museums, theaters and opera houses, moreover for universities and research institutions that in many places, especially in Europe, create successful centers of culture and research. The United States, however, demonstrates that it is also possible to rely on private initiatives, albeit under conditions rarely encountered in Europe: foundations that have existed for many generations whose capital has not been diminished by (enormous) devaluations and which, moreover, is frequently replenished with generous tax-deductible donations.

6.6
FINANCE CAPITALISM

Within the economy, the role of finance is still growing. When it plunges into a crisis, as in the grave financial crisis of recent years, many are affected: from private investors to institutional investors such as sovereign wealth or pension funds all the way to entire national economies. It is thus understandable that criticism, radical criticism, even, arises. But is there need for more than a fundamental reform? Is capitalism "as such" responsible in particular for a boundless greed, as is sometimes said, and must capitalism "as such," for that reason, be overcome? Or is it necessary to start even earlier—as Rousseau does in the *Discourse on Inequality*, Proudhon in *What Is Property?*, and Marx and Engels throughout their work—namely, with private property?

"Capitalism" is an ambiguous expression that in recent years has become ideologically charged to express a rejection, for example in Jakob Augstein's 2013 book *Sabotage*, whose subtitle reads: "Why we must decide between democracy and capitalism."[20]

A sober assessment begins with an ideologically neutral concept. Restricting it to its newer form, industrial and especially finance capitalism, I propose the following concept: a first shape, (finance) capitalism, is an economic form in which what counts is money on a grand scale, capital, which is no longer merely a means of exchange but above all a commodity. The second shape, capitalism as a general economic form, puts money to work in investments in the present in order to receive a higher profit in the future. And in the broadest conception, the third shape, capitalism is a societal form in which the profit-seeking economy so successfully permeates ever more social domains that it becomes the dominant factor of life and governs the entire lifeworld in what Jürgen Habermas has called a kind of colonization.[21]

Finance capitalism includes investing savings and profits or money raised through credit, that is, debt, in the present and expecting from one's investment a profit, as large as possible, in the future. In that sense, there is a new kind of exchange in finance. In the exchanges dominant prior to capitalism, "social" or interpersonal exchanges, the process of giving and countergiving takes place between different persons (natural or legal). Finance does not abolish this kind of exchange. To open a savings account or to buy stocks is to give one's money to someone else and to receive something in return.

At the same time, however, a second, intrapersonal and dephased, two-part exchange takes place. Leaving aside some highly complex financial transactions, one and the same person (natural or legal) exchanges present money for a profit expected in the future but subject to risk or uncertainty; this is the return on long-term investments, their profitability. Whether someone invests money in this way or whether they grant credit—someone exchanges, on the one hand, their present for the future and, on the other, the certainty of what is being given in the present, for the uncertainty of what is being expected in return (and expected to be higher) in the future.

This is based on a twofold attitude. A capacity for renunciation, namely, the willingness to subordinate present gratification to long-term benefit, combines with a certain kind of gamble: for the expectation of a future great reward, the daring, standard-setting entrepreneur sacrifices a present certainty.

The branch of the economy responsible for these transactions is finance with its institutions, banks, stock markets, loan corporations, savings banks, and insurance companies. This branch has brought an increase in rationalization, which boosts businesses, one of the pillars of the modern, capitalist "market economy," but also serves ordinary citizens, by making installment purchases or home loans possible, as well as the state, by granting loans to fund public welfare projects. Since as a result, societies as a whole have grown richer, even radical critics do not call for prohibiting capital as a commodity, for abolishing even local savings banks and credit unions, just as in such debates, no one is calling for abolishing the money economy in favor of a barter economy. A look at this first stage of capitalism, finance capitalism, thus proves to be uncontroversial, despite some wholesale criticism of capitalism.

Yet the enormous increase in social wealth is distributed very unequally, which justifies such book titles as *Freedom Doesn't Belong to the Rich Alone.*[22] Some authors demand narrowing the gap between rich and poor. Others again, like Rawls,[23] consider that envy is not reasonable and that material inequality should be permitted if a society, although it allows for an unequal distribution of material wealth, ensures equal opportunity and redistributes wealth to benefit those who are the worst off.

The new branch of the economy, finance, thus creates advantages, but it creates not only advantages. It is an error, meanwhile, to consider that "capital finance" introduced greed in the world. Greed is a general human passion ancient Egyptians warned against almost four and a half thousand years ago: "Guard against the temptation of greed, for it is an evil, incurable disease.... It is a bag filled with everything loathable, a bundle of all evils."[24] And those who prefer a philosopher and Enlightener to vouch for this view may cite Kant, who counts greed among the passions, which he considers "cancerous sores for pure practical reason" and "for the most part... incurable because the sick person does not want to be cured."[25]

Greed, or avarice, in any case, is a general human passion that is encountered in every culture and that even the world of fairy tales warns us against in the story of the fisherman and his wife. What is at stake in greed is nothing less than the future, the future of individuals, groups, and societies — when it comes to the protection of the environment and of the climate, to feeding the world's population, and to public debt, even to the future of humanity, which is why we must time and again emphatically warn against greed, which often partners with hubris. Capitalist finance, however, offers both the greed for possessions and the greed for a power a new, highly tempting field of activity, as tempting for con men like Saccard in Émile Zola's *Money* as it is for ruthless investment bankers.[26]

A sober look, of course, sees temptability impartially, that is, not just on the side of the bankers. Private investors, too, and the politicians sitting on the boards of savings and other publicly owned banks have not guarded against greed in their financial dealings. Not the least of the effects of wealth in a society is to awaken desires on the part of the public, desires that tend to grow faster than they can be fulfilled. The price to be paid has already been mentioned: while according to its idea, the financially most demanding share of public spending, the welfare state, increases opportunities for freedom, the immense public debt amassed to fund the welfare state in particular in turn restricts these opportunities significantly.

As a further consequence, society does not become dependent on personal financiers, the way princes, kings, and emperors depended on the Medicis, Fuggers, and Rothschilds. It subjects itself to an anonymous power, the impersonal financial market.

For these and other reasons, an enlightened liberalism calls on politics to acquire economic and financial expertise. Of course such expertise does not simply exist somewhere, waiting simply to be read. Practically none of the world's innumerable economists, advisory councils, and specialized journalists warned against the financial crisis that began in 2007. And when the crisis had broken out, people were at a loss or giving contradictory advice. Matters were different, it seems, when the European Economic and Monetary Union was created. There were grave concerns, which, however, were being ignored for political reasons. What was ignored, in particular, was a necessary structural interlocking: to introduce the Euro, it would have been necessary first to create a fiscal union, a banking union, and a considerable degree of political union, and to combine them with effective rules for enforcing agreed-on standards.

Here as elsewhere, politicians fall prey to imprudence and thoughtlessness and may sacrifice the autonomous laws that govern the matters at issue. The view that the state could govern economic and financial markets is a statist misconception. The state *is* able, however, to create encouraging or discouraging marginal conditions in specific domains. The fact that no polity is able to govern any one of these domains does not relieve them of intervening regulatively where necessary. They have a great responsibility especially in confronting finance because of its both far-reaching and profound effects. Yet only a polity that rejects a narrow and thereby misleading diagnosis can live up to this responsibility.

One example of a dubious diagnosis is Wolfgang Streeck's 2013 study *Buying Time: The Delayed Crisis of Democratic Capitalism.* Written with grand gestures and a great deal of activist commitment, the text looks at the recent financial, fiscal, and economic crisis and claims that the sociopolitical basis of this crisis is a "democratic capitalism" inspired by Hayek. Three chapters explain the title's thesis with explicitly Marxian concepts: "buying time" consists in delaying an impending event, the long-overdue crisis of capitalism, the disastrous consequences of the hegemony of the neoliberal market, postponed to the future and, we may add, hushed up.

Streeck can indeed evoke a number of phenomena such as the power of central banks led by financial technocrats or "the euro as a frivolous experiment," which he suggests replacing with a European version of Bretton Woods.[27] What is missing, however, are references to contradicting phenomena and a judgment to follow such a juxtaposition. Demonizing it certainly does not do justice to finance capitalism as it actually is and to its potential for usefulness.

It bears repeating, for example, that leading intellectuals fleeing National Socialism found in the United States not only a capitalistically organized economy but also a liberal democracy that protected their lives and their religious freedom. Or recall the existence of Scandinavian welfare states, socialist-governed France, as well as the German comanagement model, which Streeck mentions but does not cite as an alternative phenomenon in his harsh diagnosis.

According to a comparison of 186 countries made in 2013, the public expenditure quota even increased in the phase of globalization from 1970 to 2004, and the quota of social security benefits is high in many places, not just in the Scandinavian countries.[28] A sociological diagnosis of the present, moreover, must overlook neither the impact of local citizens' initiatives nor the rich cultural scene in many European countries. And on the global level, one must take into account a development that contradicts the reduction of globalization to the economy, which Streeck, too, does not avoid, namely, that international law, a by no means just economically oriented force, continues to make headway, even if it also continues to be violated, for example in the second Iraq war of 2003 or the Russian expansion in Ukraine. Not least of all, neither the international fight against hunger nor the fight against the feared climate catastrophe, and here especially against CO_2 emissions, is entirely without success.

A sociology that is critical in the original sense of the word would have to widen its thematic scope significantly beyond financial, fiscal, and economic policy. In its argumentation, it would have to take serious counterarguments into account, engage, for example, with Niall Ferguson's thesis that it is because of the capitalist form of the economy, among other things, that living standards and life expectancy of citizens in Western countries have risen significantly.[29] In addition, key terms such as "social justice" deserve conceptual labor. Finally, one should be able to expect a look to be taken at non-Marxist authors who are nonetheless critical of neoliberalism, such as John Rawls. With his fixation on Hayekian neoliberalism, Streeck ends up choosing too easy a target: there is no question that capitalism also poses dangers, as the example of globalized finance will show (see section 7.5).

Another criticism of capitalism against a Marxian background claims, under the title *Capital in the Twenty-First Century*, that there is an inexorable trend toward a splitting of society into rich and poor.[30] According to the author, Thomas Piketty, the real rate of return on capital *r* is greater than the rate of economic growth *g*. In consequence, wage earners become relative losers, owners of capital relative winners. To oppose this trend, of societies becoming less achievement oriented and meritocratic, and instead ever more "capitalistic," wealth in all its forms, income as well as assets and especially inheritances, ought to be taxed at much higher rates.

Piketty obtains his empirical diagnosis from research on wealth based on historical tax data from France, Great Britain, Sweden, and the United States: until 1914, enormous differences in wealth existed that diminished until the 1970s and have since been rising again. However, critics say,[31] no European country even gets close to the degree of inequality that existed before the First World War. Moreover, the "patrimonial middle class" has become much larger. And in addition, a global saturation of the markets with capital makes a period of worldwide lower rates of return likely. Finally, Piketty underestimates the new demography, the decreasing number of young people, that will lead to a shortage of manpower and thus to an increase in wages. Judicatively, then, Piketty's analysis, too, turns out to be insufficiently thorough.

7

Justice in the Name of Freedom

A freedom debate about the market economy and (finance) capitalism must not ignore the point of view of justice, especially since, as I noted in the introduction, justice seems to be pushing out freedom as the guiding ethical concept. This move, however, overlooks that one basic principle of justice consists in reciprocal restrictions of freedom. An enlightened liberalism puts emphasis on defining justice in terms of freedom, granting freedom factual primacy as well, since a reciprocal restriction of freedom presupposes that there is to be freedom; confronted with the same desire for freedom on the part of everyone else, however, this freedom is viable only in reciprocal restriction.

In opposition to the political philosophy dominant today,[1] then, the systematic starting point of this study is not justice but freedom. As I have mentioned a number of times, what ultimately counts is the individual, albeit not isolated, human being, and the essence of the individual as a moral person consists in freedom.

Tasks of justice arise only where several free beings share the same world with each other in cooperation and conflict. Thereby—and here lies an objection to a *pre*-enlightened liberalism—the notion of justice constitutes a necessary continuation of the principle of freedom that is to be operated in two dimensions, within generations and between generations.

A second point is often overlooked when the perspective of justice becomes overbearing. The welfare state demanded in the name of justice is ultimately justifiable only as a welfare state that serves a freedom function; its increasing extension, however, displays an ambiguity: in serving real freedom, the welfare state also restricts freedom again.

My continuation of the debate about the market economy and finance capitalism begins with the intercultural significance of justice (section 7.1) and the two main concepts, institutional and personal justice (section 7.2). The key term *social justice* (section 7.3) brings out the ambiguity just mentioned (section

7.4). Finally, I assess one branch of the economy from the point of view of a justice committed to freedom, choosing once more the finance sector as my example (section 7.5).

7.1
WORLD JUSTICE HERITAGE

Justice can be discussed in many different ways. Those who value rhetorical brilliance are better off speaking as moralists condemning an unjust world or as prophets who encourage everyone to change their lives for the sake of a more just world. Philosophers, however, are no Jeremiahs; their task is neither to harangue nor to prophesy. As proponents of moral philosophy or philosophical ethics, they prefer a maxim of Goethe's: those who philosophize disagree with their age.[2]

A first objection to the present declares that there is no lack of ethical or moral principles in finance. To be sure, the finance industry does not show itself to have ethical integrity and has for some time now been showered with reproaches in the name of ethical principles, reproaches that, when they are justified, are widely applauded. Ethical principles thus do not just occur in the world; they also have power. They live up to Kant's definition of power as "a capacity that is superior to great obstacles," or they are able, in Max Weber's terms, "to carry out [their] own will despite resistance."[3]

This contains another objection to the present: power is held not only by the usual four factors, namely, the medium of finance, money or capital; the authority of binding rules, government; the sword or the military; and print as well as audiovisual media. Power is held also by ethics or morality because it defines both the first and the last driving force of the usual power factors.[4] Now, within the frame of this fifth and de facto first or primary power, morality or ethics, justice plays a preeminent role, even if, from a systematic point of view, it is second to freedom. It does so for two reasons, both of which are highly welcome in an age of globalization.

The first reason: partly for the sake of their negative freedom, partly for their positive freedom, namely, to abolish coercion, oppression, and exploitation and to be able to live according to their own ideas and interests, people in all cultures yearn for justice—which thus clearly plays a subordinate role as a means to freedom rather than as a purpose. And for that reason, because no culture wants to renounce the perspective of justice, justice, along with the aspect of freedom, has intercultural, even omnicultural, we might say: cosmopolitan significance.

Humanity forms a worldwide community of justice demanded in the name of freedom. The principles of this community have the status of a world justice heritage, which, moreover, unlike the world cultural heritage, does not take different forms in different places but at its core remains the same. Skeptics of course consider justice to be a suit to be bought only in different styles and in different sizes; for them, there is no one suit called "justice" to fit all people and all occasions. In reality, an elementary awareness of justice has long united humanity. An ancient Egyptian book of wisdom, written more than three thousand years ago, already tells us concretely: "Do not displace the stone marking the boundaries of the fields / and do not move the measuring cord from its place. / Do not be greedy for an arm's length of land / and do not violate the limits of a widow's field."[5]

The outstanding value of justice openly presented here meets with global approval only because within morality, we focus on the part whose acknowledgment people owe each other. For that very reason, violations of justice deserve protest, and the articulation of that protest deserves applause. Other moral principles like sympathy, charity, love of one's neighbor, and fraternity—solidarity, in gender-neutral terms—are undoubtedly morally demanded as well but to be fulfilled voluntarily. Justice, in contrast, designates that indispensable core of morality that brooks no substitution, no "deal" in exchange for other demands. No artistic or intellectual genius may violate justice in the name of his genius, no generous benefactor in the name of his generosity. By the same token, a debtor may not give the payment he owes his rich creditor to a poor beggar instead.

Yet what does justice consist in? So far, we have named three characteristics: its intercultural significance, its being owed to one another, and exemplarily, the ancient Egyptian demand to respect property and not to take advantage of so powerless a person as a widow. Further definitions begin with the distinction between an institutional and a personal justice.

7.2
INSTITUTIONAL AND PERSONAL JUSTICE

Within the frame of institutional justice, two minimal conditions are undisputed: that the law, not arbitrariness and violence, is to govern, and that the law is to govern without regard to the person. From the second condition results the originary, still basic meaning: justice initially consists merely in an accordance with the law, *ius*.

This basic meaning contains a further objection to widespread views. Contrary to a popular misunderstanding that both neoliberals and simplistic anticapitalists succumb to, justice is not primarily a material matter. Without downplaying the economic aspect, the primary concern is with legal rules to be interpreted, in case of dispute, by an impartial jurisdiction.

Only in countries in which it has become a matter of course that the judicial system, despite the sometimes necessary criticism of details, acts free of arbitrariness and free of corruption do citizens underestimate its status and import. At most they acknowledge it in matters of "foreign" policy when they protest corruption in other countries' justice systems, and in matters of "domestic" policy because no one is willing to sacrifice a functioning justice system for more social justice. On the contrary, the long-standing expansion of the traditional judiciary to include new domains such as administrative, labor, and social security tribunals, tax, cartel, and patent courts, is being welcomed. This acknowledges the, literally, outstanding significance for justice, what Kant calls the "public justice,"[6] of the judiciary.

In the case of another justice, the form that is decisive both for the organization of society and for political philosophy, the primacy of freedom is particularly salient: the justice that normatively shapes the law is not content with just any kind of law but rather subjects the law to the principle of a generally compatible freedom, whose justification and explication in civil rights and liberties will be the subject of a later discussion (see section 11.2).

Politicians and media professionals as well as the leading actors of the economy want to change things. To that end, they seek what is generally a scarce resource: influence and power. In their search, they run the double danger of, on the one hand, saying "justice" when they mean a particular good or demand something they are not due and, on the other, employing unfair means in the struggle for influence and power.

These dangers are prevented by those who, once more, object to the zeitgeist and take personal justice into account, which many debates about justice simply ignore. This kind of justice marks the character of a person. Also referred to as uprightness, it distinguishes, in economic life, the honorable merchant. In ethics, it has the status of a cardinal virtue, for in keeping with the Latin expression, *cardo*, it belongs to those fundamental virtues on which many other virtues "hinge." In the case of personal justice, these include attitudes such as impartiality, freedom from arbitrariness, and the rejection of all kinds of bribery.

Where is this personal justice required? Members of Parliament need it to be able to live up their oath of office and ultimately serve neither their own careers nor their clients but indeed the good of the entire people. Citizens in turn need it in cases of vital injustice to be able to voice indignation and protest, where necessary even to engage in civil disobedience. And that personal justice is indispensable in the economy as well will be shown in this chapter's last section via the example of finance.

7.3
NEW SOCIAL JUSTICE

When we now turn to a further aspect of justice, the social justice so widely evoked in recent years, a sober assessment begins with a surprising finding: there is no discussion of social justice in the theorist of justice whose work predominated for centuries, Aristotle. Only more than two thousand years after him, in the course of the nineteenth century, does the expression insinuate itself in a provocatively casual way into the discourse of justice. Probably first used in Christian social ethics, the notion was to help solve the time's social difficulties, such as a high level of unemployment, absence of protection in case of accidents, illness, and old age, lack of education and training, and poverty, pauperization, even, phenomena, that is, that are undoubtedly relevant to freedom.

Even those not entirely happy with today's welfare state won't be able to dispute that in western and northern Europe, the problems just listed have largely been solved: by means of social security institutions, by means of welfare benefits that secure more than the minimum required for survival, by means of free public schools, by means of subsidized occupational retraining, and much besides.[7]

The painful experience with absolutist authoritarian states speaks in favor of negative civil rights and liberties. A liberalism content with these, at most supplementing them with democratic rights to participation, however, overlooks that humans do not possess the capacity for leading a life of their own from birth but instead must acquire it in the process of inner cultivation (see chapter 4). Partly as a precondition, partly as a frame of this learning process, humans require a number of things: goods such as food, clothing, and shelter; services that begin with the tasks of the family and continue with those of schools; not least of all numerous opportunities, today opportunities for highly developed training above all.

Because freedom becomes actual only where these tasks are fulfilled, an enlightened liberalism advocates not only negative but also positive liberties and a welfare state responsible for them. It does not, however, ignore the danger that looms here: a welfare state that is too generous financially will readily reduce the ideal values freedom and dignity to something material and thus succumb to an economization that is criticized elsewhere. Because the alternative lies in a freedom-promoting "help to help oneself," a materially expanded social justice must confront a new age-defining state of affairs and simultaneously one of the newer social questions.

Thanks to a high degree of economic and social democratization, the separation between two realms, pinpointed from antiquity to Marx, has disappeared. For not just the activity of workers but that of employees, civil servants, managers, and entrepreneurs, not least of all activities in the home and in community service have labor character. In this respect, work rather than leisure opens up the freedom opportunities that make attaining such important goals as individuation, autonomy, and self-fulfillment possible. For this very reason, the traditional separation into a realm of necessity (the needy human being leads a simple life of labor) and the realm of freedom (the "spiritual" being leads a good life of leisure) is largely abolished in reality.

Occupation and work no longer serve only to make a living and to secure a pleasant, safe, even generous life, but in an essential respect also to make a meaningful existence possible. From the perspective of the individual, they inspire and motivate the development of a broad spectrum of knowledge, skills, and capacities, including emotional and social talents, and of intercultural sensibility. They thus make an essential contribution to personal and social identity (see section 13.3), especially since the individual has the right, which according to Hegel is even an "infinite right," to "be satisfied by whatever activity or task it performs."[8] And from the perspective of the collective, they contribute to the economic and thereby also to the cultural thriving of the polity. Not least of all, they are a counterforce against the propensity toward violence particularly prevalent among youth — even if there are cultural differences here as well; this propensity is more pronounced in Great Britain and some French cities than, for example, in Italy or Greece.

Another consequence for an expanded social justice is obvious: given the opposition of the employed and the unemployed (and given the fact that long-term unemployment entails health problems and earlier mortality), neither the protection of labor nor wage setting and collective bargaining must protect those who have a job at the cost of discriminating against those who do not. Reasonable policies instead work toward a legal and economic organization that creates a globally competitive work and business climate that is fiscally and moreover socially and culturally attractive to domestic and international investors. For creating new jobs requires large capital expenditure.

In the field of education and training, ever more important today, an expanded social justice does not urge giving everyone the same thing. That would be too demanding for some, insufficiently demanding for others, and both groups would thus be denied the justice required for their freedom.

Let me cautiously phrase another task as a question: may a liberal society fight for equal opportunities for women but spare itself the effort, and the courage, too, to take up the issue of women's rights when it comes to immigrants, and to do so in time and comprehensively?

Among new but, in principle, accepted tasks there is the responsibility for the environment and for climate change mitigation. No less important but still underestimated is the responsibility toward the future when it comes to new demographic developments (which have been objectively foreseeable for some time). It is not an exaggeration to speak of a stealthy revolution that is particularly dramatic in Germany. While especially in wealthy countries people remain physically, intellectually, and emotionally agile far beyond the (current) retirement age, ever fewer children are growing up there. In addition, the willingness to bring children into the world is decreasing. The consequences for the labor market, for urban and regional planning, and for public finances are considerable. Retirement insurance, for example, has to confront two problems: on the one hand, entitlement periods become longer while, on the other hand, fewer children are growing up, and, assuming stable contribution rates, less money is being paid into retirements funds. In addition to the question of how to secure these funds—through higher contributions, lower retirement benefits, or subsidies from tax funds—a question of justice arises, which the sociologist Franz-Xaver Kaufmann puts in very clear terms: "People who take on responsibility as parents make investments, free of charge, into future human capital or human assets; people who do not take that responsibility do not make that investment."[9] The retirement policies of a welfare state that seeks to be just thus must not punish parenthood. Or, put more cautiously in the terms of a theory of freedom: the free decision to have or not to have children should not be restricted by retirement-related advantages or disadvantages.

7.4

THE AMBIGUITY OF THE WELFARE STATE

Another task arises in the relationship between generations. It is now generally agreed that the so-called intergeneration compact insofar as it relates to the natural environment is just only if it regards natural nature as the common property of all humanity. No generation is entitled to leave behind an environment that on balance is poorer in nature or its functional equivalents than what it has received. And like generous parents, generous generations, too, bestow a richer inheritance on their children and grandchildren.

As we know, in many places the opposite is the case, a "clash of generations" or even "war on our children."[10] The gap between spending on the tasks of the present and investments in the future becomes ever wider; expenditures on consumption increase; those on investments decrease.

Those who follow the rhetoric en vogue about an unjust "fairness gap" must not overlook three things. First, the concept of social justice, taken as a criterion, is vague. Above all, it does not have any internal limits, which is why not just different parties within a nation but different countries, too, have different conceptions. Second, closing one so-called fairness gap tends to be followed by the opening of another gap, which betrays a certain pleonexia, an insatiability with regard to the welfare state. The political interventions operated under the heading social justice often create new inequalities, again referred to as "socially unjust," that in turn serve to motivate new social-political interventions. That is why internal cost control mechanisms are not just contingently but structurally foreign to a social policy that aims for ever more equality.

Above all, third, public spending on social issues has increased enormously over the years. When, for example, the budget of the German Federal Department of Labor and Social Affairs amounts to almost 120 billion Euros, to be exact, €119,229,132,000, and at 39.48 percent represents the single largest item in the federal budget, then a zero-sum game for social programs seems advisable: if spending is increased somewhere or new groups of people are to be included, other items in the departmental budget are to be cut by an equal amount, since the amortization of an unimaginably high public debt brings additional costs.

For investments in young people's opportunities in life, by contrast, for investments in the area of schools, universities, and research, and in more than just the mere maintenance of infrastructure, money has become scarce. Although we have long been living in knowledge societies, entitlement spending by far exceeds the budget for education and research, in the German federal budget even by a factor of 8.7. And while the federal states' expenditures must be added, states and municipalities, as noted, have tremendous debts. These would be justifiable had they been amassed because of public investments; in fact, however, such investments have decreased enormously.

A thematically expanded conception of social justice objects to this development thanks to which the state, rich in social charges and burdens of debt, poor in investments, has become one of the greediest entities in history. It is clearly unjust that the birthday present polities give to the moreover dwindling number of newborn children is an inordinately large public debt. Those with a foible for pathos may speak of debt bondage. We must, at a minimum, be aware of this ambiguity of the welfare state: the immense increase of costs that have accumulated in the name of positive freedom diminishes the financial scope of other personal and public domains of freedom; not least of all, it restricts the freedom of the generations who follow.

Thanks to the bureaucracy that serves the welfare state, the scope of nonfinancial freedom narrows as well. In the transition from the absolutist, both paternalist and maternalist authoritarian state to liberal democracy, the state retreated to the background; in the welfare state, it is back with a vengeance although not all socially advisable tasks must be performed by the state. In any case, the welfare state, legitimate in principle, threatens to degenerate into a no longer legitimate caring nanny state that promotes a thinking in terms of entitlements, distracts from autonomy including the freedom that comes with it, and reduces the ideal value of freedom and dignity to the merely material.

The alternative is obvious. If the welfare state seeks to live up to its claim to social justice, it must develop from a welfare and social security state into a state of social investments committed to freedom. This includes, for example, provisions for young parents. For demographic reasons already, but even more so because society needs not just the economic capacities of the generation growing up but its stimulation, finally for the sake of freedom and justice, a society must provide living conditions for its young parents that include, for example, day-care facilities, flexible working hours, and higher subsidies. These aids, in turn, must not give preference to one or the other model: a society that renounces economistic fixations allows for a choice between gainful employment outside the home and the work of raising children in the family.

These brief observations urge a summary and a recommendation. The summary is that a merely allegedly social justice is fixated on the present and a maternalist (re)distribution that pushes autonomy aside or, more polemically: on justice rather than freedom. The alternative inspired by enlightened liberalism suggests a social justice that is committed to the principle of freedom and therefore provides the conditions for actual freedom. In contrast to the maternalist nanny state, it seeks to strengthen autonomy, that is, citizens' freedom, and thereby their self-respect wherever it can, or, in a word: justice in the name of freedom.

7.5

FOR EXAMPLE: FINANCE

There can be no doubt that finance today is one of the most important factors of the globalized world. It therefore suggests itself as prime example in discussing the tasks of justice as they relate to freedom. One prefatory remark: even if there is plenty of it — money does not bring happiness, certainly. But there is much to be accomplished with it, and with a lot of money, with a fortune, much can be set in motion and great things be done. Of course, money as such is an instrument that, like all instruments, is neutral toward its goals and purposes.

Those suffering from debt are entitled to curse money the way the debtor does in Hugo von Hofmannsthal's *Everyman*: "The name of Satan's net in this sad world / Is money."[11] Such demonizing, however, does not do justice to the neutrality of money. The great things enabled by a fortune manifest in three directions: neutrally as a generous mode of living; negatively as malice and violence all the way to the financing of wars or frequently obscene luxury; and finally positively in generosity on a great scale, as a philanthropy that funds buildings and parks, research institutes, hospitals, or museums, and not least of all universities — and amplifies their financial inequality: the world's most famous private universities such as Harvard, Princeton, and Stanford are all located in the United States. Their annual budget already exceeds the GDP of many small countries. And thanks to enormous endowments from their sometimes unimaginably rich alumni, they become ever richer, which makes (almost) all competition difficult.

A second, a historical preliminary remark will illustrate the current situation: the deregulation begun in the United States under the Republican president Ronald Reagan and in the United Kingdom under the Conservative prime minister Margaret Thatcher, and continued under the Democratic president Bill Clinton and Labour prime minister Tony Blair, and the liberalization of capital markets in particular, gave finance a literally undreamed of boost.

Contrary to the widespread one-sided diagnosis, both of the following rose initially: on the side of customers, savers and borrowers small and large, the scope of pecuniary freedom increased, and on the side of financial institutions, the power in matters of financial policy increased, which later developed into a general economic power and which in turn, because of its size and scope, became political power, namely, a power that now came out into the open, as in the case of the trust-like American rating agencies, now was cashed in as bargaining power over against political decision makers "over the phone" and "behind closed doors." And when the oversized financial institutions turned out to be dilapidated constructs, the state had to save them from bankruptcy with taxpayer money, on the tune of "too big to fail." Concurrently, exorbitant compensation packages were being paid out in banks, particularly investment banks.

This development obviously contradicts the avowed aims of liberalism, which is why the now common designation "neoliberalism" is misleading. For it equates a single variant of liberalism, a variant moreover criticized even by liberal thinkers, with the larger family of liberalisms. It thereby threatens to discredit liberalism as a whole instead of demanding a regeneration in the spirit of the Enlightenment.

One of the things to emerge in the course of the process just outlined were excessive mortgages for which, again, several actors were responsible, the finance industry as well as customers and public institutions such as the Federal Reserve. And because of the (in part recklessly established) international intertwinement of US finance, the earthquake that finally ensued spread across large parts of the world.

At the same time, the (pecuniary) gain in freedom made possible by a functioning financial sector reverted into unfreedom. The almost unimaginably large destruction of capital restricted the material freedom of action. In some places, this freedom was even destroyed, the freedom of action of savers large and small, of pension funds, of cultural, scientific, and university foundations; some countries almost or actually went bankrupt.

The public reaction was both understandable and justified: indignation about the consequences and a call for new laws. Both conveyed the hope that it would be possible to separate the manifold advantages and the disastrous disadvantages of a booming finance sector, to enjoy the former and avoid the latter. All experience tells us that this hope, of boosting the advantages and making the disadvantages disappear, cannot be realized anywhere, and neither can it in the finance sector. It makes sense, however, and moreover it is incumbent on us, to seek a new balance, an equilibrium that keeps advantages at a maximum and disadvantages at a minimum. The goal must be an optimal net balance. How and to what degree that can be achieved is a matter of contention even among experts, which is why a prudent nonexpert, a philosopher, does not claim to possess greater wisdom. In his role as responsible citizen, however, he may make some suggestions aimed at freedom and justice.

Let's begin with institutional justice: the two fundamental tasks of justice, law and the justice system, are accepted in a state of law; their acceptance is almost trivial. Not the least bit trivial is the matter of the advice that shapes policy. According to a procedural principle that is uncontested in the legal order and whose violation we know from Kleist's *The Broken Jug*, namely, that no one should be a judge in his own case, it is inadmissible that a leading banker advise a government concerning a country in which his bank has business interests. And there is something fishy about finance ministers, central bank presidents, and World Bank presidents increasingly being recruited from the ranks of powerful consulting and investment banking firms, to which they gladly return later.

The claim to universal validity inherent to justice demands that a minimum of justice be established between states as well. Something considered utopian by small-minded contemporaries that in truth represents a realistic vision thus imposes itself: the institution of a subsidiary and moreover federal global legal order (see chapter 15). The finance sector itself is not responsible for instituting it. Yet just out of self-interest, to alter its image as a bunch of buccaneers and gamblers, it should voluntarily advocate global, binding rules instead of discrediting them as the impositions of an allegedly populist policy.

The regulation that began with rules against the abuse of insider knowledge and against money laundering, against the tax evasion practiced by the superrich as well as against "aggressive tax avoidance" by certain multinational companies, should be continued in rules against offshore markets. Not least of all, tax havens are to be shut down. Three justice arguments speak against them. First, a number of the states serving this function behave as free riders of the global society because they hardly finance public goods such as universities and hospitals. Second, they tend to foster the opposite of law and justice, namely, embezzlement and corruption. And even if they are states under the rule of law with little corruption, they, third, enrich themselves to the detriment of the other countries.

In principle, there are two ways of shutting down tax havens. Either rules are found that apply all over the world, a global investment register hosted by the International Monetary Fund, for example, or a worldwide and moreover progressive property tax; or the governments of the criticized countries get on board and implement such rules by themselves. Which option is more promising is certainly not a matter judicable a priori; experience is needed. Presumably, a form that blends both basic options has the best chances of success. Insofar as this would include worldwide rules governing finance, they should be limited to *framing* rules. For why should finance not be allowed what the engineering, pharmaceutical, or fashion industries are granted, global competition?

The finance sector, however, has the capacity to influence particular national economies to a much greater degree than individual sectors of the real economy can. That is why a double strategy may be advisable here: on the one hand, the creation of a global legal framework whose regulations, on the other hand, are loose enough for countries to be allowed to establish their own rules to further their public welfare, be they stricter, be they more generous. Countries whose real economy and finance sector are comparable should get together, "harmonize" their rules, and establish a common regulatory authority. A globally shared set of rules and its enforcement, however, seem—especially for an enlightened liberalism seeking to strengthen the basic unit of constitutional democracy, individual nation-states—not to be necessary and, because they seem not necessary, inimical to freedom.[12]

The regulatorily loose but by no means superfluous legal framework must, for the sake of legal and judicial justice, tie global competition to the principle of generally compatible freedom. Evidently, the legal framework is to be enforced impartially, not by national-protectionist means. That is why it takes what likely began with the Basel Bank for International Settlements: a kind of international law for finance. And for this international law to be effective, it must be supplemented with a globally effective financial justice system that can, if need be, also hold leading managers of the finance industry accountable. Responsibility for administering this justice could be vested in national courts, provided three conditions are met: that one cannot avoid prosecution, that the courts all submit to the same criteria, and that it not be possible to choose the most generous courts.

A future international finance law must also address the dangers of excessive speculation, which today have a stronger negative impact on the global economy than rising commodity prices. A further task: money should flow where it is being used productively, for the finance sector is not an end itself but rather a service provider for others, an auxiliary instrument for the real economy with its savers and pension funds, its private customers, and its businesses small and large, as well as nation-states.

Let me take just a few of the immediate tasks as examples. First, even in a worldwide financial sector that relativizes national legislation, capital and returns on capital are to be taxed globally. Second, so-called systemically important financial institutions must no longer commit the obvious injustice, which evidently violates the cited principle of freedom, of reaping the profits but receiving public aid when they need to be rescued. Freedom and liability here belong together, inseparably. The overall goal here is that strict but prudent requirements render government bailouts of banks as good as unnecessary.

Speculation with foodstuffs poses more difficulties from the perspective of a theory of justice. *If* speculation is a *significant* cause for hunger in the world, it must be proscribed like slavery and serfdom in the past. Driving up the prices of wheat and corn on the back of starving people contradicts elementary conceptions of freedom. An assessment that is open to experience, however, verifies the *if*. It does not reject the objection that two other factors are much more significant in the increase of food prices: a still-increasing world population and the fact that a lot of people have joined a middle class consuming more meat, whose production in turn requires more grain for feed. Presumably, the power of all three factors must be curbed: population growth, increasing meat consumption, and speculation with foodstuffs.

Now for personal justice. One feature shared by many examples is that money is exchanged not just materially, for money, but in addition for an immaterial and nonetheless indispensable capital, trust. For a large part, the finance industry is a credit industry, and "credit" means a trustworthiness that must exist on both sides, borrowers and lenders. That is why we should take to heart the maxim articulated by a French mayor, namely, to proscribe transactions an honest person can no longer understand. For otherwise both sides, the bankers ultimately responsible and their customers, lose their freedom. When banks get involved in business models those ultimately responsible no longer understand, they violate the justice of exchange by putting someone else's money at risk.

On a second, regional level, politicians may well serve on the boards of savings and other publicly owned banks, but they must not dominate the boards. The disastrous failing of several German regional banks was partly caused by interference from politicians, partly also by state guarantees for these banks.

On the third, national yet internationalized level, the number of posts on supervisory boards someone assumes is relevant to justice. If one takes the job seriously, experts say, it requires one full working day a week, two or three times the amount of time for the chairperson. That is why accepting more than a small handful of posts is both dubious and unjust.

On the fourth, now global, level, an exemplary instance of a lack of personal justice is the Libor scandal, that is, the manipulation by British banks of reported interest rates. Because this amounts to a fraud, what is required here, too, is the opposite of the impunity for the City British politicians had long supported, namely, the continuation of the principle of freedom, just punishment.

The last example, the compensation of top executives, poses more difficulties. These difficulties begin with the fact that this problematic group includes not just investment bankers and managers but also principal conductors, say, or theater and opera managers. That for all of them, according to the law of diminishing marginal utility, the first half million is more gratifying than the second, third, or tenth, is evident. Yet a vice already denounced in the ancient civilizations, which the Greeks called *pleonexia*, wanting more and more, and is today called greed, nonetheless leads to an attitude that defies all art of living: it knows the price of everything but the value of nothing. In consequence, many are content with their remuneration, or the number of board memberships, only when they have more than their competitors.

It would be nice if it were possible to rely here on what is increasingly becoming the standard in science, for example, a flexible intermediary level between a rigid law and anarchic rulelessness, that is, efficient self-control. Compensation, however, is a positional value where the decisive factor is not the amount but the comparison with one's colleagues who, as regards positions, are also competitors. What helps here is the interplay of transparency and a collective code of conduct that declares certain amounts of compensation to be quite simply indecent.

Even a preliminary analysis of the financial debacle shows that excessive compensations first spoiled morals, then business. Our children and grandchildren will have to pay for the financial crisis, which contradicts the freedom of generations. Already, the funds for their future, for education and training, for science and research, not least of all for culture, have been limited.

Instead of citing further examples, we may conclude with two freedom-theoretical insights that must not be brushed off as moralizing. According to the first insight, a lack of personal justice harms only others but on a second look harms ourselves as well. I might not have to fear criminal law but I do have to face a loss of a self-respect that is relevant to freedom and which allows us to say to our image in the mirror: "you are one of the few honest people I know."

The second insight tells us that those who upset so valuable a good as trust only harm themselves — if it happens only occasionally. If there is an accretion of cases, however, the reputation of the entire profession is put at risk and with it the previous freedom of action. That is why the finance sector would secure its own freedom in the long term if it restricted this very freedom by itself: if the power of ethics cited at the beginning of this chapter is to manifest itself not only in the protests that unsettle the finance industry but in a reality that rebuilds trust, the sector, out of self-interest, should contribute to a just financial order, and its representatives, again at least out of self-interest, should be just in the personal sense as well.

8

Free Society

The freedom of a society includes the law, and the law includes the principle of generally compatible freedom. A free society, however, does not content itself with this core grammar enforceable through coercion. Its social grammar also includes informal sanctions, now positive, now negative.

A society committed to the spirit of the Enlightenment also designs the extended grammar, which envelops this core, in a liberal way. Every society, to be sure, has a specific history and a tradition that comes with certain habits. Without betraying its historical-social origins, an enlightened liberal society, however, claims the right to judge traditional habits as to their meaning and purpose and, if need be, to change them or give them up. Not least of all, it accepts that its origins are not homogeneous; usually, there exist not only generally shared habits but also differences, all the way to competition and the conflicts that arise from it.

As a result, a free society is open toward its traditional habits in two respects: it neither supposes the pure homogeneity of tradition, nor does it consider it to be sacrosanct and therefore unchangeable. There is a third aspect: instead of imposing unnecessary requirements on its members, individuals and groups, it permits deviating, even eccentric actions, provided they do not restrict the corresponding actions of others. With just this one restriction, a free society allows its individuals and groups to develop in whatever forms of life they choose, and in so doing to subscribe to different values and political convictions, to confess different religions or to be without religion, even to be declared atheists.

Three elements thus characterize a free society; all three are interconnected and give enlightened liberalism a clearer profile: openness (section 8.1), pluralism (section 8.2), and tolerance (section 8.3). Although an excess of each of these characteristics would threaten freedom on balance, no one who has seriously thought about them advocates such an excess. A fourth element is civic society guided by civic-mindedness (section 8.4).

8.1
OPENNESS

The introduction into philosophical debate of the characteristic of openness as opposed to closedness is probably due to a French thinker. In his *The Two Sources of Morality and Religion* of 1932, Henri Bergson, then an influential proponent of the philosophy of life, distinguishes between "closed" and "open," and also between "static" and "dynamic."

As the title of his book suggests, Bergson aims to present not a theory of society but a philosophy of morality and of the enhancement of morality in religion. The book begins with the question why we obey the prohibitions of parents and teachers, and at the same time of the society behind them. The answer points to the reciprocal support of individuals and their society: the individual and society maintain each other reciprocally; both sides amalgamate. As long as one limits oneself to one's own society — and this applies to "civilized" persons and societies no less than more simple and originary ones — a society is said to be "closed" and its members to have a "closed soul." The "open soul" in contrast "embraces all of humanity," just as the open society lives with a view to all humanity and extends the solidarity within society to become an (all-encompassing) "brotherhood of man."[1]

The corresponding "closed morality" is fixed, and if, as happens from time to time, it does change, it immediately forgets or does not acknowledge having done so. "Open morality," the morality of the open soul, in turn, is constantly changing and constantly moving. This brings in the second conceptual couple: closed morality is static; open morality is dynamic.

A closed morality according to Bergson is thus based on the principle of a society's self-preservation, thus on a collective interest that, for citizens, is ultimately a vital interest, the original force of life Bergson calls *élan vital*. It is for the sake of this force that individuals are bound to assume attitudes that, in analogy with animals' instincts, allow for conflict-free communal life.

In contrast there are, based on freedom, humanity, and an *élan d'amour* or life force of love, "open morality" and "dynamic religion," modeled on the morality of the Gospels. There is no more coercion being exercised here. Instead, great figures such as the Christian saints, the prophets of Israel, or wise Buddhists serve as models. This morality is not called "open," though, because it would allow for arbitrariness. On the contrary, the models set the bar very high. Yet their call for imitation — recall the Christian motto of an "imitation of Christ"— is directed at the freedom of those addressed by the model.

While the lower, as it were, closed morality is characterized by calm, stability, and lawfulness, the other, higher, as it were, is distinguished by movement, dynamism, and, precisely, freedom. Bergson, however, does not see this as a simple opposition. For the common morality is not being suspended but demoted to a moment in a process of progress: the dynamic absorbs the static.

A little more than a decade after Bergson's book, in Karl Popper, the notion of openness leaves its original context—primarily a philosophy of morality and religion, only incidentally also a social philosophy—and becomes the guiding concept of a theory of society. In his two-volume study *The Open Society and Its Enemies* (1945), the theorist of science and social philosopher known for his critical rationalism designates as open that social organization whose basic democratic order challenges people's critical capacities, stimulates open debate about political goals and means, votes out incapable governments, and, renouncing global control of society via a synoptic total plan, is content with incremental reforms, so-called piecemeal engineering.[2] The countermodel, tribal society, subjects people to magical powers and denies them the development and exercise of an individual will of their own.

Popper outlines his idea of an open society in opposition to the ideas of Plato, Hegel, and Marx, all of whom he sharply criticizes. The appreciation of an open society advocated here, within the frame of enlightened liberalism, shares Popper's respect for Kant, the Enlightener, but sets aside the polemic against Plato, Hegel, and Marx, as well as the crude opposition of overall planning and incremental reform.[3] It also finds Bergson's cosmopolitan impulse to be lacking in Popper's account, namely, that individuals and societies prove to be (truly) open when they live with a view to all humanity. Admirable, however, is Popper's moral-political plea for a society that entitles individuals to follow their own wills only within the frame of well-defined boundaries drawn primarily by an enforceable body of law.

Just before the publication of Popper's book, the economist Friedrich A. Hayek in 1944 warned against the notion that society as a whole was plannable.[4] As an alternative to Auguste Comte and Karl Marx, Hayek—in contrast to the claims of Streeck's attacks (see above, section 6.6)—did advocate regulatory policies that limit freedom, namely, by subjecting it to rules and embedding it in institutions. Individuals are permitted freely to fashion their lives not as such but only within these limits. According to Hayek, this also makes better use of individual potentials and moreover deploys them for freely chosen purposes, achieving a higher degree of "responsiveness" to individuals' personality. By contrast, the study Jørgen Randers presented on behalf of the Club of Rome in 2012 under the title *2052: A Global Forecast for the Next Forty Years* puts surprisingly great store by the possibility of planning.[5]

Under the title *The New Liberty*, another proponent of an enlightened liberalism advocates an "improving society" in which social conditions can be ameliorated.[6] Ralf Dahrendorf, who traveled between social science and politics, working as Max Horkheimer's assistant before studying under Popper and later serving in influential political capacities, follows his teacher Popper's notion of freedom. In Dahrendorf's own conception, the expansion of freedom in the sense of increasing opportunities in life is called for even if these opportunities do not at first benefit everyone.[7] In no event, however, must certain citizens be denied participation in the social, economic, and political process.

8.2
PLURALISM

When a society follows the ideas by Bergson just outlined, even more so those by Popper and Dahrendorf, and in addition Hayek's regulatory skepticism as well, and when, above all, it remains open to the will of its members, it will after some time unavoidably be characterized by a diverse pluralism. Here especially we might speak of a "metaphysics" of liberalism in the mitigated sense of the term that has recently become common: because of human beings' openness to the world, combined with the diversity of their interests, values, and life projects, there emerges a pluralism of religious confessions, value conceptions, and forms of life, of social groups and forces that determine policy.

This many-faceted diversity does not just emerge in fact; it is also justified. Even the pluralism of values and the resulting competition of values are legitimate, indeed positive for a number of reasons. This legitimacy, of course, does not extend so far that all duties would be abolished and both arbitrariness and indifference would be allowed to spread.

Let us take a short look at the history of the idea. An early conception of pluralism, although not part of a theory of society, can be found in Kant's *Anthropology from a Pragmatic Point of View*. In the first book, entitled "On the Cognitive Faculty," Kant discusses egoism and its "three kinds of presumption": the "logical egoist considers it unnecessary also to test his judgment by the understanding of others," while the "aesthetic egoist is satisfied with his own taste," and "the moral egoist limits all ends to himself." To all three, Kant opposes "*pluralism*, that is, the way of thinking in which one is not concerned with oneself as the whole world, but rather regards and conducts oneself as a mere citizen of the world."[8]

The later conception of pluralism in theories of society could adopt this notion easily. It took shape above all in North American pragmatism, even if its initial meaning there was metaphysical rather than social. For pragmatism precisely opposes the view, advocated by Hermann Lotze but also by Hegel and the English neo-Hegelian philosopher F. H. Bradley, that an initial pluralism according to which there is a multitude of independent things ought to make way for a monism, conceiving of the multitude as parts of a one true Being. In his homonymous 1909 book, the philosopher and psychologist William James counters with his notion of a "pluralistic universe." For him, things do not exist in a monist "all-form" but in an "each-form or distributively."[9]

While other philosophers, like Herder, the late Schelling, or Cassirer, do not work with the expression "pluralism," their ideas come close to the social-theoretical understanding predominant today. Johann Gottfried Herder's notion of a "spirit of the people" manifesting in customs and mythology, in language, songs, and tales, points to the diversity of culture. Friedrich Wilhelm Joseph von Schelling's philosophy of mythology thematizes two kinds of polytheism: the simultaneous kind of a multitude of gods among whom there is a highest god, and the successive kind of having many gods without such a god. Cassirer for his part distinguishes in his philosophy of symbolic forms a diversity of, in principle, equally valid manifestations, besides language especially myth or religion, art, and science.[10]

Even before Cassirer, James in a "study of human nature" examines "the varieties of religious experience."[11] James is thus virtually destined to become an advocate of religious pluralism. It must not be overlooked, though, that James is not a proponent of relativism but claims that religious experience develops across various degrees and levels. According to James, religious experience refers to the totality of the world that humans admire but which is also shot through with horrors, even evil. From a systematic perspective, experience begins with an originary religious feeling and, via a gradually unfolding conversion to the true self, reaches the apex of a perfectly pure stadium of sanctity that bestows peace, happiness, and inner harmony on the human.

An enlightened liberalism does not reject the succession of levels thus outlined, and for the sake of the well-being of society and politics, it welcomes that true believers, who feel a connection with a higher power, in James's view champion an ideal social order. Yet neither does it reject the experience that many orthodox, especially ultraorthodox believers show little interest in social and political matters whereas among those working for the common good, there are many nonbelievers, occasionally even outspoken atheists. Just on the empirical basis thus hinted at, an enlightened liberalism is skeptical of the thesis (which James of course does not defend in this form) that a commitment to better social and political conditions is tied to religion or faith. This skepticism is reinforced by the insight that commitment to the common good does not require a religious foundation and that, where such foundations exist, several of them are competing with each other.

With regard to society and politics, an enlightened liberalism is content with accepting the variety of worldviews, both religious and nonreligious, and with considering this acceptance to be a condition of freedom.

Not necessarily a theorist but an argumentative advocate of pluralism is the sometime professor of social and political theory at the University of Oxford Isaiah Berlin. He starts from two suppositions, from the necessity for humans to decide and from the (justifiable) experience that the mode of life one chooses may be existentially irreconcilable with the mode of life of others. On their basis, Berlin pleads for a pluralism that means more than the right to pursue one's own interests.[12]

Some remarks in his 1958 essay *Two Concepts of Liberty* are relevant to pluralism as well. Berlin here adopts the well-known distinction between negative and positive freedom along with the familiar definitions, which is why it is surprising that the essay should have become famous for making that distinction. Moreover, neither his criticism of Kant nor his thesis that human beings are allowed to detach themselves from the social contexts that constitute them because they cannot do so completely anyway is convincing. What is relevant, however, albeit to an international and no longer national pluralism, and moreover convincing, is Berlin's criticism of nationalism, where a national collective acts out its interest in self-determination and self-fulfillment ruthlessly, namely, at the expense of other collectives.

What legitimizes pluralism in social and political theory, which is important to the themes of this book? According to a first, pragmatic justification, those who permit diversity promote something denied to a society that imposes homogeneity, even uniformity: coexistence without constraint and greater, richer self-fulfillment. For in a pluralistic society, the richness of human possibilities and at the same time the limitedness of each individual form of life become apparent. A pluralistic society accepts that an abundance of paths, even a multitude of reasonable albeit incompatible paths leads to individuals' welfare. At the same time, it explores the conditions that allow for fair coexistence.

Above all, and this is the moral justification, it accepts each human being's right to take his or her own path in life as an autonomous person and responsible citizen. Because of this right, in an open society, the pluralisms listed earlier initially stand beside each other with equal rights, yet of course they often also stand against each other. They are legitimate, however, only if they fulfill the criteria of an enlightened liberal democracy and of the Golden Rule, especially their prohibition on freeloading—which ipso facto is a rejection of arbitrariness.[13]

The reasons just outlined thus do not justify an absolute pluralism. Pluralistic societies on the contrary require a unity that is first of all legal-political and, in turn, draws on such commonalities as language, culture, history, and law that prevent opponents from becoming enemies and competition from degenerating into (civil) war. The most important commonality politically, law, in turn is based on shared obligations, namely, liberties as the conditions of mutual acceptance.

8.3
TOLERANCE

Because pluralism with these restrictions is justified, it demands tolerating the various differences; pluralism is a test for the attitude of tolerance, a further characteristic of a free society. Tolerance allows for morally different convictions. Suicide is a good example, for its moral evaluation has been contested since antiquity (see above, section 3.3). A free society does not take sides in this dispute but leaves it to its members personally to follow the arguments of one side or the other.

Someone who has no convictions cannot boast with being genuinely tolerant. Someone who disdains religion is no more tolerant when she approves of exotic religions than someone who does not appreciate the traditional family when he promotes patchwork families or someone else again who has no regard for traditional marriage but favors same-sex marriage. True tolerance is lived by those who highly value something their own and nonetheless, perhaps only after an inner struggle, confront the other respectfully.

The tolerance that liberal polities cannot surrender has developed three dimensions: liberal citizens respect other people who adhere to other religions, faiths, or political convictions or pursue other life projects: personal tolerance. Liberal societies allow everyone to profess everything in religious matters, or nothing, and to develop in just about any form of life, although only just about any: social tolerance. And a liberal polity elevates existentially important domains of tolerance, especially freedom of religion, to the status of a human right, which it anchors in a lived, often even a written constitution: political tolerance or tolerance as principle of law and government.

In all three dimensions, tolerance is characterized, on the purely conceptual level, by three moments: (1) we consider someone else's convictions or conduct to be wrong or bad and therefore disapprove of it; (2) we nonetheless accept it, not for ourselves but in the other; (3) there are limits to this acceptance nonetheless. The characteristics thus are disapproval, acceptance nonetheless, and limitation.

With regard to the second moment, tolerance manifests in two stages: at the weaker, passive stage, confessions, convictions, and forms of life that deviate from our own are endured. At the stronger, active stage, they are being met with understanding and the people concerned with respect. In a word: "Freedom is always . . . freedom for the one who thinks differently."[14] For the first stage, we may speak of an (often reluctant) tolerance of permission, for the second of a (free) tolerance of respect.[15]

The minimal demand of not restricting the possibilities of others, thus the limitation operated in the third moment, remains intact. This is reflected already in the Golden Rule, that is, a modest moral principle acknowledged by practically all cultures, which in its proverbial negative form demands: "What you do not wish to be done to yourself, do not do to others." This principle is obviously violated by those who act as freeloaders and reap the benefits of a common enterprise without sharing the cost.

Although in enlightened liberal societies, the three dimensions of two-stage tolerance are a matter of course, conflicts arise time and again. Liberal intellectuals then often practice a generosity that goes far beyond what they expect from others. Many Western intellectuals, for example, cannot be bothered to protest, often not even to acknowledge, the fact that the group quantitively dominant in their societies, Christians, is being oppressed or persecuted in so many places outside the West, that Christians even constitute the most persecuted religious group worldwide. Here generosity threatens to turn into arbitrariness because it passes over a threat to freedom that exists in many places.

Cautiously put merely as a question: are we allowed to be tolerant within our own country toward practices that do not concern us directly but fellow citizens, for example, tolerant toward forced marriages, tolerant toward the discrimination of girls and women, tolerant toward the freedom-restricting supervision of girls by their brothers, even far younger brothers?

The answers to these questions should be obvious, which is why they need not be developed here. The method for finding the answers, however, may be cited. It consists in the collaboration of a moral attitude, tolerance, with a capacity for judgment, including the capacity for assessing the situation. In this method, different goods must be weighed against each other. That is why the decision made at the end, even if it is made by a supreme court or the legislature after thorough reflections, including public discourses, can be extraordinarily contested. For in such cases, the precise limits of political tolerance are not easily determined.

The reason for this difficulty, put in the terms of the theory of action, is that the decision at issue, conceptually, combines two moments, a disposition and a capacity for judgment. This helps dedramatize the conflict. For among the two moments, the first, dispositional moment is undisputed in an enlightened liberal democracy, whereas the second, deliberative moment is subject to a possibly bitter conflict, over the factual basis, for example, but also over the nature of the problem, the duties at issue, or the weighing of interests that may be required. Occasionally, liberal democracy might even find itself genuinely unable to decide. That is why not only certain demands but possible different decisions, too, should be met with tolerance. For difficult assessments and weighing of interests make it well-nigh impossible to call one decision clearly tolerant, the other just as clearly intolerant.

From this circumstance follows a new kind of tolerance, a second-degree tolerance. It resists overestimating one's own capacity for judgment, rejects all fanaticism, and remains open to creative compromise.

Like common tolerance, this new tolerance differs from two superficially similar things, first from the fig-leaf indifference that is only ostensibly but not truly tolerance, and second from a kind of skeptical abstention from judgment that somewhat rashly declares the pros and cons to be of equal strength and merit and, therefore, a just decision to be beyond reach. Meanwhile, the disputed cases await a decision. Yet the decision does not have to be made independently of context, nor does it have to be made once and for all. First of all, it can be made differently in different legal traditions (one might discuss this under the heading "right to difference") or be made anew under changed circumstances (because of a changing society). For both reasons, it can, second, be made cautiously with regard to content and, third, as regards form, be made with a kind of request for indulgence such that those who think differently have less trouble with it.

Questions of tolerance also arise in the most incisive domain of any legal order, in criminal law. May we permit what is prohibited in Western countries by criminal law as sexual abuse, sexual intercourse with a sixteen-year-old, when that person is a member of someone's household with the assent of her parents? Or how are we to judge the case of a man who comes to the West and marries a second woman, something that is permitted in his home country but prohibited in Western countries as bigamy? A more complicated version of the case: the man married in this country returns to his country with the sole purpose of marrying a second woman with whom he returns here to live with both women.[16]

Decisions that are based on cultural bias would have to be judged intolerant. In many cases, however, the opposite likely applies, namely, that the protections of criminal law overcome cultural bias, for example the attitude of patriarchal societies that do not accept that women and children have equal rights. And protection for underage women, too, does not serve the local population or to preserve a European or Western culture. It benefits all to whom the law applies, foreigners and nonforeigners alike. Nor is it an issue of a "liberty" practiced in the West but viewed with skepticism in other cultures, the sexual freedom of young people. Instead, something much more elementary and generally human is at stake: the absence of disturbance in the sexual development of children and adolescents, which is of such importance in the development of independent and autonomous adults. Such protection even has the dignity of a human right, which can be extrapolated into a general criterion: enlightened liberal polities have the right and even duty to include crimes that can be shown to violate human rights in their criminal law and to prosecute them.

After this look at possible cases of conflict, let's return to general reflections on tolerance and emphasize once more that we must not be content with the lower stage, with passive tolerance that often only reluctantly accepts and permits what is different. What is called for is the more demanding, higher stage, active and creative tolerance that freely accepts different views and conduct.

True tolerance—to repeat—is not indifferent to religious, ideological, moral, and political questions and rather presupposes, in keeping with the first conceptual moment, convictions of one's own. It thus does not fall prey to an ideophobia that, for fear of being accused of xenophobia, renounces its self-respect. In keeping with the second conceptual moment, convictions that deviate from one's own are respected nonetheless. Those who are interested in how other people think and live and who, inspired by this, accept the other—albeit, in keeping with the third conceptual moment, only within certain limits—reach the perfection of tolerance.

In our age, the age of a more than merely economic globalization, different cultures confront each other not just within a society but in a worldwide coexistence as well. Two dangers arise in this context. The first danger, which looms by no means only in the West, combines an ethnocentrism that considers one's own culture to be superior with a cultural imperialism that seeks to marginalize or suppress, in some places even exterminate other cultures. The second danger in turn is spreading primarily in the West. I mean a cultural relativism that considers all cultures, including opposing values that may even violate liberties, to be equally valid. The meaningful alternative consists in a qualified tolerance.

For cultures to live with each other, on equal terms, rather than living against each other in a violent "clash of civilizations" or indifferently alongside each other, they must at a minimum practice a global passive tolerance, a reciprocal enduring. Better, of course, is a global active tolerance by means of which all sides accept each other as, in principle, equal. This does not imply relinquishing the question of assessing which values are morally valuable and what kind of intercultural coexistence is appropriate.

In any case, an initially merely intrasocietal tolerance must be extended to become respect for the different cultures and traditions across the globe. And because for that reason, one rejects all ethnocentrism and cultural imperialism, one accepts what I have listed here as the first challenge of an enlightened liberalism: one engages in intercultural legal and social discourse on the basis of which an interculturally tolerant coexistence can develop.[17]

8.4
CIVIC SOCIETY AND CIVIC-MINDEDNESS

On the view of enlightened liberalism, a society proves its freedom in yet another different way. It supplements the two visions, the market and democracy, with a third, at the same time mediating vision, with a civic society and the civic virtues brought together in the notion of civic-mindedness [*Bürgersinn*].

A *civic* society, not the *civil* society, not the legal and political body, defends against the statist reduction of democracy. It accepts the necessity of an enforceable legal order entrusted to the state with its three public powers. But it makes this legal order a shared public matter, a *res publica* in the literal sense. Here, citizens form not only a constitutional community but also a political-social community of free and equal members, visible in an active participation in shaping the polity. This in turn manifests in two superimposed forms, namely, as civic-mindedness, in which democratic virtues, the civic virtues of a sense of right, a sense of justice, and civic sense [*Gemeinsinn*] combine, and as the exemplary form of their exercise, community service (see also section 13.6). Just one figure: more than a third of the inhabitants of the German state of Baden-Württemberg are involved in their communities.

When they deem it necessary, citizens organize civic protests. Nobody there has the right to ignore the conditions of the rule of law. Now, civic society and civic virtues resist both the emaciation of a living democracy by the growing influence of the state and the threat of the increasing power of bureaucratic thinking. When a state penetrates into ever more domains, and moreover consolidates its presence in each domain by an increased regulation and bureaucratization, it causes not just financial and personal costs. It also restricts freedom in the sense of citizens' responsibility for themselves, including their freedom to act. The civic-mindedness that opposes it neither can nor seeks to abolish bureaucratization, but it is able to limit it.[18]

Critics like to claim that liberal democracy reduces the individual to economic interests. The reality of innumerable clubs and associations, of citizens' associations and initiatives suggests the opposite. It also contradicts the popular thesis that the modern human being is increasingly individualized. In truth, there is both, often in one and the same person: a strong individual profile combined with great social involvement.

One might see civic society as the second-best solution, as surrogate or stand-in for government action: because political parties and their politicians in their struggle for power block each other more than they engage in constructive activity or because public funds have been depleted by political decisions in the past, citizens come in to perform the tasks of the state. A veritable liberalism thinks differently; it follows in this matter the notion of subsidiarity, which reverses the argumentation just sketched that points to an authoritarian conception of the state.

A viable liberalism pleads for a more civic society and for more civic sense not because the state has shouldered too heavy a financial burden and finds itself poor, despite rising tax income and a tax burden of no less than about 50 percent. Instead, it contests the state's claim to a monopoly over the public welfare and declares itself coresponsible for the concept and the reality of the common good. Civic society with its civic-mindedness and civic sense is directed against the statification of the polity; it conceives of itself as a constructive correction and free supplement. Enlightened liberalism may indeed resort to pathos here: civic society and civic-mindedness help society acquire more freedom over against the state, and they help the state concentrate on its core tasks, and in this twofold manner, a liberal-democratic culture is promoted. In this manner, in an autonomous, civic-minded involvement, citizens once and for all stop being subjects of the state, and the danger mentioned earlier (section 7.4) is completely overcome: the citizens neither reduce human dignity to the material, nor do they let the welfare stare degenerate into a patronizing nanny state; instead, they understand the state to be a function of freedom in an emphatic sense.

Committed proponents of direct democracy justifiably ask representative democracy what happens to democracy between elections. Civic society provides an important partial answer to that question insofar as it provides a counterweight to the overbearing political parties and it forces politicians to be closer to the citizens. It also strengthens public processes of reflection and consultation, whereby it helps both prepare and critically comment on parliamentary decisions as well as, if need be, stimulate change. In doing so, it undoubtedly unfolds a communicative power.[19] However, only a small part of the citizenry is participating.

In other regards as well, democracy in many places is reduced to a form of life lived by involved minorities. This introduces an element foreign, even antithetical to democracy. Democracy transforms into an aristocracy or, more cautiously put, a quasi aristocracy. Simultaneously, the new, nonhereditary aristocracy risks serving citizens' interests selectively. The selection does not have to be restricted to the very own interests of the involved minorities, who largely come from the educated upper-middle class, yet the interpretation, too, of what interests may well accord with the common good takes place from the perspective of the quasi aristocracy.

This, however, is counteracted by elements of direct democracy. At least at the local and regional level, plebiscitary elements have proven viable even in Germany, where they were long viewed with skepticism. And on the federal level, more plebiscitary elements would force politicians to rethink their decisions; at the least, however, they would constrain them to give credible explanations of such decisions as the risky introduction of the Euro and the even riskier financial aid packages launched to respond to the Euro crisis, furthermore the lowering of the retirement age despite an increase in life expectancy. Representative democracy does have the advantage of taking responsibility over against the mood that dominates a given country. Yet a greater share of direct democracy increases something that also belongs to responsibility, the responsibility to respond to the concerns of the people with convincing arguments.

PART III

Science and Art

There are two things that are indispensable for us human beings and yet are countermodels to everyday life: knowledge and art. Both are integral components of a free society and yet play a special role. Furthermore, both are essential to modernity, which once more manifests modernity's interest in actualizing basic anthropological interests, even in making them thrive. Finally, there is a formal similarity between the two and freedom: both allow humans a high degree of creativity and criticism, even if they take different forms in the two domains. And the ambivalence of freedom, too, takes different shapes.

9

Knowledge and Freedom

Since early modernity, the freedom of human reason has been a motivation and at the same time a core element of an enlightened liberalism. Both modernity and the principle of freedom, in turn, take concrete shape, an essential shape, in knowledge and its methodical amplification in science and research. Accordingly, a liberalism in the spirit of the Enlightenment practically always stands on the side of knowledge, science, and research. Of course, these three constitute neither a monolithic institution nor a homogeneous subsystem of society but rather consist of a wide variety of disciplines and topics — but this is not decisive here.

Liberal support for the world of the epistemic begins with an unyielding commitment to the relevant liberties, in negative terms the prohibition of censorship, in positive terms the freedom of science and research. Together, they relieve scientists and researchers of the constraint of having to agree with dominant social, political, or religious views. Instead, they give them the right to dedicate themselves to the truth and nothing but the truth. The consequence, the thriving of science and research, is beneficial, especially when it is joined by an excellent reputation, by a positive liberty, and by plentiful support from both private and public sources.

An enlightened liberalism is aware of and accepts a precondition of the freedom of science: trust. Institutionally, for example, it trusts the numerous scientific academies that, usually, rely "on the excellence of [their] members, on the quality of their projects, on the expertise and impartiality of project leaders, project members, and evaluators"— and the success of the research they support proves them correct.[1]

However, here, too, a closer look brings an ambiguity to light. There is both knowledge that promotes freedom (section 9.1) and knowledge that threatens freedom (sections 9.2 and 9.3).

9.1
KNOWLEDGE THAT PROMOTES FREEDOM

Among the various ways in which knowledge can be relevant to freedom, there are three salient, fundamentally different kinds that can be organized into further subspecies. In the first kind, knowledge merely promotes freedom; in the second, it liberates; and in the third, it is itself a free activity. In modernity, astonishingly, only the first two, merely subsidiarily liberal kinds find a tremendous echo, while the third, inherently liberal kind is relegated to the background. A reassessment of modernity must not pass over the fact that in so essential a domain for freedom as knowledge, the freedom balance is not wholly positive. The reason does not lie in the flipside—often stressed, not infrequently overstressed—of the first kind of knowledge relevant to freedom but in the widespread neglect of truly free knowledge.

We know the first kind of knowledge from the first part of this study. Applied research contributes to an emancipation from the constraints of external and internal nature as well as to a liberation from hunger and poverty in a number of domains, and particularly clearly in technology and medicine but also in a pedagogy committed to freedom. And by creating jobs it resists the restrictions of the freedom to act that come with joblessness. Moreover, in countries poor in natural resources, such as large parts of western Europe, economic prowess and political influence are decisively defined by scientific creativity, the science-based performance of technology and medicine, and the innovation potential of businesses.

The second kind of knowledge relevant to freedom is contained in the very qualification of liberalism as enlightened. Enlightenment has a usefulness, but this usefulness is often overlooked because it is not of the kind that immediately comes to mind, the usual use-oriented knowledge of applied research. In fact, enlightenment has a usefulness relevant to freedom because it justifies the pathos of the formula *the truth shall set you free*.

A particularly telling example is a thesis by the pre-Socratic philosopher Xenophanes. In traditional Greek myth, the rainbow is the appearance of a goddess named Iris. In opposition, Xenophanes declares: "And what they call Iris, this too by nature is a cloud, / Purple red and greenish yellow to look on."[2] There is a double enlightenment here, both an overcoming of myth by a "rational" explanation of nature and a critique of traditional religion, a critique in which the goddess is no longer a visible natural phenomenon but instead that which, in comparison with nature, is its other.

From the perspective of a theory of knowledge and, at the same time, that of a theory of freedom, the highest form of knowledge consists in a third kind. Yet modern society risks alienating itself from this kind, precisely, which in philosophy is extremely valued and has been so since one of its first great representatives, Aristotle. It consists in a knowledge free of use, a knowledge that according to the opening sentence of Aristotle's *Metaphysics* belongs to the very nature, that is, the essence of the human being.[3] The evidence Aristotle cites — no doubt imbued with experience — is the pleasure we take in sense perceptions that do not depend on being useful. Something similar applies to some higher forms of knowledge, especially the knowledge of causes and reasons insofar as it is sought for its own sake. Knowledge then acquires the status of an end in itself and carries its value within itself.

Such knowledge even cannot be appropriated by the concept of basic or fundamental research. Basic research can mean two things. *Either* it means research that is not yet aimed at any application but, as if by a ruse of research reason, makes an application possible. Research here is factually free of purposes but potentially it serves certain albeit not yet known ends. *Or* it means research that explores the systematic and methodological foundations, the basis, precisely, of a scientific discipline or group of disciplines. Research here is subjected to a known purpose, albeit one immanent to science.

A knowledge that is free of purpose in the strict sense, not just in the merely mitigated, quasi-free sense, marks itself off from both kinds of basic research. As the alternative to both, as a knowledge truly free of use, it is, despite its diversity, not just alien but even unknown to the dominant self-conception of scientists today. It is even denounced as "superfluous luxury." Let's recall, therefore, some examples.

Truly free of use are those domains of mathematics that are not in the least geared toward application in, for instance, physics, statistics, the insurance industry, or the economic and engineering sciences. Free of use, too, is the exploration of extinct cultures, languages, and scripts, Neanderthal culture, say, or hieroglyphics, or Maya script. No less free of use is that pure form of biodiversity research based in natural science museums with their research collections.

Within the framework of research on science the first example has a great advantage. Basic, pure mathematics is as highly appreciated in the scientific universe as it is in the public. There are probably several reasons for this, especially the potential usefulness of so many mathematical disciplines, but perhaps admiration for these scientists' inventiveness and acumen as well. Support for mathematics institutes, departments, or faculties and for individual mathematicians is thus largely uncontested.

The examples from the human and cultural sciences, by contrast, are facing ever greater pressure to justify themselves. And representatives of pure biodiversity research barely dare defend their research in this purity. They prefer justifying themselves with two other arguments, pointing to a sustainable use of biological resources and a more effective protection of the environment.

It has by now become a general phenomenon: if science does not want to risk losing public funding for research, it must not evoke the human value of knowledge without use but emphasize the close connection of science and social well-being. Even such wealthy societies as the Western ones thus have difficulties with the ideal of a true freedom from purpose: that there are things in human life that do not seek any use and yet are not useless. Put paradoxically, humans need things they do not need. These include love and pure friendship, mere play, all kinds of music, literature, and art, and also machines whose complicated mechanics are useful for nothing but showing, in their functioning interconnection of levers, cogwheels, and rollers, the beauty of mechanics. It is the same for the honesty of a way of life, for the acknowledgment of human dignity, and of human rights in a legal order, and not least of all for a thirst for knowledge free of use.

All these cases bring to light a humanity relieved of all purposes. It should be a matter of course that freedom from use in the domain of knowledge does not make any exclusive claim to being an end in itself and that activities that carry their purpose within themselves do not make an exclusive claim to humanity. Yet it should equally be a matter of course that a humanity free of purpose and with it knowledge free of purpose and use should not be excluded since only humans have that capacity and find in it their dignity.

The predominance of the first model of knowledge, especially of technology, furthermore the power of the economy, is criticized in some quarters today. The much more fundamental criticism is offered by the model of knowledge as enlightenment, a model, in other words, that is essential to modernity and has recently been claimed by scientists working in specific disciplines, neuroscientists, for example (we will have to assess whether this is justified; see chapter 16). An even more far-reaching amplification of the more fundamental critique of thinking exclusively in economic and technical terms, however, is offered by the model of knowledge free of use. Whether the more modest ("enlightenment") or the more demanding ("end in itself") form — both models contain the more fundamental criticism insofar as they call for a freedom of science and research that is radical in the literal sense, that is, emancipated from all technicization and economization and, moreover, refuses any appropriation for ideological and religious ends.

The disempowerment of a knowledge free all the way to its roots sets in long before modernity, with the doctor of the church Augustine, who tasks research with inquiring in a God-fearing manner. He himself thereby seeks to give research a new, a higher status. In reality, however, he burdens it with an additional task that restricts free research. It demands viewing nature as creation and seeking behind nature the artist of the creation, God. Mere wanting to know, curiosity without a use, by contrast, he denounces as a lust (*concupiscentia*) that risks turning into a vice.[4]

Without naming Augustine, the early modern scientific politician Francis Bacon rejects any "admixture of theology" and opposes this apotheosis or deification with the "sober-minded" motto, "give to faith only that which is faith's."[5] Nonetheless, he, too, does not advocate knowledge free of use but, once more, a purposive appropriation. He, the most influential prophet of a new science, thus consigns modern science to extrascientific service. And the conception that dominates epistemic modernity will follow him.

Salomon's House, the model of a republic of researchers Bacon sketches in his "fable" *New Atlantis*, explicitly pursues use. In the form Bacon gives it, such use, to be sure, is to be welcomed without reservations because it helps the human and human freedom in a variety of ways. Yet despite the humanitarian character of its obligation, research remains obligated; its service is primarily external.[6]

Even a brief overview, then, already discovers three models of knowledge relevant to freedom. In the first model, applied science, science liberates from the constraints of outer and inner nature; in the second model, that of enlightenment, it liberates from intellectual, mental constraints; and in the third model, knowledge as an end in itself, it is in itself a form of freedom.

In consequence, I cannot but reaffirm the thesis that introduced this chapter: because of this three-dimensional contribution to freedom, an enlightened liberalism takes the side of knowledge wherever possible. It does, however, regret the dominant disdain for knowledge free of purposes. In addition, it confronts the question whether there is also a flipside to the models of knowledge relevant to freedom, a knowledge that is dangerous because it threatens freedom.

9.2
KNOWLEDGE THAT THREATENS FREEDOM I

Practically unknown for a long time, it is now not uncommon to hear talk of knowledge that threatens freedom, of "dangerous knowledge." Examples of knowledge that is dangerous because it threatens freedom abound, already because in our globally connected information society, knowledge in many places has become a critical factor. Banks and insurance companies, for instance, possess data about the financial situations of their clients. Health insurance companies keep patients' medical histories, thereby creating the so-called transparent patient. The social networks popular around the globe save their users' personal data and seek to cash in on it. State agencies, especially intelligence agencies, even those of allies, spy on telephone conversations and other electronic communications. Uncertainties thus arise not just from unplanned data leaks but already from semiofficial procedures that instead should guarantee internal and external security and thereby serve freedom.

The list of threats to freedom, to be sure, can be extended at will, but its examples are all recent; moreover, the dangers derive only from the abuse of knowledge. If insurance companies keep their clients' medical histories confidential, as they are obligated to do, the transparent patient is not to be feared. And if social networks neither share their users' data nor "capitalize" them themselves, and if the state, too, does not pursue its security tasks excessively but with meaningful restrictions, either no or fewer dangers are looming. Yet, as we will see in more detail (see section 12.1), data privacy protection increasingly cannot be relied on.

The usual examples, however, implicitly assume two things: that dangerous knowledge is a fairly new phenomenon and that the dangers loom primarily when knowledge is abused. Both assumptions raise doubts. On the one hand, the phenomenon of dangerous knowledge is much older; it goes back to the beginnings of modern knowledge and, strictly speaking, even back to the beginnings of Western science and philosophy. On the other hand, these beginnings, for example the thinkers cited earlier, Xenophanes and Aristotle, show that not just the abuse of knowledge but already knowledge itself can be dangerous.

Xenophanes's twofold criticism of tradition is so radical that the tradition loses all legitimacy in both domains. For according to Xenophanes, the divine explanation of natural phenomena must make way for a rational, (natural) scientific explanation, and in opposition to any humanizing, anthropomorphizing theory, the divine figure is the radically other (see also section 10.1). Aristotle's notion of a knowledge free of all use requirements threatens, once again in a radical manner, the obligation of science to seek out technological, economic, and even humanitarian advantages. For he confronts all of them with a countermodel that restricts the legitimacy and the reach of a science with external obligations.

In addition, science cannot be sure of the advantages it commits itself to, for two reasons. Applied science, from a structural point of view, provides only the means for the advantages being sought, and these means form their own autonomous world, the domain of the instrumental, in two regards.

On the one hand, viewed on its own, applied science of the technological variety is freedom neutral. On the model of artisans and engineers, it aids in the construction of houses, bridges and roads, cars, smartphones and CT scanners, but also of cannons, explosives, and nuclear bombs. And this freedom neutrality cannot be abolished, again for two reasons: first, the knowledge bases created for constructive purposes prima facie allow for applications to serve destructive ends. Second, prima facie destructive technologies, such as explosives, can also be employed constructively, for example in building bridges and tunnels or in demolishing no longer wanted structures.

On the other hand, the triumph of modern technology, to be sure, has taken place under humanitarian auspices. Influenced by Francis Bacon in this regard, the exceptional mathematician, physicist, and metaphysician René Descartes declares that insights are worth publishing only when they contribute to "the general welfare of mankind."[7] Even if we subscribe to this privileging of a science committed to humanitarian uses, a more careful, considered assessment is required because Descartes's immediate goal, knowledge of the forces of nature, cannot be tied down to the desired final goal, the humanitarian purpose. The context of a discovery—trivial as regards the structure of the action but of tremendous practical significance—does not decide its use. And those forces, too, that are explored only for humanitarian purposes can ultimately be employed for whatever purpose one chooses.

This two-dimensional autonomization of the instrumental, of course, was not what either Bacon or Descartes was hoping for. In Bacon's scientific utopia *New Atlantis*, the already-cited name of "Salomon's House" points to a task exemplarily resolved by the biblical king, namely, to obligate all research to follow a wisdom tied to morality. Such an obligation, however, cannot be built into the structure of how research proceeds, and the autonomization of the instrumental cannot be prevented in principle. What is required are the two factors within science already evoked by Bacon, both legally binding guidelines as well as a certain ethos on the part of researchers (see the example of medicine discussed above, section 3.1).

To put all these factors aside and assume the standpoint of science alone is not necessarily to introduce a contradiction into the self-conception of applicable science, but it does constitute a structural hubris. Science makes a humanitarian claim that, taken purely by itself, it does not live up to. In a very fundamental sense, it can never escape the role of sorcerer's apprentice. Even where its exploration of the forces of nature is motivated by humanitarian considerations, knowledge, once acquired, will exist independently of the motivation and elude its power and control.

Bacon calls on science to learn to see nature in a whole new way, without baggage and bias, like little children. This comparison is more appropriate than the author thought. Children not only live without baggage; they also in a certain respect act without thinking: they often do not perceive negative side effects, prefer to overlook the costs of an endeavor. Modernity has tried for a long time to live in a state of innocence and to suppose its innovations to have no resulting costs. Innocence, however, can at most be attributed to truly use-free knowledge but not to a science that seeks to master the forces of nature. In early modernity, such a supposition may well have been productive, since it liberated immense epistemic forces; today, it would constitute a fatal blindness.[8]

Modern research is certainly not without success: as soon as they are recognized for what they are, intellectual fetters are thrown off; experimentation has attained previously unimaginable levels of precision; and humanitarian purposes are being served in a variety of ways. At most, many contemporaries succumb to a specific illusion, what sociologists call "background fulfillment": the more we are assured of a benefit, the more we subjectively underestimate the value it objectively has. If we look at the successes in the fight against infectious diseases, against maternal and infant mortality, or against organ deficiencies (from glasses to pacemakers), if moreover, although only in richer countries, we look at the overcoming of hunger, at the replacement of hard physical labor with machine labor, at the shortening of working time, and, not least of all, at a standard of living unimaginable in the past, we find an abundance of material for a success story. What Bacon expected, though, has not happened—the sciences have brought not just blessings alone.

Those who see only the accomplishments consider the epistemic project of modernity to be a success; those who perceive only the flipside dramatically speak of a failure. The former think that research deserves a blank check, the latter an absolute prohibition. The truth is that the natural sciences in particular still make dreams come true; yet they also create nightmares, albeit fortunately not nearly as many as wholesale criticism of science suggests. The sober and at the same time more precise description of science thus sees it as Janus-faced, as ambiguous. (I am leaving aside the question of the sidelining of purpose-free science for now.)

In the rich universe of the sciences, problems do not arise in the same way in all places. Let's take genetic research as an example. It is experimenting with the building blocks of life without really being able to assess the consequences for the world outside the laboratory. There are also fears, especially at the beginning, of catastrophic consequences, global epidemics for example.

Whether such threats are real and if so, how probable they are, that is, what risks exist, is not a matter philosophy can decide. In the debate about the risks and opportunities of genetic research, philosophy intervenes neither with a priori claims nor, as some self-assured moralists do, with readymade convictions. Rather, here as elsewhere, it calls on citizens and those in positions of political responsibility not to cling to ideologically contaminated prior opinions and instead to charge the relevant sciences, now the natural sciences, now the economic and social sciences, now the humanities, with the partly topical, partly general task of researching, in time, specific states of affairs and their possible dangers. Such research must — already for pragmatic reasons, moreover because of the principle of the freedom of science — be conducted independently of political expectations and interest-driven guidelines.

One integral component of this task is interdisciplinary risk assessment. Such research begins, systematically, with defining concepts and continues with the demand for a new kind of critical science, risk research in a more narrow sense that would analyze, partly for well-defined tasks, partly for broader thematic fields, both possible dangers and possible dysfunctions in the economy, society, and politics. For this task, it outlines a possible progression (see section 2.5). The consequences of so vast a field of tasks are evident; they can be articulated in three theses.

1. In our functionally organized society, the sciences are responsible for the culture of knowledge: for the criteria, for the thematic fields, not least of all for the interests that guide knowledge. At the same time, they provide a model for a life in which what counts is not economic and political power but knowledge that can be verified and something that always carries the risk of failure, intellectual creativity.

   In addition, they resist the tendency of organizing the world merely as a universal network of utility. To that end, however, they must grant sufficient weight to the two models of knowledge supplementing the applied sciences, enlightenment and research free of use.

   Science is not only a site of research; it is also a site of teaching, and here a place of both education and training. Where teaching is focused on training, science codetermines the professional and social chances students will have. Beyond that, science more and more serves as a consultant to policy makers, one that is as independent as possible of economic and political interests. And where knowledge is sought for the sake of the education and enlightenment it yields and, above all, for its own sake, there science exemplarily shows what a free and humane life can consist in.

2. Already for reasons of prudence, all the more so for reasons of honesty, the applied sciences, especially, must develop a new self-conception, in two regards. Even where they pursue humanitarian goals — and that is by no means everywhere the case — they must accept the two other models of knowledge relevant to freedom, enlightenment and knowledge as an end in itself. Moreover, without giving up the humane guiding goals, they must admit to the Janus-faced nature of their actual achievements. Science must not deny its structurally instrumental character, which consists in the two dimensions discussed earlier; it therefore requires a nonepistemic supplement, an ethics and, in more complex cases, an applied ethics. The debates to be had belong in a "discourse of responsibility." This discourse, in addition, tasks the sciences with helping to steer the civilizational process, as far as possible, in a humane direction.

It is a matter of course that genuine research enters unknown territory. Nonetheless, it is hardly permissible to enter this territory in extreme weather and, especially, to drag along others, and this includes all those who do not participate in a given project but are affected by it without their consent. The modern sciences have lost their moral neutrality insofar as through their experiments — thought experiments excluded — they have moved from "acting in thought" to "acting in and on the world." Whereas initially, this acting took place only on a small scale, and in physics and chemistry, moreover, on inorganic matter, it now happens on a large scale (as in the case of nuclear testing) or contains operational risks that cannot be known beforehand (as in the case of genetic biology labs); it concerns the building blocks (in the case of genome manipulation and cloning), the very first and the very last phases of life (see above, chapter 3); it takes place using pain-sensitive animals; and not least of all, it extends, partly in the natural, partly in the social sciences, to the human being itself.

The freedom of research is undoubtedly always bound by legal limitations. In the case of human cloning and other questions at the limits of medicine, however, it is not always clear what the traditional and accepted legal order demands and what conforms to human rights and human dignity. Science must therefore confront these questions. Not because, as hasty moralists believe, science has become more "immoral"; rather, as modernity progresses, science must take up ever more difficult and more complex moral questions. Hence I may permit myself to repeat a thesis I first put forward elsewhere.[9]

3. Rather than always lagging behind research, what is required is a discourse of responsibility, a real discourse that discusses the basic assumptions, the pros and cons of each case instead of deciding beforehand on a mere accusation or

its opposite, simple defense. And this discourse must accompany research, and even be prospective: for if it is the case that the emblematic bird of wisdom, the owl of Athena, flies only at night, why not the night before?

9.3
KNOWLEDGE THAT THREATENS FREEDOM 2

Two additional, fundamentally different kinds of knowledge that threatens freedom concern another important aspect of freedom, a life without fear. In the first case, we learn, partly in traditional, partly in new ways about hereditary diseases we or our children will possibly suffer from. And there are, in the second case, diagnoses that are dangerous insofar as they name a state of affairs that unsettles a prior sense of security and thus restricts freedom. Here, knowledge is not dangerous in the sense that its employment poses a danger, but, rather, already the known state of affairs is dangerous. Because with it, fear breaks into our lives, a good part of freedom melts away. Examples can be found in public as well as private life.

For quite some time already, politics has been sensitive to the topic of generational justice but has for many years operated a peculiar selection. While it is committed to the protection of the environment, it represses the other question of generational justice, an ever-increasing public debt that is in no way justified by investments. Even more clearly dangerous is the knowledge about a changing demographic structure defined by fewer younger and more older people. The diagnosis has long been known, but it requires profound reforms, which is why it still continues to be ignored.[10]

A good example of dangerous knowledge in personal life are medical diagnoses that tell previously healthy persons that they are suffering from a serious, possibly life-threatening disease. Another example is the already-cited early diagnosis of hereditary diseases. Furthermore, still in the field of medicine, there is what is called surplus information, things that are found incidentally to a targeted genetic test without being directly related to it. Further, there may be coincidental findings: someone who volunteers for a medical research study displays unexpected abnormalities. Should that person be told although it is well known that most abnormalities, given a closer look, turn out to be harmless, that is, should that person be confronted with a burdensome uncertainty? How much truth can this person bear?

A similar question is raised by predictive diagnostics: should a person who currently enjoys perfect mental health be told about the danger of a dementia recognized thanks to neuroimaging, knowing that early treatment is more effective but therapy still is very limited: how are the advantages of treatment and unnecessary stress to be weighed against each other? Screenings of newborn babies pose analogous questions.

In the case of knowledge that threatens freedom in the usual sense, we must try to prevent the use that poses the danger. In the case of the new kind, the authors of the knowledge, the diagnosticians, must think about whether and, where applicable, how they communicate their knowledge. In the conversations physicians have with patients to inform them of such findings, the line is difficult to draw. For according to the accepted principle of informed consent, patients must understand what jurists call the nature, meaning, and scope of a medical intervention in order for their consent to be valid. It is, however, doubtful whether this requires citing all imaginable complications, even the most improbable. Prudent physicians prefer describing how they reduce the risk of a (not highly improbable) complication, thereby naming the risk in a milder manner. They may be helped here by a proverbial Jewish commentary on the eighth commandment: "You shall not lie, but you don't have to say everything you know."

The receivers of such knowledge in turn have a right to not knowing, namely, the right not to be informed. In other cases, where neither a medical intervention nor a highly recommended screening is indicated, those concerned by a diagnosis either must live without the relevant examinations in their personal lives, and also without prenatal and preimplantation diagnoses (see sections 3.4 and 3.5), or they must learn to react to unfavorable diagnoses. The widespread reaction of repressing knowledge is psychologically understandable insofar as it is human, but it comes at a high price: it postpones a necessary reform or modification in one's lifestyle that, when it is finally taken on, becomes emotionally more difficult and financially more costly.

For both sides, for the one who transmits the diagnosis and the one who receives it, a fourth model of knowledge (beside humanitarian science, enlightenment, and unfree knowledge) is helpful. It is no longer of a methodological, scientific nature but consists in practical power of judgment, in practical wisdom. In its classic form of *phronēsis*, decisively shaped by Aristotle, it is tasked with facilitating a life led with circumspection, a life that is on the whole successful. This practical wisdom, to be sure, is responsible merely for means and ways, but as *phronēsis* it does not reflect on these with a view to any and all goals but explicitly to a goal designated in the singular and with a definite article: the successful life, *eu zēn*.[11]

A successful life requires two fundamentally different factors. While the one factor, character virtues such as collectedness, valor, and justice, is tasked with the basic orientation toward happiness, the other factor, intellectual virtue, namely, practical wisdom, ensures that the basic eudaimonistic orientation becomes concrete in specific situations. In valorous action, for example, the character virtue of valor ensures that the reaction to danger is neither cowardly nor reckless but undaunted, while prudence defines the details of the action.

The danger that looms, and once again looms not just in cases of abuse, is that this intellectual virtue degenerates into a Machiavellian prudence, the proverbial serpent's wisdom or fox's cleverness. This degenerate form even exists in two forms already discussed by Aristotle, as a morally indifferent, merely instrumental power of judgment, as cleverness, and as an amoral power of judgment, as cunning or slyness.[12]

Where dangerous knowledge is concerned, the advice practical wisdom gives in the domain of politics is evident: bound by the welfare of the citizenry, politics must confront looming danger in time and courageously; the proverbial head-in-the-sand policy is not an option. The same is true for parents, teachers, and all other persons who have taken on responsibility for others. On the one hand they must, as far as possible, acquire the necessary knowledge in time and act according to it, but on the other hand they must, in transmitting this knowledge, act sensibly and with circumspection.

In purely personal life, insofar as it is indeed purely personal, there is hardly ever such a thing as simple advice. Leaving obvious diagnoses such as lack of exercise, unhealthy diet, and excessive indulgence in various stimulants aside, it hardly seems a meaningful requirement to ponder all potentially dangerous diagnoses. Wise people take the question whether something serves their freedom as their criterion, freedom here being best understood in terms of fearlessness. Not generally—people are different—but for many people, it does not run counter to all practical wisdom to do without some kinds of knowledge for fear of having to give up a previously untroubled life, especially when it comes to danger-filled diagnoses where there is as good as no therapy available. Here, there exists a right to not knowing. From Greek tragedy, we are familiar with the tragic exaggeration of wanting to know at all cost: was it prudent that Oedipus wanted to know the truth no matter what?

These few indications suggest the following assessment: whether as private, professional, or public individuals—those who have practical wisdom can neither avoid dangerous knowledge nor cope with it according to prescribed formulas. But they do know to deal with dangerous knowledge for their own welfare and the welfare of others.

10

Freedom and Creativity: Art

Underestimated by many theorists of freedom, art and in art the principle of freedom play a central role. One reason for this underestimation is evident: only very few theorists of freedom know enough about so diverse and multifaceted a field as art, extending as it does from music to the fine arts and architecture to poetry, theater, and film.

No less diverse are the aspects that pertain to a theory of freedom. They include not just the two sets of questions that have the best chances of being discussed, two groups of legal and political frameworks, the basic rights of the freedom of art including the prohibition of censorship on the one hand and public funding for art on the other. At least as important as these, however, is the question what role art plays for the freedom of society and how important, in that regard, the diversity of the arts is.

Because of the richness of facets, both of art and of the freedom-theoretical questions, facets in turn rich in subfacets, the discussion of the topic here can present only the basic traits. Following the examples of an early philosophy of literature that develops from tying art to other purposes to the freedom of art (section 10.1) and of the notion of full aesthetic autonomy (section 10.2), I take a look at the freedom of art (section 10.3) and, by way of conclusion, present some nonsystematic reflections on the role autonomous arts play for the freedom of society (section 10.4).

10.1
FROM THE CRITIQUE OF POETRY TO AFFECTIVE RATIONALITY

Plato

The language of the oldest European literature, as of early and classical European philosophy, is Greek. It is because of the language that we may consider those authors, presumably hailing from Asia Minor, who created the oldest great poems of our culture, two epics attributed to a figure called Homer, the

Iliad and the *Odyssey*, to be European authors. It is to these two epics, precisely, that the first model of the European philosophy of poetry refers, which ties the poet and poetry to extrapoetic tasks. It can be found in Plato's major work the *Republic*.

The theory of poetry, a criticism of poets, comes up at two points in the dialog; not in passing but in detail and moreover at prominent points, first in the book that follows the independent introductory "Thrasymachus" book, that is, in book 2 with a continuation in book 3 (376c–398b), then in the tenth and last book, where it constitutes the first half (595a–608b).

The first criticism of poets is connected with the multistage emergence of the *polis*. At the intermediary stage, *pleonexia* rules, an unlimited wanting more and more. That is why guardians are needed, security forces for the interior (police) but above all the exterior (military), who defend the city's growing territorial claims against the other cities. Within the framework of discussing the education of these guardians, Plato now criticizes the polytheistic myths handed down by Homer and Hesiod as immoral. This criticism is made from a constructive standpoint, namely, from that of a "true," equally monotheistic and moral theology.

Plato's criticism of poetry has model character because of this commitment to truth. Plato criticizes Homer and Hesiod not for some lack of poetic qualities, weaknesses in the composition or the language, say. On the contrary, he admires the two poets. His criticism, rather, is based on an uncompromising commitment to truth.

Nor must we overlook another aspect, namely, that the pedagogical context of Plato's criticism practically prohibits a purely literary evaluation. For Homer's epics in particular were not simply literature but an essential component of education. It is for that reason, because of their pedagogical significance, that Plato wants to outlaw telling the leadership elite of so-called guardians what a pre-Socratic philosopher had castigated already one and a half centuries before him. Xenophanes's triple criticism of the myths about the gods (see above, section 9.1) begins with a criticism of the gods' immoral behavior: "Homer and Hesiod have attributed to the gods all things / That among men are sources of blame and censure: / Thieving, committing adultery, and deceiving each other." It continues with the reproach of anthropomorphism and culminates in a new, enlightened, as it were, concept of the gods: "One god, among both gods and humans the greatest / Neither in bodily frame similar to mortals nor in thought."[1]

Plato primarily takes up the first and the third point of criticism. For according to his philosophical concept of god, god is first good and second the cause not of everything but only of the good. Moreover, he is immutable, and if he is the author of sanctions at all, then only of salutary ones.

The context of Plato's second criticism of poets is no longer that of education but of an epistemology and an ontology. The principle of truth remains in force but is no longer limited to theology and morality and acquires a comprehensive meaning that includes the theory of knowledge and of objects. According to his criterion for increased rationality, the division of labor and specialization, Plato does not ask whether Homer, because of the many topics he discusses, is a generalist knowledgeable about many things; he merely asks about Homer's special expertise: following the model of the physician who is able to cure patients, Homer would have to have the capacity to make improvements in the fields he makes his topics, conducting military campaigns, organizing cities, and education. Yet even according to his admirers, this is not the case.

Plato thus offers his harsh criticism for moral and political as well as epistemological and ontological reasons. According to him, poets hold false views of the gods and of right and wrong, and they amplify our passions and thereby cloud our judgment. Not least of all, from a practical-political point of view, they are useless.

Aristotle

Plato's "student" Aristotle resolutely rejects this criticism. In agreement with the Greek tradition, he counts the poets among the best teachers of the people. Approvingly citing Aeschylus's line from the *Agamemnon: ton pathei mathos*, "learning by suffering,"[2] Aristotle, the author of the first formal logic and of the first theory of science in Europe, does not assess poetry by the criteria developed there. Rather, here as elsewhere, he practices an epistemological tolerance. He grants poetry a rationality of its own, a primarily affective rather than intellectual form of rationality, which amounts to a plea for a considerable degree of aesthetic autonomy. In the relevant treatise, he so naturally follows his principle *tithenai ta phainomena*, to take the object seriously in its rich reality, that the concepts and arguments he develops there shape the debate of philosophers and scholars of literature for centuries.

Aristotle addresses the essence of poetry, its various genres, and its anthropological basis. He sees the essence in *mimesis*. Such "imitation," however, does not seek to present a deceptive reality; instead, it means that even a fiction of genius remains tied to a preceding, existing reality, especially to human social and political nature and culture.

Aristotle in fact remains loyal to Plato's principle of truth, albeit in a way that differs fundamentally from Plato's criticism of poetry. According to the concept of mimesis, there is, first, a kind of truth characteristic of poetry, to which is added, second, the task of establishing an inner harmony.

Aristotle goes beyond Plato in another regard as well. He does not limit himself to Homer and Hesiod but considers the extraordinary richness of Greek literature. Here, and again for reasons internal to poetry, tragedy plays a preeminent role. Compared to epic poetry, tragedy is characterized by greater vividness; moreover, it "requires less space for the attainment of its end"; and not least of all, its mimesis achieves a greater degree of unity.[3] Because of the dramatic unities of place and time and the limitation to a small number of characters and above all because of the concentration on essential human questions—Who are we? Which competing laws define our lives? What is up to us, and what lies beyond our control?—Greek literature, to this day, is one of the most prominent dramatic forms in world literature.

For tragedy, Aristotle coins the influential concept of tragic pleasure with the twin stars of pity and fear and the concept of *catharsis*, purification or relief. With regard to the later alternative between a theater of instruction and a theater of entertainment, Aristotle rejects neither option. Tragedy exposes the audience to an *éducation sentimentale*, an education of the emotions, which intertwines the two sides of the alternative. The rationality taking place in this interlocking is not intellectual but affective and, characteristically, applies beyond tragedy: be it theater, film, or literature—many great instances show how the arts represent exemplary possible forms of life: they present great passions, force us to sympathize with the protagonists and, in so doing, to expose ourselves to a process of emotional or affective cultivation.

Because of a second element, poetry according to Aristotle's *Poetics* is more philosophical and furthermore more valuable than historiography, for although poetry gives characters proper names, it is dealing with the general, it makes statements "as to what such or such a kind of man will probably or necessarily say or do."[4] Within the framework of its mimesis, poetry presents, in an individual poetic character and its fate (for example in the figure of Oedipus in the homonymous tragedy), something exemplarily and generally human (for example an ascent followed by a deep fall). And in any case, not only good plays but good stories, too, require empathy and plausibility.

10.2
AESTHETIC AUTONOMY

The two models, Plato's and, even more so, Aristotle's, are so powerful for centuries that despite the innovations that did take place—for example, the emergence since late antiquity of a "contextual rationality," that is, literature, music, and fine arts conceived to praise God (yet already in archaic and early classical Greece, the theater and in particular tragedies and satyr plays had religious and moreover political significance)—a truly fundamental change in the script of the philosophy of poetry was a very long time in the making. Prepared in the Renaissance and humanism, continued in the early Enlightenment, a decisive transformation happens in the first part of Immanuel Kant's *Critique of the Power of Judgment.*

This part, the "Critique of the Aesthetic Power of Judgment," is concerned with two basic aesthetic concepts lacking in Plato and Aristotle, the beautiful and the sublime, as well as with two other concepts not discussed by the ancient thinkers, either, common sense and genius.

Let's focus on the beautiful, which according to Kant is characteristic of poetry or literature, albeit not specific to it; not only do other arts such as painting and architecture produce beauty; nature does as well.

Kant does not investigate the beautiful itself but judgments about it, the "judgments of taste," to which feelings of pleasure and displeasure, that is, something subjective, are considered to be essential. Yet what counts is not a feeling of what is agreeable or unagreeable guided by interest and thus by definition private; what counts is a *Wohlgefallen*, a satisfaction or delight, that is disinterested and in that sense free. For precisely this reason, its disinterestedness, it has a paradoxical property: it is capable of objectivity, albeit only of a subjective objectivity.

Objectivity prompts an immense revaluation of the aesthetic. At the same time, because it is a subjective objectivity, it does not impose any external claims on poetry but instead subjects it to criteria internal to poetry. The questions which kind of theater may be expected to provide entertainment or which kind of (cultivated) pleasure may be expected can at most be answered, on Kant's view, by generally valid rules of experience. Judgments concerning the beautiful, by contrast, are capable of that kind of subjective and yet strictly general validity that, on the basis of a common sense, the *sensus communis*, amounts to a capacity for publicity.

In Plato, the criteria of generality and necessity apply only to strictly scientific, not to poetic propositions. According to Aristotle, they apply to poetry as well but only as "generally human" in an anthropological sense. Kant by contrast significantly revaluates the aesthetic in declaring it capable of a truly general, not just anthropological validity.

According to Kant, the author of aesthetic general validity, the poet, is characterized by originality and exemplarity but also by ignorance of the reason for the exemplarity, and in this three-dimensional sense already, the poet is a genius.

Despite more recent skepticism about the notion of genius, few today would relativize the first two dimensions as traits of truly great artists. For unlike remarkable talent, true greatness is characterized in addition by a small but unlearnable Something. For some reflective artists, one might indeed want to mitigate only the third dimension. Greater skepticism, in turn, is likely to be the reaction to Kant's main reason for geniality, namely, his claim that the poet dares to give sensuous form to ideas of reason.[5]

Would emancipation from this task bring even greater autonomy? Even if so, it would be worthwhile examining whether, nonetheless, some paradigmatic works of modern literature, Baudelaire's *Fleurs du mal*, Tolstoy's *Anna Karenina*, Kafka's on occasion downright cruel stories, or Thomas Mann's novels, from *Buddenbrooks* to *The Magic Mountain* to *Doctor Faustus*, give sensuous form to ideas of reason, albeit in a new, more indirect manner. The same might be said of painters creating art that—allegedly—abolishes art: Marcel Duchamp explicitly sets out "to put painting once again at the service of the mind."[6]

What can we take from this brief sketch? The path from Plato to Aristotle to Kant can be seen as a process of emancipation. First, in Plato, literature is subjected to a criterion proper to philosophy but alien to poetry, ethical and theological, moreover epistemological and ontological truth. Already in Aristotle, it reaches a high degree of aesthetic autonomy, which is why the emancipation, if it is accepted, is not to be seen as a progress from antiquity to modernity. Aristotle liberates poetry from the extrapoetic claims of truth and morality and subjects it to the intrapoetic criteria of mimesis and tragic pleasure.

While in Plato and Aristotle, poetry is considered a *tekhnē* or *poiēsis* and thus not to be fundamentally different from artisanship, Kant delineates it and elevates its great representatives to the position of exceptional human beings, of geniuses. Even more importantly, with the category of the beautiful, namely, the beautiful liberated from both truth claims and moral claims, he declares the aesthetic to be an entirely independent domain characterized by a specific freedom, a neither agreeable nor good but rather disinterested delight.

That is why we may conclude, even after such short reflections, with the following thesis: according to Plato, the propositions of poetry should be true and morally good; according to Aristotle, poetry should be agreeable and generally humanly correct. Only Kant, and no one before him, with his concept of the beautiful as a disinterested delight achieves what may be considered perfect emancipation.

This assessment does not claim that philosophical aesthetics stopped developing after Kant. On the contrary, post-Kantian aesthetics is almost overly abundant in significant contributions. Here it must suffice to recall the enduring appreciation of art among philosophers. In Hegel's *Aesthetics*, for example, fine art is ennobled and becomes "the sensuous presentation of the Absolute itself," because "the realm of fine art is the realm of the *absolute spirit*." Yet Hegel also declares that there is no longer any need to represent a content in the form of art: "Thought and reflection have spread their wings above fine art."[7] This notion is vehemently opposed by Nietzsche, who, in a variety of ways, proffers the view that not reason but art is the element in which life fulfills its meaning. Heidegger in turn affirms Hegel's assumption, writing that in the time between Hegel and his own day, art is no longer "an essential and necessary way in which that truth happens which is decisive for our historical existence." Yet he also considers it possible that art might in the future attain that position once more.[8]

10.3
THE FREEDOM OF ART

Heidegger's view that in art a truth can happen that is decisive for human existence might be answered with a clear "no," especially since art has become a problem for itself. We may leave the question open here. To address the question what status art has for freedom and what work it does for freedom, the much more modest assumption suffices that art has not become inconsequential. Moreover, we must limit ourselves to some keywords here, and the first of these is a legal precondition, the freedom of art.

We today consider the freedom of art to be an obvious right; that is why we protest when it is not respected and criticize countries in which this happens systematically. While it is true that freedom of art belongs to the indispensable elements of constitutional democracies, as a basic right, it is relatively young.[9]

The history of the freedom of art in modernity begins with protection against censorship from state and church. The historical basis consists of the familiar processes of emancipation, especially the detachment from ties to the church and from absolutist paternalism. After absolutism includes art among the purposes of the state — a welcome development — art, also because of the aesthetic autonomy won through Kant, liberates itself from the ties that bind it to courts and estates. Many artists, however, have to pay for this liberation with social insecurity and impoverishment. This is counteracted later by democracies with a kind of indemnity bond: they take over the task of promoting culture and the arts previously performed by princes, the church, and rich patrons. This is joined by the welfare state idea of providing artists with a certain level of livelihood: the negative freedom, the liberation from tutelage, is supplemented with a positive freedom.

This supplement, because of public budgets becoming ever more strapped for cash despite surging revenues, is increasingly modest. Fortunately, part of the public support no longer available is made up for by nonstate patrons, private individuals as well as businesses, which, however, implies new demands being addressed to art.

When we look at the constitutional development, taking the German-speaking countries as our example, we find the freedom of art for the first time in the "bourgeois" Frankfurt Constitution of 1849. As a predecessor to a veritable freedom of art, its article 1, section 143 contains the freedom of artistic speech. The freedom of art becomes a component of a constitution actually in force in article 143 of the Weimar Constitution. The Basic Law for the Federal Republic of Germany takes this up: article 5, section 3 declares the arts and sciences to be free and does not allow for this freedom to be restricted by law. In Austria, freedom of art is not included until 1982 in an amendment, article 17a, of the December Constitution. And in Switzerland, jurisprudence has endowed the freedom of artistic speech with a status comparable to the situation in Austria and Germany.

What does this constitutional status mean? As a defensive right against the state, the constitutionally guaranteed freedom of art protects first of all artists, but then also their works and the works' aesthetic presentation. This gives rise to a serious problem: there is no broad consensus today about what distinguishes art and the arts from other forms of presentation and communication. Above all, precisely because of the defensive liberty of art, which cannot, moreover, be restricted by law, the state has no right authoritatively to establish a binding concept of art.

Kant's criterion of disinterested delight as well as the aspects of originality, individuality, and emotionality might still count as standards of great art. And in newspapers' arts sections and other media they are still, at least implicitly, acknowledged as criteria. For interpreting the constitutionally protected freedom of art, however, they are too narrow. Beside "disinterested" art, "committed" art, beside "free" art, "applied" art enjoys constitutional protection. The status difference between "highbrow" and "lowbrow" art is of no legal consequence and increasingly doubted in the arts sections as well.

Since, as noted, there can be no restrictions by law, freedom of art may be limited only by legal interests of equal rank. These include personality rights that may be invoked to defend against all too malevolent attacks in cartoons and satires. They also include health, which may be invoked by residents to defend against excessive noise caused by street musicians or open-air music events. Not least of all, artists are not free to pilfer the property of others.

Like any weighing of legal values, this calls for judgments that are methodologically difficult and rarely result in undisputed decisions. Different cultures with different traditions and value conceptions will reach different conclusions. What used to be rejected as immoral or an act of lèse-majesté is now in many places permitted. Believers, especially Christians, must put up with blasphemous images and texts. By contrast, such can be dangerous when they are directed against Islam; think of the death threat of the fatwa pronounced against the author Salman Rushdie, who grew up Muslim; similar threats against Lars Refn, the Danish, non-Muslim author of the Muhammad cartoons; or the terrorist attack on the satirical magazine *Charlie Hebdo*.

One consequence of the lacking consensus about the conception of art is evident: here, too, free societies follow their three criteria of openness, pluralism, and tolerance (see above, chapter 8). They do not narrow their perception of the phenomena of art down, permit a pluralism, and practice tolerance toward the wide variety of phenomena that claim to be art. The minimum of their tolerance consists in permitting a diversity of arts. A tolerance that goes further does not restrict support for the arts to a narrow concept of art. Instead, it does not promote just the diversity of the great branches of art such as music, literature, fine arts, architecture, and film, because consideration for this diversity is a matter of course. It is not as self-evident yet characteristic of a free society not just to allow but to foster competing forms within each of these branches and subbranches. An enlightened liberal society is proud of this acceptance of openness, pluralism, and tolerance even when artists like Marcel Duchamp seek to shock the audience by exhibiting an ordinary urinal under the title *Fontaine* or authors like Peter Handke explicitly go about "offending the audience."[10]

10.4
ART AS FREE CREATIVITY

The tolerant acceptance of a pluralism of conceptions of art, however, creates a further problem: the question of what contribution art makes to freedom in a free society becomes much more difficult to answer. Only a formal answer is easy. And on the question of this contribution, we are likely to encounter a multitude of facets as rich as that of the phenomenon of freedom. And as the diversity of art and the arts works against any attempt at systematicity or even completeness, so do their achievements with respect to freedom. Let me therefore enumerate some possible achievements as regards freedom, nonsystematically and without any claim to completeness. Let me begin with some less sophisticated ones.

Art serves our entertainment and enjoyment. Art can provoke or fan fears; similarly it can evoke or amplify feelings of pity and steer both, fear and pity, in certain directions. In the case of enjoyable entertainment, art serves to provide relief. Take as random examples the movie *Paulette* and Jonas Jonasson's two novels *The Hundred-Year-Old Man Who Climbed Out of the Window and Disappeared* and *The Girl Who Saved the King of Sweden*.[11] Depending on its intention and quality, art can prompt an amused smirk, occasionally even a liberating laugh, and in so doing free us from the toil and trouble of work and the drudgery of the everyday, even of worries and care, albeit — usually — only temporarily. In fortunate cases, art gives our lives new vigor or opens our eyes to new possibilities. Novels that show how people maintain their dignity even under extreme conditions are more demanding, such as John Williams's *Stoner* or Robert Seethaler's *A Whole Life*.[12]

As noted, other contributions art makes, in contrast, have an unsettling or oppressive effect. Taking these and other ways of creating art together unmasks a widely held view to be a myth, namely, that art makes up a small special domain of life today. In fact, the arts have been on the rise since about the last third of the nineteenth century and have rarely if ever been so present, in private as in public, as they have been since then and are today. Artistic activity and cultural events have long become far more than a feature of the life of the educated, more, too, than an only occasional beautification of the everyday.

The greater value of art is hard to contest, if only for the simple reason that the arts as a whole move in a space of the imagination that forms as a counterpole to the "harsh reality" of the predominance of rationality, of science, medicine, and technology, and of the economy — the "art of the possible."[13] Let's take a look at individual domains of art.

The *fine arts* help us in learning to see: in portraits, what a human being can be, in landscapes, what the peaceful or forceful or civilized environment of the human looks like; and in surrealism and abstract art, we learn to see what is different. In painting we find the full spectrum, from horror and terror (Goya, *The Disasters of War*) via the solitude of the frozen wilderness (Caspar David Friedrich, *The Sea of Ice*), and the misery of absinthe consumption (Picasso, *Absinthe Drinker*), to the joyful counterworld to the everyday, namely, the anticipation of peace and harmony, the utopia of paradise. We see the pride of aristocrats and patricians, the drudgery of the working life, the beauty of the human being, the nobility of old age, homages to woman, the praise or dream of never-ending virility. Edvard Munch succeeds in rendering visible what is invisible, the torture of jealousy, for example, the scream rising from the depths of body and soul, anxiety, torture. On the other hand, there is what in China is considered the highest praise for photographs, drawings, and paintings, poetry in images. In all these domains, the fine arts help us project both images and counterimages. They make our way of seeing more acute or question our habitual ways of seeing and challenge our judgment. Analogous points can be made for our habitual ways of listening and reading and other ways of perceiving.

Music gives countless forms to a general and originary human force of expression, to rhythms, melodies, instruments, and the human voice. It cites old forms and develops new ones. It can be opulent; it can be playful, bursting with joy, but also fearfully melancholy; and it teaches us to perceive these forms.

Music can enchant, even perform miracles, albeit rarely permanently: in a city marked by daily warfare, Sarajevo, a famous cello player performs a piece of music reconstructed from a fragment found in the burned remains of the Dresden music library, the mournful sounds of Tomaso Albinioni's *Adagio*. And although the city remains destroyed, for the listeners, it "repairs itself. . . . People stand up taller, their faces put on weight and color. Clothes gain lost thread, brighten, smooth out their wrinkles."[14]

In one of the oldest expressions of human life, in *dance*—from folk dance based on the dances of peasants to the more sophisticated ballroom dance to the high art of stage dance that derives from them, ballet—the featherlight grace of movement combines with an astonishing expressivity of the face and a no less astonishing flexibility of the entire body to present, in a literally speechless manner, psychological experiences, that is, emotions or social relationships, and often the conflicts between the two.

Even those who have difficulty deciphering facial gestures and bodily movements marvel at dancers' as well as great musicians' breathtaking virtuosity, which is even enhanced by charismatic presence. With unbegrudging admiration we perceive the human capacity for top performances we previously never even thought possible. In theater performances such as Peter Brook's New York production of *A Midsummer Night's Dream*, in ballet performances such as John Neumeier's choreographic adaptation of the same play or John Cranko's choreography for *Romeo and Juliet* to the music of Sergei Prokofiev, we experience an unbounded joy in an abundance of vitality. Peter Stein's Moscow *Oresteia* conveys a different experience, the rise of judgment from the conflagration of violence; the performance is moving even for someone who does not speak Russian. Great actors like Edith Clever in Euripides's cruel

Medea are able to embody passions and bring out, perhaps even to conquer the demons concealed in the human being.

Literature hones our sense for language, for its rich possibilities of expression, for the staccato found in many a play and the long arches of Kleist's sentences, not least of all for puns and wit, for, to quote the title of a comedy by Christian Dietrich Grabbe, "joke, satire, irony, and deeper meaning."[15] Some authors cultivate a "cold" style and, on T. S. Eliot's advice, "carve, polish, compress, and simplify" their texts. Others cultivate instead a "charismatically chatty prose," authors like F. Scott Fitzgerald or John Irving, "whose sentences unwind with glowing ease."[16]

A concert, a visit to the theater or to an exhibition can quite simply make us happy. The reaction that dominated the beginnings of music and theater, astonishment and admiration, remains intact in sufficiently many places today. And as if in passing, but by no means trivially, it expands our view of the emotional, social, and political world and at the same time of exemplary human emotions and destinies; for example, we come to view characters favorably who then become guilty or who, without incurring guilt in an emphatic sense, fail nonetheless.

Light fiction in turn meets the expectations of a wider audience and prefers happy endings. This applies not just to sentimental songs, movies, plays, or romance novels denigrated as schmaltz. In classic crime fiction and the very popular crime series, too, the criminal in the end meets his just punishment. In the ultimate victory of law and justice, evil is being domesticated.

The basic forms of all these arts belong to the oldest expressions of human life. Initially, in all likelihood, deeply rooted in cults and myths, they arise from an originary drive of the human being, to be observed across the globe and already in very early cultures, a will to create, play, and imitate. In the words of a philosopher, Hegel, "the universal need for art" is a need to elevate "the inner and outer world" into "an object in which he recognizes again his own self."[17]

Because it is based on an originary drive or universal need, art effortlessly lives on after the dissolution of its cultic-mythological roots. The arts are an essential element both of the way societies affirm themselves and of the way they confront their (relatively) natural environment and its fateful forces. They are part of the group's struggle for survival and at the same time establish a distance from this struggle, which is particularly apparent where the arts acquire a festive and solemn character.

Insofar as it is possible for an amateur to assess the art of archaic cultures, it seems that in its works, the two perspectives of life intertwine that are often considered alternatives, the simple life, or just survival, and the happy-successful, the good life. In that sense, necessity and freedom here enter into a unity.

In the course of human history, of course, one side of the arts, necessity, increasingly receded to the background until, at the very latest in Kant's notion of disinterested delight, the aesthetic achieves autonomy. At that point, the arts offer the suggested counterimage to the mere necessities of life. A society that does more vis-à-vis the arts than merely tolerating them, by giving them a jester's license to speak freely and instead welcomes them and therefore supports them and participates in their lives, relativizes the world that usually takes center stage, a utilitarian world often reduced to the economical and even to cost cutting. In this way, the arts bring out a further facet of enlightened freedom.

Human beings not only liberate themselves from the constraints of inner and outer nature; they are not just, in addition, economic citizens, called to knowledge, and moreover (possibly even cosmopolitan) state citizens. They display yet another freedom where beyond all that they live as artists or at least as people who love and are committed to the arts.

This assessment, of course, must be taken with a grain of skepticism. Neither all artists nor all recipients of art must be perceived in too "idealistic" terms. While some artists, whether they work with images, sounds, or words, consider creating art a vital necessity and follow their artistic conscience alone, others stretch, perhaps overstretch their artistic conscience or prefer silencing it. They conform to a dominant contemporary or expected taste in art; they have their eye on reputation and remuneration; they are, strictly speaking, opportunists, Sophists, as it were, just not in philosophy but in the arts instead. Others again quite simply lack talent; yet because there is no generally convincing concept of art there is not even a halfway objective criterion for this deficit.

Finally, when it comes to artistic success, we must not overlook, on the one hand, the power of literary agents, critics, and gallerists and, on the other, the vanity of art consumers, especially of art collectors of whom many buy art for the sake of their own reputation, as decoration or investment. Multinationals that adorn their lobbies with paintings, sculptures, or tapestries in fact degrade them, turn them into decorative ornaments, literally less than a "percent for art." As they think of it, of course, they put their cultural horizon on display, expand their so-called corporate identity, and convey cultural values to their employees and customers. Not least of all, they want to match or, better, outdo their competitors.

The consequence for artists: they, too, know their business; they act as entrepreneurs themselves. According to observers, the names of certain neighborhoods such as New York's Greenwich Village used to have an artistic ring to them; today, the only sound is that of money.

Risks, abuses, perversions — the world of art cannot avoid these "dark sides." They are undoubtedly part of reality, but they must not dominate in an assessment of the value the world of the aesthetic has for freedom.

By way of conclusion, let's summarize the opportunities: art gives the imagination wings of freedom. In Niklas Luhmann's terms, art aims for a "reactivation of eliminated possibilities." The result consists in more than just fiction because art "generates a reality with a right to its own objectivity."[18] As I noted at the beginning, visual artists, musicians, and writers create a world of its own freed from the constraints of reality and allow this world, which we might call a fantasy world, to establish itself: they produce counterworlds to the world of the everyday and shed light on the blind spots as well as the dangers, flipsides, and abuses of the present; through contrast and exaggeration they make us aware of what this everyday world is and how it is; they show its abysmal sides and quotidian horrors; they refine this world; perhaps they also make it more beautiful and transform or even transfigure the ordinary;[19] they dramatize, add pathos, demonize; they raise up or put down; they allow for celebration and give it expression; they distract from reality or expose it.

Even this abundant array of accomplishments does not come close to giving a complete description of what art is able to achieve. The three-dimensional significance for freedom, however, has become clear: art makes certain freedoms possible, but it is also an expression of freedom (in the singular and in the plural), and finally it accompanies freedom. In consequence, a free society appreciates art and the arts, and it does so especially when they prove to be founts of creativity and originality, when they are — the reservations voiced in recent decades notwithstanding — a source of beauty in the sense of disinterested delight or present themselves as a site of constant unrest and renewal.

PART IV

Political Freedom

In many regions of the world, in the East for example but not only there, the family and its natural continuation, the clan or tribe, are of preeminent significance. In many places, neighborhood cultures grown over centuries play a role. Nonetheless, from a global perspective, the organization of human coexistence that characterizes modernity is the political polity, the state, and, namely, in its modern form, that is to say, neither a city-republic nor an empire. Individual states, or nation-states, dominate not only in the West.

If we take membership in the United Nations as our criterion, there are now 193 instances; another ten are waiting to be admitted. Since the state constitutes the primary site of political legitimation from a normative perspective as well, it has become almost the only form of government. To justify it, two ideal types have been articulated. According to the functional model, the polity serves its citizens, whose freedom and equality have a value of their own. According to the alternative, intrinsic model, the polity, although only the liberal polity, is an end in itself. The fourth part of this study considers this alternative not to be adequate and develops an integrating, both functional and intrinsic justification.

Ultimately, the only thing that counts is the individual but not isolated human being, the free, autonomous person. The political culture of polities founded for the sake of their citizens, however, is characterized by the combination of mentalities and institutions that must be preserved as such. What is required, therefore, is a two-dimensional legitimation: polities must benefit each member, each individual citizen, that is, they must be distributively advantageous. In addition, they need the collective advantage that they serve the liberal political culture of the polity, namely, that they initiate, foster, and preserve this political culture. In the terms of the history of philosophy, this legitimation enriches a basic Kantian notion with Hegelian elements.

Now, the individual polities are not by themselves in the world. Political freedom is thus composed of two aspects that were decisive already in ancient

Greece. According to autonomy within, the opposite of dictatorship, despotism, and tyranny, a free polity makes its own laws, namely, laws that permit citizens leeway for free actions of their own. And according to outer autonomy, a free polity is not subject to any foreign rule.

As legislation by those concerned, as rule of the people, the name of the inner political freedom that is important to modernity is constitutional or liberal democracy (chapter 11). The justification of constitutional democracy leads us to one of the basic theses of this book that is at the same time an indispensable element of enlightened liberalism: restrictions of freedom are necessary, not in the form feared by philosophical anarchism, the repression of freedom, but in part to make freedom possible, in part to secure it. The other, external political freedom is characterized by state sovereignty and power (chapter 14), which cannot be unlimited either but must accept fitting in with a liberal global order (chapter 15). In between, I develop freedom-theoretical reflections on the basic rights (chapter 12) and on the question of (Western) citizen's identity (chapter 13). Chapters 13 and 14 thus discuss the two main agents of the political, the citizen and the sovereign polity, respectively.

To be sure, the question of freedom, which here is explicitly also a question of modernity, poses itself differently in each of these domains. The two-dimensionality of political freedom, its functional and at the same time intrinsic meaning, however, remains intact. Moreover, once again, ambiguities arise.

11

Constitutional Democracy

11.1

FREEDOM FROM RULE OR RULE OF FREEDOM?

The core grammar of every polity consists in law, which necessarily combines the possibility of its enforcement. That is why every polity also exercises political rule [*Herrschaft*], and it is why "ordered anarchy" cannot be "the philosophical model to guide the liberal *Rechtsstaat,* the rule of law or constitutional state."[1]

Because every government allegedly violates individuals' rights, skepticism arises even when it is those concerned by rule who exercise it. It raises a question that contemporary philosophy, surprisingly, largely ignores: does freedom in the realm of the political, political freedom, consist not, as elsewhere, in inner and outer autonomy but instead in freedom from rule?

It is in this sense that the early work *A Vindication of Natural Society* (1756) by the later critic of the French Revolution Edmund Burke offers a blunt criticism of rule aimed at what he sees as the trail of blood running through the history of political rule.[2] Given such assessments, it cannot but be surprising to see that originally, among the Greeks, the absence of rule was always judged negatively. And in political modernity, too, from Machiavelli to Montesquieu to Voltaire, say, the negative assessment prevails. Only religious "enthusiasts" such as the Anabaptists shift the abolition of political rule, which Christian thinkers had reserved for the hereafter, to this world and demand a coexistence free from law and the state already for the present. However, the notion of a freedom from rule comes back to life in Marx and Engels's thesis of the withering away of the state, in Herbert Marcuse, who is influenced by it, in Michel Foucault's subversive critique of institutions, and not least of all in antiauthoritarian movements.[3]

In Burke, the one-sidedness of the passionate criticism of rule is on display: it is right in what it says but wrong in what it leaves out. One-sided already is the emphasis on the external perspective, on the relationship between systems of political rule to each other, where in fact war often dominates, which in turn entails the well-known host of calamities and suffering. Burke, however, not only passes over times of peace, which also existed; he especially ignores the internal perspective, where rule is often exercised in the form of a legal order that proscribes violence among citizens.

Moreover, a judicative differential analysis is lacking that would first of all look for the advantages and disadvantages of both sides, of political polities and their (allegedly) rule-free alternatives among natural tribal societies, and then weigh the advantages and disadvantages against each other, perform a cost-benefit analysis. Also lacking is a neutral concept of rule that does not disqualify it from the outset. And what is lacking above all is a thorough thinking through of a strictly rule-free coexistence. In political philosophy, this thinking through takes place in a thought experiment called "state of nature" that forms the first argumentative step in contract theory.

We know approximations to the state of nature from literature, for example Lord Byron's apocalyptic 1816 poem "Darkness." During an exceptionally cold and bleak summer on Lake Geneva, Byron outlines the social disaster triggered by a climatic disaster. It consists in panic, despair, and the dissolution of all social order. Everyone fails this test Byron has set up for humanity. Hunger makes everyone everyone else's enemy: "no love was left."[4]

The philosophical thought experiment differs from Byron's poem in that it does not suppose any external catastrophe. It merely takes the notion of freedom from rule seriously but discovers that the notion is self-contradictory. For a state of lawlessness and constitutionlessness initially gives every human being the freedom to pursue purposes with the means deemed to be right. This freedom, which, as Hobbes rightly explains, includes "a right to everything, even to one another's body,"[5] threatens the corresponding freedom of fellow human beings, which is why the opposite of the state of nature, that is, an enforceable law and with it political rule, is needed.

To avoid misunderstandings, it must be emphasized that the state of nature thought experiment does not presuppose a pessimistic view of the human being as naturally egotistical, unsociable, obsessed with power, and violent. It does not even suppose an innate pugnacity but simply assumes a common, spatially limited world in which human beings with unlimited freedom of action can enter into conflicts ranging all the way to a life-or-death struggle. And this is where the inner contradiction or the dialectic of the state of rulelessness lies: the freedom to everything in the social perspective turns out to be a freedom to nothing, for ultimately neither life and limb nor goods and chattels nor any kind of free personal existence is protected. Other arguments can be added, for example protection against intruders or, at the beginnings of humanity, protection from predators.

The consequence, a special kind of paradox, is evident: for the sake of freedom, freedom must be restricted. Because without restricting and simultaneously securing freedom of action — thus without a binding order that as such constitutes political rule — the freedom of everyone is threatened with destruction at any time, humans have long left the hypothetical state of nature and created in its place a form of coexistence that secures freedom. In this move, the great Nowhere, the utopia of freedom from coercion and rule, makes place for the small utopia and realistic vision of the smallest possible coercion, of liberal rule.

In justifying liberal rule, there is an additional argument, namely, that rights do not guarantee their own actuality. Taken by themselves, rights have the (ontological) status of a merely "natural" political freedom that lacks actuality in three respects: in the precise definition of rights, in their implementation, and in the impartial decision of conflicts. Because there is a public power responsible for overcoming each of these deficits — the legislative for detailing the rights, the executive for enforcing them, and the judiciary for arbitrating conflicts — the political freedom that is more than natural, actual political freedom, requires the embodiment of the three public powers, that is state rule or a rule analogous to that of the state.[6]

11.2
BASIC FREEDOMS: HUMAN RIGHTS

The alternative to freedom from rule results from its determinate negation. Because the freedom to everything turns out to be a freedom to nothing, anarchic freedom — this is the negation — must be restricted, yet — in keeping with positive determinacy — only to the extent necessary for freedom to be actual. Here lies the basic thesis I mentioned in the introduction to this fourth part: in opposition to philosophical anarchism, political freedom, first, is possible only as a restriction of freedom that, second, is legitimate, however, merely for securing, not for suppressing freedom.

Restriction is possible in a variety of ways, for example in that the stronger claim a greater degree of freedom. There is thus a need for a normative point of view, more precisely the basic notion of justice that is equality, which demands that no one be advantaged and simultaneously that no one be disadvantaged.

Thomas Hobbes already articulates the relevant principle of freedom in the second law of nature in his *Leviathan*.[7] We owe the concise justification and formulation to Immanuel Kant, who says in the "Doctrine of Right": "Right" in the sense of elementary justice "is therefore the sum of the conditions under which the choice of one can be united with the choice of another in accordance with a universal law of freedom." John Rawls adopts this principle of the general compatibility of freedom and makes it the first principle of justice: "Each person is to have an equal right to the most extensive total system of equal basic liberties compatible with a similar system of liberty for all."[8]

This one basic principle can be spelled out, in accordance with the various aspects of human coexistence, in a large number of intermediary principles that have the meaning of basic freedoms. As universally valid conditions of beings compos mentis, they pertain to all human beings, prior to and independently of any and all individual or public actions, and for that very reason, they have the status of human rights. In the terms of the traditional rhetoric, they are innate, natural, inalienable, and inviolable rights of the human being as human being.[9]

To be able to address which freedoms have this status, the basic normative idea, the principle of equality, must be supplemented with elements of the human condition. The basic anthropological elements have been undisputed since the articulation of the human being as an organism capable of language and reason (*zōon logon echon*) in antiquity,[10] yet it is not until modernity that the legal consequences are drawn from this definition.

As living being, the human being requires a living body and, as rational being, the things that allow for developing and exercising the capacity for language and reason. We can thus expect two groups of basic freedoms, on the one hand those related to life and the body, on the other those related to language and reason.

A polity that guarantees these basic freedoms by giving them the status of positive rights, basic rights, may be qualified as at its core liberal; a state that refuses this guarantee must be qualified as unfree, in the case of enhanced unfreedom as tyrannical or even totalitarian. The political consequence is evident: no matter how well a state's laws and institutions vouch for internal and external security, even if they vouch for coordination, efficiency, and stability, and beyond that economic well-being as well: if at the same time, they contradict the basic freedoms, then the basic political organization must be changed.

Which freedoms, in detail, have this status? In general terms, the basic freedoms include first of all liberties that secure for each human being a strictly personal space, a space removed from any interference, political or from others. As objections to interference, their meaning is that of defensive rights or negative liberties. For the human as a living being, this includes the already-cited inviolability of life and limb, which is why for all fellow humans, any kind of violence, especially manslaughter and murder, rape, mutilation, and physical abuse, is prohibited.

Because the living being that is the human is also a rational being, inviolability also demands that no psychological cruelty be committed. Moreover, all interference must cease that hinders the freedom of religion and of conscience, the freedom of science and of art, of the press, of radio, and of television, and in the electronic age, data privacy as well (see below, section 12.1).

These demands, from a systematic point of view, are aimed first of all at our fellow human beings, only secondarily at the relevant public powers, which, from the perspective of the theory of freedom, are called to secure the basic freedoms. The negative liberties are primarily defensive rights against our fellows, only secondarily defensive rights against state powers. These powers obviously must not endanger the basic freedoms; hence the necessity of protection from arbitrary arrest, detention, and punishment, which is probably the oldest of the constitutional defensive rights against the state.

The basic freedoms also include the right to personal property. While this does not entail a precise organization of property, it implies not only allowing personal property as a fundamental condition of action but protecting it; theft and robbery as well as arbitrary or uncompensated expropriation must thus be prohibited.[11]

Classical liberalism is particularly committed to the "negative" liberties and conceives of these primarily as defensive rights against the state. From painful experience with the absolutist paternalist state or with what remains of it, it advocates the right of each and every individual freely to form his convictions and freely to live his own life in accordance with these convictions. Having convictions and a life "of one's own," of course, requires certain means, partly goods and partly services, and not least of all opportunities, which is why an enlightened liberalism is not content with negative freedom. In opposition to critics of the idea of social rights (and liberties) or the idea of a welfare state (see above, sections 7.3–7.4), it holds that a political community shares in the responsibility for the framework of conditions under which employment is defined and income, education, and social status are acquired, used, and transferred. The polity is responsible for the regulatory framework of professional life and situations such as old age, illness, and accidents.

Such social and cultural rights must of course not be pursued to the detriment of the negative liberties. They are legitimate as conditions of actualizing these liberties but not when they interfere with them; they thus justify less a claim to being provided for than a claim to personal and political freedom being made possible and protected. They do not legitimate the kind of maternalist nanny state that leads to a sprawling bureaucracy on the part of the state and promotes dependency on the part of citizens. Instead, they justify a freedom-promoting welfare state that secures the conditions of subsistence and provides scope for freedom.

Regional differences must be taken into account here: where supportive communities such as families, clans, or guilds are still alive and well, fewer demands are to be made than in places where the individualization of life has weakened such communities. Nor must it be overlooked that social benefits not only compensate the waning power of supportive communities but also can serve to accelerate this loss of power. Moreover, the absence of a quid pro quo for benefits, benefits as gifts, as it were, is justified only in exceptional cases, even for legitimate benefits. For unlike human kindness, the principle of liberties is set up reciprocally. Within the possibilities opened up by the principle, it is not inappropriate for the welfare recipient to do work in the community, especially since this can help increase self-respect — the assistance is earned. Avishai Margalit in *The Decent Society* rightly highlights how bureaucratized assistance interferes with individual dignity.[12]

The liberties occasion political, and also philosophical, controversies that are often blamed on a competition of values, the opposition of freedom and social justice. The truth is that there seems to be a competition only between values, when, in fact, there is a competition within each of the two values, both within freedom and in freedom-promoting justice. The alleged tension thus turns out to be a task of evaluation within both freedom and justice. The reason lies in the structural difference between negative and positive liberties: the negative rights that result from renouncing violence (excepting self-defense) can be claimed under all circumstances, even in situations of scarcity; the same is not true of social rights. When there is, for example, a pervasive shortage of food or clothing, someone's death by hunger or freezing is not necessarily a violation of his freedom.

Since, then, the positive liberties are subject to the problem of scarcity, it is more appropriate to treat them not as subjectively enforceable individual rights but as programmatic demands, and the welfare state as an objective of the state. This leaves it to the legislative to detail the objective as a function of what is possible in a given situation. Because positive liberties present a continuum that reaches from bare survival via countless nuances to the pleasant life, there is leeway that polities can and may make use of in different ways. Just as there is no single way of organizing property that follows from the notion of basic freedoms, so there is no precise welfare state agenda that derives from them. Instead, a "right to difference" emerges that is, in fact, claimed by Western democracies.

In Europe, the state is called on beyond the level of negative liberties to such an extent that critics speak of a "faith in the state." In the United States, in contrast, people quickly consider the freedom from state tutelage wrested from Great Britain in the War of Independence to be under attack. The difference is thus due to traditions that reach far into the past and to deeply rooted attitudes.

11.3
AN ADVANCE IN LEGITIMACY

A superficial conception of democracy likes to overlook two aspects in particular. Democracy, too, needs justification, and such justification is more likely to be convincing coming from a constitutional democracy than from a simple rule of the people. Indeed, constitutional democracy may well be one of humanity's greatest cultural innovations. Yet constitutional elements, of course, introduce a tension into the concept of democracy.

Democracy needs a justification because it, too, does not relinquish the core grammar of coexistence, an enforceable law, and thus constitutes a form of rule that requires justification. This justification is all the easier, evidently, when rule is exercised by those concerned themselves. The vote for democracy lived in the West is therefore justified; with regard to justifying rule, there is no serious alternative. As self-organization of coexistence, democracy has an advance in legitimacy that cannot be outdone.

That is why the notion of a constitutional, liberal democracy is indeed "exportable." Where democratization takes place only temporarily or merely apparently, where in truth a regime hostile to pluralism and freedom such as a tolerance-resistant "Islamic State" is spreading, no culturally relative liberalism is called for. As far as legitimation is concerned, there is no alternative to liberal democracy. Its effective establishment, however, requires a mentality and education that in some places will take a long time to create.

The fundamental advance in legitimacy, however, does not exclude any and all criticism of concrete democracies. For very often, their divergence from the ideal is all too great. Decreased interest in being politically active in parties, even more so lower voter turnout are clear indicators that the actual democracies stand in need of renewal. Even so, reality does not offer a uniform picture: in the elections for European Parliament in May 2014, for example, voter turnout in Germany rose by 10 percent from the previous poll, from

43.6 to 48 percent; in Slovakia, it attained a mere 13 percent, while elections taking place that same month in a neighboring country, where democratic conditions are still only a promise, Ukraine, saw very high turnout.

The striking difference between Slovakia and Ukraine is probably partly to blame on a hedonistic discount: in countries where democracy has become a matter of course, voter turnout decreases. For the difference between Slovakia and Germany, though, other, perhaps contingent domestic reasons are at least partly responsible. There is an antidote to diminishing participation rates, compulsory voting of the kind practiced in Belgium, Greece, and Luxemburg. From the perspective of a theory of freedom, however, this option is not without its problems.

Also problematic for a living democracy is the low esteem in which "the politicians" are held. It is the reason why, outside the usual reservoirs from which new generations of politicians are drawn — of political scientists, even more so jurists, especially lawyers, moreover teachers (but rarely professors), and various kinds of officials — interest in a career in politics is on the wane. Even among politicians who have already reached higher office, the passion for politics is diminishing. When politics becomes too much work, they follow the last king of Saxony in declaring, "Well, then do your own dirty work!" and switch to (much more lucrative) jobs in the private sector.

Undoubtedly, "the politicians" themselves are partly to blame for this development. There is, at the very least, a danger that politicians turn into a kind of political class. In its tendency to become a power in its own right, which includes the danger of securing advantages ("privileges") for itself and its clientele, this class neglects its strictly subsidiary task, its responsibility toward citizens and the service of the common good. At a minimum, they underestimate the task of sufficiently explaining the many, in part highly difficult issues facing them to the citizenry. Young democracies especially are not immune to relapses into autocracy, corruption, and violence, and even experienced democracies react with clear opportunism in sacrificing long-term perspectives to short-term success.

Despite the problems hinted at, many of the recent criticisms of democracy clearly go too far. The claim, for example, "that we have gone beyond the idea of rule by the people to challenge the idea of rule at all," as Colin Crouch writes in his *Post-democracy*, has garnered much applause.[13] Yet it generalizes the particular experience of Italy and, even more importantly, passes over the moments of coercion no legal order can do without; it thus amounts to a wrong diagnosis.

Emanuel Richter's thesis, in turn, that democracy is to be discovered anew, ignores that there is hardly any alternative to the three classical dimensions of democracy.[14] Even if the precise conception of democracy is a matter of dispute,[15] the core, all three dimensions — that the people rules because all power comes from the people: government *of* the people; that rule serves the people: *for* the people; and that rule is exercised *by* the people — has immense legitimating value. For in the first dimension, the people constitutes rule; in the second, it normalizes rule; and in the third, it organizes rule.

Nondemocratic forms of government might be more efficient, as is sometimes claimed, even if one may well be skeptical of such claims. The People's Republic of China, the preferred example, is not to be compared to the European democracies with their highly developed economics and entirely different cultures, but to a country like South Korea. And South Korea, with its need to catch up economically and its (neo-) Confucian cultural foundations, is much more closely related to China and has achieved, "despite" its democratic system and, moreover, market economy or perhaps even because of them, greater economic success.

Above all, from the perspective of freedom and legitimacy, citizens' political self-organization, democracy, precisely, has primacy. Astonishingly, this primacy is not always taken seriously. After Hans Jonas's (often overlooked) advocacy for an ecological dictatorship, the second world forecast commissioned by the Club of Rome, Jørgen Randers's *2052: A Global Forecast for the Next Forty Years*, too, attributes a greater capacity for promoting the welfare of their collective and that of future generations to authoritarian regimes like China. Once again, counterarguments, though obvious, are not taken seriously enough: it overestimates the viability of forecasts (the scenarios predicted by the first report, *The Limits to Growth*, have not materialized); it overestimates what planning can achieve and at the same time underestimates the possibilities market economies open up; in addition, it lacks differential analyses such as a comparison of China with another country shaped by Confucianism, yet a democracy and market economy, South Korea; and it fails to consider such highly dictatorial regimes as the one in North Korea.[16] Furthermore, even "benevolent dictatorships," if there is such a thing or can be in the long run, cannot escape the problem that states, too, can fail. Moreover, they are interested in the well-being of their country but not in what the Club of Rome is interested in, the well-being of the world as a whole. And last but not least, one must not marginalize the legitimating value constitutional democracies have as such.

11.4
SEVEN CONCEPTUAL ELEMENTS

Since democracy as we know it comes from the Greeks, one might consider the philosophical case for democracy to have a Western bias. Yet, just empirically, democracy is not a purely Western invention. The self-organization of hunter-gatherer societies, which was founded on the coordination and agreement of those concerned, already invalidates the fear that there might be some kind of legal-cultural imperialism at issue. To confront this fear, which is voiced frequently and is by no means always unjustified, the intercultural legal discourses I have called for time and again suggest themselves.

Even if democracy appears in many forms, there is the common core I mentioned. It can be defined in more detail in terms of three dimensions with a total of seven aspects, to which the most fully developed form adds a high degree of participation.[17]

1. The *first* legitimating dimension supplements (1) a formal aspect—rule comes from those concerned (government *of* the people)—with (2) the content aspect that this rule can be justified by every individual concerned ("distributively") and in addition by the totality ("collectively").

   The formal capacity for democracy to achieve a consensus, which legitimizes democratic rule, is thus joined by a universal capacity to achieve a consensus that normalizes it. This is the case where democratic rule, as the guarantee of liberties, benefits each individual (distributively) and in addition the whole (collectively). In the concept of the people, thus, two meanings enter into an indissoluble alliance: every individual must benefit, not in all respects, especially not in every material respect, but on the basic level; this corresponds to a both legitimating and methodological individualism, government *for* the people. Just as indispensably, however, beginning with a common legal order to keep the peace, democracies are communities of cooperation; the functional legitimation is thus expanded by an intrinsic legitimation.

2. Since the first two aspects are both indispensable and complementary, popular sovereignty—government *of* the people—on the fundamental level that includes the third group of human rights, the political liberties or democratic participatory rights, and the combination of a legal order to keep the peace with human rights as liberties—government *for* the people—are of equal rank and origin. This situation, however, contradicts a simple conception of democracy because it ties the pure rule of the people to binding standards.

   Not granted but merely guaranteed by the state, the two guiding tasks, a peaceful order and human rights, do not allow for majority decisions but only for a reflective affirmation and agreement. The *self*-determination of each individual they guarantee is not balanced out by any *co*determination or participation, however great. Legitimating fundamental democracy thus contradicts the kind of organizational total democracy that is unwilling to submit from the start to the guiding tasks just named. A democracy that allows majority decisions on the fundamental human rights violates its legitimacy.

Simple democracy thus must become constitutional democracy (and it is usually practiced as such), which introduces the tension mentioned earlier into the conception of democracy. For the simple conception allows for the absolutist rule of the people free of all restrictions that the well-known criticism of democracy is aimed at, starting with the most important representatives of ancient political philosophy, Plato and Aristotle.[18] Their uncompromising veto against an unbound rule of the people is sustained by the great advocate of individual freedom John Stuart Mill, with his warning against a "tyranny of the majority." Constitutional democracy elevates this veto to a principle, though the scope and import of this veto varies in different constitutions.

In states with a high proportion of direct democracy, it is generally easier to intervene in the existing constitution. If we take the example of Switzerland, however, the aims named in article 2 of the Federal Constitution of the Swiss Confederation and the basic rights such as human dignity (article 7), equality before the law (article 8), the protection against arbitrary conduct (article 9), and the right to life and to personal freedom (article 10), as well as many other elements, are hardly being restricted as to their substance; at most are they supplemented and specified here and there. Other constitutions, like the German Basic Law, for example, state explicitly: "In no case may the essence of a basic right be affected."[19] And according to article 79, section 3, the so-called eternity clause, any change to the Basic Law that would touch on, among others, article 1 (human dignity and acknowledgment of "unalienable human rights"), and the principles laid out in article 20 — the welfare state (section 1), representative democracy (section 2), rule of law (section 3), and right to resistance (section 4)— are inadmissible.

Where in addition to the constitution, there is also a constitutional court, another danger, the opposite to simple democracy, must nonetheless not be denied: the danger that power shifts significantly from the people, exercising this power directly or via elected representatives, to the courts. Not formally but in fact, the courts then engage in a good deal of politics, for which, however, no independent mechanism of control exists (see below, section 12.2).

In the concept of the rule of the people, the second component, the people, remains insufficiently defined in two respects. On the one hand, "people" may mean an entity defined by a shared language, culture, and origin, perhaps also religion and other sociocultural parameters, or it may mean the citizenry constituted by a voluntary act. The former is a "natural" or "ethnic" conception, the latter a "voluntarist" or "constitutional" one.

This juxtaposition, however, is little more than a description of ideal types. For even in ethnically highly homogenous countries such as Japan or Sweden, even more so in Iceland, the people that constitutes the state is a citizenry that has the capacity and the will to live together in acknowledging a shared legal order, a constitution, and to naturalize persons of other ethnic backgrounds according to criteria the most important of which, usually, is acknowledging the legal order. Countries, such as Canada, that are made up of many ethnicities, or multilingual countries, such as Belgium, Switzerland, or again Canada, over several generations develop sociocultural commonalities that they expect newcomers to accept. It is, in any case, the constitutional concept that has normative priority, not a fictive birth nation but a nation of state citizens.[20]

The second need for further definition concerns the normalizing of rule contained in the term "people." For it can be understood in modest or in demanding terms. In the first, "collective" conception, it serves only the whole; in the second, "distributive" conception, it also serves each individual member of the people, which makes the need for legitimacy all the more pressing and results in the already-mentioned tension.

This process begins with the rule of law and develops into the triad of human rights: the negative liberties; the positive liberties; and of course the political liberties, the democratic rights to participation. Where the justice system is corrupt or where media and NGOs cannot work freely, we do not ask whether the majority of the people is protesting. Even if in such cases, we often, albeit imprecisely, speak nonetheless of violations of democracy, we in fact criticize infringements on the rule of law, that is, on the constitutional component of the concept of democracy and not on the simple rule of the people itself.

3. When rule is not merely legitimized but also exercised by the people, the initially pre- and suprapositive notion of fundamental democracy sketched earlier becomes the principle shaping a political polity. Rule-exercising democracy emerges as the *second* dimension. According to the principle of equal freedom, it prohibits both political discrimination in the form of a politically less valuable lower class and political privileges in the form of a politically more valuable upper class. According to equal civil freedom, each citizen has the same right not just to be concerned by public decision-making processes but to participate

in them as a subject and to participate, directly or mediated by representatives, in the elaboration of a constitution, in legislation, and in governing.

When rule is organized democratically, the usual democratic politics takes place: its conflicts about issues and offices; about the goals of domestic and international policies; about the implementation of these goals in laws, decrees, and treaties; about the periodic election of officials including a possible change of government and opposition; and, as the case may be, also about popular initiatives and referenda.

According to the principle "one person, one vote," democratic decisions take place according to the majority principle. Ever since the work of mathematician and political philosopher Condorcet, however, we know that this principle has its pitfalls due to so-called cyclic preferences. Given three options, for example attending a concert (C), an opera (O), or a theater performance (T), three people (P1, P2, P3) prefer different alternatives in a different order: P1 prefers C to O to T, P2 in turn O to T to C, and P3 finally T to C to O. In such a situation, there is no democratically clear decision; what counts instead is the succession in which alternatives are put to a vote: if the first question to be voted on is "C or O," then P1 and P3 vote for C because they prefer the concert to the theater performance, overruling P2. If the alternative, however, is "O or T," the decision is in favor of O, overruling P3, while the question "C or T," finally, will result in a vote for T, and P1 loses.

Even if in political practice cyclic preferences rarely occur with such clarity, they show the pitfalls of the majority principle in two respects. First in setting the agenda for a session: determining the order of votes can influence the decision. Second, the Condorcet paradox affects voter behavior: given three candidates, a voter might like A the best, C the least. If now, instead of voting for her second favorite candidate B, she votes for her favorite candidate A knowing that A has no real chance of winning, she might help her least favorite candidate C win because candidate B is lacking the vote wasted on A.[21]

Another difficulty is concealed in the question whether citizens are willing to shoulder the consequences of their decisions, for example the costs of an energy transition that foreseeably will be very high but are initially downplayed for political reasons.

In representative democracies, the extraordinary weight of parties raises an additional serious problem. At first only political associations that sought to influence public opinion and shape state policy, they have since acquired the monopoly for naming candidates for parliament and, mediated by parliament, the members of the government. More than that: in the considerable expansion of this monopoly, in a downright imperialistic extension of their power that threatens basic democratic traits, parties increasingly name their followers to occupy key posts in government departments, federal and state agencies, public broadcasting, even the higher courts.

New parties like the Pirate Party (which, however, is already disintegrating again) raise expectations that a new method could overcome the (excessive) power of the parties and bring about what has been called a "liquid democracy."[22] Thanks to the digital revolution, each individual citizen is said to have the potential to decide on every issue, which would greatly diminish the weight of parties, should they still be needed at all. Party democracy would be replaced by computer democracy.

In political theory, this expectation is much older and was voiced already by Robert Paul Wolff, for example.[23] It overlooks three things, however: first that the place of decisions so far is not called "parliament" by accident; it is a place where issues are debated, talked about, before decisions are taken. Second, parliamentary debates are accompanied, before, during, and after, by discussions in the political public that give the citizenry an additional right to participation. And third, we must not overestimate the consequences of the digital revolution, namely, the power of social media such as Facebook, Twitter, and so on. The new media may indeed help turn internet campaigns into torrents of protest that force companies, for example, to improve working conditions in developing countries. To become a political power in a country, however, it is still necessary to engage in traditional politics, that is, found a party, organize rallies, talk to people, negotiate, and make compromises. And not least of all, spectacular cases of data theft and data hacking even by so-called allied intelligence services demonstrate the dangers and uncertainties of the digital world in general and of its huge masses of information (big data) in particular (see below, section 12.1). Of course there are gains in security as well, for example when terrorist attacks are prevented.

4. For the guarantee of liberties to become an integral component of the legal order in force that no democratic majority, however large, can override, they must be turned into positive basic rights that bind all public power. This is what a further concept of democracy, the *basic rights concept* of democracy, consists in.
5. According to its *existential* concept, democracy is a lived form of life in which citizens themselves, exercising their political rights, are concerned with and about their polity. The politicians they elect are answerable to them and must accept, especially in a democracy, that the interests, hopes, and fears of the citizens are decisive, which is why in democracies, politics is an *open-ended* form of life.

It takes supportive institutions and mentalities to ensure that the notion of citizens concerning themselves with the polity does not remain a declaration of intent without consequences. The concrete interplay and interlocking of institutions and mentalities makes up the political culture of a polity. In this culture, the liberties acquire the second meaning I announced earlier: they do not merely serve personal freedom in a distributive legitimation, but, in an additional (not, as Joseph Raz would have it, an alternative) legitimation, they serve the existential concept of democracy; they serve the living political culture.[24]

6. To prevent the unbridled exercise of power by a crowd without economic means and with little political ability, feared since Plato and Aristotle, and nonetheless avoid introducing special rights, democracy-promoting conditions must be created that, according to a further, the *social* concept of democracy, justify certain positive liberties as functions of democracy: to convey the intellectual precondition of democratic maturity [*Demokratiemündigkeit*], a certain level of education must be secured.

   Education of course must not stop at knowledge of facts but in addition, and, above all, calls for skills and judgment, which for their part do not at all depend on secondary and higher education. And financially, politically responsible citizens do not require much, something that once again speaks against a nanny state: political maturity is not a question of one's bank account. Even if citizens seek to make a generous livelihood for other reasons — for their political freedom a modest income suffices.

   The thesis that democracy is tied to wealth, or, even better, increasing wealth, is a theory myth widely proffered in the 1970s, for example. Even if it has few backers today, it points to an undoubtedly still-persisting danger, politicians promising their clientele economic advantages.

   This only parenthetically: there is, interestingly enough, a degree of confirmation of the thesis that political maturity does not require great material preconditions coming from a new discipline, socioeconomic physics. By applying the laws of nuclear physics and thermodynamics to human societies, it makes forecasts about the change of political states of aggregation, in particular about the transition of nondemocratic polities to democracy. From the perspective of this branch of research, two factors count in this transition more than others: in addition to a birth rate of less than three children per woman, it takes a certainly rather modest GDP of just \$2,500 to \$4,000 per capita, that is, for a family of four, an annual income of no more than \$10,000 to \$16,000.

7. The *third* dimension, the dimension of foreign policy, opens up a further aspect: that democracy is free not only within but also toward the outside.

Taken together, these aspects, especially numbers (1)–(6), amount to an "enlightened liberal" democracy. In such a democracy, the core of democracy, the rule borne by the participation of the people, combines with a rule of law committed to human rights and the division of powers. As the embodiment of the three powers — the legislative, the executive, and the judiciary — a legal state entity proves to be fundamentally legitimate, unlike a strict anarchism, the utopia of communication free of rule. Unlike a strict legal and political positivism, however, it must not be arbitrarily designed but is committed to the principle of equal freedom, and this combines the legitimation of law and the state with their limitation.

On the condition that the public powers serve a distributive and collective good designed according to general laws, every citizen can, after careful consideration, freely agree to political rule. This ability to agree amounts to a free self-limitation, that is, to the legal figure of a (social) contract, and proves the strictly subsidiary character of a legitimate polity: as an institution of the citizens, the state is not an end itself but instituted for its citizens, which is something it has to prove both generally and individually.

11.5
PARTICIPATORY DEMOCRACY

Further aspects are added in an even more developed form of democracy, called "participatory" or sometimes "republican" democracy. Objectively, these aspects begin with a political public, in which citizens act as the bearers of politics even where they do not directly vote or decide. When public debates acquire significant weight, we speak of deliberative democracy, in which media play a decisive role (see below, section 12.3).

The continuation in participatory democracy takes place in the broader field of self-organization on a voluntary basis, a civic society that establishes a sphere of its own between the private and the public domains (see above, section 8.4). With its large proportion of community service, civic society pursues nongovernmental activity in the general interest. Its personal ideal consists in developing the responsible citizen into an involved citizen. For that reason alone, participatory democracy does not shut the door on elements of direct democracy. Such elements also serve to confront the danger of a quasi aristocracy, for participatory democracy is borne primarily by involved minorities, whose majority in turn belongs to the educated (upper) middle class.

An appreciation of the argumentative character that participatory democracy cannot do without can already be found at the beginnings of Western democracy. In the praise of his hometown written down by Thucydides, the

Athenian statesman Pericles declares: "it is not debate [*logoi*, arguments] that is a hindrance to action, but rather not to be instructed by debate [*logos*] before the time comes for action."[25] In that sense, a democracy may call itself deliberative when its decision-making processes are based on debates, on criticism and countercriticism.

In the course of these processes, first, the four factors constitutive of all politics — interests, opinions, assessments, and values — become known more quickly, namely, even between election days. They also, second, appear in a more differentiated form, namely, not only as part of an often vague complete package embodied in the parties and people running. And not least of all, these factors are exposed to an enlightening clarification: they are given weight, weighed against each other, and declared to be either negotiable and subject to compromise or, as for example in a number of bioethical controversies, beyond all negotiation because they are said to reflect values that cannot be abandoned.

It is evident that no pure clarification can be expected. For political debates are much more short-winded than scientific disputes. Moreover, they are shot through with particular (or more intensely particular) interests and strategic conduct. Finally, the import of factors outside discourse must not be underestimated, neither access to media nor, within media, rhetorical talent, including the Sophistic abuse of this talent.

Fortunately, such dangers are much reduced in an enlightened liberal democracy: by a constitution that commits democracy to human and basic rights; by the separation of powers, especially an independent judiciary; by opening politics to science-based advice; and by a media world that thanks to a well-educated citizenry (although with a preponderance of the middle and upper classes) allows for sophisticated debates, even if in some places the threat of the opposite, an oversimplifying sensationalism, looms.

12

Liberties

According to a principle indispensable to political modernity, the principle of generally compatible freedom, there are human rights, and the core of human rights is constituted by two basic kinds of liberties: The negative liberties protect each individual from infringements coming from others with equal legal standing as well as from state powers. And positive liberties come together in the state objective of a welfare state. This chapter discusses the broad field of liberties in three of its aspects: first an example, data protection (section 12.1); then a problem of guaranteeing liberties, the rule of legal process (section 12.2); and finally a support of the liberties that has become ambivalent, the power of media (section 12.3).

12.1
FOR EXAMPLE: DATA PROTECTION

As our example of a liberty, let's take a young but by no means insignificant right, data privacy protection. If we try to characterize our age with just one word, the term "globalization" practically imposes itself, although, as noted, it must not be economistically reduced to economic and financial markets. If we try to define our age via a single technology, it must be via digitalization or the electronic global network, the internet, which is both the precondition and the dominant medium of globalization. Thanks to the internet, spatial distance becomes less important, events are perceived practically simultaneously across the globe, and information is exchanged within seconds. Not least of all, the revolutionary new forms of audiovisual communication are enormously inexpensive.

Undoubtedly, this process comes with an immense democratic gain. The web, to be sure, does not ensure a globally equal density of devices and their users. Yet wherever the devices are used, all places in the world, and also all persons, companies, and states are treated equally. To participate, neither power nor prestige nor wealth is required. Moreover, the censorship of autocratic states is being undermined, albeit with limited success in some countries.

A further democratic gain lies in search engines like Google and internet encyclopedias like Wikipedia. They offer (1) everyone (2) within seconds (3) access to (almost) the entirety of the world's knowledge. The deprivileging of the then small number of court, monastery, and university libraries begun by Gutenberg's invention of movable type is being perfected. Certainly, access to computing devices and the ability to use them are not given equally everywhere. Yet the digital foundation for a democratization of knowledge still unimaginable just a few decades ago has been laid. And it has been achieved, not from within the world of knowledge, public or private universities, and certainly not from the divisions there that would be responsible, the libraries. Credit must go to entrepreneurs of genius (section 6.2).

The democratic gains are joined by an ecological gain: surfing the web instead of taking a car or a plane saves energy and reduces the toll on the environment. Not least of all, users' legal security is improved because life and limb, at least, remain unendangered.

But the full story is not only one of gains. For in ever more domains of life, ever more data are obtained that are not just potentially but — because of hackers and spies, yet also because of intelligence agencies and internet companies — actually available. Pessimists even believe that people are being abused as *mere* providers of data and forced into modes of thinking of anticipatory conformity. Liberal democracies object to these developments and include data privacy protection in their catalog of liberties.

The topic, to be sure, is not entirely new, for successful protections have long existed as part of a professional ethos: the confessional secret for priests, doctor's confidentiality for physicians, attorney-client privilege for lawyers; and both journalists and intelligence agencies tend to protect their sources. Not least of all, there is the secrecy of correspondence, posts, and telecommunications, the fiscal secret (even if in spectacular cases, it is often violated), and the (increasingly loosened, of course) bank secret.

Yet the digital revolution has given a qualitatively and quantitatively new dimension to this familiar topic. Initially developed only as a both efficient and sophisticated aid to memory and especially to mental processing, digitalization with its almost universal applicability has now developed a power of its own that has already profoundly transformed work and leisure, private and public action, and forms of communication, institutions, as well as self-perceptions, and it will continue to do so. Already, a new relationship of human beings to their social, linguistic, probably also the natural world, and undoubtedly a new relationship of the human to itself, to both the intellectual and the emotional aspect of the self, are taking shape.[1] Fortunately, though, the digital revolution cannot create a new human being: the transformation of the *Homo sapiens* into a *Homo digitalis* is beyond its reach.

Let me preface the detailed discussion of the example of data privacy protection with a general assessment that rejecting the oppositional pair of risk and opportunity rejects two extreme attitudes, both a whining cultural criticism and a progress euphoria. The first attitude is contradicted already by the chances the internet opens up for freedom: the most famous and most used encyclopedia is no longer the *Brockhaus*, nor is it the *Encyclopædia Britannica*; it is an encyclopedia that is elaborated not by a well-defined editorial staff but, participatorily, by an anonymous community of users, an encyclopedia that is, moreover, free, and that has become quite reliable: Wikipedia. Mere euphoria, however, is tempered by the wide variety of possible misuses already hinted at. There is also the danger that we degenerate from information giants to knowledge dwarves because the fast output of "raw," unprocessed data alienates us from "cooked," processed knowledge.[2]

A presentation of data protection best begins with the observation that the name obscures the meaning the issue has for freedom, for it dries it out, narrows it down, pins it down, and at the same time plays it down. For data are givens, facts, in the domain of computing primarily in the form of encodable information. Yet what is to be protected above all is neither things nor givens but rather people. And about people, there is information that is highly sensitive and reaches to the very core of personhood: information about income, spending, fortune, investments, and debts; about possible acute, chronic, or hereditary diseases; about all sorts of preferences, temperament and emotions, skills, talents, and much more besides. In a word: the expression "data protection" sounds like a term from property law when in fact it names a personal right.

Data are not harmless facts but keys to the inner reaches of personality, to the strictly private, a realm that not only in the West, but for example also in the Arabic term *harem*, names the innermost domain that lies beyond the reach both of the polity, the state, and of other private persons. "Private" designates a free space initially prohibited to all others, exemplarily manifest in the inviolability of the home: "my home is my castle," access to which I can refuse to anyone.

In public law, the one who has the right to make the final decision is called sovereign. The analogue of this sovereignty in the private domain is freedom, and it belongs to the person concerned — and to no one else. That is why in principle, everyone is free to decide which personal data they reveal and how it is used. The question of who knows something about me, the further question of what they know about me, and finally the question of how they came to know it — concerning all three questions, everyone has a right to control.

The answer to the question why the private domain must be protected is evident: the issue is the human being in its autonomy or freedom and at the same time the moral source from which all liberties derive, namely, human dignity, here to be understood as the right to live according to one's own desires, interests, and needs. This is nothing less than the core of living one's own life. For a conventional as well as an unconventional and idiosyncratic life to be possible, this core must be protected against arbitrary intervention both by the state and by nongovernmental agents. No one is to be bound to a past, but everyone, rather, ought to have an open future, a chance at developing — with one proviso: as long as they stay within the framework of established law.

True privacy exists where — despite the difficulties of keeping electronic interactions confidential — I myself control access to my own person, where I am able, as it were, to draw up the bridge to my castle at any moment, indeed, where there is no duty that I ever let the bridge down.

To illustrate this point, let's take a look at personal behavior, then at the political arena. The first look encounters phenomena of self-exposure that quite frequently, in excessive activity on social networks such as Facebook and Twitter, for example, escalate to an "electronic exhibitionism." There are also the services by banks, insurance companies, and other institutions that are offered as "free" but are in fact paid dearly, namely, by disclosing personal data. And the price displayed on our screens when we buy movie and theater, train and plane tickets, books or other goods on the web is joined by an additional price that is not displayed, the personal data we reveal.

The second look is at law and government. If a preeminent legal value — and we may call life, limb, and liberty of the person preeminent — is under threat, not a vague but a well-defined threat, then the state may intervene. Yet the demand, articulated in a EU directive, that European Union member states retain the data of telecommunication companies and internet service providers for the purposes of future law enforcement activity can hardly be subsumed under the notion of a well-defined threat.[3] Fortunately, the European Court of Justice decided against this so-called data retention.

In addition, there is the international dimension of, for example, surveillance programs even of "friendly" states that by far exceed even a very generously conceived scope. Many generations were proud of overcoming tyranny;

now democracies turn themselves over to a "tyranny of algorithms," more precisely, of data searches and data retention, where an instrument employed to secure freedom, particularly in fighting terrorism, on balance ends up destroying freedom.

A further look at the political arena realizes that for a polity to flourish, the economy must flourish, for it is the economy that provides goods, services, and jobs, which in turn make taxes and with them financing the welfare state possible. Now, one of the main pillars of a flourishing economy is trade or business secrets. A legislature that intervenes here under the pretext of security does not only undermine the rule of law. It also threatens economic welfare, and thus the welfare of science and culture that at least in part depend on it.

If the state is to fulfill its task of providing legal protection against crime, it undoubtedly needs information; yet, also for the sake of legal protection, protecting the right to informational self-determination this time, it may not acquire this information in just any way nor to just any degree. The core of the problem thus consists in two competing aspects of protecting freedom, protection from criminal violence and protection from state power.

The therapy follows from this diagnosis: the core problem of data privacy law can be resolved only in the form of an evaluation. There is no catch-all formula; instead, just as in the case of dangerous knowledge (see above, section 9.3), it takes judgment and moderation and, in this case, functioning oversight as well. The evaluation can indeed lead to different results. Britons for example consider security to be of such importance that they quietly allow both omnipresent cameras and their intelligence services to surveil them.

There are, in all events, three objections to an unbounded greed for information on the part of the state. First, security quite often is no concrete personal equivalent I would benefit from specifically; rather, it is a general equivalent that helps an abstract collective in a general way. Second, it contradicts an elementary legal principle, the principle of proportionality: to ferret out dangerous wrongdoers, a group that accounts for probably a fraction of a fraction of 1 percent, much too large a part of society is placed under suspicion. Third, the lesson to be drawn from the fight against terrorists in the 1970s is "Less is more!" As we know, the decisive tip from a local resident about where the kidnapped president of the employer's federation, Hanns Martin Schleyer, was being held was lost at the time in the data trash produced by the dragnet investigation.

The state's hunger for information raises another problem, often overlooked: the state also owns innumerable data obtained in perfectly legitimate ways. Among other things, it collects and administers enormous amounts of data on social security, transportation, crime, and private and public finances and their transformations. Where do these data go for the citizen? Are they published in more than excerpts? Are they not a public good to which citizens should have open access? And should they not also have access to the masses of data gathered by the companies that dominate the market, such as Google, Facebook, and Amazon?

Hence this concluding thesis: for pragmatic reasons already, yet more so for reasons that pertain to the rule of law and the theory of freedom, liberal democracy declares that it does not want to know, in the form of explorable data, everything it could know.

12.2
INSTEAD, THE RULE OF LEGAL PROCESS

Undoubtedly, rule of law is required to guarantee the liberties and to guard against legal privileges as against discrimination and corruption. Only with the help of the rule of law can the danger of arbitrariness be contained and are government agencies and the courts subjected to effective control.

Theodor W. Adorno's *Minima Moralia* contains the frequently quoted phrase "wrong life cannot be lived rightly."[4] The sentence (referring in Adorno to the "Western" form of life) undoubtedly applies to dictatorships as well as to societies dominated by organized violence and corruption, for there it is possible to be compelled into actions one would prefer to refuse, for example in order to protect one's family. Where rule of law is lacking, it can become very difficult to maintain decency and dignity. Not everyone possesses or is willing to display the great deal of cleverness and courage, heroism even, that is then required. This is where the rule of law comes in, for it allows ordinary people, too, to live honestly and with self-respect.

For this unquestionably good reason, the rule of law in constitutional democracies is anchored at the most fundamental level, in the constitution (in Germany's Basic Law, for example, in article 20, section 3). If the rule of law is bound to the principles guiding constitutional democracies, basic rights and human rights and the principle that both supports and outranks them, human dignity, then pathos is not out of place: such rule of law is a civilizational achievement that must not be abandoned nor even put in jeopardy.

Nonetheless, it is not beyond all criticism. What deserves criticism, however, is not the basic idea of the rule of law but a number of aspects of its manifestations in reality. Criticism that attributes to the normative aspect of the rule of law an "ugly flipside," namely, "obstinacy" and "indeed occasionally inhumanity," thus overshoots the mark.[5] For the rightly demanded consideration of individual situations belongs to the core domain of the rule of law. Its symbol, the blindfold of Justice, stands for impartial judgment without exception of person but not for blindness to the individual case that may indeed turn out to be the exception. According to a basic principle of reaching a judgment, and undoubtedly of judges reaching their verdicts as well, the first thing to do is to explore the facts of the case in their individuality.

A possible criticism has to start elsewhere, at a more fundamental level, with the fact that to become real, the rule of law requires the rule of legal process. This is a necessity, certainly. For a rule of law that lacks efficient legal processes, that lacks ways, for instance, to ensure someone's right in a civil court or someone else's right to a fair trial in criminal court, remains a stale assurance, an empty claim, without any serious attempt being made at making the law a reality. For the sake of objecting to arbitrariness, for the sake of impartiality, legal processes must be normalized in turn. This normalization, however, must not forget that it is not an end in itself but that it serves a purpose, that the law requires it.

The rule of legal process includes an occasionally exhausting but hard-to-criticize element: the several stages of appeal. They contribute to right winning in the end, despite the possibility of error that can never be excluded in the affairs of fallible human beings.

Things are different when it comes to the fact that under the rule of legal process, legal procedure increasingly comes to dominate the state. Naturally, procedures are indispensable, but they also allow for abuse; sometimes they even invite it. The action in such instances is legal but nonetheless contributes to right being left behind. Jury trials in the United States, as if made for television, are clear evidence that de facto guilt and final verdict are two different things, that, in stark terms, guilt and verdict have nothing to do with each other.

Moreover, care is to be taken that the normalization that has been on the rise in many areas does not infringe on personal freedom. Normalization appears in different forms, of course. In some fields, in trade law, for example, norms have become ever denser; in others, "only" a tightening of existing regulations is taking place. In yet other domains, the large number of court decisions to be taken into account is reason for complaints. Within Europe, there is in addition the constantly growing number of EU directives and regulations. And in some areas, in the work of physicians, for example, documentation requirements are expanding to such an extent that here as elsewhere complaints about a freedom-restricting bureaucratization are justified.

An assessment of these different phenomena from the perspective of freedom must not take the easy way out. For at least some of them display, on closer inspection, a dilemma of actual freedom: often set up to sustain ever-new aspects of positive freedom, increasing normalization and bureaucratization on balance restrict freedom once more. In addition, administrative tasks require ever more time and effort in practically all domains. In the health-care system, in science and research, in business—presumably because of a lack of trust (and is it always justified?)—the bureaucracy restricts the freedom of doctors, entrepreneurs, and scientists if only through the sheer amount of time documentation requires. Other consequences include the spreading of defensive behavior, of defensive medical practices, for example, by doctors who for fear of litigation do not apply certain treatments.

Nor must we overlook that the increasing bureaucratization expands the power of lawyers and courts: we are approaching a rule that contradicts the basic democratic notion of the separation of powers, a rule of the justice system.

Not least of all, the natural sense of right is being disempowered. Not only are ordinary citizens no longer able to find their way through the flood of norms; their sense of right no longer even allows for making an assessment "by rule of thumb." Even more incisive from the perspective of a theory of freedom is the restriction of freedom operated in the name of freedom. Not infrequently, though, the restriction takes place no longer "in the name of freedom" but in the name of needs and interests government is expected to satisfy. In so doing, the state moves away from its core mission. The guarantee of liberties is replaced with material demands, and the state degenerates into a service provider.

There are two more phenomena to be cited, which often are not included under the heading of the rule of law. The first can be explained by way of the example of asylum law. The Western democracies are not only under the rule of law but, in their majority, wealthy as well. Understandably, they thus become a destination for citizens of poor countries. Yet since from the perspective of the rule of law, mere poverty is not a sufficient reason for a right to immigrate, the right to asylum is often invoked, a right that is undisputed in many places and, in Germany, even constitutionally guaranteed. Yet as we know, the majority by far of asylum seekers does in fact belong to the group of economic refugees. Once such refugees are in the country, asylum procedures can last for so long that a large share of this group remains in the country although there can be no question, often predictably, of granting them asylum status. Individually and structurally, one may indeed speak here of a misuse of the rule of legal process.

The second phenomenon does not directly constitute a misuse but consists in an extension or rather overstretching of competencies. The Roman Empire applied the rule *Roma locuta, causa finita*: when the appropriate legal authority in the capital has spoken, the case is closed once and for all. This privilege in Germany today belongs to the Constitutional Court. That it often makes wise decisions is undisputable, and it is highly respected not only in Germany but far beyond its borders. Yet there also is a danger that the Constitutional Court does not always evade.

Instead of giving scope to politics and the societal debates that belong to the political process, rulings are handed down that, unlike the decisions made by politicians, cannot be contested and are in practice never revised: *Karlsruhe locuta, causa in aeterna finita*.[6] The chances for a countermovement, that justices, once elected, would restrict the powers wielded by their predecessors, are slim. The culture of judicial self-restraint is much less alive in Germany than it is in one of the models, the United States Supreme Court.[7]

12.3
MEDIA DEMOCRACY?

The importance media, especially print media, have for democracy is well known and in principle uncontested. To be sure, a truly structural change has been underway in the world of media for some time, since "opinions" are increasingly formed in the new social media. Yet, with a pinch of optimism, we may still refer to newspapers as the media "where civil society encounters itself, the sphere where politics, economy, and culture are reflected."[8]

The media the public cannot do without are not just a forum where interests and opinions are voiced. They are also an arena where influence and power are fought for and a critical authority before whom all of government, including the judiciary, is held accountable. Since a functioning public also gives voice to the opposition, it moreover contributes to domestic peace.

As an essential part of a public they both create and are, media, from the perspective of a theory of democracy and of freedom, have a responsibility with at least four dimensions. If we leave the task of entertainment aside, which is (despite protests to the contrary) indifferent to democracy, media are to (1) inform citizens; (2) provide citizens with a platform for political debate; (3) control the power of the powerful and criticize where necessary; and (4) warn against looming threats before it is too late. Because no democracy and in particular no participatory democracy is possible without the appropriate media, freedom of the press belongs to the liberties that are the most important for political culture.

With regard to these four tasks, media are often called the Fourth Estate. In keeping with their very essence, however, they constitute themselves at a distance from the three "official" powers, which suggests that the moniker may not be appropriate. They also lack the transparency and moreover the legitimacy public powers usually have; at most, there is the quasi legitimation of citizens paying for media voluntarily (public media excepted).

However, the media have indeed become at least a quasi power; no longer essentially only accompanying and checking public power, they now share in it. Fortunately, though, the view sometimes voiced that democracy is degenerating into a talk show republic where television panels dispute parliament's status as the main forum of (representative) democracy derives from a superficial analysis.

An open and at the same time fair assessment does not declare that media in democratic polities have abandoned the many facets of their work for democracy. Norbert Bolz's thesis that journalists live on the delusion of revealing the truth undoubtedly has made an impact in the media and might even be welcomed by professional critics, but it overshoots the mark.[9] It is correct that not all print and visual media make an effort to explain and clarify and that where it happens nonetheless, such efforts are devalued.

Yet those of us who are interested in such enlightening efforts still find a great deal of journalism to provide them. Not just an older public, even young people aged twelve to nineteen in a recent study on media consumption credited not the internet (19 percent), nor radio and television (25 percent) but the newspapers (48 percent)—the medium, it seems, most open to enlightenment—with the greatest credibility.[10] The backdrop to these figures is an authority gained only in the long term and "in only one way": "through knowledge, prudence, dependability, through freely justified judgments that are being submitted for discussion."[11]

It is also correct, however, that further tasks infringe on the fourfold responsibility. For example, the entertainment sought for the sake of attracting a wide reader- or viewership "forces" even public television to broadcast a whole host of soap operas and crime shows that, first, reduce the chances more serious issues have at being perceived; that, second, leaving actors and cinematography aside, are of inferior quality; and that, third, increasingly operate in their subtext a popular education that some might call "enlightenment" but that annoys truly "free spirits."

In their quest for ratings and high circulation figures, media seek attention, partly for journalistic, partly for commercial reasons. This goal is more easily attained by means of exaggerations and by stirring emotions, which is why the opposite movements of enlightenment, agitation and alarmism, are so popular. Even intellectuals devoting themselves to enlightenment know that talk of an "apocalypse," for example, attracts more attention or even creates attention in the first place.[12]

The attempts made by some journalists to become masters of the contents and orientations of public debate, fortunately, come up against limits. Catastrophic flooding or movements for independence, never-ending civil wars, corruption, or poverty, are not brought about by journalists talking or writing about them. Nor can journalists really change the basic structure that dominates constitutional democracies: politics views its actions in the mirror of the media, and the media report and criticize. The criticism, however, does not have to remain fair, and where the occasion arises, media gladly make use of their power.

One example of such an exercise of power is the so-called *Energiewende*, the energy transition in Germany, which I would like to assess here not as to its merits but as to the process by which it was decided. It is without a question problematic when a generation feels entitled to leave to future generations a highly hazardous form of energy. Yet since a large number of nuclear power plants have been established around the world, what counts now, when the problem of nuclear waste repositories has existed for many years, is the way in which and the speed at which nuclear power is being phased out. This applies all the more to Germany, which decided on the phase-out as an objective quite some time ago.

Because ever since the "nuclear death" movement of the 1960s and the antinuclear movement of the 1980s, a significant portion of journalists had pursued a quick phase-out, their coverage of the Fukushima disaster was dominated not by empathy with the victims of the tsunami, the thousands of casualties and even larger number of people made homeless, but by coverage of the release of radioactivity. And even there, they were interested less in precise diagnoses, neither as relates to the earth- and seaquakes that are unlikely to occur at such amplitudes in Germany, nor as regards the higher technical safety of German nuclear power plants or the significantly better-functioning security checks. The reports and editorials, shot through with more or less partial comments, exercised a de facto constraint on the government then in place even though nuclear power had already been declared a transitional technology, that is, a source of energy to be used only for a limited time. First, instead of having detailed plans concerning future energy supplies ready and, second, having already taken significant steps toward implementing these plans, Germany's government decided the energy transition overnight.

The marine wind farms required, for example, had not been built yet and still today pose technical difficulties, and the necessary power lines are not in place either but instead are likely to encounter innumerable obstacles.

Furthermore, other challenges such as setting up an intelligent grid or standardizing the technology required for transmitting electricity and regulating the grid across Europe had hardly been considered. Not least of all, proponents denied what by now they admit: that energy costs are rising significantly.

According to an early advocate of freedom, Thucydides, one of the secrets of freedom lies in courage. Journalists and politicians alike display courage when they refuse to submit to the diktat I just outlined and demand that sober debate replace near-hysterical indignation.

From the perspective of democracy theory, the increased power of journalists is not unproblematic. Supposed to serve as constant critical observers of politics as well as the economy and culture of democratic freedom, their power forcefully intervenes in this freedom. The roles are thereby reversed: the servant becomes the master. Neither authorized by elections nor controlled by the public (even just unsympathetic letters to the editor are not infrequently suppressed), the media enter into competition with the elected representatives of the people. Largely beyond the reach of the usual democratic control mechanisms, some of them engage in what, on occasion, they reproach others with, an "economical" way of dealing with the truth.

A further development is more threatening: ambitious journalists want to produce the news rather than just report it; the story about a scandal is more important to them than the scandal itself. They even take the motto (rejected by Kant)[13] *fac et excusa*, act now, make excuses later, one step further: they do not even make excuses and instead embellish this refusal with the cynical argument that although it could not be proven that politicians or other so-called public persons were involved in the alleged scandal, the accusation is considered valid because of the way the accused reacted, because of the way they mishandled the crisis.[14] And when the whole affair turns out to have been distorted, perhaps even made up completely, the accused at best recover respect but practically never their earlier position.

Yet another problem is posed by the preponderance of the visual: succinct images leave a deep impression, certainly, but they rarely do justice to convoluted and tricky problems. Moreover, new digital techniques make it increasingly easy to manipulate images.

Finally, there are indirect manipulations, such as publishing and commenting on opinion polls shortly before an election. What looks like basic journalistic service then becomes active politics (even if the primary aim is to increase circulation) because, as we know, a considerable proportion of undecided voters switches to the suspected winner's side.

Such developments, however, might be due more to the ever more difficult market situation than to a will to political power. Thus, for example, a large share of the previously so lucrative business with classified and other ads has moved from newspapers to other media without income from electronic subscriptions being able to compensate sufficiently for the losses.

Another problem: while in the 1950s and 1960s, self-respecting politicians avoided appearing in the yellow press, they now feel honored by interview requests. Even if the influence of tabloids must not be overestimated — their political content accounts for only a small share — two tendencies are being reinforced here: the inclination of public debate toward sensationalism and the scandalization of politics just mentioned.

Allow me, for the sake of warning against this danger, to put it in stark terms: under the cloak of enlightening revelation, the yellow press offers journalistic fast food, namely, simplification, exaggeration, and an extreme personalization, while the gossip pages delight as much in glamor as in the indiscretions of the rich and famous. In addition, they move from one scandal or affair to the next, a development for which readers, of course, are partly responsible, namely, insofar as a large number of them constantly seek new thrills but dislike dwelling on a topic. Since no audience maintains its emotions in a constant state of alert, since moreover thrill seekers are better served elsewhere, namely, by watching crime shows, a good part of alarming news sinks to the level of event-driven political entertainment. Fortunately, real-life politicians still rely on reviewing a broad spectrum of news; good politicians reflect on the media situation as a whole, and superior, poised politicians do not let themselves be compelled into permanent re-action. And a responsible citizenry is impressed by familiarity with the issues rather than by spectacular statements or elegant appearances on stage.

Quite obviously the development I have sketched in deliberately bold strokes is dangerous from the perspective of democracy theory. It gravely violates the ideal of politicians explaining to citizens what policies they consider to be reasonable. In a first restriction of the ideal, politicians are guided by opinion polls; in a second, they react by anticipating the reactions they expect from the press; and in a third, they seek to appear in the media as often as possible, preferably on the television news. This triple restriction of the ideal promotes not well-considered but spectacular words and not infrequently leads less to prudent than to attention-seeking decisions.

Add to this the new electronic media. Blogs, Twitter, and the like do indeed develop a potential that fosters democracy and at the same time freedom. They allow many citizens a new kind and a greater degree of participation. And politicians are able to reach people entirely unfamiliar with the traditional ways of political presentation such as town hall meetings, rallies, and newspaper interviews.

As is the case with practically every technology, however, here too, there are abuses and negative flipsides. In particular, there is the danger of electronic mobbing and so-called shitstorms, a term that designates waves of indignation that go out of control. Moreover, the electronic network forces an ever-higher reaction speed, which superior politicians, however, refuse to follow; they neither want to be reachable at all times nor immediately voice an opinion on any and all issues because they avoid the danger, as a witticism has it, of not knowing at noon what they'll have to deny at night.

Phenomena of acceleration have long been noted; Goethe already complained about the "velociferous" (from Latin *velocitas*, rapidity, speed) character of modernity.[15] According to Hermann Lübbe, there is a shrinking of the present that is being compensated for by an increasing interest in the past, for example in exhibitions.[16] Yet Lübbe is talking about the time *before* the triumph of electronic media and the compensation he notes is more social than political. More relevant to the current situation is the thesis by a later author, Hartmut Rosa, that we are witnessing "a process of social acceleration that has been underway for almost three hundred years now,"[17] which he supports with a broad spectrum of acceleration phenomena and of which he sketches the consequences for social change and the lifestyles of individuals, including a loss of self-determined living he calls "alienation." In this section, however, we are concerned with only a small part of the phenomenon, the influence electronic media exercise on politics.

The impatience that dominates the new media, their inability to wait, their "Now!" promotes a politics constantly on the rush and thereby, as is to be expected, rushed decision-making.[18] And where little can be done, politics becomes merely symbolical. One example are the terrifyingly high unemployment rates among young people prevailing in many European countries since the early 2010s. They have occasioned summit meetings and prompted financial aid, actions that often distract from more profound causes, from structural problems.

The wide variety of phenomena indicated — pars pro toto: the rhythm of the internet — makes something that democracy generally, and participatory democracy in particular, requires more difficult: taking one's time, time to think about something, time to debate it, and the time it takes for consultation and participation in order, in the end, to make a well-considered, mature decision.

The change I have outlined raises two interlocking questions: how much speed and how much merely symbolic politics can our democracy bear? Let's look at the urgent tasks incumbent on us: in the mid-2010s, these undoubtedly include, domestically and on the European level, the still-ongoing Euro and financial crisis; the still-horrendous public debt, which is not the result of investments in the future and which is manageable only because of extraordinarily low interest rates and plentiful tax revenue; the demographic transformation, especially the decreasing number of young people in many Western societies; moreover, rising health-care costs; lack of funding for higher education; decaying transportation infrastructure.

On the international level — to add a few issues without claiming to be systematic — there are innumerable serviceable weapons of mass destruction; perennial conflicts in the Middle East; the question of Afghanistan; the many countries without a minimum of rule of law; population growth; the horribly high level of hunger and misery; and, not least of all, there is, despite impressive progress in international law, no global legal order.

None of these problems, obviously, can be solved quickly. The snail's pace, at best, at which many steps forward are taking place is enough to cause despair. But at the speed dictated by the media, we will certainly not master these things. And because it is still called on to act, politics, unfortunately, has one more reason to act now precipitately, now only symbolically.

12.4
SUMMARY

Let's summarize, at this intermediary stage, the three aspects of the liberties that are significant for freedom discussed here by way of example. In each aspect, we found, beside opportunities for freedom, a considerable potential of dangers as well. The first aspect, the World Wide Web, once hailed as the medium of communication in an unregulated freedom from all hierarchies, has over the years led to huge masses of data, so-called big data, that are being misused both commercially by private companies and politically by the intelligence services even of Western democracies.[19] We may call this development an aporia of freedom: a medium of anarchic freedom degenerates into the perfect space of control.

A similar aporia appears, although fortunately in attenuated form, in the rule of legal process. Even law committed to freedom, of course, needs clearly normalized legal processes to become real. The procedures created to this end, however, run the risk of abandoning the subservient character and to put on the airs of an end in itself that endangers substantial law.

Finally, the danger in the case of media, which are indispensable in controlling political power, is that they become a power of their own, developing, in some respects, an overwhelming power. Fortunately, there is a counterpower in which the political freedom of those who bear responsibility comes out into the open: superior politicians maintain their supremacy over against the media, and responsible citizens shy away from fast-food media and instead award those outlets that focus the power of the "Fourth Estate" on the business of democracy.

13

Minimal Citizen, State Citizen, World Citizen

For a long time, political philosophy focused on social institutions and systems. Politics appeared as an interest-driven struggle for power. The subjects from whom, nevertheless, all political power derives in a democracy were neglected. This neglect is remedied by the study of citizen identity. The decisive subject, the citizen, must however not be reduced to the citizen in the narrow sense, the citizen of a state, nor must the citizen's civic virtues be forgotten. Even if we considered the state citizen to be the most important aspect, we must not pass over the others, especially since they influence how people live as state citizens. The civic virtues — sense of right, sense of justice, and civic sense — in turn contribute to the welfare of democracy and therefore belong to the core of an enlightened liberalism.

When it comes to citizenship, recent English-language debates are often content with two, sometimes three dimensions. Citizenship begins with being a legal citizen to whom civil, political, and social rights ("legal status") pertain. It continues with the state citizen, who, as "political agent," is actively working in political institutions, evoking civic virtues, and who, because of this activity, has model character. The newer, third dimension is concerned with the citizen as member of a political, identity-instituting community, as what I call the communitarian or community citizen.[1]

Anglophone scholarship furthermore distinguishes between two models for the second dimension: one that emphasizes the negative liberties, a liberal model that foreshortens enlightened liberalism; and a republican model of state citizens governing themselves said to go back to Aristotle, Machiavelli's *Discorsi*, and Rousseau. (In the term's original meaning, of course, *republic* is opposed to monarchy, which is why the German legal tradition in this context speaks of a *free state*.) In the republican model, the citizen is regarded above all as a public person, a state citizen; in the (reductive) liberal model, in contrast, as a private person interested in commerce, as economic citizen.

At first sight, these concepts are undoubtedly helpful; a closer look finds clear weaknesses. For beside the state citizen, the economic citizen, and the community citizen, there is, at the very least, the fourth person of the cultural and educational citizen. Made up of ministers, teachers, professors, and journalists, this group plays an eminent role across generations, presumably not just in Germany. Besides, the three dimensions of citizen identity intermesh. And the third, communitarian dimension, moreover, has so many facets that it does not represent a homogeneous entity. Furthermore, it seems that a different interpretation of the first two dimensions is more appropriate to the subject. And finally, we should not forget a fifth dimension, the world or cosmopolitan citizen.[2]

Because of all these reservations and additions, this chapter does not follow the anglophone debate, which, moreover, here as elsewhere, is largely concerned only with itself. In provincial complacency, it takes advantage of its linguistic dominance and, with the exception of translations of the classics, hardly takes note of debates in other linguistic and cultural spheres.

Historically, political modernity begins with the vision of the enlightened citizen.[3] It develops or becomes more specific in the vision of the emancipated, later the responsible citizen, which in recent decades has culminated in the notion of the involved, the participatory citizen.

It makes sense to orient the identity of today's citizen toward these visions, that is, toward enlightenment, many-faceted emancipation, and involved participation, because a significant share of contemporary questions of identity can easily be referred to them. Such references tend to be reduced to current, often emotionally charged topics. In contrast, this study takes the liberty of offering a more comprehensive and, with regard to current debates and the visions just cited, more sober view. It does not, of course, shut its eyes to current difficulties. It also perceives additional, in part more fundamental problems even if such a perception contradicts the dominant zeitgeist. Serious philosophy seeks to capture its time in concepts, not to reduce it to a fashionable zeitgeist.

According to the methodological maxim *sōzein ta phainomena* (section 1.7), my reflections are structured in seven steps. I begin with a tension in the main concept (section 13.1). According to another methodological maxim, the complementarity of ascent and descent, the next step takes us down to an extreme restriction of identity, to the minimal citizen (section 13.2). The minimal citizen's identity, however, is static and abstract, which in the methodological step up urges the question of the inherently dynamic identity that is being lived concretely (section 13.3). Here, religion can occasion conflicts (section 13.4), an issue that the following reflections on intercultural penal law (section 13.5) and three figures of the involved state citizen (section 13.6) follow up on. The last step is a brief summary supplemented by a conjecture (section 13.7).

13.1
TENSIONS IN THE CONCEPT OF IDENTITY

At first sight, the content seems clear and uncontroversial: identity means a kind of equality or even sameness. Yet it occurs on two levels, on the one hand as species identity or, in the terms of social theory, as the identity of a larger or smaller group, as collective identity; on the other, as an identity in number, as numerical identity or the identity of a natural person.

This is the first complication. The question of a citizen's identity may ultimately aim at the second level, at an individual's personal identity. Yet collective identities are of such importance to individual identity that personal identity can largely be defined as a bundle of collective identities. This bundle, of course, looks different, and also more or less individual, for each person. We are born into at least a part of collective identity, especially into a polity or, more rarely, into statelessness, but also into a certain linguistic sphere and into a religious community or into not belonging to one.

Such identity factors are givens, they are not matters of personal freedom, and yet, paradoxically, they make a constructive contribution to freedom. As citizens of a state, we benefit from the protection of the state and, at least in constitutional democracies, enjoy negative and positive liberties. Without a language or a well-defined multilinguality, the capacity for thinking and communicating that real freedom requires cannot develop. And insofar as religious communities aid in leading meaningful and upright lives, they strengthen human freedom—something critics, however, deny for some or all communities. Later in our lives we can confront these givens and, as the case may be, emigrate from a polity, switch to a different linguistic sphere, or enter into a different religious community or indeed leave all such communities. States or religions that prohibit this create significant obstacles to personal freedom and are, for their part, deeply unfree.

In the modern societies of the West, the degree of individuality is probably rather high, presumably higher than in many other societies. If this hypothesis turns out to be true, it has the paradoxical consequence that collective identities shape not just the kind but also the extent of an identity's individuality. It is for that reason that we should move away from the dominant anglophone debate in yet another respect: citizen identity should not be discussed globally and generally but with reference to the modern Western type of society. In addition, contemporary globalization does not merely expand the facets of today's citizen identity. It has also led to two diametrically opposed developments that create a further problem: the first development, the global approximation of forms of societies to each other, is opposed, especially in non-Western societies, by an emphasis on the nonglobal, on what is special and one's own. This countermovement claims a right without which globalization would lose a significant measure of legitimacy: it claims a right to difference.

This fact exhorts the identity debates raging in the West to be more modest. Because from an empirical perspective, the right to difference is in fact being exercised, questions of identity come up differently in many non-Western countries. And because, now from a normative perspective, exercising this right is justified under well-defined conditions, Western identity debates should not implicitly, never mind explicitly, play themselves up as generally relevant. With the indexical "Western," they should accept their limitation, already on the level of content, and remain open to differently structured, non-Western debates; more than that: they should engage in intercultural legal discourse (see section 13.5).

Within the West, too, the right to difference must be respected. One might object to James Tully's tendency, for example, to transpose his own, Canadian situation, with its two constitutive linguistic spheres in addition to the indigenous peoples, to societies where fundamental cultural differences have largely emerged not a long time ago but only thanks to more recent immigration.[4]

13.2
MINIMAL CITIZEN

Even exclusively Western modern citizen's identity is a convoluted and tricky phenomenon. From a legal-bureaucratic perspective, it is based on elements that include legal documents such as identity cards and passports and are not specific to the West. Issued by the relevant authorities, such documents attest that someone belongs to a polity recognized under international law, to the state. This purely legal belonging makes the citizen a state citizen. Additional entries — photograph, date of birth, eye color, and so on — serve to identify the person in question as the state citizen cited.

Only parenthetically: some citizens have several passports. Under special circumstances, dual or even triple citizenship can make sense. In generously granting these, however, four aspects should be considered. First, there is a concern about justice: because the state citizen belongs to the authority, the nation, from whom all the state's power derives, double citizenship doubles this basic civil right, membership in the political sovereign. This membership is a privilege and like all privileges discriminates against the nonprivileged.

According to a second argument, citizenship can come with further, not so basic and yet significant advantages, such as the right to acquire real estate or works of art, which grants additional privileges to those who possess the citizenship of more than one country. A third concern pertains to the justice of choosing between the protections offered by different countries, possibly even using them against each other. And in the case of military service, it becomes possible to choose where one will serve, with some choosing the more comfortable options, others serving in a country whose military engages in actions criticized by the other. The fourth concern, immigrants ignoring the task of identifying with their new country, raises the question of identity. Not the least of dangers is that foreign politicians take the liberty of interfering in the other country's domestic affairs via speeches and appeals. And there is something that is quite simply shameful: an issue with such long-term consequences as multiple citizenship, not infrequently, is being sacrificed in favor of short-term party political or coalition-government interests.

Back to passport identity. It represents a minimal identity that, already because of its minimal nature but additionally because it is much older than globalization, is able to undermine the opposing developments of globalization: without infringing on the right to difference, passport identity is an identity accepted across the globe and provides one more reason for the right to be an accepted member of a polity and not to have to live as a stateless person.

Some Western citizens mock their state identity, which they often discredit as the identity of a nation-state. In our part of the world, they prefer being just Europeans, and on the global scale they think of themselves as mere citizens of the world. Yet when they travel to politically dangerous regions, are captured there, and are released only for ransom, they do not just hope for, they expect the help of the state. They claim the protection promised—promised by the heretofore discredited nation-state. Those with multiple citizenships often like to turn to the state that seems more promising politically, and perhaps also economically. The minimal identity, in any case, tends to be purely a demanding identity, that is, a form of being a citizen that reduces itself to making demands.

And those who do not contribute anything to the polity beyond what they are being constrained to contribute, taxes, for example, merely make demands as well. Mere passport holders, in any case, do not need an emotional bond to their country. There is no duty of any kind for them to feel attached, affirmatively or critically, to the history, tradition, and culture, for a long time not even the official language, of their country.

The minimalization of citizen identity can go even further. Mere citizens may consider, according to their sense of right, a law foreign to the state, the sharia, to be superior. When they then violate a legal precept of the sharia, though, they have to answer to the *qadi*, too. A pure state citizen, in any case, does not even have to cultivate the kind of minimal patriotism advocated by intellectuals skeptical of patriotism, such as Habermas's constitutional patriotism that picks up on the work of the political scientist Dolf Sternberger.[5] Despite some positive pathos, the Western state citizen as minimal citizen, even as a mere constitutional patriot is, at least from a legal-political and all the more from a cultural perspective, a "downsized citizen."

This shrinking of identity can go yet further. The enforceable contributions, the taxes, allow the state to fund the familiar tasks contributing to public welfare. These begin with legal security and continue via material infrastructure (sewers; power and gas lines; road, railway, telecommunications networks; etc.) to the health-care system, schools and universities, not least of all defense and contributions to culture. Citizens who do not pay taxes get to enjoy all these services nonetheless. And in generous welfare states, citizens can lead their entire lives as welfare recipients without ever paying taxes. Occasional attempts at demanding at least local contributions are usually abandoned very quickly.

13.3
DYNAMIC IDENTITY

Up to this point, the sketch of Western citizen identity is not only gloomy; it is evidently also insufficient. For practically no one can live with such an impoverished and atrophied, equally static and abstract citizen identity. While the purely legal citizen may well be a statistical downsized citizen, the concrete human being is attained by Michel Foucault's brilliant charge in *The Archaeology of Knowledge* in which he demands the much greater freedom potential of personal identity: "Do not ask who I am and do not ask me to remain the same: that is a registrar's morality [*morale d'état civil*]; it governs our papers. It should let us be free when we write."[6]

The protagonist of Fred Vargas's novel *Dog Will Have His Day* calls himself "son of the Rhine" and is proud, not of his statelessness but of his indeterminate statelessness. For "the advantage of belonging nowhere was that you could be from anywhere."[7] An extra step is taken by those who refuse to submit their sovereign will to change location to a document, a passport, precisely, and possibly a visa, when they want to travel to other countries. What all this shows is that even just being a state citizen, from which elementary rights and thus freedoms follow, is not untroubled by limits to freedom. Here, too, freedom turns out to be bound to restrictions of freedom.

In some countries, the simple noting of someone's religion on tax forms indicates the counterdevelopment to the downsized citizen: the step down is followed by a step up to the actual life of citizens. Here at the latest, identity acquires a dynamic component that need not modify the passport identity. The differences that come out in the now imperceptible, now eruptive processes of concrete identity formation are based on a characteristic of Western societies, pluralism (see above, section 8.2).

In officially multilingual countries such as Belgium, India, Canada, Switzerland, or Bosnia and Hercegovina, the differences begin with the official language; in Switzerland, for example, one speaks French, German, Italian, or Romansh. And Spain has a single official language, Spanish or Castilian; in the various autonomous communities, however, the country permits Catalan, Galician, and Basque as additional official languages.

While in the West, only few countries are officially multilingual, there are affiliations that are rarely associated with pluralism but do play a role in constituting identities. These are regional affiliations, partly political (in federalism, for example), partly ethnic. Let's take Germany as our example. The country is organized into federal states or *Länder* such as Lower Saxony, Baden-Württemberg, or Bavaria. And Baden-Württemberg, as the very name suggests, is inhabited by two tribes, Badeners and Swabians. The latter, however, also live in the province of Bavarian-Swabia, which shows Bavaria, too, to be made up of different tribes — in addition to Swabians and Bavarians, Franconians and the inhabitants of the Upper Palatinate.

Some feel connected with their regional origin simply by their accent, even if they have been living elsewhere, perhaps even abroad, for a long time. Others, like this author, have complicated affiliations: born in Upper Silesia, raised in Westphalia, I studied in a number of places, spent a decade in Munich, a year in New York in between, later taught in Switzerland for a decade and a half, interrupted by a year in Berlin, and have now been living in Tübingen for more than two decades. For a life lived in such conditions, home is probably best described in four dimensions: first, one's family; second, the cultural and linguistic sphere, German in my case; third, the core of what the terms constitutional patriotism but also political liberalism mean, the "pride" in law, democracy, basic rights, and tolerance that begins with one's polity and opens up, via its greater region, Europe in this case, into a cosmopolitanism; and fourth, and even more clearly transnational, the profession, philosophy.

For in today's society, one's job undoubtedly belongs to the identity-instituting affiliations. Many people also feel connected to sophisticated hobbies such as sports, chess, or music; others are active soccer fans. Others again identify with national or international charitable organizations such as Brot für die Welt, Misereor, and SOS Children's Villages, or humanitarian organizations such as Doctors without Borders, and not least of all organizations with political aims, such as Amnesty International. Some leave it at contributing money; others are actively involved but unpaid, that is, they engage in community service.

With language, profession, and hobbies, we have begun to describe something that rejects the third dimension, the communitarian concept of identity, as too narrow. For there are affiliations that cross state borders, and among them, both complementary and competing identities. Most people have only one mother tongue; some however grow up almost perfectly bilingual, a few even trilingual or speaking even more languages. Above all, it is possible to switch to another main language; examples include such spectacular cases as the Pole Korzeniowski whom we know by his first names Joseph Conrad as an English author. His anglophone colleague William Somerset Maugham initially grew up speaking French. Vladimir Nabokov writes first in Russian, later occasionally in French but mostly in English. And the Mongolian author Galsan Tschinag has enriched German with his emotionally and linguistically sensitive stories and novels, including *Dojnaa* and *Die neun Träume des Dschingis Khan* [The nine dreams of Genghis Khan].

It seems neither possible nor to make sense to try to abolish linguistic competition, for it can liberate creative forces. It should, however, be deprived of its potential for violence. In addition, it may be expected of everyone in Europe, worldwide at least of all of intellectuals, as well as of politicians and other leaders, that they speak one foreign language and understand a second. For in understanding another language, we learn something that van Parijs's plea for English as world language[8] underestimates but that must be considered more than just welcome in an age of globalization: we come to know another culture and usually also to appreciate it and draw on it in our argumentation.

Languages are not just a means of communication. Much more than just a tool in the circulation of goods, services, and capital, much more, too, than just a means for articulating information, opinions, and convictions, they have educational value in the emphatic sense of the term. They allow access to new worlds of thought; they make it possible to experience otherness; and they help us to perceive Europe's intellectual richness with its wealth of culturally highly developed languages.[9]

As for the rest, it is true what a British librarian once remarked in Paris: despite the enormous pressure to conform exercised by English, the majority of scientific texts published in Europe are still written in German.

13.4
THE CONFLICTUAL CASE OF RELIGION

With regard to one relevant factor of pluralism, the diversity of religions and faiths as well as nonadherence to any faith, Western societies have become even more pluralistic. In many majority-Muslim countries, where multireligiosity used to be common, however, religious minorities are very much under threat. An impressive counterexample: the exemplary religious tolerance practiced among Muslims, Catholics, Orthodox Christians, and Jews in Bosnia and Hercegovina, while seriously disrupted by the war from 1992 to 1995/96, has fortunately not been lost.

For a long time, the variety of Christian denominations was joined in the West by a Jewish minority whereas the few Muslims living here were an exotic exception. Later, the growing number of Buddhists was barely noticeable; followers of Bhagavan or Scientology only occasionally drew attention. The religious pluralization conspicuous today is due solely to the immigration of Muslims.

Only in this immigration do a number of differences combine that together go far beyond, for example, the differences of Jewish communities. This otherness might begin with clothing, the headscarf or even the burka, although orthodox Jews, both women and men, follow specific dress codes. It may manifest in ritual slaughter, which does not conform to animal protection guidelines, and it does not have to end with prayer in public, outside prayer rooms. Some Muslims take issue with girls participating in the usual physical education, especially swimming classes, some even with their making non-Muslim friends. There is also a tendency toward a parallel system of justice administered by Muslim justices of the peace. Honor killings deserve particular criticism.

Such differences do not necessarily form part of a Muslim citizen identity. On the one hand, just as in Judaism and Christianity, there are many different currents within Islam, and moreover both orthodox and liberal Muslims as well as those largely estranged from their religion. Furthermore, the conspicuous differences are only partly of a genuinely religious nature such that in their case, we should speak not of a Muslim citizen identity but only of an identity of Muslim citizens. And because of the differences within Islam just mentioned, this identity does not manifest homogenously.

Insofar as the differences are of a genuinely religious nature, they are habits and mentalities that depend on the economic and social environment of the region of origin. Immigrants from eastern Anatolia are perceived as foreign not only in Berlin, Basel, Madrid, or Rome but already in many neighborhoods of Turkish cities like Istanbul. And in Sarajevo, where by now about 80 percent of the population is Muslim, few women wear headscarves in public, and the mosques built in recent years with outside money are perceived, with their conspicuous minarets, as architectural foreign bodies.

Religious affiliations, incidentally, do not compete by necessity. In Japan, it is normal to practice Shintoism and Buddhism and in addition Christianity, just as Christians can practice Zen Buddhism. Judaism, Christianity (save for its first, often Jewish generation), and Islam, however, like Hinduism, mutually exclude each other, as Catholicism and Protestantism or Sunni and Shia Islam do as well.

Both, the competition between religions and, within them, competition between confessions, have manifested in often bloody conflicts; even today, the religious factor of identity can still or newly and more strongly contribute to wars. To confront this danger, we must demand tolerance (see above, section 8.3), which introduces a normative moment into the question of identity: citizens must mutually respect, as free and equal, persons who have the right to their own convictions and must be allowed to live according to them. This includes the right as a state citizen to define one's identity also via a religious affiliation, but it also includes the duty to allow others the right to an independent, perhaps even antireligious identity.

13.5
INTERCULTURAL PENAL LAW

It is a matter of course that tolerance ends where the other side disrespects the rights and freedom of others or even does so using violence. In matters of law in particular, tolerance justifiably comes up against its limits. The reference to the sharia, however, exemplarily shows that not all inhabitants, naturalized or not, accept the limits. The reason may lie in problems of identity that are particularly serious when it comes to law, especially the law in its most incisive form, penal law. The problems, although not tied to globalization, gain new importance in an age of globalization.

I have examined the question relevant here whether a legal order has the (subjective) right to apply its (objective) penal law transculturally elsewhere;[10] here, I will recall only two aspects with regard to citizen identity.

First, elements of collective identity concern much more than just well-being; they concern the freedom core of personal identity, the right to one's own religion, language, and culture. Above all, those who do not migrate at a young age become persons endangered in their identity who are much more inclined toward crime than persons with a settled identity. And second, the question of intercultural penal law has nothing to do with the bogeyman of the "dangerous stranger."

Intercultural law, not just penal law, can be justified on five patterns: (1) by the principle of equal treatment; (2) by an intercultural law such as the Roman *ius gentium*; (3) by a culturally indifferent penal law that treats people simply as legal persons; (4) by a federalism of (penal) law; and (5) by treating cases according to the law of the region of origin.[11]

The most persuasive legitimation derives from the universalist legal morality of human rights. In that case, penal law conceives of itself as possible victims' protective shield and for that very reason claims for itself intercultural validity: the restriction of freedom it forces on possible perpetrators secures, for the potential victims, trust and the freedom it nourishes.

A human rights–based penal law, for example, protects delinquents from corporal punishment, and it does not tolerate so-called honor killings. It also saves (young) women from forced marriage, from punishment for adultery, and from the—alleged—right to make them the victims of sexual aggression. Following such prohibitions should not cause identity problems for any migrant. Should it be the case nonetheless, then both the leaders of the immigrant communities and each individual are called on to resolve them. Not the least of arguments for this demand lies in the fact that no human rights violations should be allowed already in migrants' countries of origin. And in the host country, identity problems certainly do not justify human rights violations.

The problems hinted at here are usually not of an individual but of a collective nature and thus not easily resolved; but they are not unsolvable either. If the law that is at odds with human rights has a religious background—although that is unlikely—the religious groups and associations active in the host country have a great deal of shared responsibility. The polity of the host country here has not only the right but the duty to demand that they assume that responsibility: in social interaction, in the media, as *ultima ratio* also via enforceable law. In my personal experience, Western societies have ignored this task for at least two or three decades. This has allowed mentalities to solidify that are now more difficult to change. This difficulty does not, however, justify putting the task off—even if dealing with it requires immense efforts.

13.6
ANGRY CITIZENS, COMMON GOOD CITIZENS, WORLD CITIZENS

Language and religion enrich the citizen identity, which, as suggested, may be amplified in regional ties and affiliations with professional groups and leisure activities. Other factors do more than enrich and amplify because they enhance modest, simple being-a-citizen to become a demanding being-a-state-citizen. The minimum of being a state citizen consists in the acceptance of law, democracy, basic rights, and tolerance; more than the minimum consists in participating in elections and preparing for them by familiarizing oneself with political developments and party platforms. And the veritable progression manifests in an active "pride" in a constitutional democracy and liberal society: in getting involved.

It becomes visible in community service, in public statements, or in participating in local initiatives, which for some active state citizens even constitutes the most important identity. Local citizens' groups are active in the intermediary space between private and public interests. Their civic involvement, an important factor in the republican conception of the citizen, opposes a statist reduction of the concept of politics (see above, section 8.4). Yet they must not be equated with what draws the most media attention, the "angry citizens." Undoubtedly, the latter's activity institutes identity, and for some, the weekly protests may serve as a substitute for church services — an aspect with which a pluralistic society has no difficulties. Concerns arise only once "angry citizens" sacrifice so precious a political good as the rule of law to their interest in being present in the media.

For this reason alone, it would be wrong to consider local initiatives a good thing no matter what. Moreover, they do not necessarily work for the common good. Protest against infrastructure projects such as power lines, railroad tracks, or waste disposal facilities may be sustained by understandable interests, but these interests remain particular interests. And even where common good interests are being pursued, there is the danger of privileging a small part of the common good, for example in playing down justice toward future generations in the debate about retirement benefits.

An unbiased look, in any case, perceives citizen involvement not only in local citizens' groups but in the rich variety of voluntary work and community service or in participation in public discourse as well. At the same time, this view opposes a cultural pessimism critical of liberalism that considers the citizens of wealthy democracies to be egotistical monads pursuing nothing but their self-interest. In reality, participation in not-for-profit clubs, associations, and self-help groups, community service in taking care of marginalized or disadvantaged groups, or work in local citizens' initiatives — in short, social and political involvement — belongs to the citizen identity of many strongly developed individuals.

The polity at which such active citizens' involvement is directed does not have to be the state; it can also be a smaller unit, the municipality, region, canton, or province, or not least of all the global polity of a world society. Citizens involved in this way, common good citizens, are characterized by something an enlightened liberalism puts great store by, namely, civic virtues that begin with a sense of right and lead via a sense of justice including the courage of one's convictions [*Zivilcourage*] to their relative maximum, civic sense (see above, section 8.4).

The most modest civic virtue, the sense of right, is content with a compliance with the law that follows prevailing law either out of fear of punishment or voluntarily. The intermediary step, a sense of justice, speaks out, where laws are concerned, for the removal of privileges and discriminations and, where their application is concerned, for impartiality and also against the unscrupulous exploitation of loopholes. Where the sense of justice sees massive injustice and has the courage of its convictions, it reserves the right to civil disobedience. Of course there is the danger that particular interests interfere or that one shies away from the means of opposition common under the rule of law. To avoid this danger of self-privileging, serious civil disobedience submits to a sincerity test, according to which one is also willing to accept disadvantages.

A normatively yet higher level of citizen identity is attained by those who exercise a civic sense. Its first form, usually neglected in republican theories, cultural civic sense, seeks to transmit one's cultural capital, including one's language, to future generations in at least as rich a form as it has been inherited. In an age of economization, this effort can even be justified economically. Which institution a scientist decides to join or where a company establishes its European headquarters also depends on the "trade value" of the local language and the cultural infrastructure of the city in question. In the end, however, what counts in cultural civic sense is not that but the value proper of language and culture.

The value of practicing the second form, the social civic sense devoted to tasks that benefit the community, is so obvious that it needs no further presentation. One aspect already cited bears repeating, though: reality forcefully refutes the culture-pessimistic view that liberal citizens are atomized egotists.

Political civic sense, civic sense as state citizen sense, finally, has a double aspect, a domestic and an international side (something most republican theories overlook). Domestically, it works to achieve a high degree of participation in its polity, which it values for its political liberalism; internationally, it works to achieve a circumspect balance of self-esteem and esteem from others. As an enlightened patriotism, it avoids two wrong forms, both a nationalist self-praise and an idiophobia that for fear of being accused of xenophobia has nothing but disdain and criticism for what is its own and does not, not even out of self-esteem, defend itself against unqualified attacks from foreigners.

An unabridged citizen's identity has two further dimensions. Many intellectuals calling themselves critical tend to look down on the sphere of the economy, albeit often with the pragmatic contradiction that they would like to be alimented and in a good financial position. Yet the economy is indispensable not just personally but for the common good as well. Its indispensability begins with jobs, which are of existential significance in today's society shaped by labor and by professional life and are by no means limited to the aspect of earning a living but also include job training, social skills, moreover intercultural skills and, of course, the opportunity to earn respect and self-esteem. Social esteem is of particular significance in this regard, since it is respect and not income that distinguishes social strata.[12] Yet social respect must not be reduced to public reputation. Respect in the family, from neighbors, friends, and colleagues is no less important. And both, the great, public respect and the smaller, more private respect, can enter into conflict with each other.

A flourishing economy is committed to the common good not least because it increases the tax income required to fund parliaments and justice systems, health-care and education systems, the welfare state, cultural institutions, and material infrastructure. Everyone who contributes to economic welfare, as employer or as employee, has no reason to be ashamed of this aspect of their citizen's identity, their success as economic citizen.

The second dimension still missing has a rather good reputation; the expressions "world citizen" and "cosmopolitan" have a favorable ring to them. Yet they make sense for a prudent citizen's identity only when they are understood not as exclusive but as complementary, not as a rejection of being a state citizen but as a supplement to it.

We should not limit ourselves to the traditional role of citizens involved, certainly, but content with their own polity, for a number of reasons: transnational commonalities such as language, religion, and profession; the manifold economic, scientific, political, and cultural exchanges; the need for global action, for example with regard to fighting crime and protecting the climate; not least of all because of the universalist principles of law and government. Instead, we should, where necessary, expand the domains in which all three levels are active, the sense of right, the sense of justice, and civic sense, to include transregional and ultimately global challenges.

This expansion is not just up to the jet-set elites. Be it as tourists, as consumers, or as employees, as newspaper readers, as someone interested in culture, as university teachers or students, not least of all as members of multiethnic groups in schools or at work, as users of the World Wide Web, or in big-city life — practically every Western citizen experiences globalized life conditions on an almost daily basis.

13.7

SUMMARY AND A CONJECTURE

Our sketch of Western citizen's identity may conclude with these indications, and although it is a preliminary sketch, it makes one thing clear: citizen's identity is a complex phenomenon whose abstract and static core, the down-sized citizen, is being enriched in the concrete life of citizens by a bundle of factors. Its precise makeup changes in the course of our lives; lived identity is a dynamic phenomenon that usually becomes richer as we grow up and live a life of experience. In the process, internal conflicts tend to arise for immigrants, but for locals, too, and in trying to solve them, identity tends to change. Where there are breaks in a biography, identity can erode almost to the point of being lost completely. The core — "constitutional patriotism" or "patriotic liberalism"— however, should not be touched by this.

The dynamic process I have sketched suggests a question that is important for an enlightened liberalism, and I would like to conclude this chapter by attempting an answer: are citizens free in the search for their identity? My answer: undoubtedly, we depend on the collective identities of our origins and of the environments in which we life. Yet citizen's identity, especially the identity of the state citizen in a constitutional democracy, includes two things, first that we appreciate this democracy not in words alone, and second that within the framework of this appreciation we regard ourselves and our fellow citizens — children and other dependents apart — as persons responsible for what they do and do not do. For this twofold reason, because we consider constitutional democracy the inalienable framework of our lives and because, within this frame, we attribute to human beings a responsibility for their life, we consider citizens to have a responsibility to participate in forming their identities. In this formation, the civic virtues I have cited, the sense of right, the sense of justice, and civic sense, may serve as exemplary attitudes toward life.

14

Sovereignty in an Age of Globalization

The preceding chapter focused on one of the two basic agents of the political, the citizen; the present chapter focuses on the other, the polity. In discussing the meaning the two basic and main agents of the political have for freedom, enlightened liberalism rejects two one-sided views: political freedom is decided neither on the side of the citizen alone nor merely on the side of the polity. Rather, both sides, and indeed the many instances where they interlock, must be discussed.

Since it has come up several times already, the political freedom of polities can be treated here more briefly. It is called for in two dimensions, not only internally, as constitutional democracy including the liberties (see chapter 11 and 12 above), but also externally, as sovereignty. Doubts about the usefulness of the notion of "sovereignty" were voiced already in the twentieth century. Skeptics consider the concept largely to have lost its meaning in the age of globalization.[1] Undoubtedly, political conditions have changed. But as we will see, it is a matter of some debate whether this change has led only to a loosening and further development of the traditional, "classic" conception of sovereignty or to its abolition, to a break.

The concept of sovereignty brings together the various strands of a conception of the state incrementally taking shape in a long process of political modernization after a long period of war, the Thirty Years' War, that was particularly devastating for Germany. The result consists in a static and conceptually simple notion, the modern concept of the state in its foreign policy perspective (section 14.1).

After another devastating war, World War II, this concept is not abolished but modified. And this change is by no means so radical that it would be appropriate to speak of a postmodern concept of the state liberated from the notion of sovereignty. Contrary to the claims of some hasty diagnoses, the core of the modern concept, sovereignty, persists. The changes that have taken place nonetheless are more appropriately described as a second modernization in whose process, especially because of a many-faceted globalization, many states lose at least some of their freedom in matters of foreign policy (section 14.2). At the same time, the constitutional situation becomes more complicated, which is why sovereignty today is dynamic and difficult to conceptualize (section 14.4).

14.1
STATE SOVEREIGNTY

The positive and at the same time strict concept of freedom, self-determination as self-legislation, as autonomy, first emerges not in moral philosophy but in political philosophy. In Greek antiquity, in the work of the historian Herodotus writing in the mid-fifth century BCE, *autonomia* comprehends both sides, both inner and outer political freedom, and thus stands in a twofold opposition: internally to tyranny, externally to foreign rule.[2] Unknown later, foreign especially to the Middle Ages, the concept of autonomy becomes significant once more only in early modernity and then becomes important primarily in legal studies, later also in philosophy, with Christian Wolff.[3]

In the first part of his *Philosophia civilis sive politica*, published in 1756, roughly a century, that is, after the 1648 Treaty of Westphalia, which decisively shaped the European political order, Wolff's follower Michael Christoph Hanow sees autonomy as political self-determination and emphasizes not internal but external freedom, the self-determination of each state over against all other states: "Therefore beware of any transgression on another state [*civitas*] as of any intervention in its public law as in its autonomy."[4]

Hanow here brings out the decisive aspect of "external" political freedom, at least in its negative aspect. Free in relation to other polities are those states that are not threatened by what the classical Greek polities abhorred, namely, becoming the province of an empire (Persia, at the time) or the satellite state of a superpower, or simply its colony.

A lack of freedom in foreign affairs manifests in many ways. A polity is unfree not only when it is subjected militarily and incorporated as a province into an empire. Unfreedom in foreign matters begins with an obligation to pay tribute, to pay in money or goods, such as grain, wine, ore, or jewels, also tea or precious cloths. It manifests as a duty to build roads or fortifications, to provide soldiers, not least in having to adopt a foreign language, foreign weights and measures, in being forced to accept a foreign governor or viceroy, or in losing the right independently to conclude treaties with other polities.

The obligations can be so humane that they are not experienced as sacrifices and certainly not as humiliations. It is said of classical China, for example, that it answered tribute payments with countergifts that exceeded the tribute in value. Dependence might also allow for better business on more favorable terms. What remains decisive, however, is that even if pragmatic advantages predominate, one's freedom in foreign affairs remains restricted as long as the restriction takes place without inner assent.

Conceptually, the freedom in external matters that resists such constraints has two sides, and an enlightened liberalism values both: with regard to the state and to international law in particular, sovereignty is required; empirically, the force to act and create, that is, power, is required.

The first aspect, sovereignty, classically denotes the rule of a state over its territory and its inhabitants. This highest territorial rule, which no longer derives from anything else and is not subjected to any foreign ties, does of course have an internal aspect, namely, the monopoly on legitimate violence within the state territory exercised by sovereign states via a differentiated construct of authorities. The conceptually decisive point is that domestically, the bearer of sovereignty is superior to all other powers without restriction or compromise; what is sovereign is the way the state organizes authority independently of orders coming from the outside.

Yet the primary aspect of the concept pertains to international law: sovereignty as the unrestricted right to this organization, that is, the right to one's own legislative, executive, and judiciary. A political entity is sovereign in matters of foreign policy if in its territory it exclusively possesses the supreme authority, an authority not subject to any foreign power.

This modern conception of sovereignty is prepared politically-historically starting in the thirteenth century with French royal claims to independence from the Holy Roman Emperor, legal-theoretically later by Marsilius of Padua (against papal claims), and later again by Jean Bodin and Thomas Hobbes. In practice, it is "sanctioned" by the already-mentioned Treaty of Westphalia and, later again, is given the since then classic articulation by the Swiss legal scholar Emer de Vattel, who further develops the Wolffian definition. That state is sovereign "which governs itself, in whatever form, depending on no foreign" nation.[5] True sovereignty consists in a freedom from any other state's right to rule, a freedom that is absolute from the constitutional perspective as well as the perspective of international law. The related monopoly of the state on violence, on control over a specific territory, is manifest in things such as the elimination of intermediary powers, allowing for the central monopoly on rule; in mustering a standing army; in the monopoly on taxes; and in a bureaucratic administration of the country with the help of a loyal—that is, in the literal sense, subjected to the *loi*, to the law—civil service.

To be able to assess the scope of later developments, we must not overlook one thing: even at the height of classical sovereignty, there are limits to sovereignty, for there are certain constraints toward consensus and, moreover, autonomous counterforces. Even in absolutism, the sovereign does not exercise a perfectly unrestricted rule of the kind suggested by the frontispiece of Hobbes's *Leviathan*.

Self-government in foreign affairs obviously does not presuppose domestic freedom, does not presuppose a constitutional democracy, which shows the two dimensions of political freedom to be independent of each other. As we know from ample experience, sovereign states can be dictatorships or even totalitarian states in internal affairs, while the sovereignty in foreign affairs even of liberal democracies can be restricted, as that of the Federal Republic of Germany was for a long time.

And in any event, independence in foreign affairs is not to be understood comprehensively. The concept of political freedom in international law excludes neither economic nor cultural nor political dependencies. What is decisive is not that there is autarky in economic, cultural, and political respects; what is decisive is that the public powers are not subjected to any foreign public powers. Be it small or large—a state is sovereign when its legislation is not subject to any foreign legislature, its executive not subject to any other government, and its judicial system not subject any higher judiciary.

Seen this way, external political freedom is a matter of either-or: from the perspective of international law, either a state is sovereign, or it is not. Beside this conception, however, there is a second, comparative concept of external political freedom as actually available force of action, which makes this freedom a variable of power (in foreign affairs). Here, the essential role is played by actual power potentials, albeit not just military, but economic, scientific, and cultural power as well. In consequence, neither geographic extension nor population numbers are decisive. A small country like Switzerland can have a great deal of power and freedom economically and scientifically, while an economic, scientific, and cultural "middle power" like Germany for a long time was a dwarf in foreign affairs.

14.2
FREEDOM LOST, FREEDOM GAINED

Another parameter is important for freedom in foreign policy. Independently of the question whether a polity has the status of a small, middle, or large state, its freedom is codetermined by international conditions, both by the weaker form (weaker from the point of view of a theory of freedom) of international intertwinement, including the negative aspects of international terrorism, pollution, natural disasters, pandemics, and international financial crises, and by the stronger form, international dependencies. An intermediary form is constituted by the financial and currency markets. Even if it is exaggerated to declare them the real masters of the world today who are keeping states on a short leash, their power is immense.

Already in the past, few polities ever succeeded in evading the first two levels of restrictions on external freedom. The dependence of princes on bankers like the Fuggers or Rothschilds is familiar from school. Today, in an age of globalization, there is definitively no state, not even one of the so-called superpowers, that disposes of an unrestricted freedom, in the empirical sense, as regard foreign affairs. Even if perfect external independence ever existed, it would long have been forcefully undermined by the many facets of cooperation, economic, scientific, and cultural, in some places also military, and above all ecological.

Whether by design or not — the multidimensional international meshing unavoidably entails a reciprocal dependence and thereby an erosion of the classic concept of sovereignty. Not a few countries add a (legal-) moral self-commitment. It begins with international treaties and runs from the enforceable part of international law to a self-imposed prohibition of certain foreign policy measures, for example offensive warfare. And ultimately, it is committed to the notions of human dignity and of human rights. One aspect of absolute sovereignty in particular, the appeal to noninterference as a guise for permission to commit genocide, has been invalidated. Yet whether a so-called humanitarian intervention is not only justified but also advisable remains a separate question.[6]

International intertwinement, however, must not be evaluated only as a restriction of freedom. Unless one engages in cooperation foolishly, one does so to further one's interests, to advance one's own well-being, now economic, now scientific and cultural, but above all military and political. Responsible states also cooperate out of a commitment to a global justice and a global common good.

Even in the case of a restriction of freedom, a decrease of power in foreign affairs does not necessarily affect sovereignty in the sense of international law. Sovereignty is affected only where, independently of a country's power to act, the right to make the final decision is being interfered with. For sovereignty does not consist in a substantial power to act but in a (sometimes merely formal) right to act, in the entitlement, not necessarily the capacity to rule. Superpowers by definition have more power than minor or even dwarf powers, but the latter are just as sovereign.

The difference between these two concepts, freedom in foreign affairs in international law and empirically, may be illustrated once more via the example of a small country like Switzerland: neither the high degree of dependence on exports and imports nor the linguistic and cultural affiliations with neighboring countries nor the modest power to act, compared with middle and great powers, restricts Swiss sovereignty. That happens only when, and even then only in small doses, the country submits to "foreign judges," for instance to the European Court of Human Rights.

Switzerland accepted a much greater loss of freedom when in bilateral negotiations with the European Union starting in 2000 it had to learn what attentive observers had been expecting for years: if the country does not join the European Union and yet seeks the benefits, economic in particular, of a close cooperation, it will be confronted with a "take it or leave it" alternative—either adopt the rules of the European Union such as they apply in the union and accept the loss of sovereignty this implies or renounce the advantages of economic cooperation. (It remains to be seen what will become of this following the Swiss referendum on the initiative "against mass immigration" on February 9, 2014.)

When we draw the conceptual conclusions from the Swiss example, we see a comparative conception both with regard to the citizen and with regard to sovereignty. For the moment, we can distinguish three kinds of losses of freedom:

1. Both international law, for example the regional (such as the European) or global declarations of human rights, and European or worldwide courts bind state power. In the former case, they put restrictions on the national legislative, in the latter, on the national judiciary.
2. Freedom is also relinquished to some degree in joining international organizations such as the United Nations, to an intermediate degree in bilateral agreements between small states like Switzerland and much larger political entities like the European Union, and to an even greater degree in joining the European Union.
3. Finally, joining military and security alliances like NATO, in the past the Warsaw Pact, or the Organization for Security and Co-operation in Europe (OSCE) does not take place without some renunciation of freedom, for a large

share of the important responsibility for deciding questions of international security is being transferred to an inter- or supranational organization.

Yet as noted, the loss of decision-making authority and generally the losses in freedom must not be understood as pure losses. The phenomena I have mentioned — with the exception of the Warsaw Pact, which allowed the Soviet Union to station troops in the satellite states — are not pure blows of fate. On the contrary, they follow from free decisions, at most with concurrent economic interests or, as in the case of accepting human rights treaties, gentle, moral pressure.

The self-interests in whose name decisions are taken after long debates on the pros and cons are often pursued in the name of freedom interests. The military and security alliances just mentioned have just this goal: to protect one's own freedom against (feared) attacks from outside. The question whether the fear is justified or, as in the Warsaw Pact, imposed, may be left aside here. The decisive point is that freedom is restricted for the sake of freedom and that in the case of a truly free decision, the balance between restricting and securing freedom is seen as positive.

Just as important as the ultimately positive freedom balance is the (formal) moment of voluntariness: all three kinds of restricting freedom should take place not because of external constraint, a dictated peace, for instance, but rather because of free assent, free acceptance of the relevant treaties. And, again, in terms of content, military and other alliances paradoxically secure freedom by restricting freedom.

For the sake on their own freedom, states agree to a well-delimited renunciation of freedom. And in accepting international human rights treaties and international courts of justice, they affirm their liberal conception of government in domestic matters. Because of the devotion to pre- and suprapositive principles such as the freedom-guaranteeing human rights, possible violations are considered an injustice that, when it is perpetrated or tolerated by the state, is better investigated by an impartial third party, first by a judiciary within the state, if need be, however, by an international judiciary as well.

On the purely conceptual level, we can distinguish between three kinds of losses of freedom: the voluntary renunciation of freedom, which prudence advises only when on balance, it increases freedom; the forced renunciation of freedom under constraint from forces not freely controlled; and unintended self-restriction. After the three examples of the first kind above, let me cite an example of the middle kind: economic globalization. A careful analysis of economic globalization shows how in one process, all three kinds of losing freedom can interlock.

A significant share of economic globalization consists in international agreements such as the accords on currency policy elaborated at Bretton Woods in 1944 and implemented after World War II. In that regard, there is a voluntary renunciation of freedom. Yet this renunciation has side effects, which are partly unforeseen, partly foreseen but accepted and in both cases amount to a restriction of freedom not intended in this form. These include above all the collapse of some states' economic or political performance and the immense migration caused by the attractiveness of wealthy democracies, which brings significant problems both for the immigrants and for the "host countries." Moreover, the pressure of international competition can prompt the lowering of national social and environmental standards.

These and other self-restrictions, partly intended, partly imposed, and partly unintended, urge the question whether, today, external freedom is increasingly, and perhaps soon totally being lost. Let's look at a few domains of state responsibility.

Military alliances like NATO and in the past the Warsaw Pact or security alliances like OSCE demonstrate that a first classic task of the state, external security, has not been fulfilled by states on their own for a long time. Because of transborder drug, economic, and terroristic crime, the second classic task, internal security, too, can no longer be solved completely autonomously by individual states.

In a somewhat mitigated way, the restriction of state responsibility applies even to a third task, conducting foreign policy, since inter- and transnational actors like religious communities and companies, in certain political circumstances also trade unions, parties, and employer's associations, can conduct foreign policy, empirically, if not in the sense of international law. Compared to states, though, the goals they pursue are much narrower. Similar things can be said of athletic, scientific, and cultural organizations.[7]

Inter- and supranational organizations have long been reproached for democratic deficits, and rightly so. Yet such criticism merely concerns institutional deficits. The complaint is that the articulation of policy is increasingly being taken away from the nations and, in the European Union, has shifted to an intergovernmental European Council. (Time will tell if a European Parliament with expanded powers can have a profound impact on the situation.)

In Europe, in any case, the principle of subsidiarity Germany introduced into European constitutional texts threatens to become perfunctory. Instead of preserving Europe's richness, strengthening the principle *in pluribus unum*, not *e pluribus unum*, instead, that is, of reinforcing the multidimensional diversity ranging from language and law via politics to culture and mentalities with a "right to difference," this very richness is in many respects thoughtlessly jeopardized.[8]

The counterstrategy is obvious. If the achievements of constitutional democracy are not to be sacrificed on the altar of Europeanization and globalization, then international relations must be given legal form in one way or another, but this legal form must be tied back to the will of those concerned, peoples (nations) with all their differences. And that process must accept both the elementary rights of states and different traditions and mentalities.

Finally, the power of individual states is restricted by new actors such as international nongovernmental organizations. In addition, developing nations in particular are dependent on international governmental organizations—such as the World Bank, the International Monetary Fund, and the development organizations of the United Nations—whose support is usually tied to far-reaching conditions concerning economic, social, and legal policy.

The initial conclusion is evident. Neither empirically nor normatively can we speak of absolute sovereignty today. The notion of absolutely sovereign statehood makes way for that of partial sovereignty. Individual states that reconcile with this situation, their own reality, may be called "enlightened nation-states."[9]

14.3
EXCURSUS: WHO IS CONCERNED?

When a nuclear power plant is built near the border, residents on the other side of the border share in the dangers without having the right to have their say in the construction and operation of the plant. When the containment building of a power plant in Chernobyl bursts, the radioactivity released affects people living thousands of miles away, also without any say before or any compensation later. When the president of a great, even hegemonic power is elected, then his policies will have an impact, more or less strongly, on the entire world, again without the world having a say in it. The same is true of the persecution and oppression that are coresponsible for the great migrations.

These examples and many others in our time of still-increasing international intertwinements raise a question not easily answered: should those who have so far been excluded but are also concerned be given the right to have a say, and if yes, to what extent and in what form?

There is, first, a danger of one-sidedness to be mentioned. Andreas Gross, a Swiss political scientist and member of the National Council, that is, a parliamentarian, complained before the 2013 election of the German Bundestag that non-Germans were not allowed to vote and that they were not even being asked for their opinion although the parliament finally elected would significantly influence the lives of millions of Europeans.[10] Leaving aside the fact that the United States, Russia, or China could serve as examples as well, the author does not look at the opposite direction, neither at how Germans are impacted by the French, Greek, Italian, and other policies nor at how neighboring countries are affected by Swiss initiatives like the already-mentioned "Against Mass Migration" and do not have a say, either.

The argument thus expanded, however, is correct: according to the basic idea of democracy, all persons concerned by a political decision, especially if this decision concerns governance, should be allowed to codecide, directly or indirectly. Yet it is not evident how this claim can be met in the case of transnational problems.

The "negative" part of Gross's diagnosis, namely, that under current conditions of life, the nation-state is no longer the appropriate form for organizing democracy, cannot convince because, as we saw in section 11.3, constitutional democracy has so far been practiced most intensely in individual or nation-states and, moreover, because it is essentially the nation-state that has formed intensive communities in the first place.

There are indeed good reasons for creating a European Union, though they are not so compelling that they would have persuaded the citizens of Norway and Switzerland. And insofar as one is joining a European Union, this union should strengthen its democratic elements without for all that having to evolve into a federalist state, as Gross and others demand. If only because of the linguistic, political, cultural, and mentality diversity of Europe, furthermore because of the so-called principal-agent problem, that is, the problem of politicians all too often acting detached from citizens' wishes, finally because of the growth dynamic inherent to superordinate institutions, manifest in increased personnel with increasing remuneration and above all increasing power, that is, because of a proud series of arguments, a solution is advisable that is appropriate to the diversity and acts to counter numerous dangers. In both respects, then, a model imposes itself that may be called modest from the perspective of democratic theory but which may also be called more appropriate to actual democracy. Not least of all, the community is an endeavor built on reciprocity that becomes a lived reality only over time, in Europe probably only after several generations.

In addition, other issues, like geographically distant nuclear plants that, like Chernobyl, send radioactivity on its way, presidential elections in a global power, as well as internationally organized crime, terrorism, worldwide migration, climate protection, and many other phenomena require truly global solutions that exceed Europe.

14.4
COMPLEX SOVEREIGNTY

It is sometimes claimed that the losses in sovereignty and power I have sketched concern practically all states and practically all domains of state action; and taken together, these losses are said to have led to states' demotion to mere executors of the constraints of globalization. Some even believe to have found here a dictatorship of a new kind, an anonymous dictatorship, namely, the economic competition dictated by an unleashed capitalism, which is why, alarmist diagnoses would have us believe, the end of freedom in foreign policy is imminent.

A sober look shows the truth to look different. There are at least four, partly empirical, partly legitimizing reasons to oppose the rash diagnosis of a postmodern because postnational statehood. The popular declaration that the nation-state or, better, the individual state is dead may sound critical and radical, and moreover very moral because it sounds so nicely cosmopolitan. In fact, however, it overestimates both the degree of actual changes and the right to further changes, and it underestimates the still-intact core of sovereignty.

1. From an empirical perspective, states do indeed have to share certain competencies. Yet because they relinquish no area of competency in its entirety and hardly any to a significant degree, their loss of power is limited. When states do not cede competencies voluntarily (for example through uniting to form a new entity such as the European Union) and even then retain important jurisdictions, they are still largely responsible for domestic and external security, for legislation and the justice system, for education and health care, and not least of all for the welfare state and environmental protection.

   According to legal scholar Armin von Bogdandy, there are new actors that do not exercise any form of constraint and yet are powerful enough to shake up a country's domestic politics.[11] The example he cites are the PISA studies, which were conducted not by the German authorities, the conference of federal states' education secretaries, in this instance, but by the OECD, and which changed even the author's family life. These studies were of great relevance politically (even if other examples impose themselves: the terrorist attack on the Twin Towers of September 11, 2001, has changed the world of international affairs, for example, and the reactor disasters of Chernobyl and Fukushima or the report of the Club of Rome have changed the domestic policies of a good number of countries). And yet we must not overestimate their constitutional significance. On the one hand, the OECD was founded by (European) states and is supported by them. It is thus not really a new kind of organization from the constitutional point of view but a kind of actor we are familiar with from military alliances or scientific, economic, cultural, and sports associations. On the other hand, with regard to PISA, it was German media and education secretaries who assigned the studies such significance in the first place; who for that reason sought to improve the mediocre ranking of German schools; and who nonetheless preferred to sweep politically touchy results under the rug, such as the substantial differences in performance between individual federal states and between individual schools. Party politics won out over objectivity here.

Moreover, the significance of two further, at least complementary possible points of view of nonstate factors restricts the purview of von Bogdandy's interpretation. First, the politics of a country will time and again be considerably influenced by factors outside the state. And second, the fact that they let themselves be influenced and are willing to make improvements speaks to a certain learning capacity on the part of national democracies.

2. The second empirical thesis, which concerns the allegedly strongest disempowering factor, international companies as the gravediggers of national economic policies, is contradicted by reality. The few companies that are in fact highly *multi*national might have the potential to undermine the economic policies of some governments, but in practice they prefer adapting to government policies. Even if they like to threaten leaving, they do not really like to pull up stakes. Yet we must not underestimate the possibility they have to influence governments (who on occasion are very willing to listen), for example to lower corporate taxes, permit exceptions from planning requirements, lower social and environmental standards, or weaken data privacy protections (see also chapter 6).
3. A first legitimatizing argument against the alleged end of freedom in foreign affairs appeals to an achievement of political modernization: constitutional democracy can be found primarily in individual states, which is why even regional associations like the European Union should be tied back to nations or individual states. For it is these latter that still have the highest degree of constitutional-democratic legitimacy. From the separation between state and society that serves individuals' autonomy to the widespread material wealth and modern administrations to the community in the shape of public social security and finally the cultural richness tied back to the different languages, individual states have created that foundation for confidence, readiness to cooperate, and solidarity that turns subjects into veritable citizens, namely, persons that take responsibility for themselves and for others.

For these reasons, we must not overestimate the political value of individual states' competitors with respect to international law, of international organizations and companies as well as of a third kind of new actors, nongovernmental organizations. Voluntary membership in such organizations, to be sure, amounts to a certain kind of equivalent of democracy: one can join and leave, support special actions or refuse such support. Yet the organizations cannot — yet?— be controlled via elected representatives or constitutional judicial review.

At least equally important is the impossibility of addressing subjective claims to nongovernmental organizations. These organizations can influence governments via spectacular protests and public opinion. But they are unable to obtain justice either for individuals or for groups. And because they usually limit themselves to a very narrow array of issues, they shy away from a democratic task that is as important as it is difficult, the arduous weighing of competing legal values and of different groups with competing interests.

4. I have already hinted at the second legitimizing counterargument, namely, that many individual states have a property and, simultaneously, a task that their competitors are lacking: they are communities, transgenerational solidary and cooperative associations.

There are thus both normative as well as empirical reasons against the expectation that the future of the European Union and the future of a global order will lead to the abolition of the individual state. And in all events the emergence of centralistic omnicompetent units must be prevented. The only legal orders admissible from the perspective of legitimation are those that, first, come together in a federation of individual states and in so doing remain, second, committed to the notion of subsidiarity: individual states must retain responsibility for tasks they can fulfill satisfactorily. (And within individual states, it is advisable that the municipalities and regions, cantons, and other subdivisions be given as much leeway as possible.) Yet because of their European and global intertwinement, individual states can hardly consider themselves autarkic in matters of European and global policy.

When it comes to losses of freedom, then, the following preliminary assessment imposes itself: although freedom in matters of foreign policy has been restricted, there is no need, empirically, to expect its end nor, legitimatorily, to consider it desirable. Thus less is sovereignty subject to a revolutionary break than it undergoes an evolutionary development that loosens up a monolithic conception of the term.

And in any event, to speak of losses of freedom is to tell only half of the truth. Certainly, as indicated, sovereign statehood is restricted in four instances of explicit renunciations of freedom: in concluding international treaties, in joining international organizations, in joining defense alliances, and in new political constructs. But this restriction is voluntary, and as long as it does not take place blindly or thoughtlessly but is well considered, it serves the freedom of states: for example, a country seeks to strengthen its freedom to act under military threat or to establish it in the first place. Or it liberates economic and cultural powers of globalization one hopes will bring, on balance, greater economic and cultural freedom. Or issues of freedom are at stake, such as human rights, whose legal and moral status prior to and above the state is affirmed by acknowledging an inter- or supranational authority.

Evidently, the first two of these purposes amount to the contrary of a pure restriction of freedom, namely, to a strengthening, which of course can be gained only through cooperation. And agreements for the third purpose strengthen the freedom of those who ultimately count in a democracy, the freedom of individual but not isolated persons.

15

A Liberal Global Order

The current globalization is much more diverse than it is usually perceived as being. Contrary to the widespread economistic reduction to one dimension, it takes place in three dimensions that I have called "community of violence," "community of cooperation," and "community of pain and suffering."[1]

We have for a while now been living in a world where the network of economic and social, technological and ecological, scientific and cultural, not least of all legal-moral cooperation is meshed ever more tightly. Unfortunately, the same is also true of the network of criminal and other threats. In all these domains, a need for global action arises. Whether we think of environmental and climate protection or of the fight against terrorism and organized crime; of objections to the arrogance of some great powers as well as to the expanding power of multinational companies including search engines active across the globe and of ensuring a fair but not neoliberal world trade left to itself; of establishing the rule of law (including confidentiality of the mail even in the age of digitalization); of justice toward our children and grandchildren; finally, of the struggle against hunger and poverty — in confronting all these challenges, humanity is all in the same boat. It finds itself forced to develop common solutions that require conditions of law, not just within individual states but also between them, and ultimately a global legal order.

For it is an erroneous belief on the part of well-meaning but experience-resistant moralists that if only their country, Germany, say, or at least the greater region, the European Union, audaciously pressed ahead, the rest of the world would meekly follow. As the 2009 Copenhagen Climate Change Conference has shown for climate protection policy or as the bumpy road to worldwide agreements shows for the phasing out of nuclear power, a financial transaction tax, and again climate protection: shying away from the effort to reach binding global agreements without loopholes does not help to bring about the needed global change. Instead, it harms one's own country or group of countries.

That is why a global legal order is necessary, and of course this legal order must be subject to the conditions of liberal coexistence and a liberal legal and political order. It is also largely uncontested that the standpoint of political freedom requires a democratic legal order. Fundamental disagreements arise only about the scope: should something that dominates in many individual states and still requires considerable efforts in regional associations like the European Union, should the combination of law with political self-determination, separation of powers, and devotion to human and basic rights, should this quartet of legal and moral principles apply to all humanity in its global coexistence?

The standpoint of political freedom obviously admits only the positive answer: in the relationships between states, too, the dominance of particular powers must be broken and be replaced by a political freedom defined by the legal and moral quartet of principles. Because of its scope, we may speak of a world-encompassing, cosmopolitan freedom. It overcomes the international state of nature in such a way that law and democracy no longer apply only with territorial limitations but across the globe—especially since "national" law is threatened by, for example, terrorism, organized crime, and the abuse of digital communication.

These three exemplary threats suggest that a liberal global order is required not just from the international perspective, for the cooperation between states, but also from the citizens' perspective. At least two arguments, (1) citizens' need for freedom, for both negative and positive freedom, and (2) their willingness to practice civic virtues—which, confronted with global living conditions, cannot be content with the "national" perspective because narrow nationalism contradicts the universalist potential of the civic virtues—demand that citizens expand their virtues, the triad of sense of right, sense of justice, and civic sense, into a cosmopolitan practice. In this expansion, (cosmopolitically open) citizens urge their countries to establish a global legal order.

A "realist" view of the political world might dismiss the two-dimensional demand coming from citizens and from states, the global claim to political freedom, as "idealist" and utopian. Yet there is a remarkably "realist" argument in favor of a worldwide legal order, above all the need for global action evoked earlier, that includes the losses of freedom cited in section 14.2, but also globalization as it is actually experienced and lived, which inspires the civic virtues' cosmopolitan expansion. The allegedly "idealist" view of freedom here meets "realist" interests.

Let's focus on the nation-states. If they, the until now dominant collective subjects, want to keep a maximum of their capacity for action instead of ceding it to an in part economic, in part political world market, they have no other possibility but to engage with political innovations. The most important of these is a global order with a legal and democratic character. For both purposes, both for a global actualization of political freedom and for a collective capacity for action, a liberal global legal order is required.

This political innovation, of course, is so radical that objections impose themselves, of which I will name only four here.[2] According to a first objection, there are less interventionist alternatives. A liberal global order is said to be possible without having state character: as a strategic global order; as "governance without government"; or as a democratization of the world of states. These three alternatives undoubtedly have a great capacity for regulation. Yet since neither any of them separately nor all three combined are able to meet all needs for global action in a way appropriate to political freedom, a global legal order with some kind of state characteristics — in succinct terms: a world republic — remains called for.

According to a second objection, the world republic is a monster whose size and complexity render it ungovernable. Yet since polities such as the United States (316 million inhabitants), India (1.1 billion), and China (1.3 billion) are being governed nonetheless, the objection cannot be a decisive counterargument. It may at most serve as a relative and simultaneously constructive veto, not as an absolute veto. The world republic, then, remains permitted, even called for from the legal-moral perspective, provided it prevents both ungovernability and its overcompensation, be it in the form of excessive bureaucratization or even of a surveillance state.

According to a third objection, a world republic puts the great civilizational achievement of human rights and civil liberties in jeopardy. So far, the argument goes, only individual states have succeeded in guaranteeing these rights. The empirical share of this claim is correct but true only a third of the way. The second third of the truth reminds us that Western states prima facie endanger these rights. And according to the final third of the truth, a global legal order exercises restraint where human and civil rights are already being protected within a state. Not exercising such restraint in the case of massive human rights violations imposes itself, however, only when a so-called humanitarian intervention does not cause further harm; restraint is not, however, justified in principle here.

The third objection thus fares no better than the two cited earlier: it does not have the power of an absolute but of a constructive veto. Accordingly, and in keeping with the principle of global-state subsidiarity, individual states remain responsible for the primary guarantee of rights while the world republic is only a secondary state, and greater regional intermediary steps like the European Union are even merely tertiary states.

According to the fourth objection, the age of globalization threatens a leveling that demands a counterpoint, a strengthening of particularities, for the social and cultural richness of the world and the identity of individuals tied in with it to be preserved. The plea for "good fences," for national isolation instead of global unity, comes from the communitarians, who have been prominent for some time. The constructive veto that imposes itself here agrees with them, especially in the domain of history, tradition, and religion, of language, culture, and shared conceptions of the good. The second third recalls the legitimatizing individualism, which in this context means that individual states are not ends in themselves that deserve uncompromising protection. As entities that exist for the sake of people, they may be changed by and for the sake of people. And according to the last third, neither states nor foreign citizens are exempt from the universal precept of creating a legal order and a state, which in turn calls for an inter- and supranational legal order.

The principle that does justice to all three aspects is called global federalism. The world republic, the only one to be morally legitimate, is not merely a subsidiary federal unity, but it is multidimensional and includes several levels of statehood. Within it, people are citizens of the world but in a complementary, not an exclusive sense. Whether they would like primarily to be Germans, Belgians, and Latvians or rather Europeans instead is something they will have to decide. In any case, says a viable liberalism, they are primarily one or the other or, in a gradated way, both together. Secondarily or even only tertiarily, however, they are also world citizens: citizens of a federal world republic.

It is also possible to invoke the principle of subsidiarity as a cosmopolitan principle of parsimony, calling for only as much global order as is necessary. Accordingly, the global legal order must not unduly deprive individual states of power and in no case must it replace them. For it serves merely to supplement them, and moreover only where the global need for action requires it. Against the globalist thesis, which calls for abolishing them (see above, section 14.4), individual or nation-states are to be integrated into and be given priority within the global legal order. The one and only model to be legitimate, in keeping with the principle of freedom, is a complementary, that is, subsidiary and federal world republic. To establish it, more is needed than just an ever-denser and more widely applicable body of international law; just as indispensable are reliable mechanisms of control, including the separation and mutual checks of powers.

The world republic, instituted not in a coup but little by little, is thus to be established not as a homogenous, state-like unity that permits decentralization at most for pragmatic reasons. The "heroic" conception of the global state, which seeks hierarchic control of the entire world's society from a center, is to be rejected in any event. In keeping with the right to individual statehood, the parts of the world republic are not provinces given a right to administer themselves by some kind of political grace, a delegation from the top to the bottom. Rather, they are and remain states with an originary right to self-determination. Not only according to all experience so far but also in keeping with a realistic view of the facts, that is, in confronting many billions of inhabitants, hundreds of languages, and dozens of religions and faiths, moreover because of traditions grown over long periods of time, immense differences in mentalities, and not least of all the self-esteem of those concerned individually and collectively, political self-determination is in the best hands when it is left to polities that are smaller and have, above all, grown over time.

According to experience and legitimation, that is, both empirically and normatively, individual states remain the primary states. Merely for tasks they cannot solve by themselves do they ally with each other; for everything else, they maintain their competency. Here, the maxim of care and circumspection plays an important role: at no cost must they jeopardize the degree of constitutional democracy individual states and greater regions have already achieved. Two things that seem to contradict each other, individual statehood and global statehood, are connected. To make the point with a few succinct terms: what is required is a global statehood tied back to one's own state, as it were a cosmopolitanism tinged with patriotism and a patriotism steeped in cosmopolitanism.

This allows for resolving the difficulty diagnosed by the economist Dani Rodrik. According to him, there are three basic interests that drive policy. For each, good reasons can be cited although they contradict each other, and this constitutes "the fundamental political trilemma of the world economy: we cannot simultaneously pursue democracy, national determination, and economic globalization."[3] If Rodrik is correct in saying that the three political interests, in a strong democracy, in a strong nation, and in a highly developed economic globalization, cannot be stressed equally—and he makes a persuasive argument—then the legitimatizing primacy of democracy speaks in favor of the first two interests and of restraint in the case of the third, globalization.

In fact, democracy has legitimatizing primacy because legitimate rule must emanate from those concerned. Since democracy actualizes best in individual states, these latter, from the perspective of legitimacy, have the second priority, and in consequence, "the reach of global markets must be limited by the scope of their (mostly national) governance," to which we may add shared EU governance.[4] Rodrik rightly places globalization third, but he succumbs to its economistic reduction: in equating globalization with the world market, he barely pays attention to political globalization and its precept of a democracy-compatible global legal order. Since this global order also establishes the framework of economic globalization, economic globalization is given some legitimacy, albeit no unlimited right.

Individual states, if we follow the cosmopolitan principle of parsimony, that is, if we leave a great degree of individual statehood to them, can preserve their values and forms of life. Also, the identity of individuals can keep a state-related component, and the barriers of the state's borders, though diminished, are not lost. The worry of cosmopolitical skeptics is taken seriously and refuted: the diverse pluralism of humanity ought not and must not be delivered into the hands of a single, politically and culturally homogeneous polity.

One of the most important tasks of every state is to relieve citizens of the necessity of defending their rights themselves. That is the reason why the individual state takes on the protection of citizens including their rights and receives, to that purpose, sovereignty in domestic affairs (with the restrictions sketched earlier). The monopoly on violence remains in force insofar as it prohibits any kind of private justice. The same situation is replicated on the global level. Whether individuals, groups, or individual states — they all, first, have rights, among other things to life and limb, to goods and chattels, and to values of their own, furthermore to spaces and forms of living. And second, they have the second-order right to protect the common or first-order rights without recourse to private justice. In taking over this protection, the state, here understood as the embodiment of the public powers, ensures that the defense of the common rights takes place no longer personally but in common and without bias, precisely through public powers.

Yet both individual states and the global state must accept a relativization: because no state has the same legal-moral status as an individual, no state, nor any religion or tradition, is an end in itself. Instead, they serve the only (empirically known) entity to whom an intrinsic moral value can be attributed, the individual person. Yet to preserve its freedom in coexisting with others, the individual of course needs public law. In consequence, all statehood is subsidiary and yet has a legal-moral status. This presupposes that statehood serves the individuals, that it subjects itself to the legal-moral quartet discussed earlier, internally as a constitutional democracy and externally, in keeping with the notion of the enlightened nation-state, in an openness toward the complementary world republic. In this regard, but only in this regard, the political culture of a polity and ultimately also a world legal order are significant in more than just a functional sense: they also have a value of their own.

Even a merely subsidiary and federal world republic is threatened by a danger with which we are familiar from (almost) all federal states: while at the beginning, the previously independent states are not disempowered too much by the central power, federal competencies tend to grow more and more over time while a shifting back of jurisdiction happens very rarely. In this process of expansion, only a small share is due to member states freely relinquishing competencies. Generally, this takes place through a federal self-empowerment, for example by the federal powers interpreting their competencies in their own favor. (In Europe, as suggested, even an authority committed to the law, the European Court of Justice, is guilty of such an inappropriate expansion of rights.) In addition, there is often also the greater financial power of the federal authority, which is why member states welcome the assistance but repress the fact they are being weakened in the process.

The effective prevention of such dangers is among the most important tasks in detailing a global legal order. The usual principle that federal law overrides member states' law must in any event not lead to the latter's disempowerment. It is not the least of arguments *against* such a disempowerment that individual states can have, and in the case of long-standing democratic traditions in fact do have, a much greater degree of democratic legitimacy.

This argument applies already to the European Union and all the more so to a global legal order: even if the European Union reduces its democratic deficit and even if the global legal order actualizes the greatest possible degree of democracy, the sheer size of the population, moreover a wide variety of differences, and above all the social and political culture tied to different languages will unavoidably shape a development in which, the further away we move from the individual state, the less a participatory democracy that starts with the citizen can actually be put into practice. This is what is already happening on the path from the local community via a state or canton all the way to the federal state. This insight does not speak against a greater regional union like the EU or against a global legal order. It vetoes only two things: the replacement of smaller legal communities by larger ones and the accumulation or arrogation of too much decision-making power by the larger units. Whether we prefer to speak of individual states or of nation-states — to weaken them when they are democracies under the rule of law is irresponsible for reasons both of legal morality and of political prudence.

The question how these dangers are to be confronted does not fall within the purview of philosophy. What philosophy can do is obtain three criteria from the subsidiarity principle: the requirement clause, the "better" clause, and the precept of proportionality. According to them, the world republic may become active only where, first, the state is required at all and where, second, the action of the global state yields better results than the actions of individual nations acting by themselves or in coordinating themselves, all the while ensuring that, third, it acts only as much as is required.

Once more, the maxim of care and circumspection is called for. It demands a process of developing global statehood that begins with very modest solutions, gains experience with these, and emphatically remains open to necessary corrections. Above all, the level of freedom and law achieved in some places must not be jeopardized. To follow the example of the introduction of the European Monetary Union and to relinquish competencies without sufficient guarantees and reliable securities is not only to act foolishly; it is also to incur legal-moral guilt. Because there is so much more at stake here: on the path to the global legal order, in any case, we must not get involved in economic or political adventures on the pattern of the Euro.

The universal validity of the precept of law and democracy, which derives from political freedom, thus has two sides. Both can be articulated as a precept but also as a prohibition. According to the prohibition, we may neither lower nor even just endanger the level of law and freedom achieved in our own polity nor be content with the freedom within the individual or nation-state. And the precept demands a development toward a liberal global legal order that must, however, be established calmly and prudently.

PART V

Personal Freedom

For to give up a full will of my own was above all the supreme commandment
I had imposed upon myself; I, as a free ape, submitted to this yoke.
FRANZ KAFKA, *"A Report to an Academy"*[1]

Two aspects of freedom, though not they alone, of course, are essential to modernity: the freedom of thought, which makes it possible to think for oneself beyond the control of authorities and which, as freedom of science and research, grants these latter an ever-enduring thriving, and that freedom of the person that is not content with the other domains of freedom, social and political freedom, say, but one that means an inner freedom called "freedom of the will." One of the peculiarities of our time is that that the first of these freedoms turns against the second. Within the framework of the freedom of research, objections are made to the supposition of inner, personal freedom. At first some philosophers, then natural scientists oppose the assumption that the human being is free and quite simply deny personal freedom.

The last part of this study develops a three-step concept of freedom specific to the human being as a person. It also discusses, though, whether this freedom exists and whether it ought to be radically opposed: is it part of the costs of modernity that it initially grants increasing importance to personal freedom but later deprives it of all importance? Does personal freedom exist only as an illusion? Does modernity, in other words, live in the pragmatic contradiction that prominent claims of modernity are contradicted by the way modernity actually unfolds? And does the pragmatic contradiction exist not only between the freedom of research and the unfreedom of the human asserted by free research, or can it be found also in real life, since people, though they read about the skepticism concerning freedom, do not let their daily lives be influenced by it?

There is a second peculiarity, namely, that even the freedom-skeptical scientists succumb to the pragmatic contradiction. For in their own conduct, especially in their research activity, they remain as good as unaffected by the freedom skepticism they propagate.

According to the notion of personal freedom discussed in this fifth part, in any case, not only social and political units but their members, too, may be qualified as being free. In all events, societies and polities are to be considered free only if they grant their members freedom and if these members in principle know how to employ it. For if there is no kind of personal freedom, it does not make sense to demand free societies and free polities. That people do in fact make these demands and, where necessary, fight for them, already speaks against a radical skepticism and for personal freedom.

The fifth part of this study stages a new conflict of the faculties. It pursues the question whether our own experience of freedom is an illusion, as some claim anew, or whether the illusion instead does not afflict those who deny freedom (chapter 16). Because the second answer turns out to be more convincing, the following chapter develops the notion of freedom as personal autonomy (chapter 17). And a concluding outlook does not deny that humans pay a price for what, according to the great theorist of freedom Kant, constitutes their dignity, a small price and moreover a heavy price (chapter 18).

16

A New Conflict of the Faculties

Ever since its beginnings, ever since the (European) university has known the division into three higher faculties—theology, law, and medicine—and a lower, the philosophical faculty, the latter is threatened by contempt, a contempt Kant repudiates in his famous *The Conflict of the Faculties*. His thorough method is characterized by judicative argumentation. Kant first distinguishes between a "legal" and an "illegal" conflict and then rejects both the kind and the reach of the authority that the higher faculties claim for themselves.[1]

Today, some but by no means all neuro- and cognitive scientists put forward, with missionary zeal, a series of claims that force a new conflict of the faculties. This conflict is to be played out here by addressing two questions: first, the question to what extent neuroscientists have the competence, thematically and methodologically, to declare personal freedom an illusion; second, the question whether neuroscientists in their own lives as they actually live them, not (only) in their private lives but (also) in their lives as researchers, do in fact deny freedom. The first question also leads to a third: do the neurosciences have such a comprehensive authority, an eliminatory authority that excludes the other sciences? In other words, may the neurosciences repeat what has been attempted several times before in European intellectual history, namely, try to become philosophy's heir without having genuine philosophical competence? Or are there several kinds of competence, complementary, if necessary, but at the same time mutually restricting?

The term "philosophy" here is not limited to the activity of philosophy professors in the academy. It names a methodical-critical reflection for which academic philosophy does not claim exclusive competency. The conflict of the faculties played out in the pages that follow does not question the original competence of neuroscientists. It merely defends the rights of methodical-critical reflection. Neuroscientific skepticism about freedom conceives of itself as an enlightenment; the conflict of the faculties I stage here is conceived as an enlightenment about enlightenment, an enlightenment in the second degree of the kind this book is pursuing in general.

I unfold the new conflict of the faculties in four steps. I first spell out the provocations, the alleged illusionary character of freedom (section 16.1); then I outline six stages of freedom (section 16.2), encounter several fallacies (section 16.3), discuss one of them, the determinist fallacy, in more detail (section 16.4); and, after critiquing a hasty conclusion (section 16.5), I conclude by demonstrating a pragmatic contradiction on the part of freedom skeptics (section 16.6).

16.1
IS FREEDOM AN ILLUSION?

The ideas of freedom and responsibility are deeply rooted in human life. In practically all cultures we know of, people enter into friendships and partnerships. They conclude deals with one another, assume offices that come with considerable responsibility or elect others to these offices and, where necessary, demand accountability or even liability. And if they think it makes sense, they drag each other into court. In all these activities, they suppose responsibility and tacitly claim freedom for themselves.

Since the 1990s, prominent neuroscientists and cognitive psychologists have opposed this claim, practiced daily by countless generations. They claim they are able to prove scientifically what had initially been a philosophical agenda, advocated for example by materialists such as Paul Henri Thiry d'Holbach. With uncompromising severity, they declare freedom to be a delusion, a superstition even, of which we must finally rid ourselves.

The argumentative core of this Enlightener's attitude, the emancipation from the illusion of freedom, consists in a neurodeterminism that declares, to use Wolf Singer's much-cited words: "Connectivity [in the brain] determines us. We should stop talking about freedom."[2]

Before we follow neuroscientists in their freedom skepticism, we should realize what would be lost in the world we are familiar with. The loss begins with a concept that has not just dominated penal law until now but has played a role of paramount importance in everyday behavior as well, including education in the family and in school, and not least of all in public behavior: the concept of guilt. In all these domains, actions are judged according to criteria of good and bad, even good and evil. The authors of "good" actions are praised while the authors of "bad" actions are rebuked, held responsible where necessary, and held liable for the consequences of their actions. Those who excel in the good receive honors, prizes in some domains. Committing a lot of bad actions on the contrary leads to being despised and maybe even ostracized.

The loss of the idea of freedom would generally render basic concepts of our life, both of our everyday lives and of the law, obsolete: person, accountability and responsibility including liability, furthermore legal competence, religious and political maturity, as well as the idea of patient autonomy or the ideas of human rights and human dignity, not least those of political and personal morality.

A sense of history, however, reminds freedom skeptics to be modest. It is not the first time the objection against the idea of criminal responsibility is being raised, and yet it has not caught on. As early as 1876, Cesare Lombroso, the Italian forensic scientist and psychiatrist, tried to dislodge the idea of guilt with his theory of the "born criminal" in his book *Criminal Man*. Later, the German psychologist and social scientist Arno Plack, with more vehemence than argumentative force, called for abolishing guilt-based penal law altogether.[3] While these and other authors started quite a number of controversies, they have not succeeded in convincing society of the necessity of abolishing guilt-based penal law.

There is another, a systematic argument. Were we to give up the concept of guilt, communities would still be able to impose sanctions on delinquents. Yet in the absence of responsibility and guilt, these sanctions would not be penalties but merely quasi penalties, a series of measures or forced therapies that leave room for extremely unjust sanctions in both directions. Such quasi penalties could be (too) long for offenses that are likely to entail long processes of betterment or recovery and (too) short for capital offenses where there is little risk of reoffending.

Educational theorists have known for a long time something that Aristotle already articulates and common sense reaffirms, something to which we all have access: those who always follow the drives and passions of the moment are enslaved by them. They are unfree.[4] In turn, those become free who by training, accompanied by praise and rebuke, develop the appropriate attitude. We become prudent by acting prudently, brave by acting bravely, just by acting justly.

If indeed there were no personal freedom, the distinction intimated here, the difference between a free and an unfree character, would lose its justification, even if we experience it time and again in our daily interactions. At stake, therefore, is nothing less than a precondition of education, self-education, and self-respect. We must ask here whether the neuroscientists who deny freedom have realized just how broad the consequences of their claims are. Do they seriously seek to throw the educatability, the ability to educate human beings and necessity of doing so, into doubt (see chapter 4)? Do they really mean to question that, as babies and infants, humans not only need care and security but soon also need an education, which in many cases clearly succeeds but in some cases fails? The training of scientists, too, which makes them conscientious, thorough, and resistant both to plagiarism and to the falsification of data, has educational character.

The threat is thus far reaching, even if it does not, of course, concern all facts of freedom directly. Social and political freedom, or the liberation from a number of natural constraints via technology and medicine, are not immediately at stake—yet mediately they are. For why should human beings liberate themselves from natural constraints; why should society and the legal order guarantee freedom if we are incapable of making use of the framework thus provided since freedom is purely an illusion?

16.2
STAGES OF FREEDOM

When we seek a thorough assessment of freedom skepticism we agree to an effort at disambiguation. Before we stop talking about freedom, we want to know what exactly it is we should stop doing.

To get a sense of the rich significations of personal freedom, we can distinguish between six meanings. Since they build on each other, we may call them stages of freedom. The first three stages are not specific to the human being. We are dealing there with simple, not yet personal freedom. They are as it were preliminary stages. Only the next three, the main stages, are concerned with personal freedom itself.

You might wonder why these reflections cast such a wide net. There are three reasons for starting with the preliminary stages. First, it prevents a rush into anthropocentrism. The very concept that seems to lift the human from out of nature, freedom, nonetheless remains open toward the natural aspect of the human being. In this way, the popular alternative between the human belonging to nature and assuming a privileged position is unmasked as a misleading either-or. In truth, both assertions are correct: the human being is rooted in nature in a variety of ways and nonetheless falls outside nature. In a variation and application of the anthropological definition of the human being as *zōon logon echon*, an animal capable of language and reason, we may define the human as the animal that differs from other animals not by freedom as such but by a freedom of an emphatically higher stage.

Second, we thus endow the phenomenon of freedom with an inner dynamic, and, third, not least of all, we take some weight off the debate about human freedom. If freedom applies already to subhuman beings, we are no longer dealing with a question of all or nothing. What remains to be decided is not the question whether humans are free at all but the question in what way they are free and the further question whether this kind of freedom differs from the freedom we already find in the animal kingdom.

The most modest stage, a quasi self-determination, can already be observed in inorganic nature. Because of an electric charge, certain elements are pushing by themselves for a (chemical) bond with other elements. In the case of hydrogen (H) and oxygen (O), this leads to the well-known chemical formula for water, H_2O. The combination of iron (Fe) and oxygen (O), to give another example, yields ferric oxide (Fe_2O_3), that is, the phenomenon of rusting. The transmission of nerve signals via membrane potentials belongs to this first stage of freedom as well.

"Inorganic freedom" increases in the domain of the organic, since what we find there is not just a quasi self-determination but a real one. The movement takes place through the plant itself. In the three tasks of plant life—nutrition, growth, and collective self-movement, that is, reproduction—plants are *self*-moving, even if an external force usually needs to intervene to complete the third task (insects for pollination, for example).

There is a qualitative increase of these three achievements in animals, to the extent that three self-controlled and, in that regard, free activities are added: perception, locomotion, and a striving toward or away from things. In this third stage, in specifically animal freedom, in hunger and thirst, for example, the moment of the self increases to become an (albeit only sensual-practical) self-consciousness, which consists of sensations of pleasure and displeasure. This opens up a new kind of space for action, since hunger and thirst can be understood as warning signals to the brain, as sensations of a lack of food and fluids, that combine with a push, but not a compulsion, to overcome the lack.

In the inner dynamic of the concept of freedom sketched so far, we see a gradation emerge that is much more fundamental than the familiar either-or. The animals in question are not just comparatively more free than plants. They are more free in a whole new way, since moving oneself is joined by moving oneself by way of sensations, which we find in all animal species capable of pleasure and pain and by no means only in such highly developed animals as primates.

In the next three meanings of freedom, which are specific to human beings, the driving forces we already find in the animal world such as hunger, thirst, aggression, and sexuality may have some power, but they must not be overpowering. They must instead leave room for the question whether it is good to follow the impulse at issue. The specifically human capacity for language plays an essential role here. What I mean is a cognitive capacity that goes beyond the associative learning abilities of subhuman organisms because it consists in a capacity for syntactic and semantic learning. This learning opens up those practically unlimited possibilities of language that are contained in the potential for highly personal worlds of words and ideas. And because this capacity is both decisive and specific — it requires two regions of the brain that have been known for over a century, Broca's and Wernicke's areas — there may be in animals certain beginnings of the main stages of freedom. But anything beyond such mere beginnings, the real human freedom that develops in three further stages is barred for them.

To the first main stage of specifically human freedom belongs a (language-bound) knowledge. This knowledge of course is not theoretical; it is a practical, action-oriented knowledge, concerned, for example, with the scope and consequences of a given action. In affirming what we know, we combine the cognitive with a voluntary moment. We act consciously and voluntarily and are thus accountable subjects, responsible persons.

One cause of this capacity for acting from knowledge and assent lies in the object of brain research. Thanks to a brain that, especially because of Broca's and Wernicke's areas, is much more complex even when compared with that of other primates, human beings can reflect on three things: they can reflect on the scope and consequences of their actions; they can think about the criteria necessary for doing so, that is, the question what is good and the rules that go with it; and, not least of all, they are able to judge their acting according to these criteria. They do not, however, always follow them, which is why the rules for acting are not rules of what is but of what ought to be. They are imperatives, by which I do not mean arbitrary orders of a dominant power but action-oriented arguments in the interest of the action concerned. These arguments, of course, do not always manage to impose themselves.

Depending on the scope of the demand, there are three main stages of reasons and three stages of freedom corresponding to them. In the case of the first, technical or functional freedom, reasons are oriented toward a relationship of means and ends; "good" here means "good for something." In the case of the second, pragmatic freedom, "good" means "good for someone." Here, freedom concerns an as yet premoral purpose, the natural goal of a bodily and sensual being, one's own welfare or happiness. Obviously, there is in addition the next step of being able to relativize one's own welfare and setting it aside when it conflicts with other goals. This third, genuinely moral stage corresponds to moral freedom, which we will have to discuss in more detail (see chapter 17).

According to this outline of the argument,[5] there is no need for abstruse speculations to defend personal freedom. Without a moralizing undertone, it attributes freedom to the human capacity for following independently accepted reasons. This capacity, called "practical reason," suffices to defend personal freedom. Morality corresponds to that third and highest stage, the stage of independently accepted reasons, and has the status of pure practical reason.

16.3
FALLACIES

Imaging procedures are among the most important tools of recent research on the brain. Their potential for illustrating what is going on in the brain has increased so much that neuroimaging has become the most popular kind of illustration in the sciences. This contains the danger of equating the illustration of a scientific finding with the finding itself, of mistaking a means of scientific rhetoric and didactics for what is to be transmitted. The achievements must nonetheless not be brushed aside.

Neuroimaging allows for more than just illustrations. It makes it possible to draw up precise maps for localizing everyday capacities such as seeing, sensing touch, and hearing, as talking and walking. This localization has now become so exact that on the one hand, for example, it can not only identify professional musicians but moreover distinguish between pianists and violinists. On the other hand, it permits more precise and less damaging brain surgery. Brain scans also allow for the diagnosis of organic processes like inflammations, hemorrhages, and tumors, and for the early detection of Parkinson's disease and dementia as well as, in the foreseeable future, mental disorders. The causes of these diseases, though, remain unknown.[6]

The fascination neuroimaging exercises is thus understandable. Yet what is its contribution to the debate concerning freedom? In combination with a second tool, the huge capacities for data processing of the newest computers, neuroimaging is said to make it possible to watch the brain as it perceives, thinks, and feels. In reality, this supposition commits a first, a mereological fallacy: one attributes, as Aristotle already points out, properties, capacities, or actions to a part (*meros* in Greek) of an organism that can meaningfully be attributed only to the whole.[7] Not the thesis widely defended by brain researchers, *we are our brain*, but the opposite is true, *we are brain plus body* or, even more precisely, *we are our whole living body, which includes the brain*. This is how the neurophysiologist

Detlef Linke can see in freedom the decisive orientation of the human being and declare: "Even if this concept [that of freedom—OH] is supported by brains, that does not mean that freedom is only a matter of the brain."[8]

The hopes associated with neuroimaging technology must be restricted further: only in a sense is it possible to watch perceiving and thinking. For what is seen is only the objective, spatial-temporal architecture of the brain, not the subjective concomitants of neuronal processes we call "perceiving," "thinking," and "feeling." Take the plastic example of a mountain trekker: what appears on the brain researcher's screen is neither the summit the trekker is looking at nor the question *Will I be able to conquer the mountain?* The brain researcher sees neither the perceptions of our trekker nor his thoughts ready to be read. All he sees are functional connections he addresses "as" perception, "as" thinking, and so on. In so doing, he makes an addition, an interpretation, that all those neuroscientists pass over in silence who, aware of the hegemonial significance of their work in scientific policy, get ahead of themselves.

Unlike the suggestion of Gerhard Roth's title *From the Brain's Perspective*, the observed brain does not have certain views on perceiving, remembering, thinking, and feeling.[9] These views are attributable merely to the brain scientist who, constantly and at an increasing distance from what he is observing, is making interpretations. These begin with interpreting certain sense stimuli as cells or relay points and ascend via numerous intermediary steps to a physiological theory of the brain that seeks to interpret the entirety of human activities, including thinking and experiences of freedom, in neuronal terms.

To pass over this many-faceted task in silence is to succumb to another fallacy. Those who attribute already to the perception of functional connections the capacities or actions that in truth result from only the interpretation of what is being perceived commit a second, a perceptiological fallacy.

The interpretations additionally required presuppose familiarity with the patterns of interpretation, namely, knowledge of the particularities of perceiving, thinking, and feeling. To put it in institutional terms: the question of the freedom of the will is not decided in the laboratories of brain researchers and their seconds, the psychologists, but in the classroom, not in experiments but only in the interpretation of experiments. And where it becomes relevant to freedom of the will, this interpretation is by no means as uncontested as brain researchers suppose.

This situation has important consequences. If the question were decided in the lab, the relationship between neuroscientists and the lifeworld would be greatly troubled. For both in the personal and in the social lifeworld, freedom, as noted, is considered to be essential. If the brain researchers were right, a pitiful diagnosis inspired by philosophical contract theory would impose itself: brain research and lifeworld would be in an (intellectual) state of nature characterized, as in contract theory, by a state of war.

If the freedom-skeptical brain researchers were right, matters would even be worse. People in the (fictitious!) state of nature act on the basis of certain reasons. To that extent they act in accordance with a practical reason, even if this is only at the first, technical or instrumental stage, and it is precisely because of this, because they are open to reason, that they can overcome the state of nature, again for reasons, perhaps for reasons of a higher stage. Yet if, because of a lack of any practical reason, there is no freedom, neither a technical nor a pragmatic nor a moral freedom, the dangers of the state of nature escalate into an unpredictable state of nature: brain research and lifeworld would be separated by an unbridgeable abyss.

Fortunately, matters are different. Since the question is decided not in the lab but in discourse, pars pro toto in the classroom, the outlook for freedom of the will is brighter, both methodologically and factually. For while laboratory and lifeworld are methodologically separated by an abyss, the classroom is an institution that has a power of mediation. And the reconciliation resulting from the mediation transforms the alleged state of war into a state of peace.

Philosophy, in the tradition going back to Aristotle, has been making this reconciliation easier for itself by not reducing the processes inside the human being to physics and chemistry but rather conceiving of them as organic processes. In that regard, it shares the basic neuroscientific view that the dynamic within the brain is to be interpreted as an organism and is thus not to be discussed via linear procedural models but as a self-organizing process.

Philosophy thus permits itself the following preliminary conclusion: the significant objections just sketched render the neurobiological skepticism concerning freedom implausible. And an enlightened liberalism does not see any reason yet to abandon one of its basic concepts, the concept of personal freedom.[10]

16.4

FOR EXAMPLE: THE DETERMINIST FALLACY

At the argumentative core of neuroscientific freedom skepticism lies a (neuro-) determinism. Let's take a closer look. The skepticism concerning freedom, voiced already long before the neurosciences, generally goes by the name "determinism." Its core thesis, namely, that human action is determined in multiple ways, and the interest the thesis is based on, to throw a possible unlimited freedom of the will into doubt, may be convincing. It just remains to be tested whether determination—which is not controversial in principle, only as regards its scope—justifies a determinism that denies all freedom.

Undoubtedly, the human being is subjected to the laws of physics: when I lean too far over a parapet, I will fall according to the law of falling bodies. The same is true for the laws of chemistry: when I accidentally expose my hand to acid, the skin will be burned. And matters are no different when it comes to biology: our genetic code determines not only factors like hair and eye color, sex, blood type, and, largely, height, but moreover also anomalies and susceptibility for certain diseases.

The determinations investigated by the natural sciences are joined by other, emotional, social, and cultural ones. Actions may thus be explained by personal motives or social expectations and certain omissions by a relevant taboo. Yet it is not by coincidence that the social sciences investigating them see themselves as behavioral sciences, not as sciences of action. According to the expression "behavior," humans are passive rather than active beings, exposed to the overwhelming influence of the inner and outer conditions of life. The expression "action" on the contrary attributes to them a high degree of responsibility.

In its early stages, humanity was not always sufficiently persistent and clever in its search for causes and motives. It often prematurely ended the search and, especially when it came to natural occurrences, appealed to invisible powers such as gods or an anonymous fate. Yet as soon as causes and causal chains and, moreover, laws are being discovered and alleged gods unmasked as simple natural phenomena—as soon as, to take Xenophanes's example, the goddess Iris is revealed to be the rainbow that is produced when the sun behind the observers shines on a rain cloud in front of them—the traditional view may be called a superstition, outdated in any case, and its overcoming be referred to as enlightenment.

The manifold conditionality has by now become precise empirical knowledge: as a body, the human being is subject to the laws of physics and of chemistry, as a living body to the laws of biology and physiology. The driving forces, the motives and passions, depend on needs and interests, also on temperament, furthermore on constellations of drives and character traits that in turn are codetermined by genetic factors, (early) childhood impressions, and environmental factors, including education. Moreover: whom we meet, what we hear and read, and what happens to us can fundamentally change our lives. The persecutor of Christians Saul, for example, becomes the Apostle Paul, and the bon vivant Augustine a great doctor of the Christian Church.

The individual sciences, in any event, investigate causes. The question whether this turns into unfreedom, however, is no longer within their purview but within that of metareflections traditionally assigned to philosophy. Both sides have their competence proper that, for the sake of the issue, they should defend against the other side.

The metareflections begin with the insight that causes explain why something is this way and not otherwise, which is why given sufficient causes a matter of fact appears as necessary. It is, however, merely relatively, not absolutely necessary, for on the condition of another constellation of causes, the matter could have ended up quite differently. Someone falling from an upper-story window onto a hard pavement will get hurt by relative necessity. But if they do not lean out that far or if they fall onto a haystack, they will remain unharmed. Causal determination thus is merely what necessity *in each case* consists in.

Some scientists and philosophers think that, if we just look thoroughly enough, a sufficient network of causes can be found for everything, not just for physically explicable processes, and that, in the case of human behavior, this network of causes contradicts the possibility of free action. In the debate about freedom, this view, that a complete determination of human action is irreconcilable with human freedom, is called "incompatibilism."[11]

The counterthesis, "compatibilism," reproaches freedom-skeptical determinism for a wrong conception of freedom or for a conceptual confusion.[12] Freedom, on this view, does indeed consist in an independence, yet not in an independence from causes but one from coercion. A person is unfree only when she is coerced into committing or omitting an action in one of two respects. Either she is unfree in a social respect, when the coercion is coming from her social environment; or she is unfree in a personal respect, when there is something more than merely an inner drive, namely, an inner compulsion or coercion.

According to this objection, the denial of freedom needs at least one more argument, and this argument must permit inferring "coerced" from "caused." A freedom-skeptical determinism considers this permission to be given already where the usual, external causes are extended by internal causes to form a sufficient network of causes in which action appears as an inescapable effect. Yet this complete determinism does not yet yield the fatal consequence that freedom is impossible. For "caused from within" does not yet yield "coerced." To suppose so nonetheless, like the incompatibilists do, is to succumb to a further fallacy, the third by now, namely, the deterministic fallacy. According to that fallacy, in order to save freedom, it is necessary to claim an at least partial indeterminateness because complete determination is incompatible with freedom.

None of the serious defenders of human freedom deny that there are conditionalities. On the contrary, they are open to everyday experience, and in addition they gather information from the individual sciences. But they will debate the scope. Where there is a conditionality that is as comprehensive as it is profound, freedom skeptics believe they can infer something contested from something uncontested: because of determinations that are neither disputed nor surprising, they question a view that all life experience does not contest and advocate determinism.

Yet a closer look reveals more than just one determinism. The first variety, a methodological determinism, lies at the basis of all research as a regulative idea. Whether in the natural or in the social sciences — empirical research supposes of all matters of the natural and the social world that they are explainable by causes or understandable through motives, and causes and motives in turn are rendered intelligible through laws.

Methodological determinism consists in nothing but a never finally satisfied desire for knowledge in the natural and social sciences. Instead of an eternal inability to know, there is at the moment a lot of not knowing but no ignorance insurmountable as a matter of principle. Instead of expecting miracles in the strict sense of matters without a cause, one expects thorough research always to discover causes.

Critics of freedom are right insofar as all events, including human actions, may be questioned as to (natural) causes; events are thus regarded to be potentially determined. An indeterminism appealing to coincidences or miracles is excluded. This does not presuppose, as Wolf Singer claims it does, that volition is ultimately uncaused or, as Gerhard Roth would have it, that a person could have acted differently under identical external and internal conditions.[13] Nor do we have to succumb to Hume's fear, reiterated by Roth, that people will act unpredictably even more often. On the contrary, an attitude acquired through repeated practice prevents us from doing otherwise: courageous people like Achilles do not flee any danger; people willing to help like Albert Schweitzer and Mother Teresa seek to relieve distress; and honest people do not cheat.

Those who practice an epistemic imperialism for their discipline and for example consider neuroscientific knowledge to be the only knowledge relevant for freedom and who, moreover, in a generous extrapolation derive from *methodological* determinism a *dogmatic* determinism that denies freedom in general, omit the methodological restriction mentioned earlier: events are determined only insofar as we move within the domain of possible experience, be it natural or social. Beyond this domain it remains at least possible to think personal freedom, which justifies the following preliminary result.

Those who limit themselves to the domain of possible natural and social experience exclude personal freedom, that is, freedom of the will in the extended sense, from the outset and methodically. They must therefore not be surprised that they cannot find freedom as their work progresses. That is why brain researchers and psychologists ought to heed practical wisdom and stick with what they know rather than infer the nonexistence of freedom from natural and perhaps also social givens.

For the philosopher, the will is not free because it suspends natural causality but because the will despite natural causality has a capacity we will come to know better, the capacity for acting for a reason. An appropriate concept, in any case, does not declare freedom to be a deficit in knowledge, nor does it consider freedom a cognitive anarchy, an arbitrariness that arises from an absence of causes.

One position influential to this day, a strict indeterminism also known as "libertarianism," however, advocates the exact opposite view: only those are free who could also have decided differently; all those who have no alternative possibility, no way out, are unfree. According to this strict indeterminism, the concept of freedom includes a deficit of sufficient causality.

A series of arguments speaks against this conception of freedom as partial absence of causes. It begins with the freedom-threatening peculiarity that persons, including all their actions and the will they are based on, would be free only with reference to the current state of knowledge, strictly speaking even merely with reference to the current state of knowledge of the subject claiming freedom. The consequence is hardly convincing: a lack of relevant expert knowledge, ignorance, becomes the measure of freedom. The less someone knows, the more often he proclaims himself and others to be free. Inversely, the more knowledge someone has of causes, the less freedom she would have to claim for herself. For an all-knowing mind, there would even be no freedom at all, neither for itself nor for any other beings, because such a mind would foresee all beings' actions and omissions.

A second, a more fundamental counterargument notes a confusion of categories or perspectives, the mistaking of an objective for a subjective property: for as to its content, personal freedom is a property of objects, of beings capable of action. Yet according to methodological determinism, an absence of causes is due to a property of the cognizing subject, to its (preliminary) lack of knowledge. To declare an action or a volition to be free because it is without cause or reason — in a word, undetermined — asserts only a limit of human knowledge. The extreme case of asserting an absence of causes or impossibility of explanation as a matter of principle even supposes a limit that cannot be crossed, without for all that demonstrating the existence of human freedom.

Those who hold on to the "language game" of freedom and responsibility cannot accept indeterminism or libertarianism. For otherwise, the possibility no longer exists of answering to others or to oneself, to present justificatory or exonerating reasons, that is, to do what is meant by "taking responsibility."

Indeterminism fails to convince also because it succumbs to the deterministic fallacy, which omits the difference between "caused from within" and "coerced" and passes over the reflexivity that speaks against coercion and to which we will return. Incomplete but merely methodological determinism in contrast considers random action to be merely apparently random: even if we do not know the causes or reasons, we still understand all events in the world to be effects for which, in principle, causes can be found.

The great philosopher of freedom Immanuel Kant conceptualizes a determinism that is as radical as it is universal. That is why it is all the more astonishing that even philosophically trained authors from Gilbert Ryle to Peter Bieri to Ansgar Beckermann[14] shy away from engaging with this philosopher who, with arguments of rare clarity and rigor, provides a foundation for the determinism contained in scientific thinking and nonetheless develops a theory of freedom, a theory, moreover, whose subtleness has not met its match to this day. Instead, many still appeal to a pre-Kantian philosopher, Descartes, and his dualism of body and soul. Those who do not want to simplify the criticism of allegedly traditional thinking — traditional because it is dualistic — would do well to engage with the nondualistic and, moreover, scientifically supported concept of the soul Aristotle developed.[15]

Let me summarize Kant's reflections in a form detached from Kant's language.[16] Those who seek to defend the possibility of personal freedom and thereby to understand one basis of enlightened liberalism must be aware both of the scope and of the limits of the common way of thinking in terms of causality. As a matter of principle, all experiential processes, both the processes of the natural and those of the social world, and not least of all the so-called inner processes, take place as processes of causes and effects.

To explain temporal processes objectively, we must regard them as effects for which causes can be found. In consequence, the veritable freedom of a person can be thought only by detaching ourselves from temporal processes and at the same time leaving the world of external and internal causes and thereby entering into a new, fundamentally different world. It is the world of reasons, that is, a world of causes of a kind that corresponds not to (natural, social, or psychological) nature but to action-oriented reason, ultimately to pure practical reason. The usual way of thinking in terms of causes and effects is thus to be abandoned in favor of thinking in terms of practical reason. It is in its reasons that personal freedom shows that it can be thought, and it will be found, via negations, as a lived reality.

16.5
AGAINST A HASTY CONCLUSION

Following these reflections, we may conclude the new conflict of the faculties I have outlined with the question: what bearing does Libet's experiment, a paradigm of research on the brain, have on the problem of freedom? In this classic stimulus-reaction experiment, test subjects are asked to raise or not raise their hand in response to a given signal. According to Benjamin Libet's observation, the reaction that Roth calls the "jolt of the will," the raising or not raising of the hand, is preceded by the accumulation of an electric readiness potential.[17] Does it follow from this observation, first, that the jolt is the effect of the readiness potential and, second, that because of this causal relationship there is no freedom of the will in the sense of simple freedom of the will, of a technical and pragmatic freedom to act? Does it follow that we can neither choose the means appropriate to any number of purposes nor take promising paths toward the natural guiding purpose, toward happiness?

According to a standard-setting insight of Kant's, an observable change is not objectively recognizable unless four observable things are assumed. First, there must be a temporal succession: first the readiness potential, then the jolt of the will. Second, the irreversibility of this succession must be asserted: not first the jolt of the will, then the readiness potential. For the sake of irreversibility, third, a *because*, that is, causality must be presupposed: the jolt takes place *because* a readiness potential has built up *beforehand*. Yet the *because* does not follow already from the *beforehand*; a rule of association is required that, perhaps unknown for the time being, regards the event *beforehand* not as random but as a *prior to* necessary in the sense and direction of the process.

This state of affairs merely *seems* to render freedom of the will and with it responsibility, guilt-based penal law, and morality impossible. According to the enlightenment concerning enlightenment I announced at the beginning of this fifth part, it is not freedom that is an illusion. Instead, it is the alleged unmasking of freedom that turns out to be the real illusion. For beside the usual causality, the cause-effect connections investigated by the natural and social sciences, there is another, fundamentally different causality, acting for reasons of one's own, be they technical, pragmatic, or moral.

Another argument speaks against overestimating the neurobiological researches: Libet's experiment is not about a real free or unfree decision but about a minimal reaction according to a set instruction, raising or not raising one hand, an atomic action that, as we will see, is insufficient and strictly speaking inconsequential for the question of the freedom of the will. The same applies to Wolf Singer's perception experiments.[18]

Temporally, the processes of the brain relevant to the question of freedom and responsibility, that is, the neuronal processes that pertain to lying, cheating, or stealing, to being prudent, helping, or forgiving, even to threatening or appeasing, are not short but intermediary and often even long stretches, more precisely long periods of time. Human action consists of a complex connection of short-, medium-, and sometimes also long-term goals that are weighed against each other in light of guiding aspects such as happiness or morality and for which the appropriate ways and means are sought according to opportunities and resources but also according to obstacles and resistances.

We must not forget that the actions that are decisive for freedom require interpretation, too. Without interpretation, there is only a morally indifferent basic action, for example when we grasp something with our hand. How the action pertains to freedom is decided only when it comes to the question whether in this grasp, we are reaching into our own or into another's pocket and whether a possible other owner consents to this taking because he is giving the thing taken as a gift; if there is no such consent, the taking is a stealing.

Back to the reflection on ways and means: the complex of capacities and skills this requires is not something humans are born with. Rather, the capacities of thinking, evaluating, and deciding must be learned in a longer process of practice. In the course of this learning, we develop the neuronal patterns that enable (technically, pragmatically, and morally) free action.

If the learning succeeds, it becomes possible to discover reasons, to weigh them against each other, and to decide on the basis of this evaluation. By excluding all these things, atomic actions never even look at actions that are free in a sense relevant in a theory of action.

It is not a spectacular insight that making up one's mind and coming to a decision requires a brain. Nor is it spectacular that the brain, as brain researchers insist, works not with a supreme cognitive center but through a polycentric network. Nor is a philosophy of the freedom of the will surprised by the fact that mind and consciousness did not fall from the sky but developed gradually in the evolution of nervous systems or by the assumption that the I is composed "of genetic factors . . . of prenatal and early postnatal experiences as well as experiences I made as a young person and finally as an adult." It is not even necessary to assert a general "dominance of conscious reflections over unconscious driving forces."[19]

16.6
A PRAGMATIC CONTRADICTION

Reviewing the debate, one might get the impression that in everyday life, there is a natural philosophy when it comes to fundamental matters. For sober philosophers are characterized by resistance to astonishment—they do not consider everything presented to them as new to be in fact new or, in case something is new, to be convincing.

Be it everyday thinking or philosophy: neither denies that brain research has significantly extended our knowledge and might in the process have come across previously unknown or underestimated determinants. Our understanding of the neuronal bases of both the cognitive and the emotional aspect of mental processes has unquestionably improved. Yet the great successes that were announced, for medicine, for example, have not come to pass. So far, fundamental research in neurobiology has not prompted significant advances in psychiatry or in neurosurgery or neurorehabilitation either.

For the new conflict of the faculties, of course, something else is more important: the announced necessity of making a revolutionary change in our self-conception, shaped as it is by freedom and responsibility, which would have had catastrophic consequences for our lives and our living together, has vanished into thin air. Both forecasts turned out to be wrong: neither the announced revolutions nor the catastrophes have come to pass. Even what remains of the claims, their enlightening value, is meager. A dualism claiming a separation of body and mind might be advocated by Descartes and other philosophers. Since Aristotle, that is, for almost two and a half thousand years, however, there has been a more circumspect counterposition. Outside some debates in epistemology and the theory of science, in practical life, dualism hardly plays a role anyway.

A second aspect of this resistance to astonishment comes out in the following peculiarity: although freedom-skeptical brain researchers consider their work to bury freedom under a mountain of doubts, people in their everyday lives remain unaffected by it. In so doing, they can point to the scientists themselves, not to what they say but to the way they live. While what they say denies freedom, the way they live—not only their private life but above all their life as researchers—emphatically calls on freedom. In philosophy, this constellation, a person's explicit claims contradicting their actual behavior, is called a pragmatic contradiction.

Surprisingly, freedom-skeptical brain researchers and their seconds, the psychologists, have not yet noticed that they succumb to this contradiction. Although they are used to working methodically, they have not yet noticed that in their work they put conscious and voluntary action in practice as a matter of course, that is, they claim freedom for themselves in spite of their explicit statements. In any case, brain researchers who are skeptical of freedom tend not to apply this skepticism to themselves. At the least, they ignore the question how far they as investigators and the test subjects are free. When we overcome this widespread "blind gaze," we find practically all the stages of authorship and practical reasons.

On the one hand, test subjects usually participate voluntarily; they can act in accordance to the test protocol (technical freedom), expect something that will benefit them (pragmatic freedom), and are capable of honesty (moral freedom).

The investigator, in turn, is the conscious author of the experiment not just in the sense of the preliminary stages of freedom. The colleagues, at the very latest, who check the experiment take this authorship seriously, hold the investigator responsible for the three main stages of freedom, and if necessary hold him accountable (1) for the experiment's "technical" quality, including of its interpretation; (2) for its pragmatic quality in the sense of originality and explanatory power; and finally (3) for its moral quality, that is, that there has been no falsification of data or plagiarism.

Not least of all, researchers are proud of their achievements and let themselves be rewarded for brilliant performance with prestige and prizes. Despite their explicit skepticism about freedom, that is, in an obvious contradiction to the claims that deny freedom, they live a life of freedom and responsibility.

How, then, does the conflict of the faculties end? To develop their freedom skepticism, the skeptics invoke freedom, both the personal freedom apparent in their own achievement and, as political framework, a liberty, the legally guaranteed freedom of science and research. It follows that their negation of freedom is not viable without a double affirmation of freedom. In the first affirmation, the plea for (personal) nonfreedom is made in the name of freedom, and in the second affirmation, one claims for oneself the (personal) freedom one denies.

The conflict of the faculties does not merely concede to the brain researchers that they investigate determinants of human action within their thematic and methodological framework; it welcomes it. In this modest way (which ought to be expected from all disciplines), brain researchers can enrich the debate about freedom. On balance, however, the conflict ends, methodologically, in favor of a philosophical reflection, an enlightenment of enlightenment, and, in terms of content, in favor of social, political, and above all also personal freedom. For even a brain researcher, by simply reflecting on what he is actually doing, will prefer acknowledging "his" (social, political, and personal) freedom and with it the general possibility "of freedom" to denying it.

17

Personal Autonomy

17.1

SIMPLE AND FREE WILL

To recapitulate: not content with simple authorship, personal freedom, which is specific to the human being, consists in an authorship that follows reasons accepted by the acting self. Because reasons count, there is responsibility in the literal sense: the possibility to answer for oneself. And because it is reasons that count, philosophy speaks of reason, and because these reasons guide action, it speaks of practical reason.

Three conditions are met. When the acting self accepts the reasons, the action or omission is not coerced from the outside. It is undertaken freely in the sense of negative freedom and, moreover, because it is intentional, in the sense of positive freedom as well. Finally, the intention comes from "inside," from the reasons we have made our own. Together, the three conditions form a reflective acceptance: we distance ourselves from externally controlled action and follow reasons, reasons we do not simply have but on which we take a position of agreement or rejection. We thus operate a targeted, selective agreement.

Whether agreement or rejection—taking a position does not have to be making a decision; it does not require a kind of notarization. Nor do the reasons have to be pondered; they may be followed merely intuitively. What counts is taking a position that effects an action, a position present in the intentions we have or in the action-oriented reflections we engage in, moreover in the actions we perform. Not least of all, it shows in the accompanying and subsequent moral feelings such as a good or bad conscience, in apologies, satisfaction, or regrets.

This decisive moment, the practiced, lived agreement, turns conditions that may be external to the agent into practical-reflexive reasons that are her own. This transformation or metamorphosis may be called a kind of liberation; it is, of course, not a social but a personal emancipation. We liberate ourselves of otherwise all-powerful and social determinants to the extent that we act in harmony with "incorporated" reasons. This precisely makes us personally free and reveals practical reasons.

On this conception of personal freedom, the conditions of the inner world, both the physiology of the brain and the psychology of pleasure and displeasure, undoubtedly play a role, as do the conditions of the external, natural and social world. Neither one of them nor all of them together, however, have the status of a final authority sovereignly deciding that and how the person acts. What is decisive is that we follow reasons that we make our own and which, precisely because of this, are to be attributed to us. Action takes place of our own will, and therefore freedom of the will exists, even if so far only in its modest form.

According to empiricist criticism, this assigns an untenable ontological status to the will, which, the argument goes, is being reified into a mental substance, quasi-empirical but in fact withdrawn from experience. In reality, however, the will is associated with each person, its experiences, talents, interests, and character and its biography. The will is so intimately connected with the "life and soul" of the person that, as a German expression has it, we cannot "get out of" our skin.

Nor do I advocate another problematic view, the "starter model." The will is not some kind of drive unit external to and preceding the action that would get the process of action going like a starter motor getting an engine moving. The expression "will," rather, designates that practical reflexivity that explodes linearity in human action — first the willing, then its realization.

When we act in practical reflexivity, we act on our own will but not yet on a free will in the emphatic sense of the term. A person is only as free as far as his or her practical-reflexive reasons reach. We have seen three levels of these.

When reasons are restricted to the means and ways to achieve particular purposes, we are free in the technical or strategic sense. When the reasons also extend to the natural guiding purposes, our own welfare, we are free in the pragmatic sense. Yet we attain freedom of the will in the full sense, genuine freedom of the will or moral freedom, only when in the case of a conflict between morality and our own welfare we are ready to leave pragmatic freedom behind and put our own welfare aside in favor of moral obligations.

When philosophers in this context speak of something unconditional, they do not advocate the notion, dismissed by critics as absurd, that the will is independent from the body and character of the person, its thoughts, sensations, and desires. Such a will without connection with what constitutes the person would be completely foreign to the person and hence quite unsuited to grasping veritable freedom of the will.

Meaningfully, "unconditional" names something else. Reasons that are restricted to particular purposes or the guiding purpose of one's own welfare owe their status of being a reason to an external condition, namely, the particular purpose or one's own welfare. It is in reference to this precondition that these reasons are called "conditional." Those reasons, in contrast, that free themselves of such preconditions are called "unconditional."

In unconditional reasons thus defined we see a new freedom emerge that is also, compared to technical and pragmatic freedom, more radical. This perfecting form of personal freedom now explodes the widespread view that the relationship between determination and freedom must be thought as an alternative, *either* as compatibility *or* as incompatibility. In truth, the two options can be reconciled. On the surface, there is compatibility because personal freedom is compatible with determination on both levels, as freedom of action of the simple will and as freedom of the will in the strict sense. Yet freedom presupposes the transformation of "deterministic" conditions, that is, conditions external and foreign to the subject, into reasons it has appropriated, that is, internal, practical-reflexive reasons.

This state of affairs is best articulated as a paradox: the deterministic determination becomes a nondeterministic but nonetheless not indeterministic determination. Because the essence of personal freedom lies in a transformation of external into internal reasons, thus in an emancipation from pure conditionality, there is no dualism of perspectives here either, neither in its Kantian form, the dualism of the experienceable (phenomenal) and the merely thought (noumenal) world, nor in its Habermasian variant, the notion that it is possible to look at the world of action in two ways, deterministically or liberally.[1] For as soon as externally determining reasons become practical-reflexive, they are a component of the experienceable world and at the same time are of a liberal nature.

17.2
THINKING REASONS ALL THE WAY THROUGH

According to the British philosopher George Edward Moore, the basic term of all practical evaluation, "good," designates an object that is quite simply simple and is therefore "indefinable."[2] Immodestly — as happens quite often with philosophers —Moore believes that all previous moral philosophy has overlooked this point, which is why it needs to be remodeled from the ground up. As we will see, Moore greatly overestimates his achievement.

A more precise definition of the basic normative concept "good" begins with a task lacking in Moore. It points to three meanings with a different status, being good technically (good for something), pragmatically (good for someone), and morally. In addition, it distinguishes two partial stages on the intermediate stage, namely, one's own personal welfare and that of the group, collective welfare.

According to utilitarianism, the second partial stage of pragmatic being good corresponds to morality. In fact, however, this leaves two questions open that cannot normatively be dismissed and belong to a higher stage. On the one hand: why should one pursue the welfare of all, the collective welfare? Serving the welfare of others at least occasionally means restricting one's own welfare, which leads to the question why, when there is a conflict, one's own welfare should take a step back. On the other hand: how is the collective welfare to be distributed among the individuals concerned? And in addition the question: are there justified interests that must not be violated even in the name of collective welfare?

Because these questions remain open, utilitarianism does not exhaust the possibilities for evaluation, and we must move to a third, a higher level of evaluation. On the purely formal level, it contains a being good that, as regards its obligatory nature, is unrestricted: it is an *ought* with the status of a categorical imperative that applies without restrictions. To it corresponds full personal freedom, that freedom of the will in the strict and narrow sense in which the will is its own legislator, which makes it autonomous. Only here, where both one's own and the collective welfare are evaluated normatively, does personal freedom reach its highest stage.

"Autonomy" is an ambivalent expression. Originally, in the Greek polis, it designates the right of the polity to live according to its own laws (see above, section 14.1). These laws do not have to be given to the polis literally by itself; they can also be givens, divine commands or prohibitions, for example. What is decisive is that they are not imposed by another political entity but are instead accepted. Later, in early modernity, autonomy consists in the ability to decide for oneself within the framework of an overarching legal order, for example, a town deciding on a law or a citizen on his legal dealings.

As the concept develops further, the emphasis is often put on the first component of the word, the *auto* or "self." The expression "autonomy" then designates, for example, a thinking that takes place without being guided or coerced by an authority or a tradition, that is, thinking for oneself. More recently, the expression plays an important role in medical ethics, especially in the form of patients' autonomy. There is, however, no agreement on its precise definition here.[3]

Autonomy has yet another, a full significance as the perfecting form of personal morality, as its characteristic and legitimating reason. It does not mean some kind of self-determination on the part of the subject but a veritable self-legislation. And this legislation is concerned not with arbitrary, perhaps technical or pragmatic laws but with laws that derive neither from external goals or purposes nor from the guiding goal of the sensuous nature of the human, (one's own) welfare. What is decisive is a lawfulness that, independent from it, springs from the moral nature of the human being that in turn is rooted in pure practical reason.

Because the rational being that is the human remains a sensuous being, autonomous laws take the form of an imperative with unrestricted validity. This imperative, the categorical imperative, is often understood as criterion or measure of morality, a kind of moralometer. In truth it perfects, in addition, the possibilities for evaluation and thereby perfects the concept of morality.

Genuinely moral duty is no longer of the kind that can be articulated as: *assuming* I want x, *then* I should do y. Rather, it is without assumptions and preconditions, valid purely as such and for itself, thus valid unconditionally, categorically. Whether persons are concerned or institutions—viewed from this standpoint called "morality," human practice is not content with being a function of something else; it should and wants to be good for itself, that is, without restrictions.

This state of affairs, that the main object of morality, the morally good, lies in the highest stage of evaluation, brings considerable relief to the theory of personal freedom. It opposes Moore's thesis cited above that the concept of the good rejects any definition, in two ways. First, there is a formal definition after all: "good" is the name of what is evaluated positively. Second, moral philosophy is not concerned with the good in general but with the morally good, such that there is no need to dwell on the definition of the generic concept of "good." The debate Moore started is as good as inconsequential for a theory of morality. Moral philosophers who belabor the point are not being more thorough but are missing what is essential: their object is not some kind of good but quite simply the highest, precisely, the moral good.

Nor does freedom of the will consist in some kind of second-order desire. It consists in a special kind of reflexivity. When we submit to principles of practical reason, we have freedom of the will in the modest sense. But only when the principles originate from the will itself do we achieve full freedom of the will, autonomy. We do not act radically rationally, that is, morally, when we always choose the best means toward set goals nor when we seek the collective welfare at all times and in all circumstances; we do so only when we live our lives autonomously, according to categorical imperatives.

Allow me one more remark on the moral life this implies. Many things in life happen because of small, relatively unavoidable decisions. These include getting up and getting dressed, having breakfast, going to work, answering mail, and so on. Questions of morality, honesty instead of fraud, uprightness, willingness to help, in contrast, are independent from the (relative) unavoidability of many decisions. We may also put it this way: the highest stage of personal freedom, strict autonomy, does not require much technical freedom nor a lot of pragmatic freedom — except for the willingness not to seek one's welfare via immoral paths.

17.3

PROTO-OBLIGATION: FREE ACCEPTANCE

In the case of the human being, the highest claim of freedom is addressed to a being that can relinquish neither its sensuous nature nor its historical-social origin. Precisely because the human being remains a needful, historical, and social being, freedom and morality obtain an obligatory character. They encourage humans to be more than beings of needs and of society and in this *more* to find their true selves.

This obligatory character is of great scope and consequence. It does not pertain to the usual obligations such as not stealing, not cheating, and not killing. In analogy with the proto-justice that is indispensable for a thorough theory of freedom,[4] the concern is with a more fundamental obligation, a proto-obligation that asks the human being to constitute itself as being of freedom and responsibility and in so doing as a moral being.

As humans, we are not simply free and responsible; we must become so. In this process of becoming, education and social relationships play an essential role. To understand this role, it is no less essential that we find ourselves asked, even challenged to become free and responsible by others, parents, teachers, and the many people we encounter. Freedom and responsibility have the character of a challenge, a provocation. They provoke us human beings, insofar as we are sensuous beings who live in social networks defined by traditions, into acting (or not acting) autonomously, despite the impositions our living situation implies.

Biographically, this provocation initially comes from the outside, namely, from our social environment, which is indeed indispensable to our becoming subjects and selves. This provocation, of course, must be accepted by the subject; it must be absorbed by "body and soul," accepted by our whole person. Freedom and responsibility thus have, second, the character of acceptance, namely, one and the same acceptance. Personal freedom is not a natural possession. From birth, we humans have only a potential, which must be developed, first, and whose guiding purpose, freedom, including responsibility, must, second, be accepted.

We must not picture this acceptance in our individual histories as a one-time act, with the pathos of a heroic decision, *from here on and from now on, I am a person responsible for my life*. Biographically, it usually takes the form of a longer process of education and self-education. Both combine, in any case: we are not just made into free and responsible beings; in an essential way we must also make ourselves such.

In this making-oneself lies the proto-obligation, and it is for its sake that a thorough philosophical ethics or moral philosophy requires the notion of a duty, a basic duty, even, toward oneself—a point ignored or even denied in contemporary debates. Without fundamentally committing oneself to duty, without the acceptance of proto-obligation, no duty or obligation toward others can be thought.

This may be illustrated by the following thought experiment. Imagine a murderer in a country that retains the death penalty. This murderer has not been found out and lets an innocent person sit on death row in his stead. The real murderer could explain that he did not choose to be the way he is. And yet he must allow the question why he does not take responsibility, why he does not have the courage to confess his crime, which would moreover set the innocent person free.

Such courage might be considered an example of Sartre's notion of the existential choice of the self. On that view, the decisive thing is not what has been made of us but what we ourselves make of what has been made of us. A phrase from Nietzsche affirms or, historically speaking, anticipates Sartre's notion: "Willing liberates: that is the true teaching of will and liberty."[5]

When we follow this insight of Sartre and Nietzsche, we do not simply suffer a perhaps insufferable situation in our lives the way a Stoic would; we affirm it: we, precisely, want it. Neither Nietzsche nor Sartre, however, argues clearly on the third stage of practical reason. They remain indifferent to the question what concept of the good an action follows, either a more emphatic concept of one's own welfare (second stage of reason) or the moral concept (third stage of reason).

Both Nietzsche and Sartre are on to something important nonetheless: proto-obligation exists on two stages, as a pragmatic and as a moral proto-obligation. Through the first of these, the pragmatic self-obligation, we become beings responsible to ourselves, to our own welfare. But only through the second stage, moral self-obligation, do we make ourselves beings responsible both to ourselves and to others in a perfected, that is, precisely, a moral way.

17.4
ON THE REALITY OF PERSONAL AUTONOMY

Because freedom requires the acceptance I have outlined, a freedom-skeptical brain researcher can still object that assuming people, especially brain researchers, to actually operate this acceptance is an illusion. This residual skepticism, a skepticism about both the basic and the radical stage of freedom of the will along with the morality it makes possible, may be countered with a thought experiment. This experiment is inspired by Kant and in his work belongs to the both difficult and insightful theorem of a fact of reason.[6] I would like to use different examples from Kant's, however, and begin with the more modest, the pragmatic freedom of the will.

Imagine a brain researcher who considers his desire to have a brilliant career to be so coercive that he is willing to commit fraud. Now confront this researcher burning with ambition with the question how he would act if he knew that the fraud would immediately become public, that his scientific as well as personal reputation would be gravely tarnished, that he would moreover lose his position and never again be able to work in his field. Leaving clinical cases aside, his answer will be none other than *I will control my desire for a brilliant career at least to the extent that I accept the basic ethics of research and do not commit fraud.* He thereby practices the first stage of proto-obligation and accepts himself as a pragmatically free being. And this acceptance takes place in the way that counts here, not (just) verbally but in the action of controlling his desire for a career.

This is the freedom the quotation that introduced this fifth part alludes to: "For to give up a full will of my own was above all the supreme commandment I had imposed upon myself; I, as a free ape, submitted to this yoke."[7] As befits a confrontation with brain research, the quote is taken from "A Report to an Academy," written by an author attentive to the sciences, Franz Kafka.

In Kafka's "Report," an ape captured on the Gold Coast and imprisoned in a crate becomes a free ape by means of two imperatives that both ultimately serve his well-being. The first imperative is, *if you want to have a chance at succeeding in getting out of this box, you must, since the alternative of escape does not have any chance of success, qualify to join the variety show*. The second imperative is, *if you want to become a variety show artist, you must submit to the way of life of the variety show and operate the renunciation, after all oppressive ("yoke"), of any will of your own.*

Already at the pragmatic stage, then, freedom requires a renunciation; only by making an effort (in the example of the brain researcher this takes place, for instance, through the suppression, operated expressly or as a matter of course, of the inclination to cheat) does it become a real possession. Kafka of course is not concerned with the common education of a human being but with an elementary education to *become* a human being. For the "free ape" is after all capable of following a pragmatic imperative; moreover, he attains, as Kafka puts it ironically, "the average educational level of a European."[8]

A second thought experiment, this time concerning the reality of freedom of the will in the strict sense, leads via the free ape to the morally free human being. Imagine a totalitarian regime. In this regime, a neuroscientist is asked to tell a lie about a disliked but upright colleague, a lie that will destroy this colleague's professional career. The refusal to tell this lie will lead immediately to him losing his own position and finding himself without any means of subsistence.

This thought experiment expands an inclination that is overpowering for some researchers, the interest in a career, by two emotional inclinations, that of harming a competitor and that of holding on to one's job and the living it allows for. The desire for a career thus becomes a difficult-to-top superlative of self-love. To counter it, freedom of the will, if it claims to be real, would have to develop an even greater power.

By their profession, neuroscientists are no better or more courageous persons than "normal people." They will thus hardly claim the positive answer for themselves. They must realistically consider the question whether the counterpower does indeed become effective to be an open question. For no one will honestly dare guarantee that they would refuse the lie. One may even hold the pessimistic view the Vienna writer Arno Geiger voices in his novel *Alles über Sally* (*All about Sally*): "the human is a being of weak intelligence governed by its drives. Difficult to repair."[9]

Before we bring the second thought experiment to a conclusion, we would do well to look at the power or powerlessness of practical reason. When the author of an action is not just preferably but actually determined by practical reason, she follows reason in its practical, action-guiding sense. We do not possess practical reason already when we know how to judge our action under aspects of the morally good but only when we know how to live according to it. This knowing how to live manifests in three stages of increasing presence.

We have the first stage of presence when we perceive the aspects of the morally good as someone who is herself or himself concerned, when we accept our action or omission to be morally relevant, for example when in cases of contravention, we feel the pangs of conscience, regrets, and shame, or in positive cases moral satisfaction. Already at this stage, then, the good is not a pure obligation; it is at the same time a way of being. In the form of such negative or positive practical emotions, the good has a presence that is both experienced and lived. Practical reason acquires greater power when it reveals itself not merely in emotions but already in the actual action, albeit only occasionally and not yet reliably. Reason reaches the third stage, full, sovereign power, when it is practiced again and again and constantly renewed, when it finally becomes a fixed component of our person, a character trait.

Wherever practical reason rules, justifying reasons at the same time have motivating force. That is why the current dispute between the so-called internalists, who attribute motivating force to justifying reasons, and externalists, who deny them this force, cannot be resolved theoretically but only practically.[10] From a purely theoretical perspective, both options are possible for reasons. Yet which of them in fact applies is decided not externally but internally, by the particularity of the acting subject. If this subject's practical reason is characterized by power, then internalism is right; if it is characterized by powerlessness, externalism is right.

Like power in practical reason, so powerlessness, too, manifests in different stages. On a first, relatively weak stage, we momentarily lose control. On a second stage, this absence of control becomes a trait that characterizes the way we live our lives, a weakness of the will. On a third stage, a powerlessness amplified yet again, in a life driven by urges, reason becomes the slave of passion. The summit of powerlessness is bestial behavior.

Let's take up the conflict of the faculties once more. The richness of facets I have outlined, both the stages of practical reason and the stages of its power, not least of all also the stages of powerlessness, is lost when personal freedom is denied wholesale. Not the least of reasons to be skeptical in turn of the brain researchers' skepticism about freedom lies in the multidimensionality of a theory of freedom steeped in experience and, to that extent, appropriate to the phenomena.

Let's return to our second thought experiment. Even someone of weak practical reason will hardly deny that it is possible for him to give the disadvantageous but honest answer to the question whether he is able to control his desire for a brilliant career. Because he probably in his life so far has accepted moral proto-obligation often enough, he will even admit that he is aware that morality demands the answer that refuses the lie. He thus considers freedom of the will in the strictest sense and with it full personal autonomy, moral freedom, to be possible in reality. He is thus both aware of the primacy of the freedom of his will and of the moral law that belongs to it over the embodiment of inclinations, self-love empirically defined, and aware of a skepticism about the ethical skepticism that denies the reality of moral obligations.

This thought experiment inspired by Kant provides compelling counter-evidence against the twofold suspicion that freedom of the will in the strict sense including morality is either rooted in material and thus empirical principles or an invention by ivory-tower moralists: full freedom of the will and morality in the sense of pure practical reason prove their reality not only in moral actions but already in judgments people make concerning the correctness, initially pragmatic, then moral, of their actions. In these judgments, we see the presence of the acceptance of the second stage of proto-obligation and at the same time both sides of full personal freedom.

Where we contradict the inclinations, the independence from the causally determined natural order, negative freedom, is apparent. And in the capacity to act nonetheless, but according to principles of pure practical reasons this time, positive freedom proves itself. That is why Kant can claim, with a pathos rare in his work, that morality has long been "incorporated" in the essence of all human beings, "inscribed on the human soul in the broadest and most legible characters."[11]

Whether brain research will ever be able come up with an alternative *experimentum crucis* to counter the thought experiment just outlined is a matter of speculation. We don't know. So far, it hasn't. Yet as long as it simply cites Libet's experiments and more or less independent variants of them, we may follow the sketch I have given of an enlightenment about enlightenment. We may consider both simple freedom of the will, the capacity for responsibility regarding our own welfare, and the freedom of the will strictly speaking to be real. In the former case, its reality is proven in accepting to renounce fraud for the sake of one's own welfare; in the latter, in accepting the capacity for refusing a lie that saves one's own future. As soon as humans—these educatable beings, beings, that is, both in need of and capable of education—through education make self-interest and, as its corrective, honesty their attitude, as soon as through continued practice they as it were program this attitude into the central nervous system and therefore remain honest even in difficult situations and act with courage to help others in equally difficult situations, strict freedom of the will displays its full reality.

That is why the following résumé imposes itself: no doubt neuronal connections determine us, but in the reality that we can experience and that we live, the determination hardly takes place in so narrow and strict a way and above all hardly so independently from the acting and omitting we practice in the course of our lives that an enlightened liberalism would have to stop speaking of freedom of the will in both of its stages, of the simple and of the demanding moral freedom of the will.

18

On the Price of Freedom

Reflections on personal freedom that consider the advantages alone remain one-sided and even naive. Personal freedom, too, cannot be had without negative flipsides.

18.1
THE SMALLER PRICE: HAVING TO DECIDE

We are not free when we act consciously and responsibly only in certain moments but when we actualize both, voluntariness and consciousness, in the way we lead our entire lives. We are free, therefore, when we succeed in living from out of our motivation and our own reflection. Social and political developments in part facilitate this success, but they also make it more difficult. The reason does not lie outside these developments; it comes from within: the responsibility lies with legal and social freedom.

Undoubtedly many places in the last few decades have witnessed an enormous liberalization of the legal world and the lifeworld. The liberties guarantee numerous freedoms, and the rule of law ensures them. Society has largely become more open, pluralistic, and tolerant, which allows, even more than that, facilitates and often even favors not just political minorities but different, even strongly divergent lifestyles and forms of life. And in this country, a rather generous welfare state ensures a considerable degree of material security for which people in other places are willing to accept a loss of freedom.

The gain in livability these liberalizations have brought is so evident that no one seeks to undo them. On the contrary, there is a not uncommon desire to throw off *all* fetters, and sometimes this desire grows into the "tremendous desire to continue one's life without obligations, without bonds."[1] Sometimes we just want to get up and leave, disappear into the night, to begin life the next day as a new person who has left all problems behind. Some have grown tired of the daily grind of work, of the misery of a partnership gone sour, or of the pressure to fend off increasing competition. Others want to escape the monotony of the everyday or simply lead what they consider a nicer life: without legal restrictions, without societal prohibitions, without taboos and stigmatization. The "bourgeois" model of an (almost) complete new beginning is on display in Pascal Mercier's novel *Night Train to Lisbon*, the criminal model in John Grisham's *The Partner*.[2]

Not just the dreamed or fictitious emancipation from constraints, already the reality of liberalization as it has grown has a price because it comes with things that make life more difficult. On almost all levels and in almost all domains, possibilities for action have increased exponentially, as it were. Where decisions used to be facilitated or quite simply made by requirements, we may today make our own choices. Because this choice, in addition, is one between ever more options, liberalization appears only as advantageous. In truth, however, choosing is not merely being allowed to choose, not merely not being determined; it is also the task of deciding in favor of our own preferences. In many ways, choosing has become having to choose, which according to the novel by Jonathan Franzen I mentioned at the beginning (section 1.3) can become a curse: where guidelines are lacking, it is us who are being challenged.

The coercion to choose brings out an ambivalence in the two basic concepts. Hardly anyone would want to give up the negative freedom that has progressed very far in the process of liberalization, the being free from external and internal barriers and fetters. Yet it entails the new and by no means easy task of managing the increased positive freedom: where there is ever more free space for one's own life, both professionally and privately, the responsibility for this life increases as well. Even if we experience negative freedom as a blessing, we not infrequently experience the positive freedom it brings with it, the responsibility, as a burden. Some even feel exhausted by the many decisions they must make every day and enter a state of lethargy.

The fact that in many cases the freedom of choice has increased for very common things amounts to a banalization of positive freedom. To take an example from daily life, from telecommunications: Do I even want a phone and to run the risk of it being tapped? And if yes, should it be landline or a mobile phone, with the increased danger of being listened in on? And if it is to be a mobile phone, a simple one or a smart phone? Or do I want both? What model do I choose, what provider, what kind of contract? Do I need an answering service? And so on.

Yet having to decide goes far beyond these, after all, rather quotidian decisions. Already medical questions such as saying yes or no to preimplantation diagnostics (see section 3.5 above), furthermore the choice of a profession, even more so that of a life partner, or the embrace of a true calling have existential significance. This significance reaches its summit when it comes to deciding in favor of forms of life of a different order, a task already confronted by Plato and Aristotle, that appears in Kant's notion of the fact of reason, that Fichte radicalizes in the notion of the "autoproduction of the human," and that Kierkegaard reflects in a way that still shapes our conceptions today.

According to Kant, we "make" ourselves into moral beings. According to Fichte, even at the beginning of knowledge, there is an event of freedom: we have to open up not only to morality but also to (theoretical) truth and obey both of them at the same time. According to Kierkegaard and later, for example, Jaspers, there are forms of life that are of a different rank and among which we must decide: between an aesthetic, that is, sensuous, an ethical, and a religious, more precisely Christian, existence.

An only slightly less emphatic perspective is presented in modern novels. For there — and two examples, Leo Tolstoy's *Anna Karenina* and Thomas Mann's *Buddenbrooks*, will have to suffice — relationships and life plans tend largely to fail. In other novels, instability and disorientation predominate. If we suppose that, despite its fictional character, literature is steeped in experience and close to life, it seems that despite the ever-increasing life expectancy there is, although this can hardly be measured, a greater existential risk. Suicide rates are high, as are the figures for mental and other emotional disorders. In countries like Germany, to be sure, suicide rates are declining, but the number of mental disorders is increasing enormously. And according to media reports, burnout syndrome, vague as the term may be, is on the rise as well.

There is a good reason for this state of affairs. When we look at the human condition, we find only few and moreover weak biological predispositions. Impoverished and insecure when it comes to instincts and species-specific imprinting, human beings are characterized by a high degree of openness and multiple talents or polycompetence. To avoid in this situation that humans are completely without orientation, unpredictable and unreliable for others, and insecure and helpless toward themselves, research tells us, there are habits and institutions. Understood by authors like Gehlen as analogues of instinct, they offer humans a two-dimensional stability, externally (socially) and internally (personally).[3] In addition, by setting rules, they facilitate possible decisions.

We find that the ambivalence indicated earlier repeats itself here. Since habits and institutions relieve us of the constraint of permanently having to decide or at least trace out clear tracks along which necessary decisions are to be made, their requirements and obligations are helpful. Yet they also, and this is the undeniable flipside, narrow matters down significantly. Because today's liberalization reduces the flipside to a minimum, both domains, both internal and external stability are considerably weakened. The consequences are evident. The threat of danger from the outside, the violent violation of rules, and the threat of self-endangerment, all the way to drug, nicotine, and alcohol addiction, more recently compulsive gambling and cellphone dependency, are growing.

If we transpose the results of experiments with animals — although that is always problematic — then we live longer and more healthily when we have fewer opportunities for choice. Yet the high life expectancy in wealthy liberal democracies furnishes a small counterargument.

Those who want the many-faceted liberalization — and strong, self-confident people, especially, do — will of course shoulder the costs, especially since the costs are not beyond control. On the contrary, they can be influenced to quite a large extent. Early childhood education is important here, because those who in their childhood experience safety and acquire self-confidence and trust in the world become persons with a strong self who welcome the liberalizations and more easily shoulders the costs. Those who have not enjoyed the good fortune of a successful upbringing can still correct quite a few things later on. And in any case, no one, however circumspect they may act, has full control of their lives. As Theodore Decker puts it in Donna Tartt's *The Goldfinch*: "A great sorrow, and one that I am only beginning to understand . . . We don't get to choose the people we are."[4]

That is why it is advisable, also for the human being in modernity with its high degree of liberalization, to learn to live with uncertainty, even if our age has immensely increased our ability to live lives of our own.[5]

In addition, we are tied into an ever-denser network of services. This network relieves us of a plethora of tasks and decisions but also creates fetters that restrain us, often without our noticing it. Not least of all, advertising aims at hollowing out our self-determination: formally, by increasing our willingness to consume; in terms of content, by steering, sometimes even forcing, this readiness along certain paths.

One of the most important components of prudent conduct is the art of binding oneself freely: we are free when we let ourselves be bound by the right things and persons, including ourselves.[6] This includes seeking friends and partners and joining groups that offer stability but can of course be restraining. We can develop habits, learn techniques of inner control, and elaborate an art of saying no to the acceleration of life, the oftentimes mad rush, and the abundance of things on offer.

It may be objected that this is at best an ideal for an advanced age of life, although people in retirement who have not become apathetic often have a problem familiar from professional and family life: they have numerous obligations, and those who are sensitive have a bad conscience for neglecting one or the other among them; the rhythm of days, weeks, and years is set, unless we drop out or are highly independent financially.

The difficulties thus indicated are undoubtedly real, yet surprisingly they also apply, at first sight, to most citizens in wealthy societies. And yet, it is advisable to acquire at least the basics of the art of saying no. Some obligations and constraints at least can thereby be abolished.

Another problem: blows of fate occur without our contributing to them. They come without our asking for them, not rarely like a bolt from the blue. We cannot, therefore, prevent them, but we can prepare for them somewhat by developing an attitude of imperturbability. It begins with the knowledge that blows of fate occur, and it continues with the two-dimensional attempt, on the one hand, to find friends and partners who will stay with us even in difficult times the way we ourselves stay with the partner and friend, and, on the other, not to become numb or apathetic and yet not let ourselves be struck down by a blow of fate. Yet unless we are emotionally crippled, and even if someone close to us is there to help us, we cannot remain imperturbable when we fall terminally ill, lose our beloved partner in life, or are coerced under torture to give up information or to confess. The difficulties do not devalue imperturbability but rather show it to be an attitude that is neither acquired without effort nor practiced easily.

The amplified form of imperturbability is, to say it with pathos, a serene peace of mind. This does not mean an aesthetic ideal along the lines of Schiller's dictum in *Wallenstein*: "Life is serious, art is serene." What is meant here, rather, is the idea of a mode (of life), the *tranquilitas animi* familiar from the Stoa, what the Greeks called *ataraxia*. In Hermann Hesse's words, it is "nothing but an act of courage, a serene, smiling striding forward and dancing through the terrors and flames of the world."[7]

According to the ancient model, there are two variants. Serene are those whom the gods favor or whom the god saves and those who liberate themselves from fear of the gods and of death and lead a life comparable to the life of the gods. In the first variant, we need something that is out of our hands; we must be a child of fortune or a favorite of the gods. For the second variant, however, we are coresponsible. When we do not despise the goods of this world such as wealth and respect, and also power, and yet do not have our hearts set on them, when we do not fear even death all too much, we are on the path toward something that remains an ideal, toward the serenity that appears in some of

Paul Klee's pictures or in paintings by Max Ackermann that bear *Heiterkeit* in their very titles.

And there is no question that we are also free when we are sufficiently rid of our worries and cares to be able to start anew, or when we know how to do something as difficult as forgiving, generally: when we do not deny our past and yet do not let ourselves be governed by it and, in the end, are afraid of (almost) nothing and (almost) no one.

We are free also when we maintain a lifestyle that is not attached to material things. Of course we take care of our material needs instead of being supported. Yet when we are free, we do not want more and more; we are not greedy but instead are stingy neither toward ourselves nor toward others and prefer living generously, giving feely. The true, albeit not yet genuinely moral freedom that reveals itself here, in any case, contradicts the line that "freedom's just another word for nothing left to lose."

18.2
THE HEAVY PRICE: EVIL

Whether the formula is religious—*God created humanity as free*—or secular—*thanks to the human capacity for language and reason*: humans are capable of freedom, and as free beings, we are not puppets in the hands of god or fate. The consequence that is often no longer welcome and must yet be borne is that humans are capable of abuses going all the way to the radical perversion of freedom, evil. A freedom free of abuses is unthinkable. On the contrary, it permits the possibility of a libertinism à la Sade that ignores not only all conventions but also all customs and all decency, even the most elementary moral obligations.

This is not the place for a detailed theory of evil. But the topic and its place within a theory of freedom must not be passed over in silence. An enlightened liberalism does not turn a blind eye to the insight that the summit of human freedom contains the potential for a radical perversion. It thus does not subscribe to the theories of freedom and morality so common today that deny evil by remaining silent about it. Even if we regret it, a theory of freedom that gives experience its due cannot be thought without either the more private evil, libertinism in the sense just mentioned, or social and political evil such as selective oppression and exploitation, genocide and inhuman dictatorships.

George Sand, in her 1839 story *Pauline*, offers a literary example for the ambivalence of freedom. Paris, at the time the intellectual capital of Europe, is not only the privileged site of a liberal urbane life. It is also a stage of vanity, more than that, a breeding ground of vice, the preferred haunt of libertines and lechers, of speculators and freebooters of all stripes. In Paris, Pauline, after a sheltered childhood in the provinces, becomes easy prey for perfidious rakes. But the provincial world she comes from, the counterworld to Paris, too, only seems to be a world of virtuousness. In truth, it too is governed by a flipside, by a dark side of freedom, namely, by hypocrisy and bigotry.

For neither side to develop unchecked, enlightened liberalism pleads for a legal order that opposes abuses of freedom, which violate the freedom of others, with enforceable limits. In addition, it is committed to a tolerant society in which many forms of hypocrisy run out of work because they become superfluous. Finally, it takes into account evil that can arise under the conditions of freedom. An enlightened liberalism does not succumb to the naivete of passing over this danger or even of assuming the opposite. It would rather acknowledge the threat and always seeks to defend freedom against evil and evils of all kinds. For enlightened liberalism, freedom is a highest good; it even constitutes, it says, the dignity of the human being.

19

Retrospection: Freedom and Modernity

In each of its many facets, freedom has proven itself to be constitutive of the human. Human beings cannot and do not want to do without any of the domains discussed in this book. They are all important to the human, even vital in an emphatic sense: the liberation from constraints of outer nature by means of technology, aid in the case of accidents and illness by means of medicine and pharmacy, and the development of mere dispositions toward freedom into an actual capacity and readiness by means of education. Matters are no different for the economy and society, science and art, in the polity, and for humans as responsible persons—with respect to all these domains, human beings have an elementary interest in and strong desire for freedom.

For the age we call modernity, too, all these freedom aspects are essential such that we have to wonder what distinguishes the age. What really is modern, that is, specific to this age, when what dominates modernity, as regards freedom, is nothing but the general wealth of facets of freedom? On the other hand, what is essential to the human generally, that is, *not* age specifically, if the wealth of facets I have outlined is specific to the age and thus does not characterize humanity generally?

The answer to these questions still allows modernity to be self-confident but also counsels the opposite of pride and arrogance: it counsels modesty. Freedom is not an invention of modernity. What is specific to modernity is only—but that is not nothing—that it takes the principle of freedom seriously and does so to a new degree, a degree that, altogether, has probably never been known before, and seeks to make it thrive like never before. The word "altogether" is important here. For one aspect at least, political freedom, acquires extraordinary significance already among the ancient Greeks. Yet the entirety of the freedom aspects discussed in the book likely has come to be considered with such intensity and indeed such success only in modernity. Only in modernity does the whole phenomenon of freedom thrive in ways previously unknown.

Neither has the reassessment I have undertaken here in the form of a judicative critique unmasked the devotion to freedom as an unreasonable goal that on balance ought perhaps better be rejected, nor has it shown that this goal has been completely missed. Modernity is not so horrible and abhorrent a failure that it better be dismissed in favor of a (moreover conceptually vague) postmodernity. The age cannot be reproached with simply breaking its promise of freedom. The pathos-laden dismissal of modernity, in exaggerated form its declaration of death, is thus clearly off the mark. There can be no question of a predominance of losses, of a preponderance of failure.

Nonetheless, the balance is not wholly positive, neither as regards the principle of freedom nor as regards the project of modernity. For in all its facets, there is the threat of an abuse of freedom. More than that: on the one hand, a freedom free of abuse is unthinkable and, on the other, the more highly freedom is developed, the more threatening its abuse can become. The possibilities for abusing, for example, technology, medicine, and the free market are obvious, which is why here and elsewhere, counterforces and institutions to control them are required. That, however, is known, and counterforces and oversight authorities have been set up even if they are not always sufficiently established yet. Finally, the counterforces instituted in the name of freedom are themselves not beyond abuse. Moreover, they can—as the welfare state and security policies focused on domestic security concerns alone exemplarily show—endanger the purpose of freedom that guides them.

In a theory of freedom, the summit of freedom is the freedom of each individual human being. For ultimately, this personal freedom is the foundation, the core of self-esteem and integrity and of the inviolable dignity of each and every human being. Paradoxically, from the perspective of freedom, the flipside of personal freedom also contains the greatest danger. The positive apex of freedom, freedom of the will, also makes its negative nadir possible, something threatening both our private and our social as well as political, and not least of all our cosmopolitical life: evil.

To conclude with a succinct and therefore somewhat simplified thesis: there is no fundamental alternative either to the principle of freedom or to the project of modernity. And just as fundamentally, they require, again and again, a critical renewal.

Notes

PREFACE

1. See my *Categorical Principles of Law: A Counterpoint to Modernity*, 1990, trans. Mark Migotti (University Park: Pennsylvania State University Press, 2002); *Moral als Preis der Moderne: Ein Versuch über Wissenschaft, Technik und Umwelt*, 4th ed. (Frankfurt: Suhrkamp, 2000); *Kant's Critique of Pure Reason: The Foundation of Modern Philosophy*, 2003 (Dordrecht: Springer, 2010); *Can Virtue Make Us Happy? The Art of Living and Morality*, 2007, trans. Douglas R. McGaughey and Aaron Bunch (Evanston: Northwestern University Press, 2010); and *Kants Kritik der praktischen Vernunft: Eine Philosophie der Freiheit* (Munich: Beck, 2012).
2. Friedrich Nietzsche, *Werke: Kritische Gesamtausgabe*, ed. Giorigo Colli and Mazzino Montinari, pt. 3, vol. 4, *Nachgelassene Fragmente, Sommer 1872 bis Ende 1874* (Berlin: de Gruyter, 1978), 29[54]:259. [This fragment is not included in the selection in *Writings from the Early Notebooks*, ed. Raymond Geuss and Alexander Nehamas, trans. Ladislaus Löb (Cambridge: Cambridge University Press, 2009), where it would find its place on page 237.—Trans.]

CHAPTER ONE

1. Karl Marx, "Proceedings of the Sixth Rhine Province Assembly: On the Freedom of the Press," 1842, in *Karl Marx, Frederick Engels: Collected Works*, trans. Richard Dixon, Clemens Dutt, Dirk J. Struik, Sally R. Struik, and Alick West, vol. 1, *Karl Marx: 1835–1843* (Moscow: Progress, 1975), 132–81, here 155.
2. Jean-Jacques Rousseau, *The Social Contract*, in *The Social Contract, and Other Later Political Writings*, ed. and trans. Victor Gourevitch (Cambridge: Cambridge University Press, 1997), 39–152, here 41.
3. Rousseau, *Social Contract*, 45.
4. Rousseau, *Social Contract*, 41; Gotthold Ephraim Lessing, *Nathan the Wise: A Dramatic Poem*, trans. Ellen Frothingham (New York: Holt, 1867), act 4, scene 4, 155; and Johann Wolfgang Goethe, *Elective Affinities*, trans. R. J. Hollingdale (London: Penguin, 1971), pt. 1, chap. 5, 195.
5. Isaiah Berlin, "Two Concepts of Liberty," 1958, in *Four Essays on Liberty* (Oxford: Oxford University Press, 1969), 118–72.

6. Immanuel Kant, *Anthropology from a Pragmatic Point of View*, trans. Robert B. Louden, in *Anthropology, History, and Education*, ed. Günter Zöller and Robert B. Louden (Cambridge: Cambridge University Press, 2007), 227–429, §82, 7:268/369. [References to Kant's works are both to volume and page numbers of the standard Academy edition, followed by the page numbers of the English translations referenced.—Trans.] See also below section 4.2.
7. Peter Høeg, *The Quiet Girl*, trans. Nadia Christensen (London: Harvill Secker, 2007), 252.
8. See Aristotle, *Nicomachean Ethics*, trans. Benjamin Jowett, in *The Complete Works of Aristotle: The Revised Oxford Translation*, ed. Jonathan Barnes, 2 vols. (Princeton, NJ: Princeton University Press, 1984), 2:1729–867, here IV.1–3:1119b20–1125a34.
9. Sophocles, *Antigone*, in *Sophocles*, trans. F. Storr (Cambridge, MA: Harvard University Press, 1916), lines 454–56.
10. See Werner Conze, Christian Meier, Jochen Bleicken, Gerhard May, Christof Dipper, Horst Günther, and Diethelm Klippel, "Freiheit," in Otto Brunner, Werner Conze, and Reinhart Koselleck, eds., *Geschichtliche Grundbegriffe: Historisches Lexikon zur politisch-sozialen Sprache in Deutschland*, 5 vols. (Stuttgart: Klett-Cotta, 1972–97), 2:425–542; on antiquity, Kurt Raaflaub, *The Discovery of Freedom in Ancient Greece*, trans. Renate Franciscono (Chicago: University of Chicago Press, 2004).
11. Jacob Grimm, ed., *Deutsches Wörterbuch* (Leipzig: Hirzel, 1878), vol. 4, col. 94.
12. Aristotle, *Metaphysics*, trans. W. D. Ross, in *Complete Works of Aristotle*, 2:1552–728, here I.2:982b26.
13. *Herodotus*, trans. A. D. Godley, 4 vols. (Cambridge, MA: Harvard University Press, 1926–), VII.135–36:436–39.
14. Romans 6:21 and 8:21–22; Galatians 5:1; and 2 Corinthians 3:17.
15. 1 Corinthians 20 and 22.
16. 1 Peter 2:13–17.
17. On the recent debate concerning freedom, see Peter Bieri, *Das Handwerk der Freiheit: Über die Entdeckung des eigenen Willens* (Munich: Hanser, 2001); Udo Di Fabio, *Die Kultur der Freiheit* (Munich: Beck, 2005); Gunnar Hindrichs and Axel Honneth, eds., *Freiheit: Stuttgarter Hegel-Kongress 2011* (Frankfurt: Klostermann, 2013); Axel Honneth, *Freedom's Right: The Social Foundations of Democratic Life*, trans. Joseph Ganahl (New York: Columbia University Press, 2014); and Robert Pippin, *Die Verwirklichung der Freiheit* (Frankfurt: Campus, 2005); on the discourse of modernity, see, in addition, Jürgen Habermas, *The Philosophical Discourse of Modernity: Twelve Lectures*, trans. Frederick G. Lawrence (Cambridge, MA: MIT Press, 1987); Peter Gay, *Modernism: The Lure of Heresy from Baudelaire to Beckett and Beyond* (New York: Norton, 2007); and Wolfgang Welsch, *Unsere postmoderne Moderne* (Weinheim: VCH, 1987).
18. Ernst Bloch, *The Principle of Hope*, 1959, trans. Neville Plaice, Stephen Plaice, and Paul Knight, 3 vols. (Cambridge, MA: MIT Press, 1986); and Hans Jonas, *The Imperative of Responsibility: In Search of an Ethics for the Technological Age* (Chicago: University of Chicago Press, 1981).

19. Insofar as the welfare state combines with a "demeaning" bureaucracy, it even threatens human dignity; see Avishai Margalit, *The Decent Society*, trans. Naomi Goldblum (Cambridge, MA: Harvard University Press, 1996).

INTRODUCTION TO PART ONE

1. René Descartes, *Discourse on the Method*, trans. Robert Stoothoff, in *The Philosophical Writings of Descartes* (Cambridge: Cambridge University Press, 1985), 1:111–51, here 6:143 [translation modified].

CHAPTER TWO

1. For the history of the notion, see Robin G. Collingwood, *The Idea of Nature* (Oxford: Oxford University Press, 1944), even if some of his analyses raise considerable questions.
2. As John Stuart Mill already notes with clarity; see the essay "Nature" in *Three Essays on Religion*, in *Collected Works of John Stuart Mill*, ed. J. M. Robson, 33 vols. (Toronto: University of Toronto Press, 1963–), 10:373–402.
3. Jean-Jacques Rousseau, *Discourse on the Sciences and the Arts*, vol. 2 of *The Collected Writings of Rousseau*, ed. Roger D. Masters and Christopher Kelly (Hanover, NH: University Press of New England, 1992).
4. Plato, *Republic*, trans. Paul Shorey (Cambridge, MA: Harvard University Press, 1937), II.13.372d–373d.
5. See Josef H. Reichholf, *Eine kurze Naturgeschichte des letzten Jahrtausends* (Frankfurt: Fischer, 2008).
6. See Constanze Kurz and Frank Rieger, *Arbeitsfrei: Eine Entdeckungsreise zu den Maschinen, die uns ersetzen* (Munich: Goldmann, 2013).
7. See chap. 7 of my *Die Macht der Moral im 21. Jahrhundert: Annäherungen an eine zeitgemäße Ethik* (Munich: Beck, 2014), 91–103.
8. Immanuel Kant, *Critique of the Power of Judgment*, trans. Paul Guyer and Eric Matthews, ed. Paul Guyer (Cambridge: Cambridge University Press, 2000), §83–84, 5:429–36/297–303.
9. Johann Georg Hamann, "Brocken," 1758, in *Londoner Schriften*, ed. Oswald Bayer and Bernd Weißenborn (Munich: Beck, 1993), 405–17, here 406.
10. See Werner Sombart, *Der moderne Kapitalismus: Historisch-systematische Darstellung des gesamteuropäischen Wirtschaftslebens von seinen Anfängen bis zur Gegenwart*, 1902, final ed. 1928 (Munich: dtv, 1987); Ernst Jünger, *The Adventurous Heart: Figures and Capriccios*, ed. Russell A. Berman, trans. Thomas Friese (Candor: Telos, 2012), and *The Worker: Dominion and Form*, trans. Bogdan Costea and Laurence Paul Hemming (Evanston, IL: Northwestern University Press, 2017); Martin Heidegger, "The Question concerning Technology," 1954, in *The Question concerning Technology, and Other Essays*, ed. and trans. William Lovitt (New York: Harper and Row, 1977), 3–35; and Hans Freyer, *Über das Dominantwerden technischer Kategorien in der Lebenswelt der industriellen Gesellschaft* (Wiesbaden: Steiner, 1960).

11. On the philosophy of technology, see Klaus Kornwachs, *Philosophie der Technik: Eine Einführung* (Munich: Beck, 2013); on the history of the critique of technology, see Christoph Müller and Bernhard Nievergelt, *Technikkritik in der Moderne: Empirische Technikereignisse als Herausforderung an die Sozialwissenschaft* (Opladen: Leske und Budrich, 1996).
12. Jens Soentgen, "Zur Eschatologie des CO_2," *Merkur* 67, no. 4 (April 2013): 366–74, here 372.
13. Soentgen, "Zur Eschatologie des CO_2," 374.
14. On the necessary balancing of advantages and disadvantages, see Jochen Ostheimer and Markus Vogt, eds., *Die Moral der Energiewende: Risikowahrnehmung im Wandel am Beispiel der Atomenergie* (Stuttgart: Kohlhammer, 2013); on the history of the environmental movement since the 1970s in particular, see Joachim Radkau, *The Age of Ecology: A Global History*, trans. Patrick Camiller (Cambridge, UK: Polity, 2014).
15. See chap. 8 of my *Die Macht der Moral*; see also Walter Krämer, *Die Angst der Woche: Warum wir uns vor den falschen Dingen fürchten* (Munich: Piper, 2011).
16. See United Nations Scientific Committee on the Effects of Atomic Radiation, "Levels and Effects of Radiation Exposure Due to the Nuclear Accident after the 2011 Great East-Japan Earthquake and Tsunami" and "Developments since the 2013 UNSCEAR Report on the Levels and Effects of Radiation Exposure Due to the Nclear Accident after the 2011 Great East-Japan Earthquake and Tsunami," online, http://www.unscear.org/unscear/en/publications.html, last accessed September 1, 2019.
17. See Rainer Hank, "Fukushima, die Strahlenbilanz," *Frankfurter Allgemeine Sonntagszeitung*, April 6, 2014, online, https://www.faz.net/aktuell/wirtschaft/wirtschaftspolitik/strahlenbelastung-in-fukushima-12882021.html, last accessed September 1, 2019.

CHAPTER THREE

1. Otfried Höffe, *Medizin ohne Ethik?* (Frankfurt: Suhrkamp, 2002), 8.
2. Otfried Höffe, *Moral als Preis der Moderne: Ein Versuch über Wissenschaft, Technik und Umwelt*, 4th ed. (Frankfurt: Suhrkamp, 2000).
3. Sybille Lewitscharoff, "Von der Machbarkeit: Die wissenschaftliche Bestimmung über Geburt und Tod," speech given on March 2, 2014, as part of the Dresdner Reden 2014 lecture cycle at the Staatsschauspiel Dresden, online, https://www.staatsschauspiel-dresden.de/download/10591/dresdner_rede_sibylle_lewitscharoff_02032014.pdf, 4–5, last accessed September 1, 2019.
4. Émile Durkheim, *On Suicide*, trans. Robin Buss (London: Penguin, 2006).
5. Plato, *Phaedo*, trans. Harold North Fowler (Cambridge, MA: Harvard University Press, 1917), 62b–c, and *Laws*, trans. R. G. Bury (Cambridge, MA: Harvard University Press, 1926), IX:873c–d.
6. Aristotle, *Nicomachean Ethics*, trans. Benjamin Jowett, in *The Complete Works of Aristotle: The Revised Oxford Translation*, ed. Jonathan Barnes (Princeton, NJ: Princeton University Press, 1984), 2:1729–867, here III.11:1116a12–15; see also IX.4:1166b11–13.
7. Fragment IX from the Vatican Collection ("Sententiae Vaticanae"), in Epicurus,

Epicurus: The Extant Remains, ed. and trans. Cyril Bailey, 1926 (Hildesheim: Olms, 1989), 107.

8. Seneca, *Epistles*, trans. Richard M. Gummere, 3 vols. (Cambridge, MA: Harvard University Press, 1917–25), letters 70.5 and 58.32.
9. Plotinus, *Ennead*, trans. A. H. Armstrong (Cambridge, MA: Harvard University Press, 1969), vol. 1, I.9; and Porphyry, *On Abstinence from Killing Animals*, trans. Gillian Clark (New York: Bloomsbury, 2014), I.38 and II.47.
10. Thomas Aquinas, *Summa Theologiae*, trans. the English Dominican Fathers (New York: Benziger, 1947–48), II-II, q64, a5.
11. Immanuel Kant, *Groundwork of "The Metaphysics of Morals,"* in *Practical Philosophy*, ed. and trans. Mary J. Gregor (Cambridge: Cambridge University Press, 1996), 37–108, 4:397–98/53.
12. Arthur Schopenhauer, *The World as Will and Representation*, trans. and ed. Judith Norman, Alistair Welchman, and Christopher Janaway (Cambridge: Cambridge University Press, 2010), vol. 1, IV.§69:425.
13. Friedrich Nietzsche, *Thus Spoke Zarathustra: A Book for All and None*, ed. Adrian del Caro and Robert Pippin, trans. Adrian del Caro (Cambridge: Cambridge University Press, 2006), section "On Free Death," 53 [modified].
14. Albert Camus, *The Myth of Sisyphus*, in *The Myth of Sisyphus, and Other Essays*, trans. Justin O'Brien (New York: Vintage, 1991), 1–137, here 83.
15. Jean Améry, *On Suicide: A Disclosure on Voluntary Death*, trans. John D. Barlow (Bloomington: Indiana University Press, 1999), 43 and 60.
16. See article 6, section 1, of the *International Covenant on Civil and Political Rights*, 1966, online, https://www.ohchr.org/EN/ProfessionalInterest/Pages/CCPR.aspx, last accessed September 1, 2019.
17. Swiss National Advisory Commission on Biomedical Ethics, *Assisted Suicide*, opinion no. 9/2005, https://www.nek-cne.admin.ch/inhalte/Themen/Stellungnahmen/en/suizidbeihilfe_en.pdf, last accessed September 1, 2019, 62.
18. Barbara Orland, "Die menschliche Fortpflanzung im Zeitalter ihrer technischen Reproduzierbarkeit seit den 1970er Jahren," 1999, in Giovanni Maio and Hansjörg Just, eds., *Die Forschung an embryonalen Stammzellen in ethischer und rechtlicher Perspektive* (Baden-Baden: Nomos, 2003), 7–31, here 7–8; and Hans Blumenberg, "Lebenswelt und Technisierung unter Aspekten der Phänomenologie," in *Wirklichkeiten, in denen wir leben* (Stuttgart: Reclam, 1981), 7–54, here 38.
19. Lewitscharoff, "Von der Machbarkeit," 13 and 11.
20. For the outline of an argument on this point, see sections 4.2–4.4 of my *Medizin ohne Ethik?*, 79–92.
21. On the PGD debate, see also the roundtable discussion summarized by Peter Propping and Heinz Schott, "En Route to the Complete Rationalization of Reproduction? German Perspectives on the Latest Developments in Genetic Diagnostics," February 16–17, 2013, German National Academy Leopoldina, online, https://www.leopoldina

.org/uploads/tx_leopublication/2014_05_29_Discussion_Reproduction.pdf, last accessed September 1, 2019.

CHAPTER FOUR

1. Immanuel Kant, *Lectures on Pedagogy*, trans. Robert B. Louden, in *Anthropology, History, and Education*, ed. Günter Zöller and Robert B. Louden (Cambridge: Cambridge University Press, 2007), 434–85, here 9:454/447.
2. See A. S. Neill, *Summerhill: A Radical Approach to Child Rearing* (New York: Hart, 1960); for an assessment, see Peter H. Ludwig, *Summerhill: Antiautoritäre Pädagogik heute: Ist die freie Erziehung tatsächlich gescheitert?* (Weinheim: Beltz, 1997); and for an overview of progressive education, see Jürgen Oelkers, "Reformpädagogik," in Dietrich Benner and Jürgen Oelkers, eds., *Historisches Wörterbuch der Pädagogik* (Weinheim: Beltz, 2004), 783–806.
3. Kant, *Lectures on Pedagogy*, 9:448/443.
4. See chap. 22 of my *Kants Kritik der praktischen Vernunft: Eine Philosophie der Freiheit* (Munich: Beck, 2012), 403–27, on which I draw here.
5. Immanuel Kant, *Idea for a Universal History with a Cosmopolitan Aim*, trans. Allen W. Wood, in *Anthropology, History, and Education*, 107–20, here 8:25/115.
6. Kant, *Lectures on Pedagogy*, 9:441/437 and 443/439.
7. Kant, *Lectures on Pedagogy*, 448/442–43.
8. Kant, *Lectures on Pedagogy*, 9:450/444.
9. Immanuel Kant, "What Does It Mean to Orient Oneself in Thinking?," trans. Allen W. Wood, in *Religion and Rational Theology*, ed. Allen W. Wood and George Di Giovanni (Cambridge: Cambridge University Press, 1996), 1–18, 8:146/18n.
10. Kant, *Lectures on Pedagogy*, 9:481/468.
11. Kant, *Lectures on Pedagogy*, 9:441/437 [modified].
12. Kant, *Lectures on Pedagogy*, 9:442/443.
13. *ὁ μὴ δαρεὶς ἄνθρωπος οὐ παιδεύεται*; Menander quoted in Herbert Weir Smyth, *A Greek Grammar for Colleges* (New York: American Book, 1920), no. 2734:619.
14. See Aristotle, *Nicomachean Ethics*, trans. Benjamin Jowett, in *The Complete Works of Aristotle: The Revised Oxford Translation*, ed. Jonathan Barnes (Princeton, NJ: Princeton University Press, 1984), 2:1729–867, here I.5:1095b19–22; and Immanuel Kant, *Critique of the Power of Judgment*, trans. Paul Guyer and Eric Matthews, ed. Paul Guyer (Cambridge: Cambridge University Press, 2000), §83, 5:432/299.
15. Kant, *Critique of the Power of Judgment*, §83, 5:432/299.
16. Kant, *Lectures on Pedagogy*, 9:478/467.
17. See, for example, Immanuel Kant, *Groundwork of "The Metaphysics of Morals,"* in *Practical Philosophy*, ed. and trans. Mary J. Gregor (Cambridge: Cambridge University Press, 1996), 37–108, 4:414–21/67–73.
18. On the question whether animals can think, see chap. 4 of my *Die Macht der Moral im 21. Jahrhundert: Annäherungen an eine zeitgemäße Ethik* (Munich: Beck, 2014), 54–63, where I also provide detailed references.
19. [Kant, *Groundwork*, 4:416/69.]

20. Kant, *Lectures on Pedagogy*, 9:450/444.
21. Kant, *Groundwork*, 4:415/68, Kant's emphases.
22. Kant, *Lectures on Pedagogy*, 9:450/444.
23. See, for example, Kant, *Idea*, 8:20/111.
24. Yves-Marius Sagou, *Die Erziehung zum Bürger bei Aristoteles und Kant* (Würzburg: Königshausen und Neumann, 2009), 44.
25. Kant, *Lectures on Pedagogy*, 9:486/473.
26. Kant, *Groundwork*, 4:416/69.
27. Kant, *Lectures on Pedagogy*, 9:450/443.
28. Kant, *Lectures on Pedagogy*, 9:469/459.
29. See Kant, *Anthropology from a Pragmatic Point of View*, §88, 7:278–82/378–82.
30. Translated as Adolph von Knigge, *Practical Philosophy of Social Life or, The Art of Conversing with Men*, trans. P. Will (Lansingburgh: Penniman and Bliss, 1805).
31. Kant, *Lectures on Pedagogy*, 9:450/444.
32. Immanuel Kant, *The Metaphysics of Morals*, in *Practical Philosophy*, ed. and trans. Mary J. Gregor (Cambridge: Cambridge University Press, 1996), 353–603, 6:236/392.
33. Kant, *Lectures on Pedagogy*, 9:488–89/475–76.
34. Kant, *Lectures on Pedagogy*, 9:489–90/476–77.
35. Kant, *Lectures on Pedagogy*, 9:490/477.
36. Kant, *Lectures on Pedagogy*, 9:450/445.
37. Kant, *Lectures on Pedagogy*, 9:450–51/445.
38. Kant, *Lectures on Pedagogy*, 9:455/448.
39. Kant, *Lectures on Pedagogy*, 9:455/448.
40. Kant, *Lectures on Pedagogy*, 9:450/444.
41. Kant, *Lectures on Pedagogy*, 9:477/466 and 9:470/460.
42. Kant, *Lectures on Pedagogy*, 9:470/460 and 9:478:466.
43. Kant, *Lectures on Pedagogy*, 9:453/447.
44. Kant, *Lectures on Pedagogy*, 9:454/448.
45. Kant, *Lectures on Pedagogy*, 9:477/466; compare 9:470–71/460: "The child should play . . . but it must also learn to work."
46. Kant, *Lectures on Pedagogy*, 9:471/460–61.
47. Kant, *Lectures on Pedagogy*, 9:454/448.
48. Kant, *Lectures on Pedagogy*, 9:450/444.
49. See my *Wirtschaftsbürger, Staatsbürger, Weltbürger: Politische Ethik im Zeitalter der Globalisierung* (Munich: Beck, 2004).

CHAPTER FIVE

1. John Stuart Mill, *On Liberty*, in *Collected Works of John Stuart Mill*, ed. J. M. Robson, 33 vols. (Toronto: University of Toronto Press, 1963–), 18:213–310, here 217.
2. On pluralism and tolerance, see below, section 8.3; on the sources of liberalism, see Lothar Gall and Rainer Koch, eds., *Der europäische Liberalismus im 19. Jahrhundert: Texte zu seiner Entwicklung*, 4 vols. (Frankfurt: Ullstein, 1981); on its history, Rudolf Vierhaus,

"Liberalismus," and Rudolf Walther, "Exkurs: Wirtschaftlicher Liberalismus," both in Otto Brunner, Werner Conze, and Reinhart Koselleck, eds., *Geschichtliche Grundbegriffe: Historisches Lexikon zur politisch-sozialen Sprache in Deutschland*, 5 vols. (Stuttgart: Klett-Cotta, 1972–97), 3:741–85 and 787–815, respectively; on the historical semantic origins and transformations of the political concept of "liberalism" from the end of the eighteenth until past the middle of the nineteenth century, see Jörn Leonhard, *Liberalismus: Zur historischen Semantik eines europäischen Deutungsmusters* (Munich: Oldenbourg, 2001); and Edmund Fawcett, *Liberalism: The Life of an Idea* (Princeton, NJ: Princeton University Press, 2014).

3. Judith N. Shklar, "The Liberalism of Fear," in Nancy L. Rosenblum, ed., *Liberalism and the Moral Life* (Cambridge, MA: Harvard University Press, 1989), 21–38, here 21.
4. Isaiah 2:4.
5. "Fraud, Luxury, and Pride must live; Whilst we the Benefits receive"; see Bernard Mandeville, *The Fable of the Bees: Or, Private Vices, Publick Benefits* [etc.] (London: Tonson, 1724), 23; on Mandeville as a social critic, see Walter Euchner, *Egoismus und Gemeinwohl* (Frankfurt: Suhrkamp, 1973), 74–131.
6. Adam Smith, *An Inquiry into the Nature and Causes of the Wealth of Nations*, ed. Edwin Cannan (Chicago: University of Chicago Press, 1976), I.8:88.
7. Smith, *Wealth of Nations*, I.1:16; on Smith's oeuvre and influence, see Ian Simpson Ross, *The Life of Adam Smith*, 2nd ed. (Oxford: Oxford University Press, 2010); as well as Karl Ballestrem, *Adam Smith* (Munich: Beck, 2001).
8. See Stephen Conway, "Bentham, the Benthamites, and the Nineteenth-Century British Peace Movement," *Utilitas* 2, no. 2 (November 1990): 221–43.
9. See Jeremy Bentham, "Postscript" to *Defence of Usury*, in *Jeremy Bentham's Economic Writings*, ed. Werner Stark (London: Routledge, 2014), 1:195–206, here 202–4.
10. Wilhelm von Humboldt, *The Sphere and Duties of Government*, trans. Joseph Coulthard (London: Chapman, 1854), 11.
11. John Stuart Mill, *Utilitarianism*, in *Collected Works*, 10:203–59, here 212.
12. See John Stuart Mill, *Considerations on Representative Government*, in *Collected Works*, 19:371–577, here 562–77.
13. Mill, *On Liberty*, 301.
14. John Stuart Mill, *The Subjection of Women*, in *Collected Works*, 21:259–340, here 336.
15. Mill, *Considerations*, 467–82.
16. John Stuart Mill, *Principles of Political Economy*, in *Collected Works*, 2–3:IV.VII:758–96; and *Chapters on Socialism*, in *Collected Works*, 5:703–53.
17. Mill, *Principles*, II.II.§3:218–23.
18. Mill, *On Liberty*, 227.
19. Mill, *On Liberty*, 219.
20. Mill, *Considerations*, 375.
21. On Mill, see Peter Rinderle, *John Stuart Mill* (Munich: Beck, 2000).
22. John Rawls, *A Theory of Justice*, rev. ed. (Cambridge, MA: Belknap Press of Harvard

University Press, 1999), §46:266; see also Otfried Höffe, ed., *John Rawls: A Theory of Justice*, 1998, trans. Joost den Haan (Leiden: Brill, 2013).

23. John Rawls, *Political Liberalism*, exp. ed. (New York: Columbia University Press, 2005); see also the collective commentary in Otfried Höffe, ed., *John Rawls: Politischer Liberalismus* (Berlin: de Gruyter, 2015).
24. Richard Rorty, *Contingency, Irony, and Solidarity* (Cambridge: Cambridge University Press, 1989).
25. Richard Rorty, *Achieving Our Country: Leftist Thought in Twentieth-Century America* (Cambridge, MA: Harvard University Press, 1998), 98.
26. Rorty, *Contingency, Irony, and Solidarity*, 61–69.
27. Rorty, *Achieving Our Country*, 103 and 105.
28. For a plea in this sense, see chap. 7 of Richard Rorty, *Philosophy and the Mirror of Nature* (Princeton, NJ: Princeton University Press, 1979), 315–56.
29. For an attempt on the subject of penal law, see my *Gibt es ein interkulturelles Strafrecht? Ein philosophischer Versuch* (Frankfurt: Suhrkamp, 1999).

CHAPTER SIX

1. Max Weber, *Economy and Society: An Outline of Interpretive Sociology*, ed. Guenther Roth and Claus Wittich, trans. Ephraim Fischoff et al. (Berkeley: University of California Press, 1978), I.VII:635–40.
2. Axel Honneth, *Freedom's Right: The Social Foundations of Democratic Life*, trans. Joseph Ganahl (New York: Columbia University Press, 2014), 304–29.
3. Plato, *Republic*, II.11:369b–371b.
4. Karl Marx and Friedrich Engels, *The German Ideology*, ed. and trans. C. J. Arthur (New York: International, 1970), 54.
5. Adam Smith, *An Inquiry into the Nature and Causes of the Wealth of Nations*, ed. Edwin Cannan (Chicago: University of Chicago Press, 1976), I.1:7.
6. Joseph Schumpeter, *The Theory of Economic Development: An Inquiry into Profits, Capital, Credit, Interest, and the Business Cycle*, 1912, trans. Redvers Opie (New Brunswick, NJ: Transaction Books, 1983).
7. Joseph A. Schumpeter, *Capitalism, Socialism and Democracy* (London: Routledge, 1992), 81–86.
8. Karl Marx, *Capital: A Critical Analysis of Capitalist Production*, trans. Samuel Moore and Edward Aveling, pt. 2, vol. 9 of *Karl Marx Friedrich Engels Gesamtausgabe*, ed. Waltraud Falk et al. (Berlin: Dietz, 1990), III.X.1:202.
9. Smith, *Wealth of Nations*, I.2:18.
10. Otfried Höffe, *Democracy in an Age of Globalisation*, trans. Dirk Haubrich with Michael Ludwig (Dordrecht: Springer, 2007), 287–90.
11. As Julian Nida-Rümelin did in 2011 and, long before then, Erich Fromm, in 1976. See Nida-Rümelin, *Die Optimierungsfalle: Philosophie einer humanen Ökonomie* (Munich: Irisiana, 2011); and Fromm, *To Have or to Be?* (New York: Bloomsbury, 2015).

12. Michael J. Sandel, *What Money Can't Buy: The Moral Limits of Markets* (New York: Farrar, Straus and Giroux, 2012), 10.
13. On such terms as failure of the market, failure of citizens, and the rule of budget cuts, see chap. 17 of my *Ist die Demokratie zukunftsfähig?* (Munich: Beck, 2009), 247–61.
14. Alfred Müller-Armack, *Studien zur sozialen Marktwirtschaft* (Cologne: Institut für Wirtschaftspolitik an der Universität Köln, 1960), and *Wirtschaftsordnung und Wirtschaftspolitik: Studien und Konzepte zur sozialen Marktwirtschaft und zur europäischen Integration* (Bern: Haupt, 1976).
15. On business ethics, see chap. 3 of my *Wirtschaftsbürger, Staatsbürger, Weltbürger: Politische Ethik im Zeitalter der Globalisierung* (Munich: Beck, 2004), 30–51.
16. See on this point Thomas Piketty's study *Capital in the Twenty-First Century*, trans. Arthur Goldhammer (Cambridge, MA: Harvard University Press, 2014); and below, section 6.6.
17. Charles de Secondat Montesquieu, *The Spirit of the Laws*, trans. and ed. Anne Cohler, Basia Miller, and Harold Stone (Cambridge: Cambridge University Press, 1989), 20.2:338–39.
18. Immanuel Kant, *Idea for a Universal History with a Cosmopolitan Aim*, trans. Allen W. Wood, in *Anthropology, History, and Education*, ed. Günter Zöller and Robert B. Louden (Cambridge: Cambridge University Press, 2007), 8:21/111.
19. On this competition, see Kia Vahland, *Michelangelo und Raffael: Rivalen im Rom der Renaissance* (Munich: Beck, 2012).
20. Jakob Augstein, *Sabotage: Warum wir uns zwischen Demokratie und Kapitalismus entscheiden müssen* (Munich: dtv, 2013). On the controversial debates, see Luc Boltanski and Ève Chiapello, *The New Spirit of Capitalism*, trans. Gregory Elliott, new upd. ed. (London: Verso, 2013); on the history and definition of capitalism, see Jürgen Kocka, *Geschichte des Kapitalismus* (Munich: Beck, 2013); as well the still-classic studies: Max Weber, *The Protestant Ethic and the Spirit of Capitalism*, trans. Talcott Parsons, ed. Richard Swedberg (New York: Norton, 2009); Schumpeter, *Capitalism, Socialism and Democracy*; and Werner Sombart, *Der moderne Kapitalismus: Historisch-systematische Darstellung des gesamteuropäischen Wirtschaftslebens von seinen Anfängen bis zur Gegenwart*, 1902, final ed. 1928 (Munich: dtv, 1987).
21. Jürgen Habermas, *The Theory of Communicative Action*, trans. Thomas McCarthy, 2 vols. (Boston: Beacon, 1984–87), 2:332–73. On the cultural and conceptual history of money, see Felix Martin, *Money: The Unauthorized Biography* (New York: Knopf, 2014); on thought experiments for a new set of rules, see Christian Felber, *Geld: Die neuen Spielregeln* (Vienna: Deuticke, 2014).
22. Lisa Herzog, *Freiheit gehört nicht nur den Reichen: Plädoyer für einen zeitgemäßen Liberalismus* (Munich: Beck, 2014).
23. John Rawls, *A Theory of Justice*, rev. ed. (Cambridge, MA: Belknap Press of Harvard University Press, 1999), §§80–81:464–74.
24. Quoted in Otfried Höffe, ed., *Lesebuch zur Ethik*, 5th ed. (Munich: Beck, 2012), 30.
25. Immanuel Kant, *Anthropology from a Pragmatic Point of View*, trans. Robert B. Louden, in *Anthropology, History, and Education*, §81, 7:266/367.

26. Émile Zola, *Money*, trans. Valerie Minogue (Oxford: Oxford University Press, 2014).
27. Wolfgang Streeck, *Buying Time: The Delayed Crisis of Democratic Capitalism*, 2nd ed., trans. Patrick Camiller and David Fernbach (London: Verso, 2017), 174–77.
28. Stephanie Meinhard and Niklas Potrafke, "The Globalization–Welfare State Nexus Reconsidered," *Review of International Economics* 20, no. 2 (May 2012): 271–87.
29. Niall Ferguson, *The Ascent of Money: A Financial History of the World* (London: Allen Lane, 2008).
30. Piketty, *Capital in the Twenty-First Century*.
31. Karl-Heinz Paqué, "Gibt es doch Gesetze des Kapitalismus?," *Frankfurter Allgemeine Zeitung*, September 21, 2014, online, https://www.faz.net/aktuell/wirtschaft/wirtschaftspolitik/gastbeitrag-von-karl-heinz-paque-gibt-es-doch-gesetze-des-kapitalismus-13148312.html, last accessed September 1, 2019.

CHAPTER SEVEN

1. Most incisively, John Rawls, *A Theory of Justice*, rev. ed. (Cambridge, MA: Belknap Press of Harvard University Press, 1999); but see also the economist Amartya Sen, *The Idea of Justice* (Cambridge, MA: Belknap Press of Harvard University Press, 2009); and the legal theorist Ronald Dworkin, *Justice for Hedgehogs* (Cambridge, MA: Belknap Press of Harvard University Press, 2011); as well as other authors such as Jan Assmann, *Ma'at: Gerechtigkeit und Unsterblichkeit im Alten Ägypten* (Munich: Beck, 1990); Friedrich Dürrenmatt, "A Monster Lecture on Justice and Law, Together with a Helvetian Interlude," trans. John E. Woods, in *Plays and Essays*, ed. Volkmar Sander (New York: Continuum, 1982), 263–311; Christoph Horn and Nico Scarano, eds., *Philosophie der Gerechtigkeit: Texte von der Antike bis zur Gegenwart* (Frankfurt: Suhrkamp, 2002); and Paolo Prodi, *Una storia della giustizia: Dal pluralismo dei fori al moderno dualismo tra coscienza e diritto* (Bologna: Il Mulino, 2000); and see also my *Political Justice: Foundations for a Critical Philosophy of Law and the State*, 1987, trans. Jeffrey C. Cohen (Cambridge, UK: Polity, 1995).
2. Johann Wolfgang Goethe, "Plato, als Mitgenosse einer christlichen Offenbarung (Im Jahre 1796 durch eine Übersetzung veranlaßt)," in *Goethes Werke*, vol. 12, ed. Erich Trunz and Hans Joachim Schrimpf (Munich: Beck, 1981), 244–49, here 245.
3. Immanuel Kant, *Critique of the Power of Judgment*, trans. Paul Guyer and Eric Matthews, ed. Paul Guyer (Cambridge: Cambridge University Press, 2000), §28, 5:260/143; and Max Weber, *Economy and Society: An Outline of Interpretive Sociology*, ed. Guenther Roth and Claus Wittich, trans. Ephraim Fischoff et al. (Berkeley: University of California Press, 1978), I.I.16:53.
4. See chap. 14 of my *Die Macht der Moral im 21. Jahrhundert: Annäherungen an eine zeitgemäße Ethik* (Munich: Beck, 2014), 182–203.
5. Quoted in Otfried Höffe, ed., *Lesebuch zur Ethik*, 5th ed. (Munich: Beck, 2012), 31–32.
6. [Immanuel Kant, *The Metaphysics of Morals*, in *Practical Philosophy*, ed. and trans. Mary J. Gregor (Cambridge: Cambridge University Press, 1996), 353–603, here §41, 6:305–6/450–51.]
7. For a well-sourced overview and sensible assessment, see Franz-Xaver Kaufmann,

"Das Doppelgesicht des Sozialstaats," *Frankfurter Allgemeine Zeitung*, February 24, 2014, 7.

8. Georg Wilhelm Friedrich Hegel, *Lectures on the Philosophy of World History: Introduction*, trans. H. B. Nisbet (Cambridge: Cambridge University Press, 1975), 70.
9. Franz-Xaver Kaufmann, *Schrumpfende Gesellschaft: Vom Bevölkerungsrückgang und seinen Folgen* (Frankfurt: Suhrkamp, 2005), 195.
10. Laurence J. Kotlikoff and Scott Burns, *The Clash of Generations: Saving Ourselves, Our Kids, and Our Economy* (Cambridge, MA: MIT Press, 2014), esp. chap. 7.
11. Hugo von Hofmannsthal, *The Play of Everyman*, trans. George Sterling and Richard Ordynski (San Francisco: Robertson, 1917), 20.
12. On a globally decentralized regulation of the finance industry, see Dani Rodrik, *The Globalization Paradox: Democracy and the Future of the World Economy* (New York: Norton, 2011), 260–66.

CHAPTER EIGHT

1. Henri Bergson, *The Two Sources of Morality and Religion*, trans. R. Ashley Audra and Cloudesley Brereton (Notre Dame, IN: University of Notre Dame Press, 1977), 37–38 and 57–58.
2. Eberhard Döring, *Karl R. Popper, "Die offene Gesellschaft und ihre Feinde": Ein einführender Kommentar* (Paderborn: Schöningh, 1996).
3. On the polemic against Plato, see section 16.4 in my "Vier Kapitel einer Wirkungsgeschichte der 'Politeia,'" in Otfried Höffe, ed., *Platon: Politeia*, 3rd ed. (Berlin: Akademie, 2011), 259–80, here 275–79; on the critique of incrementalism, see section 10.2 of my *Strategien der Humanität: Zur Ethik öffentlicher Entscheidungsprozesse* (Frankfurt: Suhrkamp, 1985), 255–63.
4. Friedrich A. Hayek, *The Road to Serfdom* (London: Routledge, 1944). See also Friedrich A. Hayek, *Law, Legislation, and Liberty*, 3 vols. (Chicago: University of Chicago Press, 1973–79); and Ingo Pies and Martin Leschke, eds., *F. A. von Hayeks konstitutioneller Liberalismus* (Tübingen: Mohr Siebeck, 2003).
5. Jørgen Randers, *2052: A Global Forecast for the Next Forty Years* (White River Junction, VT: Chelsea Green, 2012).
6. Ralf Dahrendorf, *The New Liberty: Survival and Justice in a Changing World* (Stanford, CA: Stanford University Press, 1975).
7. Ralf Dahrendorf, *Auf der Suche nach einer neuen Ordnung: Vorlesungen zur Politik der Freiheit im 21. Jahrhundert* (Munich: Beck, 2003).
8. Immanuel Kant, *Anthropology from a Pragmatic Point of View*, trans. Robert B. Louden, in *Anthropology, History, and Education*, ed. Günter Zöller and Robert B. Louden (Cambridge: Cambridge University Press, 2007), §2, 7:128–30/240–42.
9. William James, *A Pluralistic Universe*, ed. Fredson Bowers and Ignas K. Skrupskelis, The Works of William James (Cambridge, MA: Harvard University Press, 1977), 146.
10. See Johann Gottfried Herder, *Ideen zur Philosophie der Geschichte der Menschheit*, 1784/85, vol. 6 of *Werke in 10 Bänden*, ed. Martin Bollacher (Frankfurt: Deutscher Klassiker

Verlag, 1989), 38; Friedrich Wilhelm Joseph von Schelling, *Philosophie der Mythologie in drei Vorlesungsnachschriften 1837/1842*, ed. Klaus Vieweg, Christian Danz, and Georgia Apostolopoulou (Munich: Fink, 1996); and Ernst Cassirer, *The Philosophy of Symbolic Forms*, vol. 2, *Mythical Thought* (New Haven, CT: Yale University Press, 1955).

11. William James, *The Varieties of Religious Experience: A Study in Human Nature*, ed. Frederick H. Burkhardt, Fredson Bowers, and Ignas K. Skrupskelis, The Works of William James (Cambridge, MA: Harvard University Press, 1985).

12. Isaiah Berlin, *The Crooked Timber of Humanity: Chapters in the History of Ideas*, ed. Henry Hardy, 2nd ed. (Princeton, NJ: Princeton University Press, 2013).

13. See my *Den Staat braucht selbst ein Volk von Teufeln: Philosophische Versuche zur Rechts- und Staatsethik* (Stuttgart: Reclam, 1988), 105–24; and John Rawls, *Political Liberalism*, exp. ed. (New York: Columbia University Press, 2005); on Rawls, see Otfried Höffe, ed., *John Rawls: Politischer Liberalismus* (Berlin: de Gruyter, 2015).

14. Rosa Luxemburg, *The Russian Revolution*, in "*The Russian Revolution" and "Leninism or Marxism?"* (Ann Arbor: University of Michigan Press, 1961), 25–80, here 69.

15. On tolerance, see Rainer Forst, *Toleration in Conflict: Past and Present*, trans. Ciaran Cronin (Cambridge: Cambridge University Press, 2016); chap. 8 of my *Wirtschaftsbürger, Staatsbürger, Weltbürger: Politische Ethik im Zeitalter der Globalisierung* (Munich: Beck, 2004), 103–19; and Heinrich Schmidinger, ed., *Wege zur Toleranz: Geschichte einer europäischen Idee in Quellen* (Darmstadt: Wissenschaftliche Buchgesellschaft, 2002).

16. See my *Gibt es ein interkulturelles Strafrecht? Ein philosophischer Versuch* (Frankfurt: Suhrkamp, 1999).

17. See my *Vernunft und Recht: Bausteine zu einem interkulturellen Rechtsdiskurs*, 1996, 2nd ed. (Frankfurt: Suhrkamp, 1998).

18. See also chapter 6 of my *Wirtschaftsbürger, Staatsbürger, Weltbürger*, 82–89.

19. See Jürgen Habermas, "Staatsbürgerschaft und nationale Identität," 1990, in *Faktizität und Geltung: Beiträge zur Diskurstheorie des Rechts und des demokratischen Rechtsstaats* (Frankfurt: Suhrkamp, 1992), 632–59.

CHAPTER NINE

1. *Statusschrift der Heidelberger Akademie der Wissenschaften*, 2013, online, https://www.haw.uni-heidelberg.de/md/haw/akademie/statusschrift_2013.pdf, last accessed September 1, 2019, 5.

2. *Xenophanes*, in André Laks and Glenn W. Most, eds. and trans., *Early Greek Philosophy*, vol. 3, *Early Ionian Thinkers* (Cambridge, MA: Harvard University Press, 2016), pt. 2, 3–113, D39 (B32):49.

3. Aristotle, *Metaphysics*, trans. W. D. Ross, in *The Complete Works of Aristotle: The Revised Oxford Translation*, ed. Jonathan Barnes (Princeton, NJ: Princeton University Press, 1984), 2:1552–728, here I.1:980a22.

4. Aurelius Augustinus, *Confessions*, trans. Maria Boulding, vol. 1 of *The Works of Saint Augustine: A Translation for the 21st Century*, ed. John E. Rotelle (New York: New City Press, 1997), 5.3.4 and 10.35.54.

5. Francis Bacon, *The New Organon*, ed. James Spedding, R. L. Ellis, D. D. Heath, and William Rawley, in *The Works of Francis Bacon* (London: Longman, 1858), vol. 4, 37–248, I.65:65–66.
6. For an interpretation of Bacon, see chap. 4 of my *Moral als Preis der Moderne: Ein Versuch über Wissenschaft, Technik und Umwelt*, 4th ed. (Frankfurt: Suhrkamp, 2000), 49–72; and chaps. 1 and 10–12 of *Die Macht der Moral im 21. Jahrhundert: Annäherungen an eine zeitgemäße Ethik* (Munich: Beck, 2014), 8–21 and 136–71.
7. René Descartes, *Discourse on the Method*, trans. Robert Stoothoff, in *The Philosophical Writings of Descartes* (Cambridge: Cambridge University Press, 1985), 1:111–51, here 6:142.
8. See my *Moral als Preis der Moderne* for a detailed discussion.
9. *Moral als Preis der Moderne*, thesis 10, 296.
10. See, for example, the recommendations made by the workgroup "Aging in Germany" that are by no means dominated by pessimism: Jürgen Kocka et al., "More Years, More Life: Recommendations of the Joint Academy Initiative on Aging," *Nova Acta Leopoldina* 108, no. 372 (2010), online, https://www.leopoldina.org/uploads/tx_leopublication/2009_NatEmpf_Altern_in_D-EN.pdf, last accessed September 1, 2019.
11. Aristotle, *Nicomachean Ethics*, trans. Benjamin Jowett, in *The Complete Works of Aristotle: The Revised Oxford Translation*, ed. Jonathan Barnes (Princeton, NJ: Princeton University Press, 1984), 2:1729–867, here VI.13:1145a6 and VI.5:1140a27–28.
12. Aristotle, *Nicomachean Ethics*, VI.12:1144a23–27.

CHAPTER TEN

1. *Xenophanes*, in André Laks and Glenn W. Most, eds. and trans., *Early Greek Philosophy*, vol. 3, *Early Ionian Thinkers* (Cambridge, MA: Harvard University Press, 2016), pt. 2, 3–113, D8 (B11):27 and D16 (B23):33.
2. Aeschylus, *Agamemnon*, in *Aeschylus*, ed. and trans. Alan H. Sommerstein (Cambridge, MA: Harvard University Press, 2008), 2:2–207, line 177.
3. Aristotle, *Poetics*, trans. Ingram Bywater, in *The Complete Works of Aristotle: The Revised Oxford Translation*, ed. Jonathan Barnes (Princeton, NJ: Princeton University Press, 1984), 2:2316–40, here 26:1461b26–1462b19.
4. Aristotle, *Poetics*, 9:1451b8–9.
5. Immanuel Kant, *Critique of the Power of Judgment*, trans. Paul Guyer and Eric Matthews, ed. Paul Guyer (Cambridge: Cambridge University Press, 2000), §49, 5:313–19/191–96.
6. Marcel Duchamp, "Painting . . . at the Service of the Mind," in Herschel B. Chipp, ed., *Theories of Modern Art: A Source Book by Artists and Critics* (Berkeley: University of California Press, 1968), 392–95, here 394.
7. Georg Wilhelm Friedrich Hegel, *Aesthetics: Lectures on Fine Art*, trans. T. M. Knox (Oxford: Clarendon, 1975), 1:70, 94, and 10, Hegel's emphasis.
8. Martin Heidegger, "Afterword" to "The Origin of the Work of Art," in *Off the Beaten*

Track, trans. Julian Young and Kenneth Haynes (Cambridge: Cambridge University Press, 2002), 50–52, here 51.

9. On the topic as a whole, see Friedhelm Hufen, "Kunstfreiheit," in Detlef Merten and Hans J. Papier, eds., *Handbuch der Grundrechte in Deutschland und Europa*, vol. 4, *Grundrechte in Deutschland: Einzelgrundrechte 1* (Heidelberg: Müller, 2011), 801–73.
10. Peter Handke, *Offending the Audience/Self-Accusation*, trans. Michael Roloff (London: Methuen, 1971).
11. *Paulette*, dir. Jérôme Enrico (Neuilly-sur-Seine: Gaumont, 2012); Jonas Jonasson, *The Hundred-Year-Old Man Who Climbed Out of the Window and Disappeared*, trans. Rod Bradbury (London: Hesperus, 2012); and *The Girl Who Saved the King of Sweden*, trans. Rachel Willson-Broyles (New York: Ecco, 2014).
12. John Williams, *Stoner* (New York: Viking, 1965); and Robert Seethaler, *A Whole Life*, trans. Charlotte Collins (London: Farrar, Straus and Giroux, 2016).
13. See Andreas Kablitz's homonymous book, *Kunst des Möglichen: Theorie der Literatur* (Freiburg: Rombach, 2013).
14. Steven Galloway, *The Cellist of Sarajevo* (New York: Riverhead, 2008), 187.
15. Christian Dietrich Grabbe, *Scherz, Satire, Ironie und tiefere Bedeutung*, in *Werke und Briefe: Historisch-kritische Gesamtausgabe in sechs Bänden*, ed. Alfred Bergmann (Emsdetten: Lechte, 1960), 1:213–73.
16. Eric Bennett, "How Iowa Flattened Literature," *Chronicle of Higher Education*, online, February 10, 2014, https://www.chronicle.com/article/How-Iowa-Flattened-Literature/144531, last accessed September 1, 2019.
17. Hegel, *Aesthetics*, 1:31.
18. Niklas Luhmann, *Theory of Society*, trans. Rhodes Barrett (Stanford, CA: Stanford University Press, 2012), 1:210.
19. Arthur C. Danto, *The Transfiguration of the Commonplace: A Philosophy of Art* (Cambridge, MA: Harvard University Press, 1981).

CHAPTER ELEVEN

1. Ulrich Klug, *Skeptische Rechtsphilosophie und humanes Strafrecht* (Berlin: Springer, 1981), 1:88.
2. Edmund Burke, *A Vindication of Natural Society*, in *The Writings and Speeches of Edmund Burke*, vol. 1, ed. T. O. McLoughlin, James T. Boulton, and William B. Todd (Oxford: Oxford University Press, 1997).
3. For a short overview of the history of and references to literature about anarchy and freedom from rule, see section 7.2 of Otfried Höffe, *Politische Gerechtigkeit: Grundlegung einer kritischen Philosophie von Recht und Staat*, 1987, 4th ed. (Frankfurt: Suhrkamp, 2003), 197–205.
4. George Gordon, Lord Byron, "Darkness," no. 301 in vol. 4 of *The Complete Poetical Works*, ed. Jerome J. McGann (Oxford: Clarendon, 1992), 40–43.
5. Thomas Hobbes, *Leviathan, with Selected Variants from the Latin Edition of 1668*, ed. Edwin Curley (Indianapolis: Hackett, 1994), I.14.4:80.

6. Worth reading on the emergence and functioning of the state is Pierre Bourdieu, *On the State: Lectures at the Collège de France, 1989–1992*, trans. David Fernbach (Cambridge, UK: Polity, 2018).
7. Hobbes, *Leviathan*, I.14.5:80–81.
8. Immanuel Kant, *The Metaphysics of Morals*, in *Practical Philosophy*, ed. and trans. Mary J. Gregor (Cambridge: Cambridge University Press, 1996), 353–603, 6:230/387; and John Rawls, *A Theory of Justice*, rev. ed. (Cambridge, MA: Belknap Press of Harvard University Press, 1999), §46:266.
9. The rich literature includes Wolfgang Heidelmeyer, *Die Menschenrechte: Darstellung und Dokumente*, 4th rev. ed. (Paderborn: Schöningh, 1997); and my own *Vernunft und Recht: Bausteine zu einem interkulturellen Rechtsdiskurs*, 2nd ed. (Frankfurt: Suhrkamp, 1998); as well as chap. 3 of my *Democracy in an Age of Globalisation*, trans. Dirk Haubrich with Michael Ludwig (Dordrecht: Springer, 2007), 35–60; Stefan Gosepath and Georg Lohmann, eds., *Philosophie der Menschenrechte* (Frankfurt: Suhrkamp, 1998); Michael J. Perry, *The Idea of Human Rights: Four Inquiries* (Oxford: Oxford University Press, 1998); Christoph Menke and Arnd Pollmann, *Philosophie der Menschenrechte zur Einführung* (Hamburg: Junius, 2007); and Hans Joas, *The Sacredness of the Person: A New Genealogy of Human Rights*, trans. Alex Skinner (Washington, DC: Georgetown University Press, 2013).
10. See, for example, Aristotle, *Politics*, trans. Benjamin Jowett, in *Complete Works of Aristotle*, 2:1986–2129, I.2, 1253a 9–10.
11. On property in the discourse of modernity, see Marietta Auer, *Der privatrechtliche Diskurs der Moderne* (Tübingen: Mohr Siebeck, 2014).
12. Avishai Margalit, *The Decent Society* (Cambridge, MA: Harvard University Press, 1998).
13. Colin Crouch, *Post-democracy* (Malden, MA: Polity, 2004), 21.
14. Emanuel Richter, *Die Wurzeln der Demokratie* (Weilerswist: Velbrück, 2008).
15. See Jan-Werner Müller, *Contesting Democracy: Political Ideas in Twentieth-Century Europe* (New Haven, CT: Yale University Press, 2011).
16. See Jørgen Randers, *2052: A Global Forecast for the Next Forty Years* (White River Junction, VT: Chelsea Green, 2012); and Donella H. Meadows et al., *The Limits to Growth: A Report for the Club of Rome's Project on the Predicament of Mankind* (New York: Universe, 1972).
17. For a more elaborate discussion, see section 5.2 of my *Ist die Demokratie zukunftsfähig?* (Munich: Beck, 2009), 77–84. See also Juliane Rebentisch, *Die Kunst der Freiheit: Zur Dialektik demokratischer Existenz* (Berlin: Suhrkamp, 2012); Peter Kielmansegg, *Die Grammatik der Freiheit: Acht Versuche über den demokratischen Verfassungsstaat* (Baden-Baden: Nomos, 2013); and Uwe Justus Wenzel, ed., *Volksherrschaft: Wunsch und Wirklichkeit* (Zurich: Neue Zürcher Zeitung, 2014); on a number of recent publications, see also Martin Saar "Heterogene Demokratie," *Philosophische Rundschau* 61, no. 3 (2014): 183–205.
18. See Plato, *Republic* VIII.10, 555b–557a; and Aristotle, *Politics*, III.6–8:1276a6–1279a22.
19. *Basic Law for the Federal Republic of Germany*, trans. Christian Tomuschat, David P. Currie,

Donald P. Kommers, and Raymond Kerr (Berlin: Deutscher Bundestag, 2018), article 19, section 2.

20. See chap. 6 of my *Democracy in an Age of Globalisation*, 103–29.
21. On the problems of the majority principle, see also Bernd Guggenberger and Claus Offe, eds., *An den Grenzen der Mehrheits-Demokratie: Politik und Soziologie der Mehrheitsregel* (Opladen: Westdeutscher Verlag, 1984), even if the authors' suggestions are problematic.
22. See Frieder Vogelmann, "Flüssige Betriebssysteme: Liquid democracy als demokratische Machttechnologie," *Aus Politik und Zeitgeschichte* 62, no. 48 (2012): 40–46.
23. See Robert Paul Wolff, *In Defense of Anarchism*, 1970 (Berkeley: University of California Press, 1998).
24. See Michael Kühnlein, ed., *Das Politische und das Vorpolitische: Über die Wertgrundlagen der Demokratie* (Baden-Baden: Nomos, 2014); see also Joseph Raz, *The Morality of Freedom*, 1986 (Oxford: Clarendon, 2009).
25. Thucydides, *History of the Peloponnesian War*, trans. Charles Forster Smith (Cambridge, MA: Harvard University Press, 1928), II.40.2–3:329).

CHAPTER TWELVE

1. To cite but two examples from the vast literature: Johann Bizer, Bernd Lutterbeck, and Joachim Rieß, eds., *Umbruch von Regelungssystemen in der Informationsgesellschaft: Freundesgabe für Alfred Büllesbach*, online, http://www.alfred-buellesbach.de/PDF/Freundesgabe.pdf, last accessed November 1, 2019; and Shoshana Zuboff, *The Age of Surveillance Capitalism: The Fight for a Human Future at the New Frontier of Power* (New York: Public Affairs, 2019).
2. Peter Burke, *A Social History of Knowledge*, vol. 2, *From the Encyclopédie to Wikipedia* (Cambridge, UK: Polity, 2012), 5.
3. See Directive 2006/24/EC of the European Parliament and of the Council of 15 March 2006 on the Retention of Data Generated or Processed in Connection with the Provision of Publicly Available Electronic Communications Services or of Public Communications Networks and Amending Directive 2002/58/EC, online, https://eur-lex.europa.eu/eli/dir/2006/24/oj, last accessed September 1, 2019.
4. Theodor W. Adorno, *Minima Moralia: Reflections on a Damaged Life*, trans. E. F. N. Jephcott (London: Verso, 2005), aphorism 18, 39.
5. Michael Stolleis, "Weltbürger im Allgäu," *Frankfurter Allgemeine Zeitung*, November 1, 2012, online, https://www.faz.net/aktuell/politik/staat-und-recht/gastbeitrag-weltbuerger-im-allgaeu-11945534-p3.html, last accessed September 1, 2019.
6. ["Karlsruhe has spoken; the case is forever closed." The southwestern town of Karlsruhe is the seat of the Bundesverfassungsgericht, the Federal Constitutional Court.—Trans.]
7. To cite but two fairly recent publications from the vast literature: Matthias Jestaedt, ed., *Das entgrenzte Gericht: Eine kritische Bilanz nach sechzig Jahren Bundesverfassungsgericht* (Berlin:

Suhrkamp, 2011); and Michael Stolleis, ed., *Herzkammern der Republik: Die Deutschen und das Bundesverfassungsgericht* (Munich: Beck, 2011), which includes my essay "Wer hütet die Verfassung vor ihren Hütern?" (124–36).

8. Lothar Müller and Thomas Steinfeld, "Die Zukunft der Zeitung," *Merkur* 67, no. 12 (December 2013): 1091–103, here 1093.
9. Norbert Bolz, *Blindflug mit Zuschauer* (Munich: Fink, 2005), 88.
10. kue, "Im Zweifel für die Zeitung," *Frankfurter Allgemeine Zeitung*, February 21, 2013, 31.
11. Müller and Steinfeld, "Die Zukunft der Zeitung," 1094.
12. See, for example, Jacques Derrida, "On a Newly Arisen Apocalyptic Tone in Philosophy," trans. John Leavey Jr., in Peter Fenves, ed., *Raising the Tone of Philosophy: Late Essays by Immanuel Kant, Transformative Critique by Jacques Derrida* (Baltimore: Johns Hopkins University Press, 1993), 117–72.
13. Immanuel Kant, "To Perpetual Peace," in *Practical Philosophy*, ed. and trans. Mary J. Gregor (Cambridge: Cambridge University Press, 1996), 311–51, here 8:374/342.
14. Bernhard Pörksen and Hanne Detel, *Der entfesselte Skandal: Das Ende der Kontrolle im digitalen Zeitalter* (Cologne: Halem, 2012).
15. See Hartmut Rosa, *Beschleunigung: Die Veränderung der Zeitstrukturen in der Moderne* (Frankfurt: Suhrkamp, 2012), 188.
16. Hermann Lübbe, *Zeit-Verhältnisse: Zur Kulturphilosophie des Fortschritts* (Graz: Styria, 1984).
17. Rosa, *Beschleunigung*, 15.
18. Bernhard Pörksen and Wolfgang Krischke, eds., *Die gehetzte Politik: Die neue Macht der Medien und Märkte* (Cologne: Halem, 2013).
19. Heinrich Geiselberger and Tobias Moorstedt, eds., *Big Data: Das neue Versprechen der Allwissenheit* (Berlin: Suhrkamp, 2013).

CHAPTER THIRTEEN

1. Two dimensions are discussed in Will Kymlicka and Wayne Norman, "Return of the Citizen: A Survey of Recent Work on Citizenship Theory," *Ethics* 104, no. 2 (January 1994): 352–81; three in Dominique Leydet, "Citizenship," in Edward N. Zalta, ed., *The Stanford Encyclopedia of Philosophy*, online, Fall 2017 ed., plato.stanford.edu/archives/fall2017/entries/citizenship/, section 1.1; for an older debate, see Thomas H. Marshall, *Class, Citizenship and Social Development* (Chicago: University of Chicago Press, 1977).
2. Otfried Höffe, *Wirtschaftsbürger, Staatsbürger, Weltbürger: Politische Ethik im Zeitalter der Globalisierung* (Munich: Beck, 2004).
3. For a nuanced look at modernity, see Alessandro Pinzani, *An den Wurzeln moderner Demokratie: Bürger und Staat in der Neuzeit* (Berlin: Akademie, 2009); still worth reading is Helmut G. Königsberger and Elisabeth Müller-Luckner, eds., *Republiken und Republikanismus im Europa der Frühen Neuzeit* (Munich: Oldenbourg, 1988).
4. See James Tully, *Strange Multiplicity: Constitutionalism in an Age of Diversity* (Cambridge: Cambridge University Press, 1995).

5. Jürgen Habermas, "Staatsbürgerschaft und nationale Identität," 1990, in *Faktizität und Geltung: Beiträge zur Diskurstheorie des Rechts und des demokratischen Rechtsstaats* (Frankfurt: Suhrkamp, 1992), 632–59; and Dolf Sternberger, *Verfassungspatriotismus*, vol. 10 of *Schriften* (Frankfurt: Insel, 1990). More recently, though, Habermas has emphasized embeddedness in historical-cultural narratives.
6. Michel Foucault, *"The Archaeology of Knowledge" and "The Discourse on Language,"* trans. Alan Sheridan (New York: Pantheon, 1982), 17 [modified].
7. Fred Vargas, *Dog Will Have His Day*, trans. Siân Reynolds (London: Harvill Secker, 2014), 97–98.
8. Philippe van Parijs, *Linguistic Justice for Europe and for the World* (Oxford: Oxford University Press, 2011).
9. On this point, see Jürgen Trabant, *Globalesisch oder was? Ein Plädoyer für Europas Sprachen* (Munich: Beck, 2014).
10. See my *Gibt es ein interkulturelles Strafrecht? Ein philosophischer Versuch* (Frankfurt: Suhrkamp, 1999).
11. See chap. 2 of my *Gibt es ein interkulturelles Strafrecht?*, 19–30.
12. Richard Sennett and Jonathan Cobb, *The Hidden Injuries of Class* (New York: Vintage, 1972).

CHAPTER FOURTEEN

1. For a concise outline of the problem, see Horst Dreier, "Der Ort der Souveränität," in Horst Dreier and Jochen Hofmann, eds., *Parlamentarische Souveränität und technische Entwicklung* (Berlin: Duncker und Humblot, 1986), 11–44, which includes a rich bibliography; more recent work includes Friedrich Balke, *Figuren der Souveränität* (Paderborn: Fink, 2009); Dieter Grimm, *Sovereignty: The Origin and Future of a Political and Legal Concept*, trans. Belinda Cooper (New York: Columbia University Press, 2015); and Ingeborg Maus, *Über Volkssouveränität: Elemente einer Demokratietheorie* (Berlin: Suhrkamp, 2011).
2. *Herodotus*, trans. A. D. Godley, 4 vols. (Cambridge, MA: Harvard University Press, 1926–), I.96:126–27; see also VII.140:442–45.
3. On the history of the concept of sovereignty, see R. Pohlmann, "Autonomie," in Joachim Ritter, ed., *Historisches Wörterbuch der Philosophie* (Basel: Schwabe, 1971), vol. 1, col. 701–19.
4. *Cavende igitur est omnis invasio alterius civitatis, omnisque usurpatio jurium ipsius publicorum, uti autonomiae*; Michael Christoph Hanov, *Philosophia civilis sive politica*, 1756, in Christian Wolff, *Gesammelte Werke, Materialien und Dokumente*, ed. Jean École et al. (Hildesheim: Olms, 1998), vol. 47, I.VI.§485:456.
5. Emer de Vattel, *Droit des gens ou principes de la loi naturelle: Appliqués à la conduite et aux affaires des Nations et des Souverains*, 1758 (Geneva: Slatkine Reprints, 1983), I.1.§4:18.
6. On this point, see chap. 14 of my *Wirtschaftsbürger, Staatsbürger, Weltbürger: Politische Ethik im Zeitalter der Globalisierung* (Munich: Beck, 2004), 209–22.
7. On "societal constitutionalism and globalization," see Gunther Teubner, *Constitutional*

Fragments: Societal Constitutionalism and Globalization, trans. Gareth Norbury (Oxford: Oxford University Press, 2014).

8. On the coresponsibility of the European Court of Justice, see Dieter Grimm, "Europa: Ja—aber welches?," *Merkur* 68, no. 12 (December 2014): 1045–58.
9. See chap. 6 of my *Democracy in an Age of Globalisation*, trans. Dirk Haubrich with Michael Ludwig (Dordrecht: Springer, 2007), 103–29; for fundamental reflections on sovereignty, see Grimm, *Sovereignty*.
10. Andreas Gross, "Betroffen, aber ausgeschlossen," *Frankfurter Allgemeine Zeitung*, September 19, 2013, online, https://www.faz.net/aktuell/politik/staat-und-recht/bundestagswahl-betroffen-aber-ausgeschlossen-12581460.html, last accessed September 1, 2019.
11. Armin von Bogdandy and Ingo Venzke, *In Whose Name? A Public Law Theory of International Adjudication*, trans. Thomas Dunlap (Oxford: Oxford University Press, 2016).

CHAPTER FIFTEEN

1. See chap. 1 of *Democracy in an Age of Globalisation*, trans. Dirk Haubrich with Michael Ludwig (Dordrecht: Springer, 2007), 1–17; for a synopsis of recent literature on globalization, see Duane Swank, "Globalization," in Francis G. Castles, Stephan Leibfried, Jane Lewis, Herbert Obinger, and Christopher Pierson, eds., *The Oxford Handbook of the Welfare State* (Oxford: Oxford University Press, 2010), 318–30.
2. For more detail, see my *Democracy in an Age of Globalisation*, esp. pt. 2, 157–248.
3. Dani Rodrik, *The Globalization Paradox: Democracy and the Future of the World Economy* (New York: Norton, 2011), xviii.
4. Rodrik, *Globalization Paradox*, 250.

INTRODUCTION TO PART FIVE

1. Franz Kafka, "A Report to an Academy," in *A Hunger Artist, and Other Stories*, trans. Joyce Crick (Oxford: Oxford University Press, 2012), 37–45, here 38.

CHAPTER SIXTEEN

1. Immanuel Kant, *The Conflict of the Faculties*, trans. Mary J. Gregor and Robert Anchor, in *Religion and Rational Theology*, ed. Allen W. Wood and George Di Giovanni (Cambridge: Cambridge University Press, 1996), 233–327.
2. Wolf Singer, "Verschaltungen legen uns fest: Wir sollten aufhören, von Freiheit zu sprechen," in Christian Geyer, ed., *Hirnforschung und Willensfreiheit* (Frankfurt: Suhrkamp, 2004), 30–65.
3. Arno Plack, *Plädoyer für die Abschaffung des Strafrechts* (Munich: List, 1974).
4. Aristotle, *Nicomachean Ethics*, trans. Benjamin Jowett, in *The Complete Works of Aristotle: The Revised Oxford Translation*, ed. Jonathan Barnes (Princeton, NJ: Princeton University Press, 1984), 2:1729–867, here 1095b19–22.
5. For a detailed exposition, see my *Can Virtue Make Us Happy? The Art of Living and Morality*,

2007, trans. Douglas R. McGaughey and Aaron Bunch (Evanston, IL: Northwestern University Press, 2010), esp. chap. 16.

6. On the history and current state of brain research and its contributions to neurology, see Johannes Dichgans, "Können wir Gehirne kurieren?," *Frankfurter Allgemeine Zeitung*, August 20, 2014, N2.
7. See Aristotle, *On the Soul*, trans. J. A. Smith, in *Complete Works of Aristotle*, 1:641–92, here I.4:408b13–17; and M. R. Bennett and P. M. S. Hacker, *Philosophical Foundations of Neuroscience* (Malden, MA: Blackwell, 2003), I.3:68–107.
8. Detlef B. Linke, *Die Freiheit und das Gehirn: Eine neurophilosophische Ethik* (Munich: Beck, 2005), 11.
9. Gerhard Roth, *Aus Sicht des Gehirns* (Frankfurt: Suhrkamp, 2003).
10. For a critique of contemporary neurosciences from the perspective of the philosophy of science and the philosophy of language, see Peter Janich, *Kein neues Menschenbild: Zur Sprache der Hirnforschung* (Frankfurt: Suhrkamp, 2009); for a balanced account of the debate, see Ulrich Pothast, *Freiheit und Verantwortung: Eine Debatte, die nicht sterben will—und auch nicht sterben kann* (Frankfurt: Vittorio Klostermann, 2011); and see also the issue "Réduction et emergence dans les neurosciences" of the *Revue Philosophique de Louvain* 111, no. 1 (February 2013).
11. See, for example, Derk Pereboom, *Living without Free Will* (Cambridge: Cambridge University Press, 2006); and Geert Keil, *Willensfreiheit und Determinismus* (Stuttgart: Reclam, 2009).
12. See Peter Bieri, *Das Handwerk der Freiheit: Über die Entdeckung des eigenen Willens* (Munich: Hanser, 2001); and Michael Pauen, *Illusion Freiheit? Mögliche und unmögliche Konsequenzen der Hirnforschung* (Frankfurt: Fischer, 2004).
13. Singer, "Verschaltungen legen uns fest"; and Roth, *Aus Sicht des Gehirns*, 166.
14. Gilbert Ryle, *The Concept of Mind* (New York: Routledge, 2009); Bieri, *Das Handwerk der Freiheit*; and Ansgar Beckermann, *Gehirn, Ich, Freiheit: Neurowissenschaften und Menschenbild* (Paderborn: Mentis, 2008).
15. See section 8.3 of my *Aristotle*, trans. Christine Salazar (Albany: State University of New York Press, 2003), 91–94.
16. See chap. 8 of my *Kants Kritik der praktischen Vernunft: Eine Philosophie der Freiheit* (Munich: Beck, 2012), 130–63.
17. Benjamin Libet, *Mind Time: The Temporal Factor in Consciousness* (Cambridge, MA: Harvard University Press, 2004); and Gerhard Roth, "Das Zusammenwirken bewußt und unbewußt arbeitender Hirngebiete bei der Steuerung von Willenshandlungen," in Kristian Köchy and Dirk Stederoth, eds., *Willensfreiheit als interdisziplinäres Problem* (Freiburg: Alber, 2006), 17–38.
18. See Singer, "Verschaltungen legen uns fest."
19. Gerhard Roth, *Fühlen, Denken, Handeln: Wie das Gehirn unser Verhalten steuert*, new compl. rev. ed. (Frankfurt: Suhrkamp, 2003), 335.

CHAPTER SEVENTEEN

1. See Immanuel Kant, *Critique of Pure Reason*, ed. and trans. Paul Guyer and Allen W. Wood (Cambridge: Cambridge University Press, 1998); and Jürgen Habermas, "Freiheit und Determinismus," in *Zwischen Naturalismus und Religion: Philosophische Aufsätze* (Frankfurt: Suhrkamp, 2005), 155–86.
2. George Edward Moore, *Principia Ethica: With the Preface to the Second Edition and Other Papers*, rev. ed., ed. Thomas Baldwin (Cambridge: Cambridge University Press, 1993), §13:66–67.
3. See Claudia Wiesemann and Alfred Simon, eds., *Patientenautonomie: Theoretische Grundlagen—Praktische Anwendungen* (Münster: Mentis: 2013).
4. See section 3.5 of Otfried Höffe, *Democracy in an Age of Globalisation*, trans. Dirk Haubrich with Michael Ludwig (Dordrecht: Springer, 2007), 50–56.
5. See Jean-Paul Sartre, *Being and Nothingness*, trans. Hazel E. Barnes (New York: Washington Square, 1992); and Friedrich Nietzsche, *Thus Spoke Zarathustra: A Book for All and None*, ed. Adrian del Caro and Robert Pippin, trans. Adrian del Caro (Cambridge: Cambridge University Press, 2006), section "On the Blessed Isles," 66.
6. On this point, see chap. 8 of my *Kants Kritik der praktischen Vernunft: Eine Philosophie der Freiheit* (Munich: Beck, 2012).
7. Franz Kafka, "A Report to an Academy," in *A Hunger Artist, and Other Stories*, trans. Joyce Crick (Oxford: Oxford University Press, 2012), 38.
8. Kafka, "Report to an Academy," 45.
9. Arno Geiger, *Alles über Sally* (Munich: Hanser, 2010), 193.
10. On this dispute, see Nico Scarano, "Motivation," in Marcus Düwell, Christoph Hübenthal, and Micha H. Werner, eds., *Handbuch Ethik* (Stuttgart: Metzler, 2011), 448–53.
11. Immanuel Kant, *Critique of Practical Reason*, in *Practical Philosophy*, ed. and trans. Mary J. Gregor (Cambridge: Cambridge University Press, 1996), 133–271, here 5:105/224; and "On the Common Saying: That May Be Correct in Theory, but It Is of No Use in Practice," in *Practical Philosophy*, 273–309, here 8:287/288.

CHAPTER EIGHTEEN

1. Arthur Schnitzler, *Der einsame Weg* (Stuttgart: Reclam, 1962), III.8:64.
2. Pascal Mercier, *Night Train to Lisbon*, trans. Barbara Harshav (London: Atlantic, 2008); and John Grisham, *The Partner* (New York: Island, 1998).
3. Arnold Gehlen, *Der Mensch: Seine Natur und seine Stellung in der Welt*, 4th ed. (Bonn: Athenäum, 1950), 84–85.
4. Donna Tartt, *The Goldfinch: A Novel* (New York: Little, Brown, 2013), 761.
5. See Ulrich Beck, Wilhelm Vossenkuhl, and Ulf Erdmann Ziegler, *Eigenes Leben: Ausflüge in die unbekannte Gesellschaft, in der wir leben* (Munich: Beck, 1995).
6. For a more detailed discussion of the ideal of a free person—undoubtedly a recommendation in the subjunctive, but not an impossible one—see pt. 3 of my *Can Virtue*

Make Us Happy? The Art of Living and Morality, 2007, trans. Douglas R. McGaughey and Aaron Bunch (Evanston: Northwestern University Press, 2010), 187–351; and, more succinctly, *Ethik: Eine Einführung* (Munich: Beck, 2013), esp. pt. 5, chap. 2, 86–90.

7. Friedrich von Schiller, *Wallensteins Lager*, online, https://www.gutenberg.org/files/6518, last accessed September 1, 2019, line 138; and Hermann Hesse, *Magister Ludi (The Glass Bead Game)*, trans. Richard and Clara Winston (New York: Bantam, 1970).

Index